Lecture Notes in Computer Science   14537

Founding Editors

Gerhard Goos
Juris Hartmanis

The series Lecture Notes in Computer Science (LNCS), including its subseries Lecture Notes in Artificial Intelligence (LNAI) and Lecture Notes in Bioinformatics (LNBI), has established itself as a medium for the publication of new developments in computer science and information technology research, teaching, and education.

LNCS enjoys close cooperation with the computer science R & D community, the series counts many renowned academics among its volume editors and paper authors, and collaborates with prestigious societies. Its mission is to serve this international community by providing an invaluable service, mainly focused on the publication of conference and workshop proceedings and postproceedings. LNCS commenced publication in 1973.

Philipp Richter · Vaibhav Bajpai ·
Esteban Carisimo
Editors

Passive and Active Measurement

25th International Conference, PAM 2024
Virtual Event, March 11–13, 2024
Proceedings, Part I

 Springer

Editors
Philipp Richter
Akamai Technologies
Cambridge, MA, USA

Vaibhav Bajpai (iD)
Hasso Plattner Institute
Potsdam, Germany

Esteban Carisimo (iD)
Northwestern University
Evanston, IL, USA

ISSN 0302-9743 ISSN 1611-3349 (electronic)
Lecture Notes in Computer Science
ISBN 978-3-031-56248-8 ISBN 978-3-031-56249-5 (eBook)
https://doi.org/10.1007/978-3-031-56249-5

This Springer imprint is published by the registered company Springer Nature Switzerland AG
The registered company address is: Gewerbestrasse 11, 6330 Cham, Switzerland

Paper in this product is recyclable.

Preface

We are excited to present the proceedings of the 25th Annual Passive and Active Measurement PAM Conference. With this program, PAM continues its tradition as a venue for thorough, compelling, but often early-stage and emerging research on networks, Internet measurement, and the emergent systems they host. This year's conference took place on March 11–13, 2024. Based on learnings from recent years, this year's PAM was again virtual, both to accommodate the realities of modern travel and to ensure the conference's accessibility to attendees who may not otherwise be able to travel long distances.

This year, we received 64 double-blind submissions from over 100 different institutions, of which the Technical Program Committee (TPC) selected 27 for publication, resulting in a program similar in size to previous years. As with last year, submissions could be of either long or short form, and our ultimate program featured 14 long papers and 13 short papers. The 27 papers of the final program illustrate how network measurements can provide essential insights for different types of networks and networked systems and cover topics such as applications, performance, network infrastructure and topology, measurement tools, and security and privacy. It thus provides a comprehensive view of current state-of-the-art and emerging ideas in this important domain.

We built a TPC that included a mix of experience levels, backgrounds, and geographies, bringing well-established and fresh perspectives to the committee. Each submission was assigned to four reviewers, each providing an average of just under 5 reviews. Following in the footsteps of previous years, we established a Review Task Force (RTF) of experienced community members who could guide much of the discussion among reviewers. Finally, 21 of the accepted papers were shepherded by members of the TPC who were reviewers of each paper. As program chairs, we would like to thank our TPC and RTF members for volunteering their time and expertise with such dedication and enthusiasm.

Special thanks to our hosting organization this year, Northwestern University. Thanks to the PAM steering committee for their guidance in putting together the conference. Finally, thank you to the researchers in the networking and measurement communities and beyond who submitted their work to PAM and engaged in the process.

March 2024

Philipp Richter
Vaibhav Bajpai
Esteban Carisimo

Organization

General Chair

Esteban Carisimo   Northwestern University, USA

Program Committee Chairs

Philipp Richter   Akamai Technologies, USA
Vaibhav Bajpai   Hasso Plattner Institute and University of
                                    Potsdam, Germany

PAM Steering Committee

Marinho P. Barcellos   University of Waikato, New Zealand
Fabian E. Bustamante   Northwestern University, USA
Michalis Faloutsos   University of California, USA
Anja Feldmann   Max Planck Institute for Informatics, Germany
Oliver Hohlfeld   University of Kassel, Germany
Jelena Mirkovic   University of Southern California, USA
Giovane Moura   SIDN Labs, The Netherlands
Cristel Pelsser   UCLouvain, Belgium
Steve Uhlig   Queen Mary, University of London, UK

Program Committee

Alessandro Finamore   Huawei Technologies, France
Alexander Gamero-Garrido   UC Davis, USA
Andra Lutu   Telefonica, Spain
Anna Sperotto   University of Twente, Netherlands
Aqsa Kashaf   Carnegie Mellon University, USA
Arash Molavi Kakhki   ThousandEyes/Cisco, USA
Audrey Randall   UC San Diego, USA
Daphné Tuncer   Ecole des Ponts ParisTech, France
Diana Andrea Popescu   University of Cambridge, UK
Enric Pujol   SAP, Germany

Gautam Akiwate — Stanford University, USA
Giovane Moura — SIDN Labs and TU Delft, Netherlands
Idilio Drago — University of Turin, Italy
Jayasree Sengupta — CISPA, Germany
Johannes Zirngibl — TU Munich, Germany
John Heidemann — University of Southern California/ISI, USA
Karyn Benson — Meta, USA
Kensuke Fukuda — National Institute of Informatics, Japan
Kevin Vermeulen — CNRS, France
Kyle Schomp — ThousandEyes/Cisco, USA
Lars Prehn — Max Planck Institute for Informatics, Germany
Lucianna Kiffer — ETH Zurich, Switzerland
Marcin Nawrocki — NETSCOUT, Germany
Marinho Barcellos — University of Waikato, New Zealand
Matteo Varvello — Nokia Bell Labs, USA
Mattijs Jonker — University of Twente, Netherlands
Michael Rabinovich — Case Western Reserve University, USA
Moritz Müller — SIDN and University of Twente, Netherlands
Nguyen Phong Hoang — University of Chicago, USA
Nitinder Mohan — TU Munich, Germany
Olaf Maennel — The University of Adelaide, Australia
Oliver Gasser — Max Planck Institute for Informatics, Germany
Pawel Foremski — IITiS PAN, Poland
Ramakrishna Padmanabhan — Amazon, USA
Ramakrishnan Durairajan — University of Oregon, USA
Ricky K. P. Mok — UC San Diego/CAIDA, USA
Robert Beverly — Naval Postgraduate School, USA
Robin Marx — Akamai Technologies, Belgium
Roland van Rijswijk-Deij — University of Twente, Netherlands
Romain Fontugne — IIJ Research Laboratory, Japan
Sangeetha Abdu Jyothi — UC Irvine/VMware Research, USA
Shuai Hao — Old Dominion University, USA
Simone Ferlin-Reiter — Red Hat AB/Karlstad University, Sweden
Stephen McQuistin — University of St Andrews, UK
Stephen Strowes — Fastly, USA
Taejoong Chung — Virginia Tech, USA
Tanya Shreedhar — University of Edinburgh, UK
Thomas Krenc — UC San Diego/CAIDA, USA
Waqar Aqeel — Google, USA
Zachary Bischof — Georgia Institute of Technology, USA

Review Task Force

Alberto Dainotti	Georgia Institute of Technology, USA
Anna Brunstrom	Karlstad University, Sweden
Georgios Smaragdakis	TU Delft, Netherlands
Jelena Mircovic	University of Southern California/ISI, USA
Mark Allman	ICSI/Case Western Reserve, USA
Oliver Hohlfeld	University of Kassel, Germany

Contents – Part I

Applications

From Power to Water: Dissecting SCADA Networks Across Different
Critical Infrastructures 3
   *Neil Ortiz, Martin Rosso, Emmanuele Zambon, Jerry den Hartog,
   and Alvaro A. Cardenas*

Inside the Engine Room: Investigating Steam's Content Delivery Platform
Infrastructure in the Era of 100GB Games 32
   Christoff Visser and Romain Fontugne

Network Anatomy and Real-Time Measurement of Nvidia GeForce NOW
Cloud Gaming 61
   *Minzhao Lyu, Sharat Chandra Madanapalli, Arun Vishwanath,
   and Vijay Sivaraman*

IPv6

Exploring the Discovery Process of Fresh IPv6 Prefixes: An Analysis
of Scanning Behavior in Darknet and Honeynet 95
   Liang Zhao, Satoru Kobayashi, and Kensuke Fukuda

A First Look at NAT64 Deployment In-The-Wild 112
   Amanda Hsu, Frank Li, Paul Pearce, and Oliver Gasser

Machine Leaning

Dom-BERT: Detecting Malicious Domains with Pre-training Model 133
   Yu Tian and Zhenyu Li

Data Augmentation for Traffic Classification 159
   *Chao Wang, Alessandro Finamore, Pietro Michiardi, Massimo Gallo,
   and Dario Rossi*

Measurement Tools

Towards Improving Outage Detection with Multiple Probing Protocols 189
   Manasvini Sethuraman, Zachary S. Bischof, and Alberto Dainotti

WHOIS Right? An Analysis of WHOIS and RDAP Consistency 206
  Simon Fernandez, Olivier Hureau, Andrzej Duda, and Maciej Korczynski

Spoofed Emails: An Analysis of the Issues Hindering a Larger Deployment
of DMARC 232
  Olivier Hureau, Jan Bayer, Andrzej Duda, and Maciej Korczyński

Designing a Lightweight Network Observability Agent for Cloud
Applications 262
  *Pravein Govindan Kannan, Shachee Mishra Gupta, Dushyant Behl,
  Eran Raichstein, and Joel Takvorian*

Crawling to the Top: An Empirical Evaluation of Top List Use 277
  Qinge Xie and Frank Li

Author Index 307

Contents – Part II

Network Security

Swamp of Reflectors: Investigating the Ecosystem of Open DNS Resolvers 3
Ramin Yazdani, Mattijs Jonker, and Anna Sperotto

Out in the Open: On the Implementation of Mobile App Filtering in India 19
Devashish Gosain, Kartikey Singh, Rishi Sharma, Jithin Suresh Babu,
and Sambuddho Chakravaty

On the Dark Side of the Coin: Characterizing Bitcoin Use for Illicit
Activities 37
Hampus Rosenquist, David Hasselquist, Martin Arlitt,
and Niklas Carlsson

Routing

Insights into SAV Implementations in the Internet 69
Haya Schulmann and Shujie Zhao

A Tale of Two Synergies: Uncovering RPKI Practices for RTBH at IXPs 88
Ioana Livadariu, Romain Fontugne, Amreesh Phokeer,
Massimo Candela, and Massimiliano Stucchi

Anycast Polarization in the Wild 104
A. S. M. Rizvi, Tingshan Huang, Rasit Esrefoglu, and John Heidemann

Ebb and Flow: Implications of ISP Address Dynamics 132
Guillermo Baltra, Xiao Song, and John Heidemann

Satellite Networks

Watching Stars in Pixels: The Interplay of Traffic Shaping and YouTube
Streaming QoE over GEO Satellite Networks 153
Jiamo Liu, David Lerner, Jae Chung, Udit Paul, Arpit Gupta,
and Elizabeth Belding

Can LEO Satellites Enhance the Resilience of Internet to Multi-hazard
Risks? 170
   Aleksandr Stevens, Blaise Iradukunda, Brad Bailey,
   and Ramakrishnan Durairajan

Topology

Following the Data Trail: An Analysis of IXP Dependencies 199
   Malte Tashiro, Romain Fontugne, and Kensuke Fukuda

You Can Find Me Here: A Study of the Early Adoption of Geofeeds 228
   Rahel A. Fainchtein and Micah Sherr

Transport Protocols

Promises and Potential of BBRv3 249
   Danesh Zeynali, Emilia N. Weyulu, Seifeddine Fathalli,
   Balakrishnan Chandrasekaran, and Anja Feldmann

QUIC Hunter: Finding QUIC Deployments and Identifying Server
Libraries Across the Internet 273
   Johannes Zirngibl, Florian Gebauer, Patrick Sattler,
   Markus Sosnowski, and Georg Carle

User Privacy

Trust Issue(r)s: Certificate Revocation and Replacement Practices
in the Wild 293
   David Cerenius, Martin Kaller, Carl Magnus Bruhner, Martin Arlitt,
   and Niklas Carlsson

SunBlock: Cloudless Protection for IoT Systems 322
   Vadim Safronov, Anna Maria Mandalari, Daniel J. Dubois,
   David Choffnes, and Hamed Haddadi

Author Index 339

Applications

From Power to Water: Dissecting SCADA Networks Across Different Critical Infrastructures

Neil Ortiz[1]([✉]) [iD], Martin Rosso[2], Emmanuele Zambon[2] [iD], Jerry den Hartog[2] [iD], and Alvaro A. Cardenas[1] [iD]

[1] University of California, Santa Cruz, USA
{nortizsi,alvaro.cardenas}@ucsc.edu
[2] Eindhoven University of Technology, Eindhoven, Netherlands
{m.j.rosso,e.zambon.n.mazzocato,j.d.hartog}@tue.nl

Abstract. In recent years, there has been an increasing need to understand the SCADA networks that oversee our essential infrastructures. While previous studies have focused on networks in a single sector, few have taken a comparative approach across multiple critical infrastructures. This paper dissects operational SCADA networks of three essential services: power grids, gas distribution, and water treatment systems. Our analysis reveals some distinct and shared behaviors of these networks, shedding light on their operation and network configuration.

Our findings challenge some of the previous perceptions about the uniformity of SCADA networks and emphasize the need for specialized approaches tailored to each critical infrastructure. With this research, we pave the way for better network characterization for cybersecurity measures and more robust designs in intrusion detection systems.

Keywords: SCADA traffic · Network measurement · ICS · Modbus/TCP · IEC 60870-5-104

1 Introduction

Supervisory Control and Data Acquisition (SCADA) systems represent the technology used to monitor and control remote large-scale physical processes such as the power grid, gas distribution, and water treatment. These systems manage several Critical Infrastructures so vital to society that their incapacitation or malfunction could have a debilitating effect on national security, the economy, and public health.

Despite their criticality to our modern way of life, these networks have received limited attention from the academic measurement community. SCADA systems have migrated from serial communications to IP-based and Ethernet networks in the past two decades, and they can be analyzed with the same tools we have developed for measuring other modern networks.

Most previous network measurement studies of SCADA networks focus on a single network using a single industrial protocol. As a result, they study real-world SCADA networks (and protocols) in isolation, one at a time, rather than as

P. Richter et al. (Eds.): PAM 2024, LNCS 14537, pp. 3–31, 2024.
https://doi.org/10.1007/978-3-031-56249-5_1

a unified whole. Consequently, generalizability of these studies is limited by the scope, physical process, network layout, and used network protocols, i.e., does not describe SCADA as a whole. By studying real-world network traffic from three different physical processes, we create an overview of similarities and differences between SCADA systems. We highlight how implementation decisions and observations made on the network traffic are directly caused by the physical process and context it resides in. Our results can help putting network measurement studies of SCADA networks into context. Further, understanding the core differences and similarities between different operational SCADA systems is necessary to create better cyber security solutions (e.g., better best-practices and Intrusion Detection Systems for SCADA systems).

2   Related Work

While there is a growing interest in analyzing SCADA networks, previous measurement studies fall into two categories: (1) Use of emulated/simulated networks, i.e., testbed or laboratory environment. (2) Studies based on a single (real-world) network or single SCADA protocol.

Due to the difficulty of obtaining real-world data from operational systems, analyzing emulated or simulated data is the most popular approach [12,17,19]. However, simulations or testbeds do not represent the complexity and behavior of complex real-world systems. In fact, datasets emulating the power grid are prone to simple and regular patterns [16,20]. Therefore, in this paper, we exclusively focus on data obtained from real-world operational SCADA systems, i.e., systems that monitor and control physical processes that deliver critical services for a large population.

Some papers study operational (real-world) SCADA networks, but they do not provide details of the system under study. For example, Yang *et al.* [24] captured network traffic data from a real-world SCADA system without adding details of the type of system they analyzed. Similarly Hoyos *et al.* [14] and Wressnegger *et al.* [23] indicate that their dataset comes from a power plant network, but they do not specify which network protocols are used or add any details of the network topology. Likewise, Jung *et al.* [15] analyze the TCP connections of a power distribution network without specification of protocols.

The works most closely related to ours are the 2022 PAM publication by Mehner *et al.* [20], the 2020 IMC publication by Mai *et al.* [18], and the Sigmetrics 2017 publication by Formby *et al.* [9].

Mehner *et al.* conducted a network characterization study in a Distributed Control System. They examined packet traffic at the network layer, focusing on the field, control, and HMI levels. At the field and control levels, most traffic was from a proprietary protocol, while at the supervisory level, there was no legacy ICS protocol.

Mai *et al.* conducted an analysis of IEC 104 traffic from a real-world bulk power grid. They characterized traffic at the network, transport, and application level, including topology configuration, TCP flows, IEC 104 message types, and measurement and control commands. Their findings showed topological changes from one year to the next, with 90% of TCP connections lasting less than one second, as well as non-standard IEC 104 packet configurations. This research focused only on one protocol in one part of the power grid, whereas our study covers a wide range of protocols in all parts of the power grid.

Finally, Formby *et al.* conducted a flow analysis of substation networks using the DNP3 industrial protocol, focusing on the timing analysis of TCP connections.

While these three papers discuss a real-world SCADA system in detail, they focus only on one infrastructure. In contrast, our paper focuses on three different infrastructures (power, gas, and water) and tries to find the similarities and differences of SCADA networks under different operating conditions.

3 Background

3.1 Power Grid

Electricity grids are the foundation for generating, transmitting, distributing, and providing electricity to end-users. These systems are divided into four interconnected grids: generation, transmission, distribution, and end-consumer. Generation plants are connected to the transmission grid through high-voltage substations and transmission lines (usually rated at 220 kV and above). The combination of generation plants and the transmission grid makes up the Bulk Power System, which typically covers a large geographical area, such as an entire country. Transformer stations step voltage down, often around 50 kV for the distribution network. Constant monitoring and control actions by (human) grid operators is necessary, often from a remote control room. The main activities of grid operators include monitoring, coordination of power production, import and export, as well as load balancing intervention to mange offer and demand and ensure network and frequency stability. The power grid, especially the bulk power grid, has a redundant configuration to ensure resilience against unexpected events. This paper focuses on the Bulk Power grid, and the associated central control room monitoring and remote-controlling different substations spread geographically hundreds of miles apart to get the big picture of the operation of the power grid.

3.2 Gas Distribution

The gas transport and distribution grid follows a similar structure as the power grid. At specific locations, ingest stations receive and de-pressurize gas from the high-pressure nationwide transport grid (usually $>= 50\,bar$) and inject it into medium-pressure regional transport networks (around $10\,bar$) and finally the local distribution grid. Local distribution grids operate at the level of cities or metropolitan areas. Small gas distribution closets can be found within neighborhoods at regular intervals. These stations contain a mechanical pressure regulator that decreases pressure (often to $>= 1\,bar$) for the last mile. Usually, residential consumers are connected to more than one distribution station to avoid service interruptions in case of unexpected faults or maintenance.

Similar to power distribution, gas distribution is considered part of a nation's critical infrastructure. However, gas distribution does not require consistent supervision or operator control, as gas "just" flows to where it is consumed, as long as there is sufficient supply. As a result, there is a smaller need for redundancy, supervision, and digital control equipment. Nonetheless, stations are usually equipped with network connections to allow the operator to remotely monitor their system.

3.3   Water Treatment

Unlike the Power and Gas distribution networks that span a wide geographical area, water treatment plants are confined to a single, often relatively small, facility. Facilities highly differ based on the supply needs, ranging from a few thousand square feet for a few hundred thousand gallons per day in small communities to several acres for millions of gallons per day for cities or industrial complexes. The purpose of these plants is to remove contaminants and pathogens from water to make it safe for drinking, use in industrial processes or for safe return the natural water cycle. The treatment process varies depending on the source of the water (natural sources like reservoirs or wastewater), the type of expected contaminants (e.g., based on geographical region), and its intended use. It can be drinking water, wastewater, or a water recycling facility.

Treatment processes can be divided in three major types. (1) Physical treatment involve separating pollutants by physical characteristics such as weight (sedimentation) or size (filtration) including e.g., micro-filtration or reverse osmosis. (2) Biological treatment uses microorganisms to metabolize pollutants and convert them into biomass that can be physically removed by settling and filtration. Coagulants aid in forming solid clumps in water (coagulation), which settle as sludge (sedimentation) and are filtered out. (3) Chemical treatment purifies water by adding chemical substances, such as chlorine or ozone, to inactive pathogens (disinfection). Ozone precedes filtration, while chlorine follows to ensure the elimination of any lingering pathogens. Ultraviolet light at specific wave-lengths is used to break down cellular structures as part of the disinfection process. Individual treatment steps are prolonged or repeated until the water meets the required characteristics to move to the next treatment process.

In terms of operation technology, water treatment plants are equipped with a range of sensors and actuators that are connected to programmable logic controllers (PLCs).

PLCs are in turn connected to a supervisory control and data access (SCADA) server, acting as a centralized data concentrator for operator stations (HMIs) which allow operators to monitor the treatment process and to carry out (manual) process control when necessary. Sensors measure different parameters, such as water flow rate, turbidity, and chemical levels. Actuators include different valve types (e.g., filter flow control, aeration blower inlet, chemical addition), different damper types (e.g., for incinerator exhaust gas or incinerator fan) as well as pump motors. The PLCs are responsible for running the water treatment logic by changing valve positions, controlling pump speeds, or adding chemicals based on the different sensor readings, as well as monitoring safety conditions and raising process alerts. Process data and alarms is collected by the SCADA server and shown to Operators that monitor its correct execution and can carry out manual process control if needed.

3.4   Datasets

Our SCADA traffic dataset consists of network packet captures from three different infrastructures. Our analysis is focused on the primary SCADA protocol, i.e.,
the protocol used to monitor and control the respective physical process. For the
power grid and gas distribution dataset, this is IEC 104, a SCADA protocol initially developed for electrical engineering and power system automation. For the
water treatment process, the primary SCADA protocol is Modbus/TCP, a commonly used, non-proprietary SCADA protocol. A brief summary of the datasets
is depicted in Table 1. In the remainder of this section we briefly describe each
dataset and the modalities of how it was captured.

Table 1. Summary characteristics of the datasets.

ICS	Protocol	# hosts	Duration (hours)	# Packets	Name
Power	IEC 104	42	8.2	7.1 M	Power
Gas	IEC 104	157	2037	86 M	Gas
Water	Modbus/TCP	100	24.5	71 M	Water

Power Grid. The network capture was collected at the border router of the
SCADA control room of an Independent System Operator (ISO) in the Ameri-
cas, capturing traffic from the control room to the remote controlled sites (transmission and generation substations, as well as other control rooms). This ISO
manages a bulk power grid serving a population of around 40 million people
over a wide geographical area. The primary SCADA protocol in this dataset is
IEC 104. Additionally, this dataset contains other domain-specific protocols like
e.g., the Inter-Control Center Communications Protocol (ICCP), which is used
for information exchange with other control rooms. Using IEC 104, the ISO's
Energy Management System monitors and controls generation plants, e.g., by
using Automatic Gain Control (AGC). The control room also monitors frequency
at a few transmission substations. Lastly, the control room indirectly monitors
(via ICCP) other transmission substations directly connected to other control
rooms. For the purposes of this study, we will focus on analyzing the traffic
related to the IEC 104 protocol. This network consists of 4 control servers and
38 RTUs (IEC 104 outstations) on 23 remote sites. Each remote site is either
an electric generator (17) injecting power into the grid, or transformer (6) to
connect medium- or low-Voltage networks to the high-Voltage bulk power grid.

Gas Distribution. The network capture was collected at a core switch inside
the control center of a local distribution network operator of a European
metropolitan area. The primary SCADA protocol in this dataset is IEC 104,
used by the SCADA system to collect data and control 155 geographically spread
Remote Terminal Units (RTUs). The capture also contains internal communication among devices in the control center (among others, typical IT network

protocols like DHCP, DNS, SMB, Telnet, ... and proprietary protocols, including Oracle TNS and two unknown and probably vendor specific ICS protocols between ICS services). Most RTUs are installed at "distribution stations", however, a small number of RTUs control and monitor a gas turbine, biogas generation and injection, and testing equipment.

Water Treatment. The network capture was collected at a core switch of a large (approx. 800 square meters) wastewater treatment plant. The facility collects wastewater from a population of approximately 650 thousands people in an American city and, after treatment, releases the purified water into a river. The control system comprises field devices (40 mid/large size PLCs, 18 small size PLCs and other 16 field devices, mostly serial-to-Ethernet gateways), two redundant SCADA servers in hot standby configuration, two application servers, one historian server, one engineering workstation and 15 operator stations. The primary SCADA protocol in this dataset is Modbus/TCP, with the primary SCADA server being the only one actively communicating with field devices. ICS endpoints in the control center (SCADA servers, application servers, historian servers, and the operator stations) communicate with each other using standard IT protocols (SMB, Kerberos, DNS, etc.) and two proprietary protocols of the General Electric iFIX SCADA software suite. The ICS network segment is mostly flat, with endpoints from both the control center and field devices belonging to the same collision domain.

4   Analysis

For simplicity, in the remainder of this paper, any endpoint that reports data will be referred to as an **agent (A)**, while any endpoint that collects data will be referred to as a **controller (C)**. For example: we will consider any PLCs or RTUs as "agents" and HMI or SCADA server as "controllers". In this way, we can focus on the characteristics of the network to facilitate our comparisons and diagrams, and not dwell on protocol-specific naming conventions.

Figure 1 illustrates how our research questions create a general framework for analyzing SCADA networks. We start by understanding the topology of each network (RQ1), and then we start zooming in to understand the traffic differences between networks (RQ2), then traffic differences within a network (RQ3), the data types handled by the network (RQ4), and finally, the types of measurement and control commands sent back and forth between a controller and the agents (RQ5).

RQ1: What are the topology differences between the three SCADA networks?
RQ2: How are the three SCADA networks different in terms of packet size and timing?
RQ3: How are the three SCADA networks different in terms of packet size diversity?
RQ4: What type of information is carried by the ICS protocols in the three SCADA networks?

RQ5: How much monitoring vs. control is done in these networks, and what types of control commands are sent?

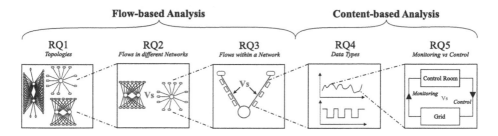

Fig. 1. Framework for our research questions.

4.1 RQ1: Network Topology

Our first goal is to understand the differences in topology of the three SCADA networks, as well as reasoning about the underlying choices that induced the respective topologies. Figure 3 is a visual representation of the network topology of all three SCADA networks. Even though the network topologies seem different at first glance, all networks are constructed around one or two central controllers.

Power. We observe that the power grid topology from Fig. 2a forms a complete bipartite graph. A complete bipartite graph $K_{p,q}$ consists of a set of p vertex and a set of q vertex (in our case, $p = 2$) and pq edges joining the vertex of different types [13]. This type of topology is known as spine leaf topology [11,22] in cloud data centers. The difference is that the spine leaf topology is used to forward packets through the spine (the central nodes), while in SCADA networks, the central nodes consume data (they do not forward it).

In our power network, each agent is connected to two controllers. This dual-purpose setup offers fault tolerance and load balance, which are essential for a network that focuses on the operational status of the process (see Sect. 4.3). This reduces the risk of the operators losing visibility in the event of a controller or link failure. If one controller fails, the other will take over, allowing control applications such as the Automatic Generation Control (AGC) algorithm to access the input data needed for its control operation. Furthermore, the operator can still monitor the grid from their HMI [3,4].

Upon looking at the traffic of each connection, we find that from the two connections to a pair of controllers, one of these connections is used to send process data to one of the controllers (active link), while the other is used to keep the connection with the other controller alive, serving as a backup. The heartbeat signal consists of U-Format messages (TESTFR) described in the IEC 104 protocol.

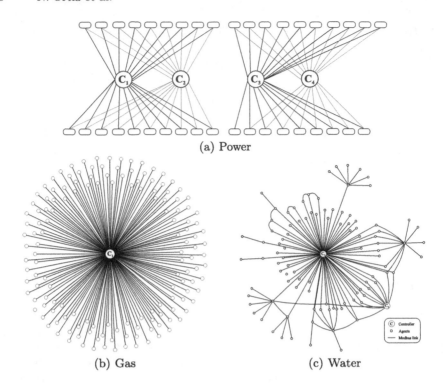

(a) Power

(b) Gas   (c) Water

Fig. 2. Type of topology structure: (a) Complete bipartite, (b) Star, (c) Star-Hybrid: a star topology with other structures.

This type of load balancing makes sense as we only require one active connection between a controller and an agent while the other connection is on standby, ready to be used in case of a failure.

In summary, we see two bipartite graphs: $K_{2,18}$ and $K_{2,14}$. We further confirm with the ISO that all four controllers are physically in the same control room, so this network represents a control room with four servers arranged in pairs, each monitoring a different part of the grid. In contrast to the other topologies, we believe these $K_{2,q}$ graphs represent networks that are more critical, such as networks for control operations, than the simple star graphs and, therefore, need standby connections to the controllers.

Gas. The gas network exhibits a star topology, with a controller connected to 155 agents, as illustrated in Fig. 2b. By number of agents, this is the largest network in our dataset.

Contrary to the IEC 104 standard that requires agents to have a second fail over TCP connection to a backup control server open at all times, agents in this gas distribution network do not open a secondary TCP connection. However, a second control server is present in the network, as we can see agents switching to a different control server during a network maintenance period recorded in our dataset.

The observed star topology can be explained by two considerations. First, some form of redundancy is provided at the network level (e.g., configured on network switches), that is not captured by our IP topology. If there was no additional fail-safe mechanism, an outage of the single control server would render the control room inoperable. Secondly, the distributed control structure of the gas distribution network does not require constant supervision from a central control server. Instead, agents run a local control loop that ensures the correct execution of the process. Thus, availability of the control server is not essential for the execution of the physical process and short interruptions "only" inhibit monitoring of the current process state.

Water. Finally, the water network is characterized by a star-hybrid topology, as seen in Fig. 2c.

We see that this network has the same single point of failure as the gas network; however, we also notice that the endpoints collaborate and exchange data at the edge of the network.

One major difference between our water network and the power and gas networks is that the water network is a LAN, and the gas and power networks are WANs. We cannot see the MAC addresses of remote devices in the power and gas networks; however, in the water network, we can see them and we can identify them as mainly Programmable Logic Controllers (PLCs). In addition, a LAN network suggests that the water treatment facility is not spread over a large physical area, all devices are setup in relatively close proximity. It can be assumed that the water treatment plant prioritizes operational reliability and simplicity.

Discussion. Network topology is shaped by the needs of the physical process under control. Managing offer and demand in the power grid requires constant and timely interventions from a centralized control room. Gas distribution, on the other hand, is a distributed process that agents can execute without constant connection to the control room. As a result, redundancy and fail-over techniques are more sophisticated in the power grid. Each agent is always connected to the primary control server *and* a backup control server. By spreading agents over multiple control servers, the impact of a failing control server on the physical process is limited. This is not necessary for gas distribution and may even result in unnecessary complexity. Instead, the topology of the gas network is kept simple.

The topology of the water treatment plant shows that most agents communicate directly with the control server. However, it also shows agents communicating among each other, as well as sub-controllers connecting multiple agents indirectly to the main controller.

The water purification process is relatively complex and divided into sub-processes. Often, it is enough to know and control the state of the process (e.g., water draining) and have the different agents take care of driving the actuators according to the desired state.

4.2   RQ2: Packet Size and Timing

We now turn our attention to the traffic flows in these networks, to identify if and how they differ. The classical traffic analysis metrics are packet sizes and the timing (or inter-arrival times) of transmissions.

Figure 3a and Fig. 3b visualize the distribution of packet sizes in bytes and the inter-arrival time between two packets for all three datasets.

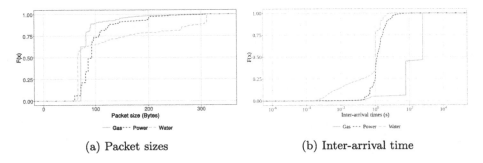

(a) Packet sizes   (b) Inter-arrival time

Fig. 3. CDF for (a) packet sizes and (a) IAT for each ICS network.

Power. The majority of packets (75%) in the IEC 104 traffic of the power grid dataset are smaller or equal to 100 bytes. Almost all (99.99%) of all observed packets are shorter than 200 bytes. The largest observed network packet was 1378 bytes, combining multiple IEC 104 messages in a single TCP segment.

The distribution of packet inter-arrival times (see Fig. 3b) shows no discrete steps or plateaus. This implies that the agents do not have a regular reporting pattern but instead that their communication pattern constantly changes. This is a result of the many spontaneous messages of this network, i.e., messages that an agent automatically sends to the control server when a value or status changes. The continuous yet varied slope in Fig. 3b implies that most messages are spontaneous or event-driven. This is a sign that the network constantly responds to the dynamic conditions of the grid and the power delivery process.

Gas. The vast majority (80%) of messages in the IEC 104 traffic of the gas distribution dataset are 100 bytes or less, with 99.99% of the messages being shorter than 200 bytes. Figure 3a indicates that most packets ($\sim$65%) are $\sim$70 bytes, which indicates a limited variety of message types being predominantly sent over the network. The largest packet observed (744 bytes) is roughly half the length of the largest packet observed in the power grid dataset and is also here combining multiple IEC 104 messages in a single TCP segment.

When looking at packet frequency, the gas distribution network is the least active. The transmission rate of network packets is one order of magnitude lower than for the other two SCADA networks (see Fig. 3b). In fact, 94% of all agents in the gas distribution network transmit IEC 104 packets in the order of minutes, indicating that the controller does not need fast updates, because process control operations are automatically done at the substation (i.e., the agent) with a local control program.

Figure 3b shows several clearly distinct steps: less than 1 s (5.5%), 1 min (40%), and 10 min (54.5%). These steps suggest that, for most agents, there is a predefined schedule based on which messages are sent.

Water. For the water treatment dataset, 65% of all messages are shorter or equal to 100 bytes. In contrast to the power and gas systems, we observe a significantly larger amount of packets in the 100–200 bytes range.

In Fig. 3b, we observe that inter-arrival times begin at the milliseconds rates. However, this is the case only for a small fraction of data points (less than 1%). A quarter of all network devices have a transmission rate interval of less than a second.

The controller interrogates 43% of the agents every second (there are no spontaneous or agent-initiated messages in the Modbus/TCP protocol, so all message exchanges are the response to a query from the controller). There is a degree of consistency in the configuration of the devices in the Modbus/TCP protocol.

Discussion. For all three networks, most of the SCADA protocol messages are shorter than 100 bytes. This is not surprising, as SCADA protocols usually do not transfer large amounts of variable length (textual) content: setpoints, sensor readings, commands, status changes, etc., are all fixed, and relatively short length, binary encoded, messages.

The high difference in packet lengths (see Fig. 3a) can be explained by the differences between the IEC 104 and Modbus/TCP protocols. A Modbus/TCP message can encapsulate a large number of (contiguous) registers in a single packet. IEC 104 packets also include overhead for the address of data points and typically need to divide large responses into multiple messages. For example, a Gas network agent might respond to an Interrogation command with 105 status data points spread across five packets, while Modbus/TCP would consolidate the same amount of data into a single reply, or even 2000 status data points in a single packet as seen in the biggest packet size (313 bytes).

The notably high messaging intervals in the gas distribution network reflects the distributed control strategy of the process. While the power grid is centrally managed and controlled, in the gas distribution grid each agent runs a local control program and centralized control is not necessary. Thus, the gas distribution control center does not need real-time information about the current state of the grid. For the water treatment process, although process control happens locally at the agents (similar to what happens in gas distribution), the agents are local to the control center and frequent data polling is "cheap", giving plant operators a more real-time view of the process being monitored.

In summary, we can see some similarities and differences among these networks. Further, we observe similarities and differences in terms of message intervals, caused by different monitoring strategies. In Modbus/TCP, agents do not act or send data independently, but instead monitoring data has to be actively polled by the controller in an interrogation process. In contrast, IEC 104 has the ability to configure agents to automatically report whenever a tracked value exceeds a threshold (the standard calls this "spontaneous"). As we discuss later, our power grid network takes advantage of this, and therefore, the transmission patterns are more diverse. Even though the gas network also uses IEC 104, it does not utilize this feature but instead is configured so that the controller explicitly interrogates the agents in regular intervals.

This difference in monitoring philosophy also explains difference in our packet size analysis. Almost half of the packets in both the Gas network and the Water network are interrogation queries, thus these packets have the same size. Every interrogation query requires a response from an agent. As the response contains a process variables, it is larger than the interrogation packet. This explains the big step in Fig. 3a for gas and water. For the power grid network, however, there are no repeated interrogation queries (that would have the same packet size). Because the distribution of message types is more diverse and spontaneous messages can push monitoring data without request, we observe a greater variety of packet sizes in the power grid.

Finally, we also observe that the power and water networks have shorter transmission times (for different reasons). Having said that, since both IEC 104 networks operate in a WAN, the minimum inter-arrival time in our datasets for any of them is 100 ms. This may identify a time constraint for these networks managing assets in large geographical areas.

4.3   RQ3: Packet Size Diversity

We now look at the diversity within networks. Entropy is a helpful metric for understanding the diversity (in terms of randomness) of data, and we can use it to evaluate the randomness of packet sizes within a network.

In the context of packet sizes, a higher entropy value (values close to 1) suggests a wide range of packet sizes being sent/received by an agent, while a lower entropy (closer to 0) implies that most packets have similar sizes. The spread and range of entropy values for each network provide insights into how varied the packet sizes are within each system. By comparing the entropy distribution using a cumulative distribution function (CDF), we determine which network has the most predictable packet size distribution.

We use the Shannon entropy formula:

$$H(X) = - \sum_{i=1}^{n} p(x_i) \log(p(x_i))$$

where $p(x_i)$ is the probability of occurrence of a particular packet size for a particular agent. For each agent, we count the occurrence of each unique packet size. Then, we divide each count by the total number of packets for that agent to get the probability distribution. Then, we add all the packet sizes a particular agent has sent at least once.

Figure 4 shows the distribution of packet size entropy values for the three networks. In the context of this plot, higher entropy values represent greater packet

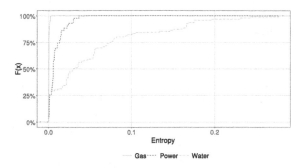

Fig. 4. CDF of packet size entropy

size diversity. The network with more agents (y-axis) having higher entropy values (x-axis) and more variability in its curve is likely the network that is less predictable in terms of packet sizes. Complementary to this view, Fig. 5 shows the packet size distribution for the three datasets.

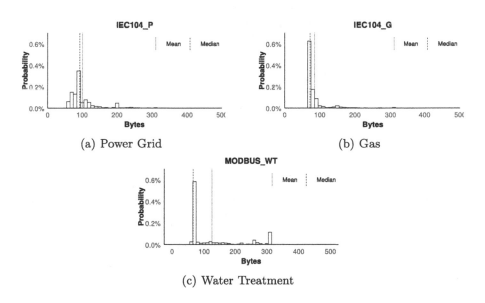

Fig. 5. Packet size distribution. Bin width 10.

Power. From Fig. 4, we see that ∼25% of the agents have an extremely low entropy value (close to 0). An additional ∼30% of the agents also have very low entropy. For the remaining agents the entropy is also low, in the range 0.02–0.04. From Fig. 5b, we identify that packet sizes are primarily concentrated around 50–100 bytes. There are two modes: a primary mode in the 100-byte bin (90–100 bytes), which is the highest peak in the distribution. A secondary or minor peak at 200 bytes (exactly at 198 bytes). The former are spontaneous, and the latter are periodic (1-s) packets containing information (I-format in IEC 104).

Gas. From Fig. 4, we see that ~85% of the agents have an extremely low entropy value (close to 0). For the remaining agents the entropy is also very low (below 0.01). From Fig. 5b, we notice that the vast majority of packets are small. 70% of them are, in fact, S-format and U-format messages (packets defined in IEC 104 to acknowledge the receipt of data and for checking the status of a connection). While the default rate for acknowledging packets is higher in IEC 104, the gas network needs to send pretty much an S-format acknowledgment for every I-message received because of the long interval of time between transmissions.

Water. From Fig. 4, we see that ~25% of the agents have an extremely low entropy value (close to 0). An additional ~50% of the agents have an entropy below 0.1. For the remaining agents the entropy is also relatively low, in the range 0.1–0.3. From Fig. 5c, we see a heavy tail of large packets. We identify that most of the small packets correspond to `Read Coil` operations (function code 1). These are binary values and usually represent the status of an actuator or the presence of a certain process or diagnostic alarm signal. In contrast, we see that the large packet sizes correspond to `Read Holding Registers` operations (function code 3).

Discussion. From the entropy analysis, we can see that a quarter of agents have uniform packet sizes. The three networks show a sharp increase at first until 25% (y-axis), meaning that a large proportion of agents in the three networks have extremely low entropy values. This implies that one-fourth of their agents have a consistent packet size or lack of diversity in packet sizes. For example, the agent with the least entropy in Power, sends repeatedly the same packet size of 72 bytes.

Most of the agents in the Gas network exhibit extremely low entropy values, implying a lack of diversity or uniformity in packet sizes for these agents. Therefore, most of the packets have a fixed length.

The Water network has the highest entropy of the three, which means that there is more uncertainty about the packet size that the controller will receive.

4.4   RQ4: Information Handled by ICS Protocols

We now turn our attention to the information contained within the packets themselves. Each protocol has its own specific standard with clearly defined object model and associated data types that are included in the packets. We start with a general overview in Fig. 6. On the x-axis, we see the number of data types defined by the standard's object model, and on the y-axis, we see the number of data types present in our capture. There are two clusters: on the top right corner, we see the IEC 104 networks, with over 100 data types defined in the standard's object model but only using around 10% in the capture. On the bottom left-hand corner is the Modbus/TCP network. The Modbus/TCP

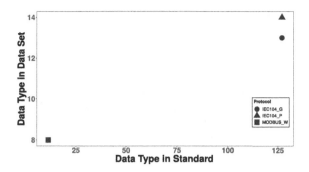

Fig. 6. Data Types.

Table 2. Power ASDU types and their description

Type	Reference	Description	%
1	M_SP_NA_1	Single-point information	<0.001
3	M_DP_NA_1	Double-point information	0.08
5	M_ST_NA_1	Step position information	0.05
7	M_BO_NA_1	Bitstring of 32 bit	<0.001
9	M_ME_NA_1	Measured value, normalized value	1.97
13	M_ME_NC_1	Measured value, short floating point number	39.71
30	M_SP_TB_1	Single-point information with time tag CP56Time2a	<0.001
31	M_DP_TB_1	Double-point information with time tag CP56Time2a	<0.001
34	M_ME_TD_1	Measured value, normalized value with time tag CP56Time2a.	0.51
36	M_ME_TF_1	Measured value, short floating point number with time tag CP56Time2a.	57.21
50	C_SE_NC_1	Set point command, short floating point number.	0.41
70	M_EI_NA_1	End of initialization.	<0.001
100	C_IC_NA_1	Interrogation command.	0.019
103	C_CS_NA_1	Clock synchronization command.	0.001
135	Unknown	not defined.	0.03

standard's object model does not define many data types so, obviously, the data types in the capture are fewer in absolute terms.

An IEC 104 packet can be either in Information (I), Supervisory (S), or Unnumbered (U) APCI format. I-format packets are used to exchange sensor and control data, while S and U-format packets are only used for network signaling (acknowledgments and heartbeats, respectively). For I-format packets, the standard [1] defines 127 different data types. However, in the power dataset we only count 14, and in the gas dataset 13 being used.

In contrast to IEC 104, other standards do not have the same diversity. Modbus/TCP is one of the oldest and simplest protocols used in SCADA systems. Its object model only defines three types of data: (Coils) single bit variables for binary values such as ON/OFF, (Registers) 16-bit variables for continuous values, and file records. Modbus/TCP defines 11 function codes to interact with these data types.

It is possible that we have not observed all the data types used in the power and water networks, due to the brief duration of our traffic captures. Nevertheless, since our traffic is consistent with steady-state conditions, our capture

Table 3. Gas ASDU types and their description

Type	Reference	Description	%
1	M_SP_NA_1	Single-point information.	27.85
3	M_DP_NA_1	Double-point information.	0.03
9	M_ME_NA_1	Measured value, normalized value.	17.92
30	M_SP_TB_1	Single-point information with time tag CP56Time2a.	1.13
34	M_ME_TD_1	Measured value, normalized value with time tag CP56Time2a.	11.38
45	C_SC_NA_1	Single command.	0.01
48	C_SE_NA_1	Set point command, normalized value.	0.01
58	C_SC_TA_1	Single command with time tag CP56Time2a.	<0.001
70	M_EI_NA_1	End of initialization.	<0.001
100	C_IC_NA_1	Interrogation command.	36.38
101	C_CI_NA_1	Counter interrogation command.	<0.001
102	C_RD_NA_1	Read command.	3.79
103	C_CS_NA_1	Clock synchronization command.	1.47
200	Unknown	not defined.	0.03

Table 4. Modbus/TCP types and their description

Type	Description	%
1	Read Coils	9.52
2	Read Discrete Inputs	0.39
3	Read Holding Registers	89.1
4	Read Input Registers	0.66
15	Write Multiple Coils	0.34
16	Write Multiple Registers	<0.001
22	Mask Write Register	<0.001
23	Read/Write Multiple Registers	<0.001
90	Schneider Unity	<0.001

reflects the most frequent data types in use during the operating stage of the respective processes.

Power. Table 2 reports the 14 (known) information types recorded in the power dataset. We see that 99% of the messages exchanged corresponds to only two types of messages: type 36 (Measured value, short floating point value with time tag) and Type 13 (Measured value, short floating point). These data types are used for exchanging power, voltage, and current measurements. The next most frequently used message (at only 0.845%) is perhaps the most critical message sent in this network: type 50 (Set point command, short floating point number). It is by means of these setpoint command messages that the SCADA system influences the behavior of (possibly large) power generators to keep the stability of the grid under control.

Gas. Table 3 reports the 13 (known) information types recorded in the gas dataset. Approximately 36% of the messages exchanged in the gas network are interrogation commands (the controller requesting information from agents), reflecting the polling-based use of IEC 104 in this setup. While the data types in the power network are dominated by continuous values, in the gas network we see an almost equal split between discrete (28.98%) and continuous (29.3%) values. Messages communicating discrete values are in turn split between type 1 (Single-point information) and type 30 (Single-point information with time tag CP56Time2a). The difference between the two is the presence (or absence) of a timestamp next to the point value, indicating the time at which the point value was measured. Reported discrete values in the gas network include several process and diagnostic alarm signals, as well as the state of the valves in the distribution network. Messages communicating continuous values are in turn split between type 9 (Measured value, normalized value) and type 34 (Measured value, normalized value with time tag CP56Time2a). As for the discrete types, the difference between the two is the presence (or absence) of a timestamp next to the point value, indicating the time at which the point value was measured. Reported continuous values in the gas network include several measures about gas (pressure, flow, temperature), as well as the position of gas pressure reduction valves (in percentage). Apart from interrogation, counter interrogation, read and clock synchronization commands, we also observe a small percentage of messages containing commands to set the value of discrete points (types 45 and 58), and of continuous points (type 48). While the vast majority of the set commands for discrete points are used to acknowledge process and diagnostic alarms, and all the set commands for continuous ones are used to adjust the value of alarm thresholds, a minority of the discrete set commands are also used by operators to manually control the gas network (e.g., by opening/closing a specific valve) during localized maintenance.

Water. Table 4 reports the 8 standard Modbus/TCP function codes recorded in the water dataset as well as the Schneider Electric proprietary function code 90. As with the power network, we can see that measuring continuous variables with function code 3 (Read Holding Registers) and function code 4 (Read Input Registers) makes up most of the Modbus/TCP messages (89.1% in total) in the water network.

While input registers contain the value of analog sensor signals acquired by the agent (e.g., a PLC), holding registers contain a variety of continuous values, from internal variables used by the PLC logic program to output signals.

Measuring discrete variables with function code 1 (Read Coils) and function code 2 (Read Discrete Inputs) is the next most prevalent type of Modbus/TCP message (9.91% in total).

While discrete inputs contain the value of binary sensor signals acquired by the agent (e.g., a PLC), coils contain a variety of discrete values, from internal variables used by the PLC logic program to output signals.

A very small percentage of the messages are control commands changing the value of discrete or continuous variables. As for the gas network, most of these commands are related to alarm management.

Discussion. While the IEC 104 standard's object model defines a large amount of data types, not all of them are used at any given IEC 104 network.

Although very similar in the use of IEC 104 data types (see Fig. 6), the two IEC 104 networks show some differences in use of data types. We now discuss the three most notable differences. (1) The representation chosen for continuous values is mostly floating point numbers in the power network (types 13, 36 and 50), and exclusively normalized values in the gas network (types 9, 34 and 48). Normalized IEC 104 data points only use two bytes for representing values, while floating points use four. We deduce that in the gas network engineers chose to favor space efficiency on wire over precision of transmitted values, a choice that could be possible in the gas distribution domain, where the purpose of data acquisition is for operators to oversee a process that runs autonomously, but not in the power transmission domain, where the precision of transmitted values is important for the correct functioning of the grid stability algorithms that run in the control center. (2) Differently from the power network, in the gas network the controller sends commands to set discrete points (types 45 and 58). This can be explained by the differences in the process control at the two scenarios. In the power transmission control system, the controller is responsible to ensure the stability of the grid by computing how much power each generation site should introduce in the grid at any given time, thus requiring to send messages to generation sites to set the value of continuous data points (the generation setpoint). Instead, in the gas network the process is controlled locally at each substation and the main goal of the central controller is for operators to check the process is running as expected (e.g., by processing alarm signals) and to carry out manual intervention in case of faults or maintenance. As we have seen previously, the latter two operations involve setting the value of discrete points, i.e., to acknowledge alarm signals or to manually trigger valve open/close procedures. (3) In the gas network, we observe more messages sending commands sent by the controller to explicitly interrogate agents (types 101 and 102). This can be explained by our previous observation that in the gas network, rather than leveraging the spontaneous reporting normally adopted in IEC 104 networks, the controller is configured to poll at set time intervals the value of all points exposed by the agents. This involves interrogating agents for data types that are not covered by the general interrogation command (e.g., counters) and, in some cases, explicitly issuing a read request for specific data points.

Finally, including also the water network in our analysis, we also notice that the power and water networks monitor and control mostly continuous signals, while the gas network monitors and controls an equal amount of continuous and discrete signals. This can be explained once more by the by the differences in the controlled processes.

4.5   RQ5: Monitoring vs. Control

We now address our last research question, which relates to the direction of network flows, in particular the initiator of a flow. Intuitively, we expect SCADA networks to have more messages sent from agents to the controller(s) than commands send by the controller(s) to the agents. However, we do not see this pattern in most of our networks, mostly because of interrogation commands.

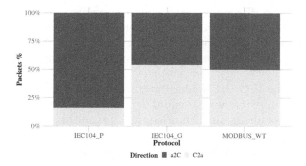

Fig. 7. Flows: Controller to agent (C2a) and agent to Controller (a2C)

We define a2C (short for $a \to C$) as the flow direction from the agent to the controller and C2a (short for $C \to a$) as the controller to the agent (Fig. 7).

Power $(a2C > C2a)$. In the power dataset $a2C = 83.7\%$ and $C2a = 16.3\%$. That is, most of the packets come from the remote substations (agents) to the controller. We also make the following two observations.

Event Driven. Four-fifths of the traffic is in the monitoring direction $(a2C)$. From that, the vast majority of the traffic (97.06%) are I-format messages. 90% of those are spontaneous packets (cause of transmission (COT) code '< 3 > spontaneous'). That means that 88% of the traffic from agents to controllers is generated by the occurrence of a particular event. Thus, most of Power's agents report changed data to the controller rather than sending static data (cyclic/periodic). For example, a change in the state of a binary point (e.g., a switch that passes from off to on), or in the case of analog points, when the values exceed a certain threshold (e.g., a frequency passes the 60.2 Hz threshold). In addition, as shown in Table 2, around 60% of the packets are time-stamp data. This is important for logging events, forensic analysis, and real-time control.

This indicates a network that prioritizes real-time monitoring and rapid response to changes in order to be able to react more quickly to real-time changes, making it an event-driven network. This is crucial to the stability of the power grid.

Minimal Overhead. In an event-driven architecture resources are utilized more efficiently, given that data transmission is primarily triggered by significant events. This minimizes the amount of 'noise' in the system by reducing the transmission of redundant or unnecessary data. The approach also ensures that the network bandwidth is optimally used, making it easier to scale the system in the future or allocate bandwidth for other critical applications. Moreover, by focusing on real-time, event-triggered data, the system is better equipped to quickly identify and respond to abnormal conditions, thereby enhancing the overall reliability and security of the power grid.

Only one-fifth of traffic is generated by the controller, mainly for flow control: 80.7% for message control (*S-Format*[1] packets), and connection control (16.7% *U-frame*[2]). This means that most of the C2a data (80.3%) is dedicated to message acknowledgment, which is a small percentage (16%) of total traffic (a2C + C2a).

By inspecting the IEC 104 header data, we observe that the controller has a large acknowledgment window (w)[3] equal to 8. This means more data packets can be in flight before requiring an acknowledgment, resulting in better throughput. Additionally, an agent can send multiple packets before waiting for an acknowledgment, thus reducing round-trip time and improving latency.

Gas $(a2C < C2a)$. In the Gas network, more traffic is sent out from the controller than what is sent by the agents. There is a noticeable difference in the distribution of packets between controller-to-agent $(C2a)$ and agent-to-controller $(a2c)$: $a2C = 45.8\%$ and $C2a = 54.2\%$. This imbalance can be attributed to two factors.

(1) *Polling Mechanism:* The controller employs Interrogation Commands to solicit data from the agents. These commands are sent as I-Frame packets, increasing the packet count in the $C2a$ direction.

(2) *Acknowledgment Scheme:* Unlike the controller, which acknowledges the receipt of each I-frame from the agent with an S-frame $(w = 1)$, the agent does not reciprocate. When the agent receives an I-frame (Interrogation command) from the controller, it sends back the requested data in an I-frame but does not acknowledge it with an S-frame. This unidirectional acknowledgment contributes to the imbalance in packet distribution.

In essence, for each cycle of data exchange initiated by a polling command, the controller sends two types of frames (first an I-frame to request data and then an S-frame to acknowledge receipt) while the agent only sends one I-frame in response. This results in a higher packet count in the $C2a$ direction. We add the following two observations.

One-to-One Acknowledgment. Unlike the Power network, which waits until it receives 8 I-frames before it sends back an acknowledgment $(w = 8)$, the Gas network operates with a smaller (average) window size of just 1. This is due to the inter-arrival time between I-frames being so large that they need to be acknowledged separately.

A Non-standard Use of the IEC 104 Protocol. In the Gas network, the controller utilizes station interrogation (Interrogation commands) instead of Cyclic data transmission to synchronize the process data of the agents. The difference is that

---

[1] *S-format* is a control field packet used for controlling the transport of information (ASDU packets). This protects against loss and duplication of I-format messages.

[2] *U-format* control field used to control the connection between stations. It is used as a start-stop mechanism for information flow. As a heartbeat to check connection. Also, as a mechanism for changeover between connections without loss of data when there are multiple connections available between stations.

[3] w specifies the maximum number of received I-format APDUs that the receiver should ACK at the latest. e.g., a $w = 8$ means that the controller will send to the agent an S-format message to ACK the last 8 I-format messages it receives.

Interrogation commands acquire a full set of data, while polling only gets the data that is of interest. Interrogation commands are used to update the controller after initialization or after data loss or corruption of data [8]. On the other hand, cyclic data is used to provide periodic updating of the process data to current values. Interrogation commands are event-based (loss of communication) or manually initiated (start a communication). Another difference between data acquisition by the Interrogation command and cyclic is that the former requires a request, while the latter does not. Interrogation commands are used to poll data from the agent, while cyclic does not require any commands; it is generated automatically by the agent (less traffic). Polling data by using interrogation commands is like a request/response; however, the agent can send the response in several messages, unlike Modbus/TCP, which sends the response in one message. The Gas network does not use cyclic data transmission, only general interrogation for polling data from agents. This is a non-standard use of the IEC 104 protocol in an ICS. It appears to be using a legacy approach like the one used in Modbus/TCP, but it implements it in IEC 104, without taking advantage of the transmission mechanism that the more modern IEC 104 protocol provides.

Water ($a2C = C2a$). In the final case, our Water network has an equal amount of packets being sent by the controller to the agent, as well as from the agent to the controller. Like the Gas network, our Water network operates on a polling mechanism. Given its request-response protocol architecture, Water exhibits an equal traffic flow in both directions ($a2C = C2a$). In essence, for every data report the agent sends, the controller initiates the communication by sending a request. This implies that the controller frequently queries the agent to retrieve the latest state information or execute specific commands.

Response Granularity. Both Water and Gas utilize a polling-driven mechanism, but they diverge in how responses are sent by agents. For instance, in Gas, an agent might respond to an Interrogation command with 5 packets, each containing 21 IOA of ASDU type 9. This results in 7 packets for the entire transaction: 3 for an Act, ActCon, ActTerm packet, and 4 for the actual data points. This increases the total number of packets in the transaction for one request. In contrast, Water adheres to a one-to-one request-response model, with each request from the controller receiving a single packet response from the agent. Consequently, a complete transaction in Water consists of just 2 packets: one for the request and one for the response. This streamlined approach minimizes packet loss and reduces network latency, making it more suitable for the time-sensitive operations in a water treatment facility.

5   Discussion

In the previous section, we showed that not all SCADA networks are built the same way. In different domains we observed differences in their topology, the industrial protocols, the traffic characteristics, and the protocol data types used. These results can help us dispel past misconceptions about SCADA networks.

5.1   Dispelling Misconceptions

SCADA communications have been analyzed by the community for some 20 years, but previous research has focused on results from testbeds or only single real-world networks. Therefore, the observations of previous research are sometimes inaccurate or not representative of diverse, real-world, operational conditions.

The common wisdom we have seen repeated in the literature is that all SCADA networks are similar, and they tend to be painted under the same broad strokes. Below we discuss some observations from past research and compare them with our observations.

Polling. "Due to the polling mechanisms typically used to retrieve data from field devices, industrial control network traffic exhibits strong periodic patterns" (Barbosa *et al.*) [5]. "most of the SCADA traffic is expected to be generated periodically due to the polling mechanism used to gather data." (Barbosa *et al.*) [6]. "Due to the use of request-response communication in polling, SCADA traffic exhibits stable and predictable communication patterns." (Lin *et al.*) [17].

Our Observations. Our analysis reveals that Request/Response is not always the mode of communication employed. Specifically, only Modbus/TCP has a flow that reflects a pure polling flow pattern with an equal percentage of traffic in both directions.

In IEC 104 networks, and all networks employing protocols that implement the report-by-exception paradigm, this assumption does not hold.

Flow Direction. "the bulk of the traffic is generated from field devices regularly reporting data to the master and the master occasionally sending commands as needed" (Formby *et al.*) [9].

Our Observations. We saw in Sect. 4.5 that for gas, this relationship can be reversed. In this case, the controller (i.e., the IEC 104 master) sends more data to the other endpoints of the connections (C2a > a2C). Furthermore, in the water treatment scenario (Modbus/TCP), the controller (i.e., the Modbus/TCP master) periodically queries sensor readings. While the responses containing the readings are bigger packets, communication is *always* initiated by the controller.

Simplicity of Network Topology. "control systems tend to have static *topology, regular traffic, and simple protocols.*" (Cheung *et al.*) [7].

Our Observations. The *topology* of SCADA networks is dynamic. Mai *et al.*, [18] shows topological differences in a bulk power grid over two consecutive years. They found that processes such as energy dispatch can affect the topology daily by adding or removing generation nodes regularly according to the demand needs. In addition, the frequency of maintenance in electrical elements, such as generation machines and transformers, removes nodes temporally. Expansion projects, which add new nodes to an existing network, are not infrequent. For instance, we observe addressing changes and maintenance work in the gas distribution network [21].

Additionally, the IEC 104 protocol is newer and more complex when compared to Modbus/TCP. Features like spontaneous messages (i.e., agents pushing measurements to the control server when the signal changes) allow, among others, for monitoring large(r) networks (including e.g., the wide-area networks of the power grid and the gas distribution network) without an unmanageable increase in the amount of traffic. The development of IEC 104 (or IEC 101) is the result of restrictions with existing protocols. It is reasonable to assume that new (and potentially proprietary) SCADA protocols are developed to meet new requirements and usage scenarios, e.g., for mobility and automotive scenarios.

"SCADA systems typically use primary-backup approaches to provide disaster recovery capabilities. Specifically, a hot backup of the central control server (the SCADA master) can take over immediately if the primary SCADA master fails, and in many SCADA systems, a cold-backup control center can be activated within a couple of hours if the primary control center fails." (Babay *et al.*) [4].

Our Observations. As we showed in this paper, there are several SCADA topologies, and some do not follow the typical primary-backup paradigm. As we saw in the power dataset, the backup controller in a $K_{2,q}$ network is not in hot or cold stand-by configuration; it is a secondary server helping also load-balancing and taking an active part in the monitoring of the system even if the primary server is operational.

More in general, IEC 104 has built-in support for redundancy. The features defined in the IEC 104 protocol soften the definition of a primary control and a (hot) backup server, as both controllers are regarded as equal and can stem the load alone, if necessary. Whether a controller is the primary control server or backup for a specific agent is a matter of choice (i.e., can be selected arbitrarily).

Simplicity of Traffic Patterns. "control systems tend to have static *topology, regular traffic, and simple protocols.*" (Cheung *et al.*) [7].

Our Observations. Figure 3b shows that in several cases there are no regular traffic patterns. Protocols that use spontaneous transmission, such as IEC 104, present high variability in traffic because the data report depends on the status of the physical process being monitored. Furthermore, some SCADA networks are composed of heterogeneous devices configured by different contractors, as we observed in the power transmission network we studied: therefore, they may have different configurations resulting in diverse traffic patterns.

Simplicity of Network Protocols. "control systems tend to have static *topology, regular traffic, and simple protocols.*" (Cheung *et al.*) [7].

Our Observations. As discussed in our analysis, early SCADA protocols such as Modbus/TCP were fairly simple. However, newer protocols like IEC 104 (or IEC 101 in this regard) have a more complex structure, with an object model defining a rich set of data types, and less simple communication features like spontaneous (asynchronous) messaging.

Protocols like BACNet (a control protocol commonly used for building automation and management) or OPC-UA, for example, support alerting, push-pull notifications and subscriptions, define a variety of different value and data types, reading and writing of files, and encapsulation of foreign protocol messages. Overall, we argue that, due to evolving requirements and usage context, industrial protocols are becoming more complex than what initially expected.

Timing and Periodicity of Traffic. "SCADA systems for the power grid must deliver device status updates and supervisory commands within 100–200 ms." (Babay *et al.*) [4].

Our Observations. As we saw in our analysis, requirements for data reporting can change significantly, not only among networks but even among different endpoints in the same network. Most of the status updates in our networks took more than 200 ms.

While substation equipment can report their status back to a control center with latency > 200 ms, protection equipment within the substation network requires faster device status updates (e.g., in the range of 10 ms).

Summarizing, we contend that the prevailing academic perspective on SCADA protocol usage in real systems is analogous to observing just a fraction of a larger puzzle. Often, researchers draw conclusions based on an isolated SCADA network, overlooking the broader context because they don't have access to other operational networks. Our paper aims to shed light on the multifaceted and evolving nature of SCADA systems within the power grid, striving for a more comprehensive understanding.

5.2   Limitations

Our three datasets, even if meaningful in size and diversity, do not represent the entirety of all SCADA networks. While we expect to see similarities in two IEC 104 power transmission networks, our study already showed that networks using IEC 104 can be build differently, i.e., with different design strategies in mind, and thus make use of IEC 104 differently.

Neither the power nor the water dataset span a timeframe that would allow us to make conclusive statements over the entire physical process. Changes in demand throughout the day, and depending on the time of year, would require a much longer capture duration for the power grid. Though, from another paper we know that we can expect that 24 h are likely enough to contain at least one entire (water treatment) process cycle [10] – though details may depend on other factors including plant location and water purity.

Nevertheless, even if our data might not provide a complete overview of the systems, to date, this is the most comprehensive comparison available. Our comparison offers valuable insights into the diversity of SCADA traffic within Industrial Control Systems. Our dataset is the most diverse ever reported in an academic context, boasting broad coverage across different organizations, device types, and protocols within ICS.

6   Conclusion

In this paper, we uncovered revealing patterns and operational behaviors across different Industrial Control Systems. Through detailed analysis, it became evident that while the power and water treatment networks adhered to conventional protocol applications, the gas distribution network deviates, reflecting intriguing operational choices, particularly in its data synchronization strategy.

Notably, some degree of consistency was observed in the ICS traffic across all networks: approximately a quarter of their traffic exhibited uniform packet sizes. Furthermore, a predilection for small packet sizes, falling within the 0–100 bytes range, was dominant in all three networks, accounting for more than half of their communications. This can be attributed in part to the specification of the two ICS protocols at hand (IEC 104 and Modbus/TCP), defining a relatively small maximum packet size ($\sim$255 bytes). More in general, we argue that parameters such as the average size of packets are influenced more by the ICS protocol and process control technology being used than the specific process being controlled. When exploring transmission timings in ICS, data update frequencies typically spanned from seconds to minutes, with millisecond-order updates being rare exceptions, as exemplified by the relatively inactive gas network.

In general, the update frequency of process data is a parameter that depends on the process control application being observed. In the three examples we observed, real-time fast updates were not necessary nor possible in the case of large geographically distributed networks. In other application contexts (such as the communication among protection equipment within an electrical substation), real-time and fast updates are necessary and implemented by means of specific real-time protocols (such as GOOSE).

IEC 104 networks, a pivotal focus of our study, revealed two consistent operational tendencies: a minimal inter-arrival time that hovers around one second and an (average) maximum packet size capped at 200 bytes. Additionally, our findings highlighted the predictability of packet sizes for polling-oriented networks: here, the controller sends a fixed-length request and receives a fixed-length response, depending on the requested data. In networks with event-driven notifications, the arrival of messages is not easily predictable and message sizes present a richer tapestry of diversity and fluctuation.

This exploration emphasized the heterogeneity within SCADA networks and the importance of customized and specialized approaches for each infrastructure. Our findings challenge generalized views on SCADA networks, advocating for more nuances in the studies of these industrial systems networks.

A better understanding of the nuisances of SCADA networks will give the research community better tools to both evaluate the practical applicability of network and security monitoring approaches and to design new security monitoring approaches based on assumptions that hold in a large(r) amount of real-world setups.

Acknowledgements. This work was supported in part by NSF CNS-1929410, CNS-1931573 and by the INTERSECT project, Grant No. NWA.1162.18.301, funded by the Dutch Research Council (NWO). Any opinions, findings, conclusions, or recommendations expressed in this work are those of the author(s) and do not necessarily reflect the views of the funding organizations.

A   IEC 60870-5-104

IEC 104 is an application layer protocol standardized by IEC 60870-5-104 [1]. Designed for the monitoring and control of industrial systems, it finds widespread application in sectors such as power grids and gas systems. Operating over TCP/IP, it employs a client/server model for communication.

There are distinct features of the IEC104 protocol:

(1) **Message Types**: Supports both synchronous and asynchronous messages, often referred to as spontaneous or periodic messages. (2) **Balance and Unbalance Communications:** In balanced communication, either the controller device or the agent device can initiate the interaction. In contrast, unbalanced communication allows only the controller device to initiate, with the agent responding. (3) **Message Attributes:** IEC104 messages can carry timestamps and quality attributes, enhancing the information's reliability and context. (4) **Synchronous and Asynchronous Modes:** In the synchronous mode, the agent sends a new message after a fixed period. However, in the asynchronous mode, the agent sends a message whenever a variable's value strays from a predefined deadband.

Inside these TCP packets of IEC 104, there is one or more Application Protocol Data Units (APDUs). Each APDU is composed of: (1) **Application Protocol Control Information (APCI):** This acts as the header of the message and is essential for the proper transmission and receipt of the message. (2) **Application Service Data Unit (ASDU):** This is the main content of the message and carries sensor and control data that is shared between the field agent and the controller.

APDUs are categorized into three types:

- **I-Format APDUs:** These are the primary carriers of sensor and control data. An ASDU within this format includes a Data Unit Identifier and Information Objects. Each Information Object is a representation of a specific device in the field, and each one is linked to a unique address called the Information Object Address (IOA). Apart from this, the ASDU holds the Type Identification, which denotes the specific data format or command type, and the Cause Of Transmission (COT) that outlines the reason behind the message's dispatch.
- **S-Format APDUs:** These are simpler and serve as acknowledgments. They are dispatched after a specified number of I-Format APDUs are successfully received by the other end.
- **U-Format APDUs:** These have a special role in managing the overall connection. They can command the beginning or cessation of I-Format APDUs and also transmit keep-alive requests to ensure the connection's stability. When a new connection is initiated, it is in the "STOPDT" State by default.

IEC 104 was designed with reliability in mind. Typically, a primary connection is established between a controller and an RTU. Alongside this, there is a secondary or backup connection with another controller server. While the primary connection handles the main data transfer and acknowledgments (I-Format and S-Format messages) and occasionally U-Frame, the secondary focuses on periodic keep-alive checks (U TESTFR messages) to test the status of the connection. If the backup server ever sends a communication initiation command, roles are swapped, with the backup server taking the primary role and vice-versa [18].

B   Modbus/TCP

Modbus is a widely used industrial protocol that is easy to implement, maintain and has open specifications [2]. It has several versions, such as Modbus RTU for serial communication and Modbus/TCP for TCP/IP communication. This paper focuses on Modbus/TCP, which is a client/server architecture with a simple request/response protocol. The controller (client) is the only one that can initiate communication with the agent (server). The agent never sends a message unless requested by the controller. Modbus has four data types: input register, holding registers, discrete inputs, and coils. The two "register" types are 16-bit elements commonly used for measurement values, while discrete inputs and coils are one-bit elements used for status values. The message structure of Modbus consists of three parts: a header called Modbus Application Protocol (MBAP), a Function Code that identifies different operations, and a Payload (Data) that carries the content of the message. The format and size of the payload depend on the function code.

The MBAP includes the following components:

- **Transaction Identifier:** A numerical identifier to match request and response messages.
- **Protocol Identifier:** This is set to zero for Modbus/TCP.
- **Length:** The number of bytes in the frame.
- **Unit ID:** This is used in serial communication as the address of the device when multiple agents are connected to a single controller. It is set to zero for Modbus/TCP. This includes the Unit ID, Function Code, and Data.

In contrast to IEC 104, Modbus does not include timestamp or quality attributes in its packets. For instance, IEC 104 utilizes the attribute CP56Time2a as a timestamp in the ASDU process with a long time tag, such as "M_ME_TF_1" (No. 36), to register the time when the measurement was taken; thus, there is no assurance that the information object sent is current or that the data is accurate. Furthermore, Modbus does not have a standard method for data object description. For example, to determine if a register value represents a voltage value between 0 and 220 V.

References

1. IEC 60870-5-104, June 2006. https://webstore.iec.ch/publication/3746
2. Modbus application protocol specification v1.1b3, April 2012. https://www.modbus.org

3. Babay, A., et al.: Deploying intrusion-tolerant SCADA for the power grid. In: 2019 49th Annual IEEE/IFIP International Conference on Dependable Systems and Networks (DSN), pp. 328–335 (2019). https://doi.org/10.1109/DSN.2019.00043
4. Babay, A., Tantillo, T., Aron, T., Platania, M., Amir, Y.: Network-attack-resilient intrusion-tolerant SCADA for the power grid. In: 2018 48th Annual IEEE/IFIP International Conference on Dependable Systems and Networks (DSN), pp. 255–266 (2018). https://doi.org/10.1109/DSN.2018.00036
5. Barbosa, R.R.R., Sadre, R., Pras, A.: Difficulties in modeling SCADA traffic: a comparative analysis. In: Taft, N., Ricciato, F. (eds.) PAM 2012. LNCS, vol. 7192, pp. 126–135. Springer, Heidelberg (2012). https://doi.org/10.1007/978-3-642-28537-0_13
6. Barbosa, R.R.R., Sadre, R., Pras, A.: Exploiting traffic periodicity in industrial control networks. Int. J. Crit. Infrastruct. Prot. **13**, 52–62 (2016). https://doi.org/10.1016/j.ijcip.2016.02.004. https://linkinghub.elsevier.com/retrieve/pii/S1874548216300221
7. Cheung, S., Dutertre, B., Fong, M., Lindqvist, U., Valdes, A., Skinner, K.: Using model-based intrusion detection for SCADA networks. In: Proceeding of the SCADA Security Scientific Symposium, p. 12 (2007)
8. Clarke, G., Reynders, D., Wright, E.: Practical Modern SCADA Protocols: DNP3, 60870.5 and Related Systems, January 2004
9. Formby, D., Walid, A., Beyah, R.: A case study in power substation network dynamics. Proc. ACM Meas. Anal. Comput. Syst. **1**(1) (2017). https://doi.org/10.1145/3084456
10. Hadžiosmanović, D., Sommer, R., Zambon, E., Hartel, P.H.: Through the eye of the PLC: semantic security monitoring for industrial processes, pp. 126–135 (2014). https://doi.org/10.1145/2664243.2664277
11. Harsh, V., Jyothi, S.A., Godfrey, P.B.: Spineless data centers. In: HotNets 2020, New York, NY, USA, pp. 67–73. Association for Computing Machinery (2020). https://doi.org/10.1145/3422604.3425945
12. Hodo, E., Grebeniuk, S., Ruotsalainen, H., Tavolato, P.: Anomaly detection for simulated IEC-60870-5-104 trafiic. In: Proceedings of the 12th International Conference on Availability, Reliability and Security, ARES 2017, New York, NY, USA. Association for Computing Machinery (2017). https://doi.org/10.1145/3098954.3103166
13. Hoffman, A.J.: On the line graph of the complete bipartite graph. Ann. Math. Stat. **35**(2), 883–885 (1964). https://doi.org/10.1214/aoms/1177703593
14. Hoyos, J., Dehus, M., Brown, T.X.: Exploiting the goose protocol: a practical attack on cyber-infrastructure. In: 2012 IEEE Globecom Workshops, pp. 1508–1513 (2012). https://doi.org/10.1109/GLOCOMW.2012.6477809
15. Jung, S.S., Formby, D., Day, C., Beyah, R.: A first look at machine-to-machine power grid network traffic. In: 2014 IEEE International Conference on Smart Grid Communications (SmartGridComm), pp. 884–889 (2014). https://doi.org/10.1109/SmartGridComm.2014.7007760
16. Lin, C.-Y., Nadjm-Tehrani, S.: A comparative analysis of emulated and real IEC-104 spontaneous traffic in power system networks. In: Abie, H., et al. (eds.) CPS4CIP 2020. LNCS, vol. 12618, pp. 207–223. Springer, Cham (2021). https://doi.org/10.1007/978-3-030-69781-5_14
17. Lin, C.Y., Nadjm-Tehrani, S., Asplund, M.: Timing-based anomaly detection in SCADA networks. In: D'Agostino, G., Scala, A. (eds.) Critical Information Infrastructures Security. LNCS, vol. 10707, pp. 48–59. Springer, Cham (2018). https://doi.org/10.1007/978-3-319-99843-5_5

18. Mai, K., Qin, X., Ortiz, N., Molina, J., Cardenas, A.A.: Uncharted networks: a first measurement study of the bulk power system. In: Proceedings of the ACM Internet Measurement Conference, Virtual Event USA, pp. 201–213. ACM, October 2020. https://doi.org/10.1145/3419394.3423630

19. Maynard, P., McLaughlin, K., Haberler, B.: Towards understanding man-in-the-middle attacks on IEC 60870-5-104 SCADA networks. In: 2nd International Symposium for ICS & SCADA Cyber Security Research 2014. BCS Learning & Development, September 2014. https://doi.org/10.14236/ewic/ics-csr2014.5. https://ewic.bcs.org/content/ConWebDoc/53228

20. Mehner, S., Schuster, F., Hohlfeld, O.: Lights on power plant control networks. In: Hohlfeld, O., Moura, G., Pelsser, C. (eds.) PAM 2022. LNCS, vol. 13210, pp. 470–484. Springer, Cham (2022). https://doi.org/10.1007/978-3-030-98785-5_21

21. Qin, X., Rosso, M., Cardenas, A.A., Etalle, S., den Hartog, J., Zambon, E.: You can't protect what you don't understand: characterizing an operational gas SCADA network. In: 2022 IEEE Security and Privacy Workshops (SPW), San Francisco, CA, USA, pp. 243–250. IEEE, May 2022. https://doi.org/10.1109/SPW54247.2022.9833864. https://ieeexplore.ieee.org/document/9833864/

22. Roig, P.J., Alcaraz, S., Gilly, K., Juiz, C.: Modelling a leaf and spine topology for VM migration in fog computing. In: 2020 24th International Conference Electronics, pp. 1–6 (2020). https://doi.org/10.1109/IEEECONF49502.2020.9141611

23. Wressnegger, C., Kellner, A., Rieck, K.: ZOE: content-based anomaly detection for industrial control systems. In: 2018 48th Annual IEEE/IFIP International Conference on Dependable Systems and Networks (DSN), pp. 127–138 (2018). https://doi.org/10.1109/DSN.2018.00025

24. Yang, Y., McLaughlin, K., Littler, T., Sezer, S., Pranggono, B., Wang, H.F.: Intrusion detection system for IEC 60870–5–104 based SCADA networks. In: 2013 IEEE Power Energy Society General Meeting, pp. 1–5 (2013). https://doi.org/10.1109/PESMG.2013.6672100

Inside the Engine Room: Investigating Steam's Content Delivery Platform Infrastructure in the Era of 100GB Games

Christoff Visser[✉][iD] and Romain Fontugne[iD]

IIJ Research Lab, Tokyo, Japan
{christoff,romain}@iij.ad.jp

Abstract. As the size of video games continues to get bigger, new games and updates are becoming more visible in network operations. This research, coinciding with the 20th anniversary of the Steam store, provides an insightful exploration of a large-scale video game distribution platform. We place the operations of Steam under the lens and break down the details of its content delivery infrastructure. As part of this, we undertake a deep analysis of its data centres and cache locations. Recognising the trends in game development, this investigation acknowledges the dawn of the 100GB game era and the increasing pressure on distribution systems as a result.

Our research showcases the significant impact of major video game releases and provides an extensive investigation into the capacity of Steam cache servers, illuminating the strategies deployed when demand overshadows capacity. Players downloaded a monumental 44.7 exabytes from Steam in 2022 alone. With no signs of slowing down in 2023, Steam served an average of 15 Tbps of traffic between February and October, with peaks of up to 146 Tbps. This study lays bare the intricacies and operational challenges inherent to the digital game distribution landscape.

1   Introduction

For almost as long as modern computing has existed, so have video games. The Manchester Baby [16] ran its first program in 1948, giving birth to what we now consider the first modern computer. Shortly thereafter, Josef Kates built Bertie the Brain [34], one of the earliest examples of a modern video game.

Both computers and video games have come a long way since their early days. The launch of the Atari Video Computer System in 1977 exemplifies this monumental progress [50]. Its introduction of 2 kB cartridges significantly increased the capability and complexity of what developers can include in their games. However, cartridges still limited the storage available to developers, packing only up to 4 MB of space in the early '90 s [3]. The introduction of CD-ROMs dramatically expanded the available capacity to 650 MB. The move to CD-based storage also introduced the possibility of distributing a game over multiple discs. Notably, in 1995, Sierra released *Phantasmagoria* across eight discs for the Sega Saturn in Japan [32]. Later, the increase in Internet availability and bandwidth

P. Richter et al. (Eds.): PAM 2024, LNCS 14537, pp. 32–60, 2024.
https://doi.org/10.1007/978-3-031-56249-5_2

gave developers the ability to move beyond the limitations of physical storage media and transition to digital releases.

Valve was one of the first adopters of digital game distribution when it released Steam, its video game distribution platform and storefront, in 2003 [7]. Since the introduction of the first digital game in the store in 2004 [24], Steam has grown exponentially over the past 20 years. In 2022 alone, players downloaded 44.7 exabytes of data from Steam [56]. Due to their increased file sizes and rising popularity, the release and updates of video games can have a significant impact on Internet traffic, causing record traffic peaks in broadband networks [15] and Content Delivery Networks (CDN) [11].

To better understand how Steam manages video game distribution, this paper investigates Steam's infrastructure and traffic data. First, we examine the data made available by Steam's public REST API [71], as well as the statistics they provide on their storefront [68]. Furthermore, we explore the insights that can be obtained from these data regarding Steam's infrastructure and its correlation with their traffic statistics.

This study offers a rare insight into the operation of a large-scale video game distribution platform. Using publicly available data from Steam, this study investigates how Steam manages the ever-growing traffic demand for the distribution of video games. We explore various aspects of the Steam infrastructure, from the data center level up to how they offload traffic to third-party CDNs. This gives us a better understanding of how Steam sustained a 36% growth in total content delivery between 2021 and 2022.

The main contributions of this study are:

– Characterising infrastructure requirements for a game distribution platform.
– Mapping Steam's presence at data centres and cache locations.
– Show the impact of big game releases and how Steam load balances traffic.
– Quantifying the effectiveness of Steam's infrastructure to serve their content.
– Estimating the capacity of Steam cache servers and quantifying Valve's usage of third-party CDNs to cope with peak traffic.
– Finally, we publish nine months of Steam aggregated traffic and cache load data [73].

2   Characterising Content Distribution

The Internet has enabled the digital distribution of software updates and media content. This section discusses the characteristics of digital distribution and the differences between popular content platforms (summarised in Table 1).

Urgency: A key benefit of digital distribution is the immediacy of content availability. Users no longer need to wait for a CD to update their system or a DVD to watch a movie. Instead, companies can now break down software and system updates into smaller parts and gradually roll them out. Microsoft, for example, famously has "Patch Tuesday" to roll out security updates [39]. For system administrators, this is a critical day to patch their systems. However,

Table 1. Characteristics of different content delivery providers

	Steam	Sports	Windows	Netflix
Urgency	ASAP	1 h+ / streamed	'Patch Tuesday'	1 h+ / streamed
Time	World Wide Sync On-demand	World Wide Sync	Rolling Update	On-demand
Localization	Steam cache + CDN	Multi CDN	Multi CDN	Netflix cache
Catalogue	++++	−	−	++
Users	132+ Million	3 Billion	1.4 Billion	232.5 Million
Size	Up to 128 GB	1 to 7 GB/h	Avg 114 MB - up to 5.4 GB	1 to 7 GB/h
Frequency	1 shot	1 shot	Low frequency	Daily

most end users will patch at their convenience. Services like Netflix and sports broadcasting use streaming to allow users to start watching videos right away and conserve traffic. Consequently, the video download is transparent to the user, as long as their throughput can provide a smooth experience. *Contrarily, upon purchasing a new video game, or during the release of a significant update for a multiplayer game, users are eager to play right away. However, since the user needs to download the entire game, the traffic load cannot be spread over a longer period of time, as seen in video streaming. The only limitation on the download time is the bandwidth available to the user.*

Time: User requests exhibit different temporal characteristics depending on the content provider. Netflix users request videos on-demand, meaning that Netflix traffic occurs when both content and users are available. Microsoft moved towards a rolling updates model, spreading downloads out over a longer period of time. Similar to Steam game releases, sports streaming is usually independent of time zones, as audiences prefer to watch events in real time. *Users download Steam games on-demand, but Steam can automatically dispatch pre-ordered games and updates to users globally. This enables users to consume the latest content as soon as it is available.*

Localization: To improve user experience, content providers aim to bring the content as close as possible to their end users. Sports streaming and Windows Updates use multiple CDNs for widespread availability. Netflix relies mainly on its Open Connect Appliance (OCA) program [43] to deploy its caches within Internet Service Providers and Internet Exchange Points [8,20]. *Valve takes a different approach, using a combination of its own infrastructure (Steam caches) and CDNs. We investigate this further in Sect. 4.5.*

Catalogue: Content variety is a crucial factor in the allocation of cache resources. Content providers need to carefully balance storage space and the availability and regional preferences of items as the variety increases. Due to the live aspect of sports events, the variety of events per provider is quite limited. Likewise, the most frequently downloaded Windows updates are typically the latest ones. As Netflix and Steam focus more on content consumption, they offer a significantly larger library for their users. In March 2023, Slovakia had the largest Netflix library with more than 8,400 titles [64]. *In comparison, Steam has more than 150,000 products listed in its global store* [70].

Users: When comparing the total number of users for each platform, we found that the number of users is inversely proportional to the variety of content. According to Microsoft, there are currently 1.4 billion [41] monthly active devices running Windows 10 or 11. For sports, the number of unique viewers for the Tokyo Olympics 2020 reached 3.05 billion [31]. Unlike other content providers, sports broadcasting includes both TV and streaming. At the beginning of 2023, Netflix reported 232.5 million subscribers [65]. *In 2021, Steam reported an average of 132 million active monthly users* [53].

Size: The shift away from physical media has had varying effects for each of these providers. Streaming platforms are striving to optimise the size of the content they deliver, without compromising quality. Netflix, for example, typically uses a maximum of 7GB of traffic per hour [42]. Microsoft has been working over the past few years to optimise its cumulative update process for Windows. This includes reducing the size by up to 40%, with the average update size now around 114MB [19]. Although Microsoft occasionally provides larger updates, we estimate that these updates should be smaller than the Windows 11 installation media (5.4GB [40]). *Conversely, the size of video games has increased significantly in the past few years* [47]. *Games exceeding 100GB are becoming more common, requiring users to download very large files. For example, the download size for the base file of Baldur's Gate 3 on Windows is 105GB. However, this is only one of the files required for the game, and the game requires 150GB once installed* [61].

Frequency: Finally, the frequency of content acquisition by users can vary significantly between content providers. Even during repeated viewings, viewers must stream content from Netflix servers, although download options are available for mobile devices. Additionally, a viewer can typically only watch one title at a time. This encourages frequent streaming for users who want to explore the variety of content available. Due to the live aspect of sporting events, most people will watch the event as it occurs. Microsoft deploys its updates gradually, keeping the frequency of its updates relatively low. Although the size of video games is significantly larger than that of video content, the frequency of content acquisition differs significantly. *Users are only required to download a video game once, with the vast majority of games requiring only occasional updates.*

Summary: Considering all the characteristics described above, Steam has unique cache requirements. They must accommodate a wide variety of products while also providing sufficient global bandwidth for major game releases. We classify a major game release by download size and global popularity. With video games having a global release and update time, combined with the necessity that users need to download the entire game, distinctive traffic patterns emerge when compared to content from other content providers. We discuss these patterns in more detail in Sect. 4.

Table 2. REST API return table

Parameter	Description
cell_id	Region ID
type	SteamCache or CDN
load	Load
weighted_load	Weighted load
host	hostname
preferred_server	Preferred or not
https_support	optional or Mandatory

(a) Cache Return

Parameter	Description
endpoint	hostname:port
type	websockets or netfilter
load	Load
wtd_load	Weighted load
dc	Data Centre code
realm	Realm identifier

(b) CM Return

3   Peeking into the Engine

In this section, we describe our methodology to collect the data used in this study. We also describe the data itself and how we processed it.

3.1   Web API

Steam provides a public API [71] that game developers [59], third-party sites [23,26,62], and the Steam client itself use. The parameter names are self-explanatory; however, documentation lacks details about the returned values. Of the 26 top-level interfaces that the API exposes, 2 are relevant to our study.

The `ISteamDirectory` interface provides the `GetCMListForConnect` method, which provides a list of *connection managers* (CM). The Steam client application contacts these CM endpoints for user authentication and manages updates and content for the application itself. The configuration file of the Steam client ('`config.vdf`') confirms these findings. This file also includes a parameter `CMWebSocket` with a list of CMs and a `LastPingTimestamp` for each CM.

Furthermore, the `IContentServerDirectoryService` interface offers the method `GetServersForSteamPipe`, which returns a list of Steam cache servers and a few third-party CDN endpoints that are used to download games and updates. Both methods use an optional `cell_id` parameter, a unique identifier for the location of the user. Querying these methods without a `cell_id` parameter instead returns results based on the IP of the client. Specifying an id value overrides this behaviour and returns the servers for that location instead. For example, using a `cell_id` parameter value of 4 returns the same results as clients querying from London. To confirm how the Steam client uses this, we refer to an older Steam client that includes a CellMap.vdf file with a list of cells [63]. Starting from January 2022, Steam clients no longer include this mapping file.

Table 2a presents the cache format from the list returned by the `GetServersForSteamPipe` method. Each server includes a `cell_id` indicating the Steam cache location. Table 2b illustrates how the `GetCMListForConnect` method returns a DC value, but not the `cell_id`.

Table 3. Cache and Connection Manager locations

cell_id	CM	Cache	Interconnects in PeeringDB	City	Country
116	eze1		Cirion	Buenos Aires	Argentina
52	syd1	syd1	Equinix	Sydney	Australia
92	vie1	vie1	Digital Realty	Vienna	Austria
25	gru1	gru1	Equinix	São Paulo	Brazil
117	scl1		Cirion	Santiago	Chile
14	par1	par1	Digital Realty	Paris	France
5	fra1	fra1	Digital Realty, Equinix	Frankfurt	Germany
5	fra2	fra2	Digital Realty, Equinix	Frankfurt	Germany
33	hkg1	hkg1	Equinix, Equinix	Hong Kong	Hong Kong
32	tyo1	tyo1	Equinix, Equinix	Tokyo	Japan
32	tyo2	tyo2	Equinix, Equinix	Tokyo	Japan
15	ams1	ams1	Equinix	Amsterdam	Netherlands
118	lim1		Cirion	Lima	Peru
38	waw1	waw1	Equinix	Warsaw	Poland
35	sgp1	sgp1	Equinix, Equinix	Singapore	Singapore
26	jnb1	jnb1	Teraco	Johannesburg	South Africa
8	seo1			Seoul	South Korea
40	mad1	mad1	Digital Realty	Madrid	Spain
66	sto1	sto1	Digital Realty, Equinix	Stockholm	Sweden
66	sto2	sto2	Digital Realty, Equinix	Stockholm	Sweden
4	lhr1	lhr1	Telehouse	London	United Kingdom
50	atl1	atl1	Digital Realty, Digital Realty	Atlanta	United States
65	dfw1	dfw1	Equinix	Dallas	United States
63	iad1	iad1	Equinix	Ashburn	United States
64	lax1	lax1	CoreSite, Equinix	Los Angeles	United States
1	ord1	ord1	Equinix	Chicago	United States
31	sea1	sea1	Equinix	Seattle	United States
			Equinix	Dubai	United Arab Emirates

We map each DC to the `cell_id` by examining the hostnames of the caches and connection managers. For example, `cache1-sea1.steamcontent.com` shows the type of server, followed by the DC, where the DC is associated with a 3-letter IATA location code. Table 3 contains a detailed list of all caches and connection managers.

Server Preference. Both caches and CMs contain a load and a weighted load value. Steam's API always returns the results in order of the weighted load, with the lowest value on top. Based on our findings discussed in the next section, we can infer that Steam clients use this to prioritise which server to use.

The load value shows the server's current load, with the highest observed value being 95, while the weighted load peaked at 280. Although the weighted load calculation is unclear, we found that it appears to be related to server load and the distance between client and server, as it increases when queried from a `cell_id` that differs from the Steam cache `cell_id`.

Steam caches also include an additional field, `preferred_server`, with a boolean true or false value. We found that Steam considers servers to be preferred when their weighted load value is less than 130. Unlike Steam cache servers, third-party CDN endpoints always have a `prefered_server` value of false and a fixed weighted load value of 130. In Sect. 4.5 we discuss how Steam uses CDNs when no preferred caches are available. Although each of the Steam cache servers has a unique hostname, a CDN endpoint always has the same hostname endpoint regardless of the location queried. To map which `cell_ids` have caches, we query the ids found in `CellMap.vdf` using the `GetServersForSteampipe` method. We also query IDs of up to 100,000 to find undocumented cells; however, we were unable to find additional locations. In total, we found 20 locations that contained caches. The same process was repeated to find the CMs. In general, we found 27 DCs that contained CMS, compared to 23 that contained caches.

```
[08-24 07:57:48] AppID 740 state changed : Update Required,
[08-24 07:57:48] AppID 740 update changed : Running Update,Reconfiguring,
[08-24 07:57:48] Got 5 download sources and 0 caching proxies via
ContentServerDirectoryService::BYieldingGetServersForSteamPipe (CellID 32 / Launcher 3)
[08-24 07:57:48] Created download interface of type 'SteamCache' (7) to host cache4-tyo2.steamcontent.com
[08-24 07:57:48] Created download interface of type 'SteamCache' (7) to host cache1-tyo2.steamcontent.com
[08-24 07:57:48] Created download interface of type 'SteamCache' (7) to host cache3-tyo2.steamcontent.com
[08-24 07:58:01] Increasing target number of download connections to 4 (rate was 0.000, now 537.271)
[08-24 07:58:01] Created download interface of type 'SteamCache' (7) to host cache4-tyo1.steamcontent.com
[08-24 07:58:13] Increasing target number of download connections to 5 (rate was 537.271, now 807.634)
[08-24 08:00:19] AppID 740 state changed : Fully Installed,
[08-24 08:01:08] HTTP/2 (SteamCache,67) - cache3-tyo2.steamcontent.com: Closing connection
[08-24 08:01:14] HTTP/2 (SteamCache,94) - cache4-tyo1.steamcontent.com : Closing connection
[08-24 08:03:19] stats: (SteamCache, 67) cache3-tyo2.steamcontent.com: 2721675904 Bytes, 105 sec
(206.63 Mbps). 19295 Hits / 538 Misses (97 %, 96 % bytes)
[08-24 08:03:19] stats: (SteamCache, 68) cache4-tyo2.steamcontent.com: 2231609202 Bytes, 78 sec
(229.86 Mbps). 12637 Hits / 4 Misses (100 %, 100 % bytes)


[08-24 08:29:31] AppID 740 state changed : Update Required,
[08-24 08:29:31] AppID 740 update changed : Running Update,Reconfiguring,
[08-24 08:29:31] Got 2 download sources and 0 caching proxies via
ContentServerDirectoryService::BYieldingGetServersForSteamPipe (CellID 32 / Launcher 3)
[08-24 08:29:31] Created download interface of type 'CDN' (2) to host steampipe.akamaized.net
[08-24 08:29:31] Created download interface of type 'SteamCache' (7) to host cache6-hkg1.steamcontent.com
[08-24 08:32:11] AppID 740 state changed : Fully Installed,
[08-24 08:33:06] HTTP/2 (SteamCache,290) - cache6-hkg1.steamcontent.com: Closing connection
[08-24 08:33:11] HTTP/2 (CDN,11) - steampipe.akamaized.net : Closing connection
[08-24 08:35:02] stats: (invalid, 0) : 14707081285 Bytes, 157 sec
(750.42 Mbps). 72373 Hits / 2129 Misses (97 %, 96 % bytes)
[08-24 08:35:02] stats: (SteamCache, 290) cache6-hkg1.steamcontent.com: 703437715 Bytes, 142 sec
(39.55 Mbps). 2377 Hits / 9 Misses (100 %, 100 % bytes)
[08-24 08:35:02] stats: (CDN, 11) steampipe.akamaized.net: 14003643570 Bytes, 156 sec
(718.19 Mbps). 0 Hits / 0 Misses (0 %, 0 % bytes)
```

Fig. 1. Condensed download logs for Steam Client in Tokyo as traffic and load increases. Although the first download is made exclusively from caches in Tokyo, the second download 30 min later comes from Hong Kong and a CDN hosted by Akamai.

Validation with Steam CLI. To confirm our findings, we set up five virtual machines (VMs) in the following cities, each of which had a `cell_id`: Chicago, São Paolo, Frankfurt, Tokyo, and Sydney. Using Steam's command line interface [67] we downloaded an instance of *Counter Strike: Global Offensive (CS:GO)* on each VM. During the download, Steam provided verbose logging for the CMs it connects to, as well as the cache servers it uses. Although we were only able to retrieve a maximum of 20 download sources via the web API, we found that the Steam client can reach up to 30 download sources. However, when the available sources dropped below 20, we were able to match the number of sources with what we see in the Web API.

Figure 1 shows the Tokyo VM logs during a CS: GO download, highlighting increased traffic and load. The logs' `cell_id` correspond to Tokyo's data in Table 3. Initial download data shed light on Steam's cache load balancing. The download speed correlates with the intended number of connections, which increased to five, although only four Steam caches were used without initiating the fifth. Once done, a summary provided detailed statistics for each connection, including bytes downloaded, time taken, speeds, and cache hits.

Just 30 min after the initial download, Tokyo's Steam cache load had intensified. This time, the client connected to only two sources, a CDN endpoint from Akamai and a Steam Cache server in Hong Kong, compared to the previous five. The logs also showed an 'Invalid' entry, with no further explanation from Steam. Notably, unlike Steam Caches, it was not possible to ascertain cache hit or miss information from CDNs. Discussions on how Steam uses caches from various cities and their use of CDN are presented in Sects. 4.2 and 4.5.

3.2 Steam Stats

The Steam store provides an extensive list of statistics [68] about its games and players. These include the number of players online, current players engaged in a game, and the maximum daily player count per game. Steam also conducts monthly hardware and software surveys [69]. Steam publishes the results of these surveys to help both users and developers gain a better understanding of the landscape surrounding PC gaming.

The study concentrates on Steam traffic data, the data displayed on their web statistics Web page [68] is also accessible via a Cloudflare endpoint. This displays regional bandwidth, country-specific total bytes, and top Autonomous System Numbers (ASNs) per country. Each endpoint has a date parameter; however, only data for the last 48 h are available. This restricts the historical analysis to the data collected during this study. The bandwidth API provides granular results, showing bandwidth usage per region every 10 min. Steam's website uses this API to plot the download bandwidth used by Steam users [68]. The total number of bytes per country and the top ASNs per country contain only the daily volume of traffic.

Table 4 summarises the countries that consume the most bandwidth and the availability of the cache and connection manager servers per country. In particular, despite China's ranking as the top consumer of Steam traffic, its caches and connection managers are absent from the dataset. Section 5 discusses in more detail the unique way that Steam manages their infrastructure, explaining their absence. Similarly, no API endpoints were found within Russia.

Table 4. Examining the countries with the highest download rates on Steam and the presence of cache and connection managers.

Rank	Country	Cache	CM		Rank	Country	Cache	CM
1	CHN	False	False		13	AUS	True	True
2	USA	True	True		16	ESP	True	True
3	RUS	False	False		17	ARG	False	True
4	DEU	True	True		19	NLD	True	True
5	BRA	True	True		20	SWE	True	True
6	GBR	True	True		24	HKG	True	True
7	CAN	False	False		25	CHL	False	True
8	FRA	True	True		34	AUT	True	True
10	KOR	False	True		38	PER	False	True
11	JPN	True	True		44	SGP	True	True
12	POL	True	True		45	ZAF	True	True

3.3   PeeringDB

Steam's API offers insight into the distribution of Valve's facilities, particularly its content delivery network. PeeringDB [49], another tool for researching Internet infrastructures. Table 3 cross-references the data centre locations found in the Web API with the facilities listed for Valve (AS32590) [48]. This cross-referencing reveals a near perfect match, with the exception of Seoul and Dubai.

Although Seoul does contain CM servers, they do not have any Steam cache servers. Dubai is a more interesting case study. Not only could we not find any CM or Steam Cache servers related to Dubai, but it is also the only presence that we see in the Middle East region.

As of December 2023 there were 1296 ASes in PeeringDB with a 'Content' network type. When ranking ASes based on the number of IXPs the AS is a member of, Valve comes in 21st with 64 IXPs. It ranks just below Apple, which is a member of 67 IXPs, and above Sony Interactive Entertainment (PlayStation) and Twitter, which are members of 38 IXPs each.

Valve's notes section in PeeringDB confirms the findings of Sect. 3.1, noting that "Clients automatically find the closest location".

3.4   Data Collection

We queried each of the API endpoints every 30 min from February 17, 2023, to October 31, 2023. Each API endpoint was queried to obtain the weighted load values experienced within all locations, we queried all APIs multiple times using all valid values of `cell_id` found in Sect. 3.1. We stored the collected data in a MongoDB database to ease data cleaning and processing. As part of the study, both the code used for the collection and the dataset itself are made publicly available [73].

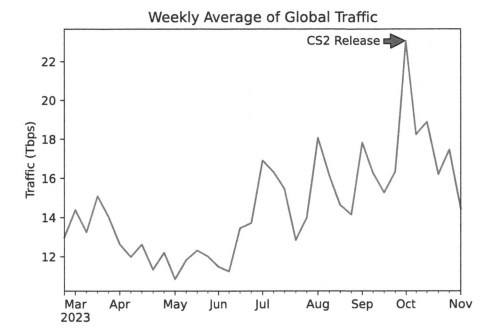

Fig. 2. Weekly average of traffic sent from Steam to end users.

Figure 2 shows the overall trend of Steam traffic. Steam sees an overall increase in traffic throughout the year. Of the five distinct traffic peaks depicted in Fig. 2, four are attributed to a week that contains one or two popular video game releases. The only exception is the peak seen in July, which is attributed to the annual Steam Summer Sale [54]. The large spike at the end of September/start of October is due to the release and update of multiple games [21,57,58], including Counter Strike 2.

Table 5 contains the time intervals used throughout this paper and the names of the relevant datasets. The release of *Counter Strike 2 (CS2)* is a great case study to illustrate how Steam handles sudden increases in traffic, reaching a peak of 85 Tbps. For the baseline, we used two time frames from the dataset. The first is `Prerelease`, based on the same period of three days but two weeks before the release of CS2. The week prior to the CS2 release has multiple popular game releases that made it ineligible to use as a baseline. The other baseline, `Postrelease`, is set a week after the release of CS2. In mid-September we added the metadata of `cell_id` from which the query originated into our dataset. This means that unlike the `Prerelease` dataset, the `Postrelease` dataset includes the origin `cell_id` used to poll the Web API. The origin `cell_id` in `Origin id` is particularly useful to determine how Steam caches are shared between `cell_ids`. Finally, the `Latest` dataset is the most recent 2 months of data representing the most up-to-date information on Steam's infrastructure.

Table 5. Data set properties and notable dates studied.

Dataset Name	Start	End	Notes
Whole dataset	2023/02/18	2023/10/31	Complete dataset
Prerelease	2023/09/13	2023/09/15	Two weeks prior to CS2 release
CS2 release	2023/09/27	2023/09/29	Release period of Counter Strike 2
Postrelease	2023/10/04	2023/10/06	One week after the CS2 release
Origin id	2023/09/25	2023/10/31	Origin cell_id present in metadata
Latest	2023/09/01	2023/10/31	Most recent 2 months

4   Steam Under Pressure

4.1   Load Balancing Within a City

Methodology. Our analysis begins by looking at the traffic and cache load patterns seen during popular game releases. As stated in Sect. 3.2, the Steam API returns a varying number of caches for a DC. To illustrate this behaviour, the load values of each cache server are plotted over time. When a cache is not visible, we assign an artificial load value greater than 100 and mark these events as 'x' in Fig. 3. The study also examines traffic data observed during this period. While the Steam Stats page updates daily for each country, a more detailed analysis utilises regional traffic statistics, available at 10-minute intervals. However, these statistics offer a broader geographic perspective, lacking the finer granularity of country-specific data.

Discussion. Figure 3 depicts an example of traffic in the Asia region compared to the load on Steam cache servers in Tokyo, Japan. Figure 3a shows a baseline using the Prerelease times. The load values follow the typical daily peak and trough pattern expected with daily Internet use. Overlaying the traffic data for the Asia region shows a matching pattern emerges, which indicates that the loads on the servers are related to how much traffic Steam serves.

The loads on all the cache servers remain uniform to each other throughout the day. This demonstrates that Steam shares traffic fairly between each of their cache servers. The other observation we make is that less Steam cache servers are visible in the Steam API during peak times, which suggests that the API is not returning overloaded cache servers. However, while there are fewer Steam cache servers advertised, we do not observe traffic volume flattening, or even decreasing. This is another indication that Valve effectively offloads traffic when there are no Steam cache servers available within a city.

Figure 3b illustrates the traffic and cache load during the Counter Strike 2 (CS2) release. This release sees Steam serving nearly six times more traffic compared to the average traffic they serve. Although traffic volume follows the trend of cache load during off-peak times, the two patterns are different during large releases.

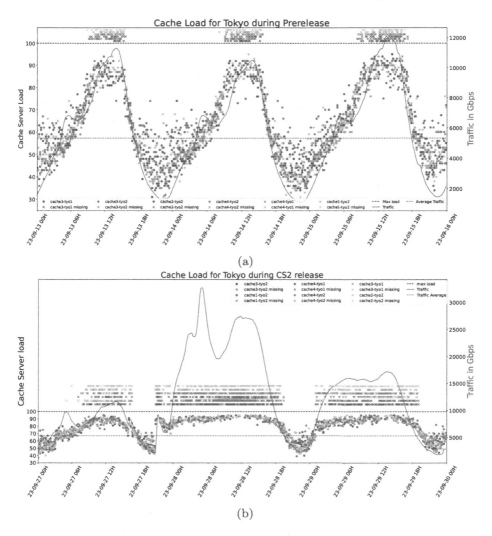

Fig. 3. Load on Steam's cache servers for Tokyo against traffic for Asia. Figure 3a represents a typical week (Sept 13 to Sept 15) while Fig. 3b shows the behaviour for the same period two weeks later during the release of CS2.

Steam usually sees a significant increase in traffic for new games or updates, but the release of CS2 had a combination of factors that contributed to the large increase in traffic shown in Fig. 3b. First, CS2 completely replaces its predecessor Counter Strike: Global Offensive. This means that it behaves more like an update and that Steam clients will download the update as soon as it is available. Whereas new game releases require user interaction to start the download when available. Second, since CS2 does not use any of the already downloaded data from its predecessor, the client needs to download the entire game. The storage requirements for CS2 also increased from 15GB to 85GB, resulting in a significantly larger download compared to a normal update. Finally, Counter Strike is consistently the most played game on Steam, peaking daily at just over a million concurrent players. During the week of CS2's release, the peak concurrent player count grew to over 1.4 million.

Figure 3b shows a sharp increase in traffic and load at 21:00 UTC on September 27 for the release of CS2. However, peak traffic is not reached until 06:00 on September 28. This can be attributed to time zone differences, with it releasing at 06:00 local time in Japan. The traffic volume continues to grow as the rest of Asia wakes up and updates the game. Although the traffic decreases after the peak, it does not drop below the typical peak that normally allows the Steam Cache servers to recover. Traffic returns to its normal pattern in the evening, but at double the traffic levels compared to the previous evening.

The popularity of the game extends to the next day. However, instead of a sharp spike, the traffic is a lot flatter but still sits well above the peak traffic of the 27th (i.e. the day before the game release).

4.2   Load Balancing Between Cities

Methodology. This section investigates how and when Steam redirects users to caches located in other cities and regions. However, the geographic isolation of Tokyo makes it difficult to study how Steam does load balancing between cities. Thus, the focus is on the two regions that have the most Steam cache servers, namely Europe and North America.

During our experiments, we found that Steam often returns servers from other `cell_ids` than the one specified in the request query. Starting in mid-September, the origin `cell_id` was added to the metadata to keep track of servers not based in the origin city.

We create a mapping between the city we searched for and the city of the caches returned by the API. In this study, we focus only on queries that originate from Europe and North America. These regions have the highest number of caches and are therefore more likely to serve other parts of the world. In order to prevent any favoritism towards cities that have a high number of Steam cache servers, such as Frankfurt which has 30 servers, only the top five servers returned from Steam are considered. Due to the large number of servers in Frankfurt, it frequently acts as a secondary cache destination for various European cities. By limiting the selection to the top five entries, it also enhances the assurance that the Steam servers are utilized by the Steam client to download content.

Because the query id metadata was not added until mid-September, we are unable to use the same time frames as the load data in Sect. 4.1 and instead focus on the datasets `CS2 Release` and `Postrelease`. However, to increase readability and maintain consistency with our other figures, Fig. 4 shows the baseline week first followed by the release week.

Discussion. Figure 4 shows a heat map of the cities that request Steam caches versus the cities that advertise available caches. Each row represents the preferred cache servers used to offload traffic by certain cities. As expected, Steam

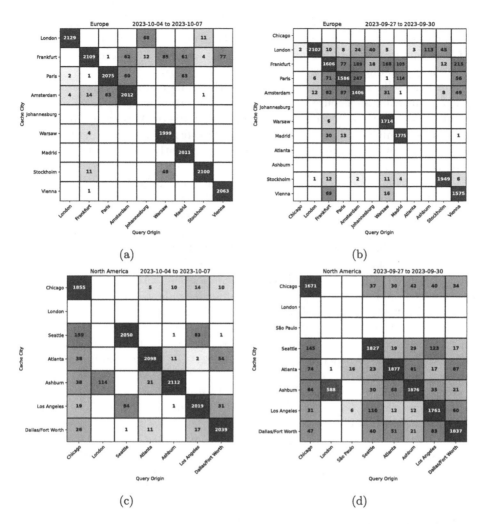

Fig. 4. Load balancing between cities within the same region. (b) and (d) show the state during the release of CS2. (a) and (c) one week after release.

caches mostly serve clients querying from the same `cell_id`. However, when the cache servers of the origin city become overloaded, the Steam API also returns cache servers from other cities. We found that Steam mainly advertises cache servers which are geographically close to the origin `cell_id`. For example, during the `Postrelease` baseline dataset, both Europe and North America contain each only one city, Johannesburg and London, querying from outside their region (Figs. 4a and 4c).

First, we look at Johannesburg, which is the only city in the African region that contains Steam caches. The geographic isolation of Johannesburg in the Steam infrastructure means that there are no other cache servers within the

Africa region to offload traffic when overloaded. Although Europe is the closest region to Africa, there is still a large geographical distance between Johannesburg and London or Frankfurt. Despite this, London and Frankfurt caches frequently serve clients in Johannesburg.

London itself, however, does not follow the same distance logic when overloaded. Unlike Johannesburg, London is not a geographically isolated city. The expectation is that traffic would be offloaded to Paris or Amsterdam because of the close proximity of these cities. However, Figs. 4c and 4d, featuring the North American region, indicate that London is significantly more likely to offload traffic to Ashburn instead.

Figure 4 shows a clear geographic preference for cache entries that appear outside of the origin city. The clearest examples of this are Frankfurt, Paris, and Amsterdam. All three cities are geographically close to each other, and cache entries for each show up in each other's queries. Amsterdam and Paris stay exclusively within this cluster, while Frankfurt also offloads traffic to Warsaw, Vienna, and Stockholm. Even with the limitation of the top five preferred servers, Frankfurt is still the most seen backup cache location in Europe. Madrid also shows a geographic preference, as it often offloads traffic to Paris and Frankfurt, but given its limited number of cache servers, Madrid does not serve other cities.

For North America, there is a geographical preference amongst the East and West Coast servers. Figure 4c shows this best with Seattle on the West Coast during the usual load, where the queries do not return any servers from Chicago, Ashburn, or Atlanta.

The plots on the right of Fig. 4 show the state during the release of CS2. As the cache servers become overloaded, there is an increase in the number of servers retrieved outside the query city. Figure 4b shows that in Europe, cities such as Vienna, Warsaw, and Amsterdam go from two backup cities to five. The North American plots in Fig. 4d show a more uniform distribution of the servers seen from the city from which the query originates. Despite the remaining geographical preferences, when under heavy load, Steam increasingly serves caches to clients on the opposite side of the region. In addition, both regions see new cities from which queries originate. Europe only sees additional requests from the North American region, receiving servers from London. In North America, there is only one new origin city, São Paulo, which received servers from Los Angeles and Atlanta.

4.3 Impact of Video Game Releases for a Region

Methodology. Previous sections focus on the impact of a game release on a city and inter-city level. Where Fig. 5 instead looks at the impact on a regional level. The average load for a region is calculated by combining the load values for Steam caches per region and calculating the average value per timestamp. As described in Sect. 4.1 during peak times, caches no longer advertise being available. In these circumstances, we designate a load value of 100% to that cache.

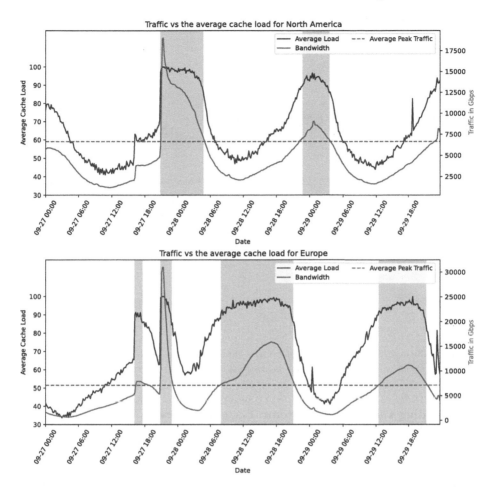

Fig. 5. Traffic and cache load for Europe and North America during the release of the game *Counter Strike 2* on March 28.

Discussion. Unlike in Fig. 3, Fig. 5 shows that both Europe and North America have a much more dramatic increases in traffic. In Europe, there is an almost immediate drop in traffic after the release that can be attributed to the game releasing at 11 PM Central European time. Compared to the North American region, where the game is releasing in the early evening.

We found that when the average cache load for a region reaches around 90, we start to encounter cache servers as no longer being available. The areas highlighted in red show when cache servers start to get overloaded. At this point, Steam no longer advertises these as being available. The cache load starts to plateau during these periods of time, although the traffic still increases. Thus, Steam offloads traffic to third-party CDNs.

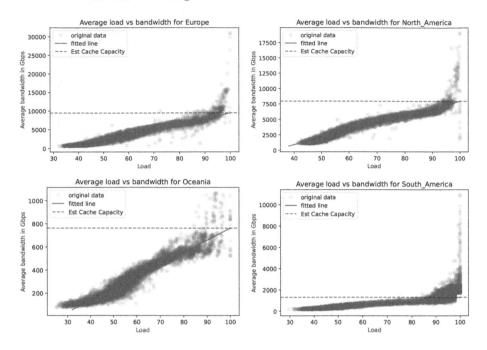

Fig. 6. Traffic against cache load per region. The linear regression is computed for the range $x = [0, 90]$. The cache capacity is derived from linear regression at $x = 100$.

4.4   Finding the Limits of Steam Cache Servers

Methodology. Figure 5 shows the synchronised trends for the cache server load and the traffic data per region. The relationship between these two metrics reflects the capacity of the cache servers in terms of traffic. We compute the linear regression between the load and traffic values for each region and exclude the periods when Steam sends traffic to third-party CDNs.

Similarly to Sect. 4.3, when a cache is no longer available, a load value of 100 is assigned. Although the highest load returned was 95, the inflated load value of 100 helps to increase the average load for the region when caches are no longer present. To find the maximum capacity that Steam caches can provide, we calculate the linear regression against a maximum load value of 80 to 100. Using a maximum load value of 90 gives the highest average r^2 value across all regions of 0.931. We plot the average load and traffic values for each region using data collected from September 1 to October 30.

Discussion. Figure 6 shows the linear regression results along with the data collected from server load and traffic. Each region has a strong positive linear relationship until the cache loads reach 90 and then only the traffic data continue to increase. This is more evidence that Steam sends traffic to third-party CDNs when their cache servers are overloaded. For South America, where load values

Table 6. Estimated effectiveness and capacity (Gbps) of Steam caches per region.

Region	Cache served %	Cache traffic %	Est Cache Cap	Peak traffic
Africa	90.95	82.88	106	281
Asia	96.09	89.50	13556	32657
Europe	97.75	93.42	9470	30954
North America	98.60	96.24	7940	19025
Oceania	99.17	97.66	763	1064
South America	59.22	33.79	1303	10883

are routinely high, we assume a limited cache capacity in that region. In the next section, we quantify the Steam cache capacity for each region and the amount of traffic offloaded to CDNs.

4.5 Pushing Past the Limits

Methodology. To estimate the maximum capacity of a region's cache servers, we use the linear regression results from the previous section and estimate the traffic value for a load value of 100. Figure 6 shows the estimated cache capacity with a dashed line, which corresponds to the change in traffic behaviour shown in Fig. 3. The volume of traffic served increases significantly after crossing the cache capacity line. This indicates that Steam uses CDNs when its cache servers are unable to cope with the increase in traffic.

Based on the estimated cache capacity, we infer the effectiveness of Steam cache servers in distribution over time and in terms of traffic volume. The cache served percentage is identified as the percentage of time when traffic remains within the cache's handling capacity. The cache traffic percentage represents the ratio of the total estimated traffic managed by the caches to the aggregate traffic observed in that region.

Discussion. Table 6 shows the computed cache served and traffic percentages, as well as the estimated cache capacity and the peak traffic seen for each region. These results highlight the effectiveness of Steam caches in Oceania, Europe, and Africa. This is especially apparent in Oceania, where we see limited use of third-party CDNs. CDNs offer a solution to alleviate cache load, allowing increased capacity during periods of high traffic, such as game releases or significant updates. This is particularly beneficial when there is a sudden surge in traffic in a short period of time. The clearest example is South America, where the observed peak traffic is 8.3 times the estimated cache capacity, giving a much flatter representation in Fig. 6. All other regions see peaks between 2 (North America) and 3 (Europe) times their cache capacity.

The South American region would benefit the most from adding more Steam cache servers. Only 59% of the traffic values fall below the cache capacity line. More importantly, caches can only serve 34% of the total traffic in that region.

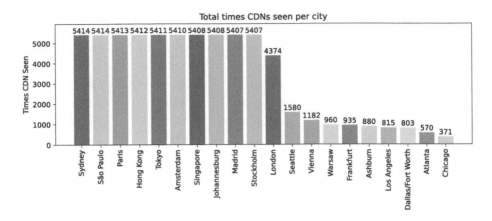

Fig. 7. Frequency of CDNs seen per city

4.6   Third-Party CDNs per City

Methodology. The `Origin id` dataset allows us to gain insight into how Steam uses third-party CDNs around the world. By querying the Steam API with different `cell_id` we can discover where Steam advertises different third-party CDNs to clients and the discrepancies between different cities.

Discussion. Figure 7 depicts the number of third-party CDNs returned per city. Although we performed the same number of queries for each city, the total number of third-party CDNs seen in our queries varies drastically from one city to another. The Steam API appears to be configured to return no more than four CDNs in each query, accounting for the peak values observed near 5400, and does not consistently advertise CDNs for certain cities, with 63% of requests including at least one CDN. The findings of Sect. 4.5 suggest that regions like South America experience frequent traffic offloading, in contrast to Oceania, where this is a rarity. This would lead to the expectation that a city like São Paulo would receive the highest number of CDNs in queries, while Sydney would see the fewest. However, both see the same number of CDNs. Manual inspection of the data reveals that Steam's API only returns third-party CDNs either (1) during peak hours when all the caches in a city are overloaded or (2) for cities that are far from other Steam caches; hence, CDNs are preferred backups. São Paulo and Sydney are both geographically isolated, which explains their high values in Fig. 7. In contrast, cities where Steam rarely advertises CDNs (e.g., Frankfurt and Ashburn) commonly host a larger number of Steam caches and have a close geographical proximity to other host caches.

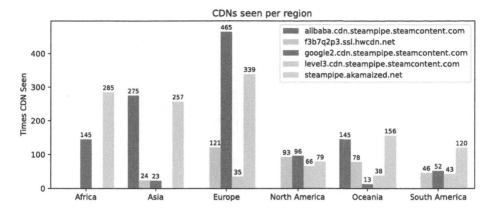

Fig. 8. Number of times CDNs are encountered in each region over a three day period during the release of Counter Strike 2. (27–29 September 2023)

4.7   Global CDN Trends

Methodology. Our dataset reveals that Valve relies on multiple third-party CDNs and that the advertised CDN endpoints may vary depending on the queried `cell_id`. To understand the mechanisms behind this multi-CDN setup, we now focus on which CDNs Steam advertise for different regions and during different loads. In this section, we leverage the `Origin id` dataset to correlate the queried `cell_id` with the domain name of the CDN endpoints returned by the Steam API and look for discrepancies between regions and time periods. Similarly to Sect. 4.3, we limit our results to the top five entries to increase the confidence that the Steam client will download content from the CDNs.

Discussion. Figure 8 shows the third-party CDN providers seen per region during the release of CS2 and the frequency with which each provider was seen. Steam uses five different third-party CDN providers: Google, Akamai, Alibaba, Highwinds, and Lumen (Level 3). However, Google and Akamai are the only providers that Steam returns for all regions. Only Oceania has access to all five CDN providers. In contrast, Africa only receives endpoints for Google and Akamai. Alibaba is the least prevalent CDN in all regions, being present only in Asia and Oceania. Notably, Alibaba is the only provider that lacks HTTPS support.

The preference for CDN providers per region is apparent in Fig. 8. Although Google and Akamai are available in all regions, Steam shows a preference for Google in Europe and North America. Akamai consistently ranks as the first or second most preferred CDN provider. Although Alibaba is only present in two regions, it is also highly preferred as a CDN provider for both of these regions. North America stands out with a more distributed preference among CDN providers. Whereas South America has a strong preference towards Akamai and a balanced preference between the other providers.

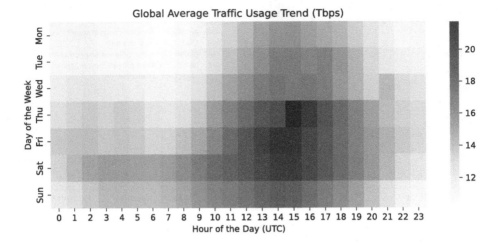

Fig. 9. Traffic trends for Steam based on the time of day and the day of the week. Users are most likely to download from Steam at 15:00 on a Wednesday (UTC), and least likely at 06:00 on a Monday.

4.8   Hourly/Weekly Traffic Insights

Methodology. In previous sections, we compared the traffic within a region during a game release with a baseline time period. Traffic patterns per region tend to follow the normal day-night cycle, except during game releases and updates.

Instead, this section focuses on the trend of traffic usage on a global scale. Mapping the average traffic per hour of the day and per day of the week highlights the most popular times worldwide to download content from Steam.

Discussion. Figure 9 illustrates average traffic usage patterns by time of day and day of the week. The data indicates that Thursdays at 15:00 (UTC) experience the highest average traffic volume, reaching 21.8 Tbps. A significant increase compared to the average of 10.2 Tbps observed on Mondays at 06:00. Analysing the Steam charts for new releases in 2023 offers insight into this trend. In particular, of the twelve top new games based on gross revenue in 2023, five were released on Thursdays and another four on Fridays. Interestingly, Counter Strike 2, despite being the most played game, is absent from the list of new releases in 2023. This is attributed to its classification as an update rather than a new release, underlining the importance of considering game updates as a factor in traffic spikes. Although updates contribute to increased traffic, tracking them poses challenges. Unfortunately, Steam does not provide specific data on update sizes or release timings. However, through SteamDB, we can monitor when new builds are submitted [60], although these do not always correlate with the updates distributed to users.

5   Limitations

Steam Data: The main constraints of this research are related to the reliance on the data provided by Steam's API. Although our findings regarding Steam's promotion of their Steam cache are supported by the Steam client, we lack information about the inner workings of the Steam caches themselves. For instance, the significance of the 'weighted load' remains unclear, and we were unable to get further clarification from Valve regarding this. However, based on our experiments, we could determine that this value fluctuates depending on the load and proximity to the cache and that it serves as a priority indicator. Unfortunately, the exact method used by Steam to calculate this value remains unknown on the basis of the data accessible through the APIs.

There are also insufficient data on cache infrastructure in the Middle East, Central America, and Russia regions. By examining the Cisco Umbrella [12] top 1 million domains and subdomains, we identified two companies that host caches using the same top-level domain as Steam's caches. These companies include RETN ltd [52], which specialises in connecting networks between Europe and Asia, and CTM [17], a Macau-based telecommunications company.

Another constraint is the expansive interpretation of the term 'region'. Consequently, it becomes challenging to determine the specific geographical location where user traffic is attributed to one region rather than another. This issue is particularly significant in regions with limited caches, such as Africa, where only one datacenter is available in South Africa.

Splinternet: In our study, fully incorporating or disregarding China is a challenging task. The launch of Steam China in early 2021 makes it a relatively new platform. However, unlike Steam Global, Steam China lacks access to community features, such as discussions or the Steam marketplace. Furthermore, the public statistics we use in this study do not include data from Steam China. As shown in Table 2b, the only 'realms' present are 'steamglobal' and 'steamchina'. This limitation is the result of the strict regulations imposed on game releases in China [45].

According to the public statistics provided by Steam [68], China is often ranked as the top country for global Steam traffic. However, when using the Web API, no Chinese cache servers or connection managers are returned. By changing the API domain name from *steampowered.com* to *steamchina.com*, we can access an API similar to that described in Sect. 3.2. However, the naming convention of the returned values is significantly different, making it difficult to include them in our study. We also attempted to query the SPSVERBc8s we found in Sect. 3.1 against the Steam China API. However, the API only returned CDNs, similar to cases where there are no Steam caches for a `cell_id`. Given the increasing awareness of the 'Splinternet', we believe that investigating the differences between Steam China and Steam Global could serve as an interesting case study.

6   Related Work

6.1   Gaming

Past networking studies on video games have focused on the characterisation of game traffic [10,22,27]. More recent studies have focused on the impact of cloud gaming on Internet traffic [5,9,14,18,74,76]. Others focus on game security issues, such as DoS attacks [33], account theft [51], and cheating detection [35].

To the best of our knowledge, there is only a limited number of research papers on the Steam platform. Using Steam's API, studies focus primarily on the social impact of Steam users [46], and Steam communities [6]. Lin et al. [36] analysed the growing trend of popular games that require urgent updates. While they are using Steam as an example, this work's primary focus is on the patch update cycle of games.

6.2   CDNs

The research community has dedicated substantial efforts to uncovering the infrastructure of large content distribution networks. Gigis et al. [25] studied hypergiant off-net cache deployments and demonstrated the massive deployment of cache servers in access networks to bring content closer to users and reduce inter-domain traffic.

The hybrid-CDN approach used by Steam is not uncommon for large content providers to use, with multiple companies advertising such services [4,38,72]. One of the key benefits of using this approach is to increase availability in geographically distributed regions. The other benefit, which is one of the primary focuses of our study, is to use third-party CDNs as an overflow as caches reach their maximum capacity.

Similar multi-CDN solutions are commercially available [2,13,37], with the same goal of making content available in more regions. Hohlfeld et al. [29] studied one of these multi-CDN solutions, providing insights into the infrastructure employed, its usage, and performance (mainly in terms of RTTs). We found that Valve closely follows the strategies described in the survey among EBU members surrounding the use of CDNs [66]. In particular the following:

- Use own CDN until max capacity and CDNs as overflow.
- Use a content management system to provide the CDN location to the client.
- Use Multi-CDNs.

Online video streaming services, and in particular Netflix, have also received a lot of attention in recent research. A measurement study [20] from residential networks has shown the extensive deployment of Netflix caches and their effectiveness. Other studies have emphasised how Netflix leverages IXPs [8] and third-party CDNs [1] to cope with the ever increasing amount of video traffic.

Another approach to hybrid CDNs is to incorporate peer-to-peer into the design architecture, creating a Hybrid CDN-P2P. Research into this design aims to lower cost, increase scalability, and reduce latency for content delivery, especially in video content streaming [28, 30, 44, 75]. In March 2023 Steam introduced a feature that allows users to copy existing game installations and update files from one PC to another over a local network [55]. Although this is on a much smaller scale compared to other P2P networks, this reduces Internet traffic in networks with multiple Steam clients. We can foresee a possibility of Steam expanding the capabilities of this to work outside the local network, further reducing the load on their infrastructure.

7   Conclusion

In this paper, we characterise the properties of video game distribution on the Internet and investigate the case of the Steam platform. Our study documents the physical infrastructure of Steam, the impact of video game releases, the capacity of Steam cache servers, and its usage of third-party CDNs. We found that Steam infrastructure handles most of the traffic load but offloads to CDNs the substantial traffic peaks due to popular game releases and updates. Overall, our study shows that Valve does a good job with its Steam distribution platform, especially during game releases. However, regions such as Africa and especially South America could benefit from more caches within the region.

Infrastructure Design: The notably large spikes observed for video game distribution are mainly due to the size of the video game files, the synchronised worldwide releases, the urgency to download all the files to play a game and the increasing popularity of video games. Handling these relatively short but intense traffic spikes with only Steam infrastructure would require them to more than double their infrastructure capacity. This is an interesting example that illustrates a cost trade-off to develop an infrastructure that is effective about 95% of the time and leverages the flexibility of CDNs to deal with overloads. Valve serves as an exemplary case study, illustrating why EBU members advocate for their specific strategies in the management of CDNs [66].

Public Dataset: The ephemeral nature of our data availability during collection makes our dataset a valuable resource for insights into Steam's inner workings. We actively maintain and update this dataset and have made it publicly available [73]. We believe that the combination of granular traffic statistics, infrastructure overview, and Internet performance per country and per Internet Service Provider gives a better understanding of global Internet usage trends.

Future Work. The main objective of this exploratory study is to collect information about Steam's infrastructure from data that Steam provides. However, this is not the end, as Steam is continually growing. Since the start of our study, Steam has increased the total number of caches they operate from 152 up to 193. Over time, we plan to document and monitor further changes to their infrastructure and the resulting impact.

Other future work also includes monitoring long-term trends of performance by Internet Service Providers and download statistics per country. Although these were not granular enough to include for this study, they could prove valuable for following long-term trends.

References

1. Adhikari, V.K., et al.: Unreeling Netflix: understanding and improving multi-CDN movie delivery. In: 2012 Proceedings IEEE INFOCOM, pp. 1620–1628 (2012). https://doi.org/10.1109/INFCOM.2012.6195531
2. Altomare, F.: Multi Content Delivery Network Explained (2021). https://www.globaldots.com/resources/blog/multi-content-delivery-network-explained. Accessed 31 Oct 2023
3. Arsenault, D.: Super Power, Spoony Bards, and Silverware: The Super Nintendo Entertainment System. MIT Press, Cambridge (2017)
4. Barcelona, A.: Why and When Do You Need a Hybrid or Multi-CDN Strategy? https://info.varnish-software.com/blog/why-and-when-do-you-need-a-hybrid-or-multi-cdn-strategy. Accessed 31 Oct 2023
5. Barman, N., Zadtootaghaj, S., Schmidt, S., Martini, M.G., Möller, S.: GamingVideoSET: a dataset for gaming video streaming applications. In: 2018 16th Annual Workshop on Network and Systems Support for Games (NetGames), pp. 1–6 (2018). https://doi.org/10.1109/NetGames.2018.8463362
6. Becker, R., Chernihov, Y., Shavitt, Y., Zilberman, N.: An analysis of the steam community network evolution. In: 2012 IEEE 27th Convention of Electrical and Electronics Engineers in Israel, pp. 1–5 (2012). https://doi.org/10.1109/EEEI.2012.6377133
7. Bode, K.: Steam Powered - Broadband distribution system to go live — DSLReports, ISP Information (2003). http://www.dslreports.com/shownews/32475. Accessed 25 May 2023
8. Böttger, T., Cuadrado, F., Tyson, G., Castro, I., Uhlig, S.: Open connect everywhere: a glimpse at the internet ecosystem through the lens of the Netflix CDN. ACM SIGCOMM Comput. Commun. Rev. 48(1), 28–34 (2018)
9. Carrascosa, M., Bellalta, B.: Cloud-gaming: analysis of Google Stadia traffic. Comput. Commun. 188, 99–116 (2022)
10. Chen, K.T., Huang, P., Huang, C.Y., Lei, C.L.: Game traffic analysis: an MMORPG perspective. In: Proceedings of the International Workshop on Network and Operating Systems Support for Digital Audio and Video, pp. 19–24 (2005)
11. Cimpanu, C.: Last week's Fortnite update helped Akamai set a new CDN traffic record (2019). https://www.zdnet.com/article/last-weeks-fortnite-update-helped-akamai-set-a-new-cdn-traffic-record. Accessed 25 May 2023
12. Cisco Umbrella: Cisco Popularity List. https://s3-us-west-1.amazonaws.com/umbrella-static/index.html. Accessed 30 Oct 2023
13. Citrix: Best practices for evaluating and implementing a multi-CDN strategy (2023). https://www.citrix.com/content/dam/citrix/en_us/documents/whitepaper/best-practices-for-evaluating-and-implementing-a-multi-cdn-strategy.pdf. Accessed 31 Oct 2023
14. Claypool, M., Finkel, D., Grant, A., Solano, M.: Thin to win? Network performance analysis of the OnLive thin client game system. In: 2012 11th Annual Workshop on Network and Systems Support for Games (NetGames), pp. 1–6 (2012). https://doi.org/10.1109/NetGames.2012.6404013

15. Collins, B.: What's Caused The Biggest UK Broadband Traffic Spike In The Past Week? 'Call Of Duty', Not Coronavirus (2020). https://www.forbes.com/sites/barrycollins/2020/03/19/whats-caused-the-biggest-broadband-traffic-spike-in-the-past-week-call-of-duty-not-coronavirus. Accessed 25 May 2023
16. Copeland, B.: The Manchester computer: a revised history part 1: the memory. IEEE Ann. Hist. Comput. **33**(1), 4–21 (2011). https://doi.org/10.1109/MAHC.2010.1
17. CTM: About CTM. https://www.ctm.net/en-US/company/about.html. Accessed 30 Oct 2023
18. Di Domenico, A., Perna, G., Trevisan, M., Vassio, L., Giordano, D.: A network analysis on cloud gaming: stadia, GeForce now and PSNow. Network **1**(3), 247–260 (2021). https://doi.org/10.3390/network1030015. https://www.mdpi.com/2673-8732/1/3/15
19. DiAcetis, S.: Windows 11 cumulative update improvements: an overview (2021). https://techcommunity.microsoft.com/t5/windows-it-pro-blog/windows-11-cumulative-update-improvements-an-overview/ba-p/2842961. Accessed 16 May 2023
20. Doan, T.V., Bajpai, V., Crawford, S.: A longitudinal view of Netflix: content delivery over IPv6 and content cache deployments. In: IEEE INFOCOM 2020 - IEEE Conference on Computer Communications, pp. 1073–1082 (2020). https://doi.org/10.1109/INFOCOM41043.2020.9155367
21. EA Sports: EA SPORTS FC^{TM} 24. https://store.steampowered.com/app/2195250/EA_SPORTS_FC_24. Accessed 11 Jan 2024
22. Feng, W.C., Chang, F., Feng, W.C., Walpole, J.: A traffic characterization of popular on-line games. IEEE/ACM Trans. Netw. **13**(3), 488–500 (2005)
23. Galyonkin, S.: Games sales. https://steamspy.com. Accessed 27 May 2023
24. Gamespot: Half-Life 2 now preloading via Steam (2004). https://www.gamespot.com/articles/half-life-2-now-preloading-via-steam/1100-6105848. Accessed 25 May 2023
25. Gigis, P., et al.: Seven years in the life of Hypergiants' off-nets. In: Proceedings of the 2021 ACM SIGCOMM 2021 Conference, pp. 516–533 (2021)
26. Gray, J.: Steam Charts - Tracking What's Played. https://steamcharts.com. Accessed 27 May 2023
27. Gu, L., Jia, A.L.: Player activity and popularity in online social games and their implications for player retention. In: 2018 16th Annual Workshop on Network and Systems Support for Games (NetGames), pp. 1–6 (2018). https://doi.org/10.1109/NetGames.2018.8463415
28. Ha, D.H., Silverton, T., Fourmaux, O.: A novel Hybrid CDN-P2P mechanism for effective real-time media streaming. Semantic Scholar, pp. 1–8 (2008)
29. Hohlfeld, O., Rüth, J., Wolsing, K., Zimmermann, T.: Characterizing a meta-CDN. In: Beverly, R., Smaragdakis, G., Feldmann, A. (eds.) PAM 2018. LNCS, vol. 10771, pp. 114–128. Springer, Cham (2018). https://doi.org/10.1007/978-3-319-76481-8_9
30. Huang, C., Wang, A., Li, J., Ross, K.W.: Understanding hybrid CDN-P2P: why limelight needs its own red swoosh. In: Proceedings of the 18th International Workshop on Network and Operating Systems Support for Digital Audio and Video, pp. 75–80 (2008)
31. International Olympic Committee: Olympic Games Tokyo 2020 watched by more than 3 billion people - Olympic News (2022). https://olympics.com/ioc/news/olympic-games-tokyo-2020-watched-by-more-than-3-billion-people. Accessed 24 May 2023

32. Kalata, K.: Hardcore Gaming 101: Phantasmagoria (2023). https://web.archive. org/web/20170109174423/http://www.hardcoregaming101.net/phantasmagoria/ phantasmagoria.htm. Accessed 26 May 2023

33. Karami, M., McCoy, D.: Rent to PWN: analyzing commodity booter DDoS services. Usenix Login **38**(6), 20–23 (2013)

34. Kates, J.: Bertie the Brain. Canadian National Exhibition, Toronto (1950)

35. Kim, H., Yang, S., Kim, H.K.: Crime scene re-investigation: a postmortem analysis of game account stealers' behaviors. In: 2017 15th Annual Workshop on Network and Systems Support for Games (NetGames), pp. 1–6 (2017). https://doi.org/10. 1109/NetGames.2017.7991540. ISSN 2156-8146

36. Lin, D., Bezemer, C.P., Hassan, A.E.: Studying the urgent updates of popular games on the Steam platform. Empir. Softw. Eng. **22**, 2095–2126 (2017)

37. Lumen: How does a multi-CDN strategy work for my business? https://assets. lumen.com/is/content/Lumen/how-does-a-multi-cdn-strategy-work-for-my-business. Accessed 31 Oct 2023

38. Medianova: Hybrid CDN: A combination of Private and Multi-CDN! https://www. medianova.com/hybrid-cdn-a-combination-of-private-and-multi-cdn. Accessed 31 Oct 2023

39. Microsoft: Security Update Guide FAQs. https://www.microsoft.com/en-us/msrc/ faqs-security-update-guide. Accessed 24 May 2023

40. Microsoft: Download Windows 11 (2023). https://www.microsoft.com/software-download/windows11. Accessed 24 May 2023

41. Microsoft: Microsoft by the Numbers (2023). https://news.microsoft.com/ bythenumbers/bythenumbers/en/windowsdevices. Accessed 24 May 2023

42. Netflix: How to control how much data Netflix uses. https://help.netflix.com/en/ node/87. Accessed 24 May 2023

43. Netflix: Requirements for deploying embedded appliances (2023). https:// openconnect.zendesk.com/hc/en-us/articles/360034538352-Requirements-for-deploying-embedded-appliances. Accessed 24 May 2023

44. Ni, J., Tsang, D.H., Yeung, I.S., Hei, X.: Hierarchical content routing in large-scale multimedia content delivery network. In: IEEE International Conference on Communications, ICC 2003, vol. 2, pp. 854–859. IEEE (2003)

45. Niko: Game regulations in China: everything you need to know (2020). https:// nikopartners.com/game-regulations-in-china-everything-you-need-to-know. Accessed 31 Oct 2023

46. O'Neill, M., Vaziripour, E., Wu, J., Zappala, D.: Condensing steam: distilling the diversity of gamer behavior. In: Proceedings of the 2016 Internet Measurement Conference, pp. 81–95 (2016)

47. Orland, K.: Despite 100GB video games, average download times are decreasing (2020). https://arstechnica.com/gaming/2020/06/ars-analysis-were-spending-less-time-downloading-games-on-average. Accessed 24 May 2023

48. PeeringDB: AS32590 - Valve Corporation. https://www.peeringdb.com/net/4782. Accessed 18 Sept 2023

49. PeeringDB: PeeringDB. https://www.peeringdb.com. Accessed 18 Sept 2023

50. Perry, T.S., Wallich, P.: Microprocessors: design case history: the atari video computer system: by omitting lots of hardware, designers added flexibility and gave video-game programmers room to be creative. IEEE Spectr. **20**(3), 45–51 (1983). https://doi.org/10.1109/MSPEC.1983.6369841

51. Prather, J., Nix, R., Jessup, R.: Trust management for cheating detection in distributed massively multiplayer online games. In: 2017 15th Annual Workshop on Network and Systems Support for Games (NetGames), pp. 1–3 (2017). https://doi.org/10.1109/NetGames.2017.7991547. ISSN 2156-8146
52. RETN: About RETN. https://retn.net/about. Accessed 30 Oct 2023
53. Steam: Steam - 2021 Year in Review (2022). https://store.steampowered.com/news/group/4145017/view/3133946090937137590. Accessed 24 May 2023
54. Steam: 2023 Official Steam Sales and Fests Schedule (2023). https://store.steampowered.com/news/group/4145017/view/3645136358931000680. Accessed 11 Jan 2024
55. Steam: News - Steam Client Update Released (2023). https://store.steampowered.com/oldnews/191068. Accessed 11 Mar 2024
56. Steam: Steam Year In Review 2022 (2023). https://store.steampowered.com/news/group/4145017/view/3677786186779762807. Accessed 25 May 2023
57. Steam Community: Cyberpunk 2077: Phantom Liberty (2023). https://steamcommunity.com/games/1091500/announcements/detail/3725096176290982673. Accessed 11 Jan 2024
58. Steam Community: Cyberpunk 2077: Update 2.0 (2023). https://steamcommunity.com/games/1091500/announcements/detail/3725096176290982673. Accessed 01 Nov 2024
59. Steam Support: Documentation Home Page (2023). https://partner.steamgames.com/doc/home. Accessed 27 May 2023
60. SteamDB: Patchnotes. https://steamdb.info/patchnotes. Accessed 11 Jan 2024
61. SteamDB: Baldur's Gate 3 - SteamDB (2023). https://steamdb.info/app/1086940/depots. Accessed 31 Sept 2023
62. SteamDB: SteamDB (2023). https://steamdb.info. Accessed 27 May 2023
63. SteamDB: Steamtracking - Cell Map.vdf (2024). https://github.com/SteamDatabase/SteamTracking/blob/0aac5ea77a74acd76194b7b8eaca43ecd6c997d6/ClientExtracted/steam/cached/CellMap.vdf. Accessed 11 Jan 2024
64. Stoll, J.: Netflix library by country for March 2023 (2023). https://www.statista.com/statistics/1013571/netflix-library-size-worldwide. Accessed 16 May 2023
65. Stoll, J.: Netflix: number of subscribers worldwide 2023 (2023). https://www.statista.com/statistics/250934/quarterly-number-of-netflix-streaming-subscribers-worldwide
66. Tullemans, B.: CDN Architectures Demystified (2022). https://tech.ebu.ch/publications/tr068. Accessed 31 Oct 2023
67. Valve: SteamCMD: - Valve Developer Community. https://developer.valvesoftware.com/wiki/SteamCMD_Linux. Accessed 20 Sept 2023
68. Valve: Game and Player Statistics (2023). https://store.steampowered.com/stats/content. Accessed 16 May 2023
69. Valve: Steam Hardware & Software Survey (2023). https://store.steampowered.com/hwsurvey. Accessed 16 May 2023
70. Valve: Steam Search (2023). https://store.steampowered.com/search?ndl=1. Accessed 24 May 2023
71. Valve: Steam Web API - Valve Developer Community (2023). https://developer.valvesoftware.com/wiki/Steam_Web_API_GetNewsForApp_.28v0001.29. Accessed 25 May 2023
72. Vecima: Hybrid CDN — Vecima Networks, Inc. https://vecima.com/hybrid-cdn. Accessed 31 Oct 2023

73. Visser, C., Fontugne, R.: Steam Content Delivery Network Study (2024). https://belthazaar.github.io/ExploringSteamPage
74. Wang, P.C., Ellis, A.I., Hart, J.C., Hsu, C.H.: Optimizing next-generation cloud gaming platforms with planar map streaming and distributed rendering. In: 2017 15th Annual Workshop on Network and Systems Support for Games (NetGames), pp. 1–6 (2017). https://doi.org/10.1109/NetGames.2017.7991544. ISSN 2156-8146
75. Xu, D., Kulkarni, S.S., Rosenberg, C., Chai, H.K.: Analysis of a CDN-P2P hybrid architecture for cost-effective streaming media distribution. Multimedia Syst. **11**, 383–399 (2006)
76. Zhao, S., Abou-zeid, H., Atawia, R., Manjunath, Y.S.K., Sediq, A.B., Zhang, X.P.: Virtual reality gaming on the cloud: a reality check. In: 2021 IEEE Global Communications Conference (GLOBECOM), pp. 1–6. IEEE (2021)

Network Anatomy and Real-Time Measurement of Nvidia GeForce NOW Cloud Gaming

Minzhao Lyu[1]([✉]) [iD], Sharat Chandra Madanapalli[2] [iD], Arun Vishwanath[2] [iD], and Vijay Sivaraman[1] [iD]

[1] University of New South Wales, Sydney, Australia
{minzhao.lyu,vijay}@unsw.edu.au
[2] Canopus Networks Pty., Ltd., Sydney, Australia
{sharat,arun}@canopusnet.com

Abstract. Cloud gaming, wherein game graphics is rendered in the cloud and streamed back to the user as real-time video, expands the gaming market to billions of users who do not have gaming consoles or high-power graphics PCs. Companies like Nvidia, Amazon, Sony and Microsoft are investing in building cloud gaming platforms to tap this large unserved market. However, cloud gaming requires the user to have high-bandwidth and stable network connectivity – whereas a typical console game needs about 100–200 kbps, a cloud game demands minimum 10–20 Mbps. This makes the Internet Service Provider (ISP) a key player in ensuring the end-user's good gaming experience.

In this paper we develop a method to detect Nvidia's GeForce NOW cloud gaming sessions over their network infrastructure, and measure associated user experience. In particular, we envision ISPs taking advantage of our method to provision network capacity at the right time and in the right place to support growth in cloud gaming at the right experience level; as well as identify the role of contextual factors such as user setup (browser vs app) and connectivity type (wired vs wireless) in performance degradation. We first present a detailed anatomy of flow establishment and volumetric profiles of cloud gaming sessions over multiple platforms, followed by a method to detect gameplay and measure key experience aspects such as latency, frame rate and resolution via real-time analysis of network traffic. The insights and methods are also validated in the lab for XBox Cloud Gaming platform. We then implement and deploy our method in a campus network to capture gameplay behaviors and experience measures across various user setups and connectivity types which we believe are valuable for network operators.

1 Introduction

Cloud gaming, also known as Game-as-a-Service (GaaS), allows users to play graphics-intensive games without having to own expensive hardware such as

P. Richter et al. (Eds.): PAM 2024, LNCS 14537, pp. 61–91, 2024.
https://doi.org/10.1007/978-3-031-56249-5_3

gaming consoles (*e.g.*, PlayStation and X-Box) and PCs equipped with high-end graphics cards. Instead, game graphics is rendered on powerful cloud-hosted servers, and the resulting video is streamed instantaneously to the end-user's device. Though cloud gaming is still nascent, it is estimated to grow 58.75% each year to become a $22.53 billion industry by 2030 [5,13,31]. Entities such as Nvidia, Amazon, Sony, and Microsoft, as well as a slew of smaller companies, have commercial cloud gaming offerings in the market already.

A significant barrier to the growth of cloud gaming is the high bandwidth that it demands from the network. Whereas a typical game (*e.g.*, shooting game like Call-of-Duty or sports game like FIFA) played on a console or PC requires only a few hundred kilobits-per-second (kbps) from the network [26], a cloud game demands two orders of magnitude more, namely tens of Megabits-per-second (Mbps). If such higher bandwidth (coupled with low latency) is not consistently available, gaming experience becomes frustrating due to drop in frames-per-second (fps), poor resolution, and jerky movements. Internet Service Providers (ISPs) often bear the brunt of this frustration, leading to complaints, churn, and reputational damage.

ISPs have historically overprovisioned their networks with respect to peak aggregate volumes, agnostic to the application mix. This is ceasing to be cost-effective as access speeds increase, because elastic applications (like large downloads) can grab unconstrained amounts of network bandwidth at any instant, degrading performance for experience-sensitive applications (like cloud gaming). ISPs are therefore looking for ways to distinguish (and potentially segregate) the latter – as one example, Comcast recently announced [25] it will support low latency forwarding in its cable broadband network for application streams marked by specific content providers (such as Apple and Nvidia). ISPs are therefore seeking to gain visibility and control into which content is worthy of preferential bandwidth or latency treatment, custom tune their network provisioning by locale in an on-demand manner to retain cost-efficiency, and continuously monitor user experience on cloud gaming and other sensitive applications to protect brand reputation.

To the best of our knowledge, little research has been done for ISPs to measure the prevalence of, and experience on, cloud gaming over their network infrastructure with fine visibility into user setups and functionalities of traffic flows, so that they can configure their networks (*e.g.*, via network APIs and slices) for guaranteed user experience. Prior works have analysed website browsing [44], video streaming [24,39,43], live video [27], console/PC gaming [26], *etc.*, but not cloud gaming. Existing studies of cloud gaming have considered video processing delays on client devices/cloud servers [17], energy consumption on mobile devices [4], differentiating cloud game RTP flows [20] from UDP traffic, impact of wireless/edge network conditions on gameplay RTP flows [7,21,22], which are not of relevance to ISPs who seek insights to better manage their networks.

Our objective in this work is to develop practical methods that can be deployed by ISPs to gain fine-grained visibility into cloud gaming behaviors and experience, so they can be actively involved in, rather than be cut out of, managing service delivery quality. We have chosen to primarily focus on Nvidia's cloud gaming platform, GeForce NOW (GFN), in this paper for a few reasons: (a) it is currently recognized as the leader in the global cloud gaming market [29]; (b) it supports a rich collection of multiplayer games from all major game publishers like Steam, Ubisoft, and Epic Games; (c) it has local servers hosted in the geography where our experiments were conducted; (d) the research team has access to the personnel operating the GFN servers for the region, making it easier to seek clarifications and corroborate findings; and (e) it is accessible broadly, both via the browser and a bespoke app, on desktops (*i.e.,* macOS and Windows) and mobile devices (*i.e.,* android and iOS), thereby providing a rich set of conditions under which it can be studied. The obtained insights and developed methods are also preliminarily validated in our lab for XBox Cloud Gaming that together with GeForce NOW dominate over 90% of market share globally [35] and in Australia.

Our *first contribution* (Sect. 3) reveals the detailed anatomy of GeForce NOW cloud gaming. We identify the establishment of various flows, and benchmark their volumetric patterns, associated with gameplay management, user input, and audio/video streaming, while highlighting the differences between the user playing on a browser versus the app. We also identify attributes in the traffic that aid in user experience estimation, such as sequence numbers for measuring latency and marker packets or stochastic patterns in packet payload sizes for detecting frame boundaries.

Our *second contribution* (Sect. 4) develops a practical network traffic analysis method to detect cloud gaming sessions and measure gameplay experience. We use a stateful mapping mechanism that tracks service domains accessed by active user flows so as to detect the start of a cloud gaming session, as well as identify the user setup (*i.e.,* operating system and software agent type). We then categorize the gameplay flows as gaming management, user input, and video streaming based on volumetric attributes. Network operators can therefore prioritize certain gameplay flows for guaranteed user experience such as mapping user inputs into low-latency network slices (*e.g.,* URLLC) while assigning gaming video to high-bandwidth slices. Finally, we derive user experience measures, including client-platform latency (between the gamer device and cloud platform), video frame rate, and video graphic resolution.

For our *third contribution* (Sect. 5), we implement our methods as a prototype and deploy it in a University campus network[1] with on-premise student housing. We evaluate the accuracy of our method via gameplay in the lab on-campus. We then collect data in the wild, and present some interesting insights obtained over the course of a month spanning 362 h of playtime. We found about 36% of playtime was via browsers, which were all in low resolution (Standard Definition)

---

[1] We have obtained ethics clearance (UNSW Human Research Ethics Advisory Panel approval number HC211007) which allows us to analyze campus network traffic to infer application usage behaviors. Note that user identities remain anonymous – no attempt is made to extract or reveal any personal user information, and all results presented are aggregated across the campus.

Table 1. Popular cloud gaming platforms on the market and their specifications.

Platform	Operator	Operating System	Soft. Agent
GeForce NOW [32]	Nvidia	Windows, macOS, iOS, Android	app, browser
XBox Cloud Gaming [30]	Microsoft	Windows, iOS, android, XBox	app, browser
PlayStation PLUS [42]	Sony	Windows, PS4, PS5	app
Luna [2]	Amazon	Windows, macOS, android, iOS	app, browser

- probably because the browser is not as optimized as the app. The laptop app accounted for 51% of playtime, and was for the most part in High Definition, though interestingly it tended to reduce frame rate from 60 fps to 30 fps more often, most likely so it could preserve the higher video resolution. The mobile app accounted for 14% of playtime, and was largely in high resolution. Knowing the mix of user setups will help ISPs tune and troubleshoot their networks to uplift user experience in a cost-efficient manner.

2 Cloud Gaming Background and Workflow

In this section, we provide an overview of current development in cloud gaming and highlight the challenges that arise for Internet service providers (Sect. 2.1). We then discuss typical operational process of gameplay on a cloud gaming platform (Sect. 2.2).

2.1 Development of Cloud Gaming

In order to provide gamers with the opportunity to play graphic-intensive games on their everyday PCs without the need to invest in high-end devices, leading companies in graphic processing (*e.g.*, Nvidia), cloud services (*e.g.*, Amazon), and gaming operations (*e.g.*, Sony) have embarked on the development of the "cloud gaming" business model, also referred to as Game-as-A-Service. This model moves on-device gaming processing to the powerful cloud compute clusters. Under this model, gamers can subscribe to the service and gain access to a dedicated cloud platform that supports a wide range of graphics-demanding games. The gameplay scenes are then rendered in real-time on the cloud servers and streamed to the user's device.

The popular cloud gaming platforms operated by the above-mentioned tech giants are listed in Table 1, with their specifications including operator, supported operating systems (OS), and software agents. It is clear that all of the four platforms are accessible on major OSes and support both console applications and browsers, except that XBox Cloud Gaming does not support macOS and only available via its console application.

However, such operational mode shifts the requirement of running high-end games from expensive graphic processing and computing hardware on user device to the network's capability of streaming high-resolution live video, along with

Fig. 1. A typical cloud gaming process.

other essential gaming requirements such as low latency and jitter. This can result in significant data consumption, often exceeding several tens of Megabits per second. In comparison to traditional online games that primarily exchange lightweight flags consisting of user inputs and server responses, which typically require only a few kilobits per second, cloud gaming places unprecedented burdens on carrier networks. If not properly managed, the increased network demands can lead to customer frustration and even prompt users to switch network providers. Recognizing the emerging challenges for ISPs, as an early step, we undertake a study that focuses on the network traffic characteristics of a representative cloud gaming platform, GeForce NOW with the aim to detect cloud gameplay and measure gamer experience.

2.2   Operational Process of Cloud Game Sessions

Cloud gaming platforms serve as intermediaries that connect user devices and individual game servers. These platforms receive input from gamers including mouse movement, keyboard input, and upstream audio, and perform graphic and gaming computations on their behalf. Real-time gameplay scenes are streamed back to users via video and audio services. Therefore, a typical cloud gaming process involves two types of sessions that are in charge of platform administration and actual gameplay, respectively.

We now walk through an example play of a popular first-person shooting game (*i.e.,* Counter-Strike: Global Offensive or its abbreviation CS:GO) on GeForce NOW platform. As shown in the leftmost window of Fig. 1, after logging into the cloud gaming platform via either console application or browser, the gamer is directed to the "**platform session**", during which the gamer can browse available games and choose the one to play. In addition, some of the graphical settings such as resolution and frame rate are also options to be set by the gamer during the platform session. Once a gameplay is about to start, as shown by the second left-most window in Fig. 1, the optimal cloud server for this gameplay is selected via a set of network measurements for key performance metrics, such as latency and throughput between the gamer device and candidate clusters.

After initial setup, the "**gameplay session**" begins, such as the CS:GO shooting gameplay visually depicted in Fig. 1. As will be soon discussed in Sect. 3, the gameplay session places significant demand on network throughput and latency, which directly impact the quality of experience (QoE) for cloud gaming. After exiting a gameplay session, a gamer returns to the platform session (the rightmost window of Fig. 1) to select/start next gameplay or finish the cloud game session.

3   Cloud Gaming Network Traffic Characterization

We now delve into the network traffic characteristics of gameplay on the GeForce NOW platform obtained from our labeled traffic traces captured in our lab environment (Sect. 3.1). We begin by discussing the anatomy of service flows (Sect. 3.2) in both platform and gameplay sessions, and then focusing on the profile of critical flows in gameplay sessions (Sect. 3.3). We also characterize XBox Cloud Gaming to demonstrate the general applicability of our insights/methods for platforms sharing similar underlying technologies (Appendix B).

3.1   Dataset

The GeForce NOW cloud gaming platform is available via both console applications and browsers on PCs (*i.e.,* macOS and Windows) and mobile devices (*i.e.,* iOS and android). Therefore, we capture packet trace files (PCAP) during cloud gaming sessions of a real-time shooting game (*i.e.,* CS:GO) and a massive multiplayer role-play game (*i.e.,* Path of Exile) on the above user setups, which can be categorized as either **desktop console application, mobile console application**, or **browser**. In what follows, we primarily focus on the insights from gameplays on the console application installed in a macOS desktop, while the differences in other supported setups (*i.e.,* Chrome browser in macOS, console application in Windows, Chrome browser in Windows, console application in android, and Safari browser in iOS) are also discussed throughout the section. To validate our obtained insights, we further collected traffic traces of 20 cloud game sessions for each type of user setups. The 20 cloud gaming sessions for each setup type cover three commonly available graphic resolutions from full high-definition (FHD), high definition (HD), to standard definition (SD), with either 30 fps or 60 fps video frame rates.

3.2   Anatomy of Service Flows

As visually shown in Fig. 2, we first look at the anatomy of network communications between a gamer device and the cloud gaming platform as obtained from our analytical results. There are three types of flows that collectively serve a cloud gaming session, namely for **platform administration, platform management**, and **gameplay** that are illustrated as blue, yellow, and green arrows in Fig. 2, respectively.

Specifically, once a user opens the cloud gaming console application or browser, *i.e.,* entering a platform session, a series of administration flows (*i.e.,* ① in Fig. 2) are initialized for administrative support, such as content management system (CMS), API utilities, login portals, and account management. After the

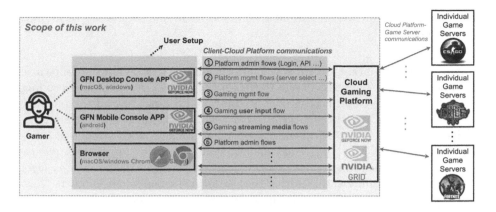

Fig. 2. Anatomy of cloud gaming communications via GeForce NOW (GFN) platform. (Color figure online)

user selects a game to play, a number of platform management flows (*i.e.,* ② in Fig. 2) are started for network diagnosis and cloud server selection. Those flows are mapped to the second screenshot in Fig. 1 and hold critical roles in the successful initiation of the subsequent gameplay. During actual gameplay sessions, three types of flows are initialised, each serving a specific purpose. Firstly, there are gaming management flows (*i.e.,* ③) responsible for controlling the gameplay session (*e.g.,* measuring run-time latency) and exchanging metadata (*e.g.,* coordinating interactions between the client and the platform). In addition, there are specific gameplay flows dedicated to user input (from mouse, keyboard and microphone) and streaming media contents (*i.e.,* downstream video and audio), annotated as ④ and ⑤ respectively After a gameplay session, the platform administration flows are restarted as the user is returned to the platform session.

We now give a representative example of the above-discussed service flow usage as a time-series plot in Fig. 3. In this example, we played two games on the macOS PC console application. Our user activity could be separated into six stages. We logged into the cloud game platform and selected our first game (*i.e.,* CS:GO) to play in stage 1; played the CS:GO game in stage 2; returned to the platform in stage 3; entered the login and character selection page of our second game (*i.e.,* Path of Exile) in stage 4; entered the world of Path of Exile in stage 5, and finished our cloud gaming play in stage 6. We note that each of the six activity stages are either platform or gameplay session as defined in Fig. 1, thus, in Fig. 3, they are annotated by blue or red labels for the two session types, respectively.

In Fig. 3, we could see the timespans of all relevant flows that are with identical color indicating their flow types as consistent in Fig. 2. The median throughput of each flow is indicated by the line thickness in Fig. 3. A representative collection of flows are labeled (as y-axis ticks) in the format of simplified service prefix (extracted from SNI or DNS records) and identifiable port numbers. The labels for other flows are not included for readability. Now we discuss the details per flow type.

Platform Administration Flows. Platform administration flows are shown as blue lines in Fig. 3. They are all sent to the service port $TCP|443$. After decoding packet headers, we confirm that they are all HTTPS flows toward the provider root domains (*i.e.*, *nvidia.com*, *geforcenow.com*, and *geforce.com*) for administrative services as indicated in their subdomain prefixes, such as content management system (CMS) [19] (*cms*) and frontend APIs (*gx-target-experiments-frontend-api*). Depending on their service purposes, some of the flows (*e.g.*, *login* and *userstore*) are only active during the platform session, whereas others (*e.g.*, *cms* and *events*) remain active during the subsequent gameplay sessions. As for their volumetric profiles, all of them are having small (or even negligible) amount of volume usage, *i.e.*, less than several Megabytes.

Upon comparing the platform administration flows across different user setups, we have observed that the sessions via Chrome browser (an example is shown in Appendix Fig. 12(a)) has most of the service flows seen in our discussed example, except for *cms* and *als* which are related to high-performant graphics. Besides, unlike PC setups, cloud game sessions via android mobile console application have limited usage of platform administrative flows (an example is given in Appendix Fig. 12(b)) that seem to only cover essential services such as *login*, *event*, and *userstore*.

Platform Management Flows. As depicted by the yellow horizontal bars in Fig. 3, the platform management flows exhibit a relatively lower quantity compared to the platform administration flows. They are all HTTPS flows sent to service port $TCP|443$ of the GeForce NOW cloud server clusters, which are all associated with the cloud cluster domain *nvidiagrid.net*.

Unlike the above-discussed administration flows that provide support to the user administration on the platform, such as login, events, and user store, the platform management flows service critical tasks relating to the delivery of subsequent gameplay session. In stage 1 of Fig. 3, we observe the first management (yellow) flow directed towards the subdomain prefix *gfnpc.api.entitlement-prod*, which grants the client access to the GeForce NOW production system. This is followed by multiple flows toward subdomain prefixes in the format of *server_[location]_pnt*, which serve the purpose of cloud server selection by measuring network performance metrics between the user and various available vantage points. As indicated by the service prefixes in Fig. 3 from top to down, the selection process progresses from the regional node to the city node and ultimately to each individual cloud server.

Given the indispensable roles of platform management flows, *i.e.*, system access and server selection, there is no significant difference that can be observed across different user setups, except that four flows toward the service prefix *img* of the production system domain *nvidiagrid.net* are seen in platform sessions on android mobile but not on PC setups.

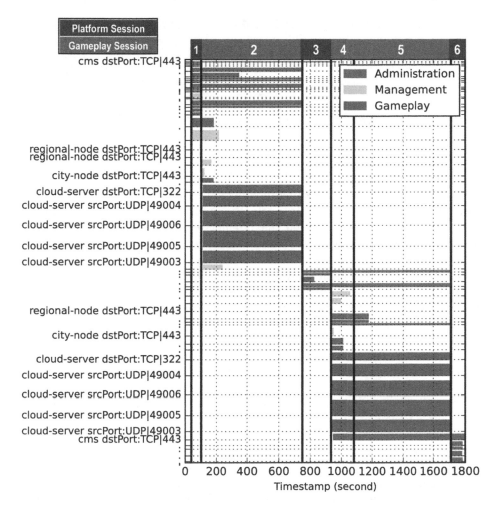

Fig. 3. Flow profiles of example gameplay via GeForce NOW desktop console application. Service prefixes and port numbers of representative flows are shown by their respective y-ticks. Throughputs of flows are indicated by their bar thicknesses (normalised by logarithmic functions). (Color figure online)

Gameplay Session Flows. Once a suitable cloud server is successfully selected by the platform management flows, the actual gameplay session is started. As depicted by the green lines in stage 2 of Fig. 3, five gameplay session flows are initiated for the CS:GO gameplay. This observation remains consistent for all gameplays via console applications on both mobile and PC devices. Similarly, in stage 4 and 5 of Fig. 3, the same combination of five gameplay session flows can be observed for the Path of Exile gameplay.

Specifically, the first gameplay session flow is always directed to destination service port $TCP|322$ on the cloud server. This is followed by four Real-Time Transport Protocol (RTP) flows originating from client ports $UDP|49003$,

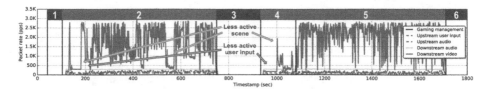

Fig. 4. Volumetric profiles of gameplay session flows (the green lines in Fig. 3 (Color figure online)).

$UDP|49004$, $UDP|49005$, and $UDP|49006$ toward dynamically selected service ports on the cloud server. According to Nvidia Support [33], the four client ports are assigned for downstream audio, upstream audio, downstream video, and user input, respectively. We believe that the dynamic selection of service ports is performed by the first TCP flow for gaming management purpose, as illustrated in Fig. 2.

Notably, the flows originating from $UDP|49005$, responsible for downstream video, consistently consumed larger amounts of bandwidth than all other gameplay session flows. In the 10-minute CS:GO gameplay (stage 1), this resulted in downstream video data transfers of 1422MB, while in the Path of Exile gameplay (stages 4 and 5), it reached 1961MB. As for the flows for downstream audio, upstream audio, and upstream user input, they consumed several MB, several tens of MB, and several tens of MB data transfers, respectively.

Similar insights are observed for gameplay session flows across console applications on both mobile and desktop devices. However, in browser-based gameplay, their gaming management flows is delivered using WebRTC protocol toward the service port $TCP|49100$ [34], as shown by Fig. 12(a) in the Appendix. Additionally, gameplays on browsers utilize a single UDP flow to carry both downstream media contents and upstream user input, in contrast to the separate flows seen in console applications.

Given that the user gaming experience on cloud platforms is predominantly influenced by the gameplay session flows, in what follows, we will focus on examining their flow-level volumetric profiles and packet statistics.

3.3 Profile of Gameplay Session Flows

We now focus on gameplay session flows (represented by the green lines in Fig. 3) that are critical to the cloud gaming experience. For flows that are active during a gameplay session, we analyze their volumetric profiles (Sect. 3.3); benchmark their bandwidth consumptions across different levels of graphic quality including frame rate and resolution (Sect. 3.3); and explore how video frame rate could be identified by packet size patterns of flows carrying downstream video data (Sect. 3.3).

Flow Volumetric Profile. For our example gameplay discussed in Fig. 3, the inbound and outbound packet rates of the five gameplay session flows, including gameplay management, upstream user input, upstream audio, downstream audio, and downstream video, are presented in a time-series plot shown in Fig. 4.

First, the **gameplay management flow**, represented by the inbound and outbound packets towards the service port $TCP|322$, exhibits a low packet rate of one pair of packets every two seconds (*i.e.*, 0.5pps), which may appear negligible in the plot. It can serve as a reliable indicator for measuring network latencies between the user and the cloud platform by tracking the sequence and acknowledgment numbers in TCP packet headers.

Second, the upstream **user input flow** for keyboard and mouse actions exhibits a packet rate ranging from 11 to 267 pps, depending on the user's activity level. As depicted by the green lines in Fig. 4, the baseline packet rate (11pps) occurs when the user is actively moving the mouse or typing on the keyboard, such as during the matching phase of a shooting game (beginning of stage 2 in Fig. 4) or the opening cinematic of a role-play game (beginning of stage 4). It is worth noting that the outbound and inbound packet rates of this flow are often equal. Regarding the throughput of the user input flow, the outbound direction exhibits minimum and maximum values of 1k and 82 kbps, respectively, which are approximately ten times larger than those observed in the inbound direction.

Third, the two flows for **upstream and downstream audio** both have constant packet rates and throughputs in their respective directions. Specifically, the upstream audio flow exhibits a packet rate of 100pps with a throughput of 15 kbps, while the downstream audio flow has a packet rate of 300pps with a throughput of 37 kbps. These values remain consistent regardless of the status of the input/output voice, such as being muted, at low volume, or at high volume, which we thoroughly tested during our experiments. In their opposite directions (*e.g.*, inbound direction for upstream audio flow), both of them constantly have 2 pps packet rate with 156bps throughput.

Table 2. Representative *Peak* bandwidth consumption of downstream video flows across graphic resolutions and frame rates during active gameplay. The green, yellow, and red cells are for full high-definition (FHD), high-definition (HD), and standard-definition (SD), respectively.

	FHD	HD	SD
60FPS	23 – 35Mbps	15 – 21Mbps	<=13Mbps
30FPS	15 – 22Mbps	9 – 13Mbps	<=8Mbps

The most bandwidth consuming flow type, *i.e.*, **downstream video flows**, exhibit a packet rate that ranges from approximately 300pps during less active scenes (as shown in Fig. 4) to 3000pps. The corresponding bandwidth consumptions for these packet rates are 3Mbps and 34Mbps, respectively. It is important to note that during active gameplay periods, such as stage 5 in Fig. 4), the bandwidth consumption mostly remains at the upper bound level. On the other hand, the low packet rate is observed during inactive periods, which often coincide with the inactivity of the user input flows. However, there are exceptions during static scenes with frequent user inputs, such as the login scene of a gameplay.

Similar patterns in terms of packet rates and bandwidth consumption are observed for gameplay session flows across both desktop and mobile console applications. However, for gameplay sessions on browsers, there is only one gameplay session flow that combines all four flows for user input and media. In this case, the volumetric pattern of the flow is primarily dominated by the downstream video content.

We note that the numerical results presented earlier were specific to the video configuration with 60 fps for the frame rate and a resolution of 1920 × 1080 (FHD). However, users have the flexibility to choose from a wide range of frame rates and resolutions, either statically or dynamically adjusted based on the network conditions during gameplay. In the following analysis, we will discuss the bandwidth consumption of downstream video flows for different graphic configurations.

Bandwidths of Downstream Video Flows Across Video Configurations. Frame rate and graphic resolution are configurable parameters for a cloud gameplay. To analyze the bandwidth consumption for downstream video flows, we manually selected various available frame rates (30 or 60 fps) and graphic resolutions (ranging from 1920 × 1200 to 1024 × 768). For browser sessions where only one gameplay flow is present, we also measured the bandwidth consumption as it is primarily influenced by downstream video content. As discussed for Fig. 4, the packet rate and throughput for downstream video flows stay at a peak range during active gameplay scenarios. In Table 2, we report the observed peak bandwidth consumption of those downstream video flows under each different graphic configuration.

Each cell in Table 2 is color-coded into three groups based on the resolution types including full high-definition (FHD), high-definition (HD), and standard definition (SD). Green cells represent the ideal FHD graphic quality, while yellow and red cells indicate less optimal graphic configurations (HD and SD) that may result in a subpar gaming experience. In general, lower frame rates and coarse-grained graphic resolutions always result in lower bandwidth consumption, both in active and less active scenarios. It is worth noting that by examining the peak bandwidth consumption of video flows and the current frame rate (which could be inferred from packet size patterns and will be discussed soon), it is possible for an ISP to infer the current graphic resolution of an active cloud gameplay by its user.

Packet Size Patterns in Downstream Video Flows Across Frame Rates. Identifying the number of packets with a frame marker set in the RTP header of downstream video flows is a straightforward method to benchmark the current frame rate. In RTP flows, the frame marker indicates the completion of the currently transmitted video frame [38]. By counting the packets with the frame marker in the downstream video flow, we can accurately determine the frame rate of a cloud gameplay. However, in a high-speed network, this method requires decoding RTP packets that could introduce non-negligible overheads

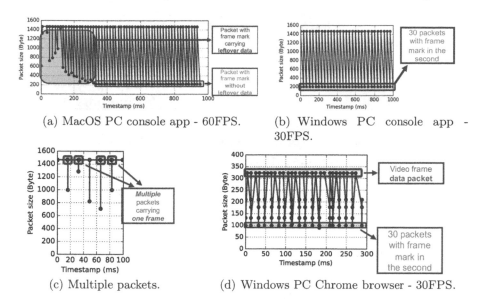

(a) MacOS PC console app - 60FPS.

(b) Windows PC console app - 30FPS.

(c) Multiple packets.

(d) Windows PC Chrome browser - 30FPS.

Fig. 5. Packet payload sizes in representative downstream video flows (each packet is represented as a blue dot) as time-series plots. (Color figure online)

(*e.g.*, via multiple sequential packet parsers each decoding one packet layer). Besides, frame marks may not always be set correctly or being encrypted, makes RTP headers not decodable. For a lightweight and robust method, we have observed certain patterns in the packet sizes of downstream video flows to determine the frame rate without decoding the Ethernet/IP/UDP/RTP headers. This approach ensures resilience even when frame marks are not available. Now we look at several example downstream video flows shown in Fig. 5.

In general, a video frame is carried by two types of RTP packets. The first type carries all or the majority of video frame data and has a fixed large packet size (*i.e.*, 1466 bytes in console applications). The second type consists of smaller-sized packets (*e.g.*, 216 bytes) that carry frame markers, indicating the completion of a frame transmission. During gameplay sessions, the number of data packets required to transmit a video frame is dynamically adjusted based on the amount of video data in the frame. This can range from one packet to multiple packets, as visually depicted in Fig. 5(c). Importantly, there is always one small-sized marker packet indicating the end of each frame, which is highlighted by the green box in Fig. 5(a). These frame marker packet may have larger sizes (still smaller than the size of data packets) to accommodate any remaining video data from the previous packets. This is indicated by the red box in Fig. 5(a).

We observed a consistent pattern in the downstream video flows, where the number of packet groups (comprising several data packets followed by one marker packet) aligns perfectly with the current frame rate. An example of this pattern can be seen in Fig. 5(b), where we observe 30 packet groups within one second for a frame rate of 30 fps. By analyzing the size patterns of these packet groups,

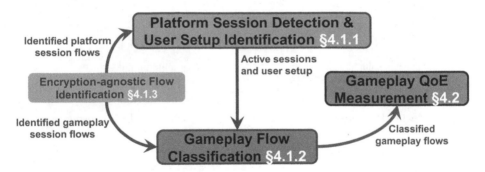

Fig. 6. The abstract view of our cloud gameplay detection and experience measurement framework in Sect. 4. (Color figure online)

we can accurately identify the frame rate being received by a cloud gamer in real-time.

In contrast to gameplay via console applications, the scenario for browsers is slightly different as there is only one RTP flow responsible for carrying downstream video, audio, and user input data. As illustrated in Fig. 5(d), each vertically aligned group of packets consists of several data packets corresponding to a video frame, followed by a frame marker packet, and three additional packets for downstream audio, upstream audio, and user input. Despite this difference, the consistent pattern observed in each packet group via browsers still aligns with the delivery of video frames.

4   Gameplay Detection and Experience Measurement

In this section, building upon the insights gained from Sect. 3, we present the development of our network traffic analysis framework that detects cloud gaming sessions, identifies user setups, and continuously measures the quality-of-experience (QoE) metrics of each cloud gameplay session, as illustrated in Fig. 6. We also discuss the generalizability of our method to other cloud gaming platforms and briefly discuss limitations of our QoE metrics (Sect. 4.3).

4.1   Detecting Cloud Game Sessions

As previously shown in Figs. 1 and 4, a cloud gameplay typically goes through two types of sessions, namely platform session (for platform administration, game browsing, and cloud server selection) and gameplay session. From our analysis, platform sessions exhibit identical usage of service flows in terms of user setups, which are important for a network operator to better understand their customer segments and potential causes of QoE degradation. The flows in gameplay sessions directly determine users' cloud game experience.

Note that our method uses the identification of flows directed towards specific service domains based on the Server Name Indication (SNI) field in the SSL

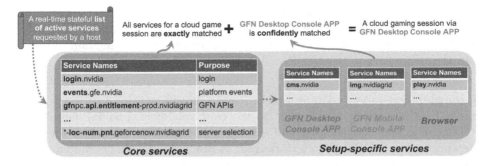

Fig. 7. Process for the detection of platform sessions and identification of user setups.

headers, which may not be available due to the potential adoption of encrypted-SNI (ESNI). Therefore, we have also devised an encryption-agnostic approach (Appendix Sect. 4.1) to overcome this challenge in the near future.

We now present our method to detect both platform and gameplay sessions.

Platform Sessions and User Setup Identification. User enters platform sessions either in the initial phase after launching to the cloud game platform (*e.g.*, stage 1 in Fig. 3) or in a subsequent phase after finishing each gameplay session (*e.g.*, stage 3 and 6 in Fig. 3). As discussed in Sect. 3.2, when a platform session begins, a series of HTTPS flows are initiated towards different service prefixes of the cloud gaming domains. These HTTPS flows contain service names in the server name indication (SNI) [10] fields of their SSL handshakes, which precede the encrypted application data communication. Therefore, we detect platform sessions by monitoring flows toward each service domain, extracted from their respective SNI records.

After analyzing our traffic traces across all user setups, we categorize the flows into two types including core services and setup-specific services. Core service flows are always initiated during the starting phase of platform sessions, regardless of the user setup type. There are also service flows specific to certain user setups. For instance, flows directed toward *login.nvidia* are always active, while flows toward *play.nvidia* only occur in platform sessions via browsers. Additionally, we have observed that the majority of core service flows follow a sequential order, starting from user login and progressing to server selection. In contrast, the occurrence of setup-specific service flows often exhibits randomness in their sequence.

As shown in Fig. 7, we have developed a codebook correlation of domain names to detect the start of a cloud gaming play (through core services) and identify the user setup type (*i.e.*, desktop console application, mobile console application, or browser). A wildcard match of domains in the corresponding table will trigger a successful detection. For example, as demonstrated by the top portion of Fig. 7, the exact match of flows in core service table triggers the successful detection of a cloud gaming session. Additionally, a confident match in the desktop console application table (compared to the other tables) determines that the cloud game session is being played on a desktop console. Please note that for simplicity, we have provided only a snippet of our matching tables rather than the entire list.

Gameplay Sessions and Gameplay Flow Classification. As a recap from Sect. 3.3, after starting a gameplay on the cloud platform, one SSL-encrypted TCP gaming management flow and several (one for browser and four for console application) UDP flows are started for media and user input. Cloud gaming sessions from console applications have their TCP gaming management flows directed to service port numbers $TCP|322$, while browsers use port $TCP|49100$. Irrespective of the user setup types, all gaming management flows have their service name (extracted from SNI) following a consistent pattern of *a-b-c-d.pnt.nvidiagrid.net*. It is important to note that the *a-b-c-d* in this pattern represents the IP address *a.b.c.d* of a cloud server assigned to a gameplay session, which is also the server IP for the subsequent gameplay UDP flows.

We devise our method to identify gameplay session flows based on their service names and five-tuples for active users detected in the platform sessions (Sect. 4.1). Subsequently, the gameplay session flows are then classified for their purposes as defined in Sect. 3.3, based on their user setup types, flow five-tuple, and volumetric profiles (*i.e.*, packet rate and throughput). The generalized classification process is shown in Fig. 8. The models in this process can be obtained either using machine learning algorithms on standardized input attributes (shown as the yellow banner in Fig. 8) that can be directly applied to cloud gaming platforms implemented using similar mechanisms, or heuristically derived for a certain platform (*e.g.*, GeForce NOW) according to the specific profiles of its gameplay flows. In this work, based on our insights obtained for GFN flow characteristics, we developed an automatic training script to derive flow classification criteria using ground-truth traffic traces (*i.e.*, PCAP files). We also provide flow charts showing the process for GFN and XBox Cloud Gaming with heuristically simplified classification criteria in Appendix C Figs. 14 and 15, respectively.

The first step of the classification process, depicted in the left blue model in Fig. 8), is to **classify gameplay management flows**. For GeForce NOW, a candidate TCP flow (identified by its service name) sent to port $TCP|322$ or $TCP|49100$ from an active user are for console application or browser, respectively. As indicated by the dashed arrow, the five-tuple (including client and server IP addresses) of the gameplay management flow will be stored in a runtime database for the detection of subsequent gameplay UDP flows that are initiated shortly afterward (*e.g.*, within 0.5 s).

The second step, illustrated in the right blue model of Fig. 8, is to **classify gameplay media and user input flows**. In the case of browser-based GFN sessions, a gameplay UDP flow can either carry media and user input data or provide support for the STUN WebRTC service, which can be differentiated based on its packet rate. Specifically, a STUN WebRTC service flow has its packet rate less than 2pps while a combined media and user input flow has over hundreds

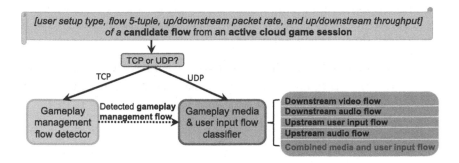

Fig. 8. Process for the classification of gameplay session flows, wherein the models can be either obtained using generalized machine-learning algorithms or heuristic criteria for a specific cloud gaming platform. (Color figure online)

of packets per second. For gameplay UDP flows in console application-based GFN sessions, they can serve different purposes, including downstream video, downstream audio, upstream audio, or user input. Classification of these flows is based on their volumetric profiles, specifically the packet rate and throughput, in both inbound and outbound directions. From our training process on GFN traffic traces, criteria on volumetric attributes are obtained including > 5Mbps inbound throughput for downstream video flows, matched inbound and outbound packet rates (*i.e.,* $\Delta <= 10$pps) for user input flow, and inbound or outbound dominant packet rates (*i.e.,* $\Delta > 10$pps) for downstream or upstream voice flows, respectively. It may be argued that the functionality of a gameplay UDP flow from GFN console application can be easily determined by its client port number as discussed in Sect. 3.2. However, the presence of network address translation (NAT) in ISP networks often obfuscates the client port numbers of users, rendering them unreliable in comparison to our method that is based on volumetric profiles.

In Sect. 4.2, we will discuss the continuous monitoring of the downstream video flows via console applications, the flows carrying media with user input via browsers, and gaming management flows as an effective approach to infer user experience per cloud gameplay session.

Encryption-Agnostic Service Flow Identification. The recent proposals of SNI encryption techniques have sparked discussions in the industry and could potentially be adopted in the near future. If that happens, current network analysis relying on SNI signatures will become ineffective. To tackle this anticipated issue, we develop an encryption-agnostic technique (the blue module in Fig. 6) as an enhancement to our existing flow detection using service names extracted from the SNI field. This enhancement allows us to identify flows with their service names associated with platform and gameplay sessions by analyzing packet payload sizes, without the need to inspect SSL headers.

According to prior research, flows with specific functionalities, such as console gaming [26], VoIP/video/file transfer/chat/browsing [36], and encrypted

Table 3. Packet payload sizes (in byte) after three-way handshakes of gameplay TCP management flows for different user setups (OS and software agent) observed in both **upstream** ↑ and **downstream** ↓ directions.

OS	dstPort numbers and payload sizes across software agent types
Windows	TCP|322 *(APP)* or TCP|49100 *(Chrome)*: [**517**↑, **1460**↓, **1460**↓, **502**↓]
macOS	TCP|322 *(APP)* or TCP|49100 *(Chrome)*: [**517**↑, **1412**↓, **1412**↓]
android	TCP|322 *(APP)*: [**517**↑, **3455**↓]
iOS	TCP|49100 *(Safari)*: [**517**↑, **3450**↓]

web [1], can be detected by the distinctive distribution or sequence of packet sizes they exhibit. Building on these findings, to detect platform and gameplay management flows without inspecting SNI, we leverage the sequence of payload sizes in the first few packets of a TCP flow, which contain predefined service requests after TCP three-way handshakes. As obtained from our training process, representative upstream and downstream packet payload sizes in gameplay management flows with their destination port numbers across different operating systems are provided in Table 3. The signatures for platform flows are not explicitly provided here for simplicity. With the precise specification of these signatures, we have achieved 100% accuracy in detecting cloud gaming sessions during our lab evaluation.

It is important to note that our technique is designed for platform HTTPS flows and gameplay management TCP flows. The detection of gameplay UDP flows does not rely on service name signatures and is already encryption-agnostic, meaning it is not affected by future SNI encryption.

4.2 Measuring Gameplay User Experience

The user's experience in a cloud gameplay session is primarily determined by three factors: the synchronization speed of the user's mouse/keyboard input with the cloud platform (measured by client-platform latency in Sect. 4.2), the smoothness of the streamed gaming scene (measured by video frame rate in Sect. 4.2), and the clarity of the gaming graphics (indicated by graphic resolution in Sect. 4.2).

In this section, we propose metrics to monitor these three key performance indicators derived from real-time volumetric statistics of gameplay session flows. Our metrics are computed from transport-layer headers and packet sizes, therefore, are agnostic to the encryption of application-layer headers and payloads.

Client-Platform Latency. The first metric is client-platform latency, which represents the response time from the moment a gamer inputs commands with their keyboard or mouse till those commands are executed by the cloud platform. As discussed in Sect. 3.2, there is a single gaming management flow over TCP that remains active throughout the entire gameplay session. This flow is detected by our methodology proposed in Sect. 4.1.

Algorithm 1. An algorithm for measuring the video frame rate (*i.e.,* frame count of an interval) of cloud gameplay using packet size patterns of downstream video flows.

Input: *packets* in gaming video flow; measurement interval ΔT; payload size margin $\Delta size$

Output: measured *frame_count*

1: $frame\_count \leftarrow 0$
2: $t_{start} \leftarrow packets[0].arrival\_timestamp$
3: $size_{max} \leftarrow packets[0].payload\_size$
4: $flag_{max} \leftarrow FALSE$
5: **for** p **in** packets **do**
6:     **if** $p.arrival\_timestamp > t_{start} + \Delta T$ **then**
7:         **print** $frame\_count/\Delta T$
8:         $frame\_count \leftarrow 0$
9:     **end if**
10:     **if** $p.payload\_size > size_{max}$ **then**
11:         $size_{max} \leftarrow p.payload\_size$
12:         **continue**
13:     **end if**
14:     **if** $p.payload\_size < size_{max} - \Delta size$ **then**
15:         **if** $flag_{max}$ **is** $TRUE$ **then**
16:             $frame\_count \leftarrow frame\_count + 1$
17:             $flag_{max} \leftarrow FALSE$
18:         **end if**
19:         **continue**
20:     **end if**
21:     $flag_{max} \leftarrow TRUE$
22: **end for**

The gaming management flow exhibits a constant packet rate of one pair of TCP packets every two seconds, where each pair consists of an upstream and downstream packet with matching **sequence** and **acknowledge numbers** in their TCP headers, as explained in Sect. 3.3.

To measure the real-time latency experienced by the cloud gamer, we continuously monitor the arrival timestamps of each packet pair (identified by their sequence and acknowledge numbers) within the gaming management flow. Specifically, we track the timestamps t_{up} and t_{down} and calculate the latency Δt between t_{down} and t_{up}.

Gaming Video Frame Rate. The second metric we consider for user experience is the video frame rate being streamed to the cloud gamer. As discussed in Sect. 3.3, a higher frame rate, such as 60 fps, imposes stricter network requirements in terms of higher bandwidth and lower packet loss. In return, it offers the user a smoother gaming video experience.

To track this QoE metric, we leverage the periodic patterns of packet payload sizes observed in downstream video flows for both console applications and browsers during each gameplay session. These periodic patterns serve as a **direct** measure of the video frame rate, as explained in Sect. 3.3 and illustrated in Fig. 5. Considering that GeForce NOW offers frame rate options of 30 fps and 60 fps, we expect the observed count of periodical patterns per second to closely align with one of these two values.

The pseudocode block in Algorithm 1 shows our approach for measuring frame rate from downstream video flows. The method takes as input the downstream packets in a gameplay video flow. It also requires an interval ΔT (set to 1 s in our implementation) that determines the frequency of measurements, and a payload size margin $\Delta size$ (fine-tuned using ground-truth sessions to 1 byte) that allows for variations in the payload size of full-size video packets in the flow.

To begin, the algorithm initializes four assisting variables from line #1 to line #4. Within the loop that processes the packet streams (line #5), the measured frame rate per interval is reported and reset from line #6 to line #9. Additionally, the algorithm determines the full payload size of video packets in the monitored flow from line #10 to line #13. From line #14 to line #21, the algorithm captures the stochastic periodical pattern observed in the packet payload sizes of a video flow. This pattern includes sequences of full-sized video packets followed by smaller-sized ones carrying frame markers and/or remaining data.

Gaming Graphic Resolution. Our third QoE metric is graphic resolution, which represents the visual quality of the graphics being streamed to the cloud gamer by the cloud platform. The graphic resolution, along with the video frame rate, determine the bandwidth consumption of a downstream video flow, as discussed in Sect. 3.3. As just discussed, we can directly determine the current level of **video frame rate**. Therefore, to diagnose the real-time graphic resolution, we measure the current **bandwidth consumption** of the video flow and refer to the mapping provided in Table 2. This mapping enables us to deduce the current graphic resolution based on the given throughput and frame rate.

4.3   Discussion on Generalizability and Limitations

First, we have validated in our lab environment that the developed methods on cloud gaming detection, user setup identification, and gameplay QoE measurement can also be generalized to XBox Cloud Gaming platform with platform-specific signatures obtained from training traffic traces, including service domains, packet payload sizes, RTP port number, and flow volumetric criteria. Also, in the limited lab evaluation, the measurement methods for client-platform latency and video frame rate do not require signatures thus are directly applicable. However, the conclusions may need additional field evaluation to become fully valid. Other popular platforms (listed in Table 1) are not currently available in our region and we are not able to evaluate them in our lab. However, from a recent research [22] studying the cloud gaming RTP flows, the platforms that are not covered in this study (*i.e.,* Playstation PLUS and Amazon Luna) share a common technological structure. Therefore, these can also be included in our method if lab setup for training trace collection is available.

Second, due to potential future variations in the implementation of cloud gaming services, the alterations in the value of considered metrics (such as protocol type, volumetric statistics, and flow service domains) may diminish the effectiveness of a trained classification model. Consequently, retraining the model becomes necessary for optimal performance. Additionally, if significant modifications occur in the network anatomy of cloud gaming sessions (as briefly captured in Fig. 8), such as the introduction of different categories of gameplay session flow types, adjustments to our model training process will be required.

Third, we acknowledge the limitations in our QoE metrics that are valuable topics for future research. The QoE metrics considered in this paper are directly related to network conditions, including graphic resolution and video frame rate impacted by available bandwidth and client-platform latency impacted by routing conditions. There are many other QoE metrics describing the capability of client devices and cloud servers [17], such as processing delays for frame encoding, decoding, rendering and game engine processing. While they are not directly impacted by the network conditions, it is worth investigating the correlation between those device-related QoE and network traffic characteristics such as signaling packets and inter-arrival timing, which may be predictable using statistical models. Also, the two gaming video metrics (*i.e.,* frame rate, resolution) may not always indicate true user experience as cloud gaming providers can dynamically adjust video settings for different in-game scenes [3,11].

5   Evaluation and Field Insights

We have implemented a fully-functional prototype of our cloud gaming detection and experience measurement framework in a large University campus with tens of thousands of students, including several hundred who reside in the dorms. Our system takes as input a raw feed of all traffic to/from the campus, obtained via optical taps on the fibres connecting the campus to the Internet. We begin by evaluating the accuracy of our system by playing cloud games from our lab on campus and comparing it to ground truth (Sect. 5.1), and then collect data in the wild over a 1-month period to demonstrate insights of interest to network operators (Sect. 5.2).

5.1   Lab Evaluation with Ground-Truth

Once our models were trained and deployed, we had volunteers play a total of 90 sessions of GeForce NOW gaming from our lab, and the ground truth they recorded was compared against the outputs reported from our system monitoring campus-wide traffic for the specific IP address of the lab devices. The sessions were designed to encompass various configurations, including user setups (PC app, mobile app, and browser), frame rates (60 fps and 30 fps), and video resolution bands (FHD, HD, and SD).

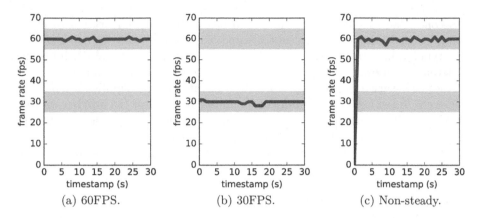

Fig. 9. Example variations of the received video frame rate measured by our prototype.

Our system correctly reported detection of all the cloud gaming sessions immediately upon commencement of actual gameplay, and the user setup (PC app, mobile app and browser play) was also identified with 100% accuracy. The client-side latency recorded by our system (based on tracking TCP sequence numbers), the frame rates (measured from stochastic payload size patterns using the algorithms discussed in Sect. 3.3), as well as the video resolution (inferred based on the real-time bandwidth usage and corresponding frame rate) corroborated accurately (*i.e.*, less than 2 fps deviation for frame rates and over 95% accuracy for resolution) with the ground-truth collected on the client side, where traffic traces were recorded and analysed.

An interesting observation is that although the platform dynamically adjusts the frame rate to either 60 fps or 30 fps, in practice, the received frame rate may vary slightly (*e.g.*, within a range of 5 fps) around the set rate. This variation is visually shown in Fig. 9(b) for the 30 fps setting and Fig. 9(a) for the 60 fps setting. Indeed there can be significant variations in the frame rate, particularly during the beginning of a gameplay session (as illustrated in Fig. 9(c)), or in situations where the network conditions are unstable.

5.2   Field Deployment Insights

We now present some insights obtained in the wild, as measured by our system over the entire month of May 2023 in the University campus network, that are of potential interest to ISPs on how user settings in GeForce NOW cloud gaming impact network bandwidth demand and end-user experience. This equips ISPs to better understand their cloud gaming customer profiles, troubleshoot experience problems, and optimize network policies to better support cloud gaming flows using network slices, priority queues, and network APIs.

User Settings and Bandwidth Demand. During the month of May, our system detected 233 cloud game sessions in the wild (*i.e.*, excluding the ones played

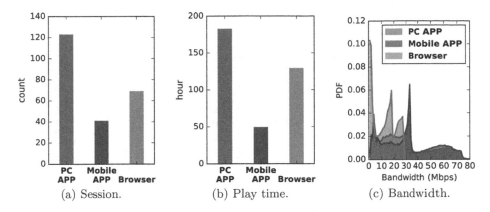

(a) Session.   (b) Play time.   (c) Bandwidth.

Fig. 10. GeForce NOW cloud gaming usage patterns from our 1-month campus deployment.

by our volunteers), corresponding to 362 h of playtime and 3.8 TB of data volume consumption. The majority of gameplay sessions (53%) and gameplay time (51%) were via the PC app, as shown in Fig. 10(a) and 10(b) respectively, followed by browsers (29% of sessions and 36% of total playtime), and finally the mobile app (17% of sessions and 14% of playtime). This is of relevance to ISPs because the bandwidth demanded by the gaming streams vary across these platforms – Fig. 10(c) shows the bandwidth distribution (measured over 1-second intervals) on the three platforms. The browser almost never exceeds 30 Mbps, while the PC and mobile app have significant durations with bandwidth demand in the range of 30–75 Mbps. While the underlying reason for this becomes clear when we examine video frame rates and resolutions next, visibility into app/browser mix may better equip ISPs in planning and provisioning their network capacity as cloud gaming grows.

User Settings and Gaming Experience. We saw in Sect. 5.1 that frame rate can vary significantly, so for ease of depiction we group it into three bands: Low (<40 fps), Medium (40–50 fps) and High (>50 fps). Video resolution has already been banded into FHD, HD, and SD, as shown in Table 2. For the three user settings (PC app, mobile app, and browser), we depict the percentage of time that the cloud game video operates at the three frame rate bands in Fig. 11(a), and the percentage of time the video renders in the three resolutions in Fig. 11(b). It is very interesting to note that browser gaming almost always has high fps but never goes to Full-HD resolution, whereas the PC app has FHD resolution 42% of the time but drops fps to medium or low about 10% of the time. The mobile app provides the best mix of fps and resolution overall, due to the advantage that it only has to work on a smaller screen. ISPs might use such visibility into the trade-offs on frame rates and resolution of cloud gaming sessions to better troubleshoot and support their customers on specific platforms.

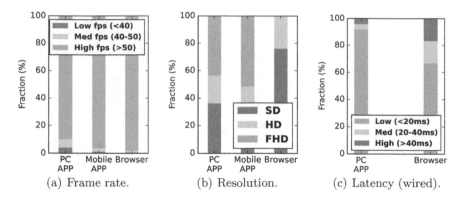

(a) Frame rate.   (b) Resolution.   (c) Latency (wired).

Fig. 11. GeForce NOW cloud gaming experience insights from our 1-month campus deployment.

Another interesting observation made by our system is in regards to the in-game latency across the platforms. To keep the comparison fair and not be influenced by wireless characteristics, we limited it to wired end-hosts (which are identifiable by IP address being on a different subnet to the WiFi network). Figure 11(c) shows that latency (averaged over 1-second intervals) stays under 20 ms (the recommended threshold provided by Nvidia) 90% of the time when played via the app, compared to 70% when played via the browser. We believe this is because the app is better optimized for gaming than the browser – indeed, we had shown in Sect. 3.3 that the app maintains separate flows for user input and media, whereas the browser mixes all traffic into the one flow, which can lead to degraded jitter performance. ISPs may use such information to encourage customers who receive degraded experience to move from browser-based to app-based cloud gaming user setups.

6   Related Work

Cloud gaming has been the subject of prior studies that have explored various aspects [6], including cloud architecture [8,15,40], computing resource provisioning [12,23,46], gameplay video encoding [16,41]. In chronological order, we discuss representative examples of prior works that have focused on enhancing gamer experience for different stakeholders, including cloud platform operators and mobile developers. It is important to note that our work specifically focuses on the cloud gaming experience for ISPs. The authors of [9] discussed several elements in the cloud platform that can have signifiant impact on user experiences if not well optimized. Through a measurement study across Europe, the authors of [18] suggested optimal sever selection and control methods to achieve minimized latency for cloud gamers using mobile platforms. In [37], the authors quantified user perception of graphic delays in different game genres (*e.g.*, card game, shooting, adventure, and racing) each with a unique sensitivity. *DECAF* [17] analysed the user-perceived experiences such as visual response received by user across different game genres. The authors highlight that networking issues like round trip delay, limited bandwidth, and packet losses could significantly degraded the user-perceived experience, which is quantitatively measured by our work using network QoE metrics. S. Bhuyan *et al.* [4] characterized the user-perceived performance (*e.g.,* frame rendering/decoding and hardware energy consumption) specifically for cloud gaming plays on mobile platforms over wireless networks.

As for network traffic analysis of cloud gaming platforms, M. Carrascosa *et al.* [7] identified generic traffic statistics (*e.g.,* utilized protocols, distribution of packet size, and packet inter-arrival time) of cloud gaming sessions on Google Stadia platform and their reactions toward sudden changes of network capacity. X. Xu *et al.* [45] measured the change in bandwidth of cloud gaming flows when competing with TCP Cubic and BBR flows. Existing works such as [14,20] developed NFV/SDN-based traffic processing systems to extract generic network attributes (*e.g.,* bitrate) of UDP flows to detect those carrying downstream video content of cloud games without considering other critical flows. X. Marchal *et al.* [7,28] studied the network traffic patterns of cloud gaming platforms under constrained (cellular) network conditions. The works described in [21,22] analyzed performance anomalies (*e.g.,* channel degradation) of cloud gaming sessions served by 4G networks with time-series network KPIs.

In this paper, our objective is to address the lack of actionable visibility for ISPs. Compared to other works that analyze cloud gaming network traffic to investigate performance impact on RTP flows caused by suboptimal network conditions, we characterize network traffic patterns covering all service flows used in all stages of a cloud gaming session, carrying different gameplay functionalities, and across user setups. The comprehensive and unique insights obtained in our work are leveraged for gameplay detection, user setup identification, and measurement of cloud gaming user experiences.

7   Conclusion

In this paper we developed a network traffic analysis method that provides ISPs visibility into cloud gaming sessions over their networks, specifically those served by Nvidia GeForce NOW platform. We first analyzed network traffic characteristics of cloud game sessions to establish benchmarks for critical service flows that exhibit unique patterns based on user setups and gameplay experiences. We then design a method to detect cloud game sessions across various user setups by stateful matching of service flows, classify critical gameplay flows using volumetric attributes, and track experience metrics (*i.e.,* client-platform latency, frame rate, and graphic resolution) on those flows. The method is prototyped in a large university network, evaluated using ground-truth sessions, and demonstrated for its operational insights from real-world cloud game sessions.

Acknowledgements. We thank our shepherd Alessandro Finamore and the four anonymous reviewers for their insightful feedback. Funding for this project is provided by the Australian Government's Cooperative Research Centres Projects (CRC-P) Grant CRCPXIV000099.

A   Flow Profiles of GeForce NOW Cloud Game Sessions Across User Setups

As complimentary to the flow profiles for cloud game sessions via desktop console application given in Fig. 3, the ones via browser and mobile console applications are shown in Fig. 12. Comparing the three figures, they all have different usage of service flows for platform administration and game session management purposes. Sessions via both mobile and desktop console applications have five gameplay flows each with a unique functionality, whereas those via browsers only have two gameplay flows, one for management, and one for combined user input and game media streaming.

B   Network Traffic Characteristics of XBox Cloud Gaming Sessions

We have conducted similar lab experiments on another cloud gaming platform Microsoft's XBox Cloud Gaming that is currently available in Australia. We discuss flow profiles of gameplay sessions on XBox Cloud Gaming platform and the applicability of our developed methods.

Figure 13 shows the usage of service flows during cloud gaming sessions on XBox Cloud Gaming platform accessed via three supported user setups including XBox hardware console (Fig. 13(a)), PC browser (Fig. 13(b)), and mobile browser (Fig. 13(c)), respectively. Compared to the evolution of service flows in Nvidia GeForce NOW we discussed in Sect. 3, we observe similar insights. First of all, the purposes of flows are also categorized into platform administration, platform management, and gameplay; second, prior to each gameplay session, platform management flows (annotated as "*regional-node*") are started to check current network connectivity and select appropriate cloud server; third, RTP flows that are destined to a certain range of port numbers (*e.g.,* $UDP|1040$ to $UDP|1190$) on the cloud server are used for gaming media and user input. Similar to GeForce NOW, the services being accessed in platform sessions of XBox Cloud Gaming vary across user setup. As shown by example service names in Fig. 13(a), 13(b) and 13(c), sessions accessed by XBox hardware console, PC browser and mobile browser uses different graphic services namely *xgpuconsole*, *xgpuweb* and *xgpu*, respectively.

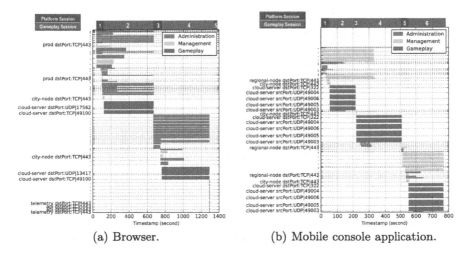

(a) Browser.   (b) Mobile console application.

Fig. 12. Flow profiles of example gameplay via different user setups. Service prefixes and port numbers of representative flows are shown by their respective y-ticks, and the throughput of each flow is shown by its thickness (normalized by logarithmic functions).

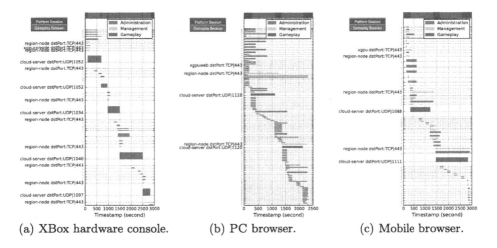

(a) XBox hardware console.   (b) PC browser.   (c) Mobile browser.

Fig. 13. Flow profiles of XBox Cloud Gaming sessions via different user setups. Service prefixes and port numbers of representative flows are shown by their respective y-ticks, and the throughput of each flow is shown by its thickness (normalized by logarithmic functions).

Apart from specific domain name (*e.g.*, XBox Cloud Gaming uses *xboxlive.com* as its gameplay domain while GeForce NOW uses *nvidiagrid.net*) and range of service port numbers used on the cloud server that are different between XBox and GFN, we observed that XBox uses a single RTP flow for both streaming media and user input even on its native hardware console, while

GFN uses separate RTP flows each only carry one type of traffic for sessions from console application.

It is not surprising to observe the above commonalities as cloud gaming platforms are built on similar technological paradigms and communication protocols. Therefore, our methods in detecting cloud gaming session, identifying user setup, and measuring gameplay QoE metrics are evidently applicable to XBox Cloud Gaming and other platforms with similar underlying structures.

C   Charts Illustrating Classification of Gameplay Flows Using Heuristically Simplified Criteria

Figures 14 and 15 visually show the gameplay session flow classification processes for GeForce NOW and Xbox Cloud Gaming derived from our generic process shown in Fig. 8 with heuristically simplified criteria obtained from our training process on ground-truth traffic traces.

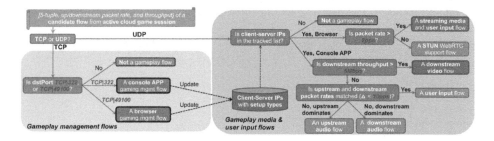

Fig. 14. Illustrative process for the classification of Nvidia's **GeForce NOW** gameplay session flows, wherein the criteria obtained from our training process is annotated with **blue text**. (Color figure online)

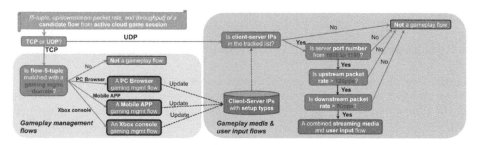

Fig. 15. Illustrative process for the classification of Microsoft's **XBox Cloud Gaming** gameplay session flows, wherein the criteria obtained from our training process is annotated with **blue text**. (Color figure online)

References

1. Akbari, I., et al.: A look behind the curtain: traffic classification in an increasingly encrypted web. Proc. ACM Meas. Anal. Comput. Syst. (2021)
2. Amazon. Luna (2023). https://www.amazon.com/luna/landing-page. Accessed 12 Jan 2023
3. Bartolomeo, G., Cao, J., Su, X., Mohan, N.: Characterizing distributed mobile augmented reality applications at the edge. In: Proceedings of ACM CoNEXT, Paris, France (2023)
4. Bhuyan, S., Zhao, S., Ying, Z., Kandemir, M.T., Das, C.R.: End-to-end characterization of game streaming applications on mobile platforms. In: Proceedings of ACM Measurement and Analysis of Computing Systems (2022)
5. Business. Microsoft, Activision Blizzard and the Future of Gaming. The Economist (2022)
6. Cai, W., et al.: A survey on cloud gaming: future of computer games. IEEE Access 4, 7605–7620 (2016)
7. Carrascosa, M., Bellalta, B.: Cloud-gaming: analysis of google stadia traffic. Comput. Commun. 188, 99–116 (2022)
8. Chen, H., et al.: T-gaming: a cost-efficient cloud gaming system at scale. IEEE Trans. Parallel Distrib. Syst. 30(12), 2849–2865 (2019)
9. Chen, K.-T., Chang, Y.-C., Hsu, H.-J., Chen, D.-Y., Huang, C.-Y., Hsu, C.-H.: On the quality of service of cloud gaming systems. IEEE Trans. Multimedia 16(2), 480–495 (2014)
10. CloudFlare. What is SNI? How TLS Server Name Indication Works (2022). https://www.cloudflare.com/en-gb/learning/ssl/what-is-sni/. Accessed 12 Jan 2023
11. Di Domenico, A., Perna, G., Trevisan, M., Vassio, L., Giordano, D.: A network analysis on cloud gaming: stadia, GeForce now and PSNow. Network 1(3), 247–260 (2021)
12. Ghobaei-Arani, M., Khorsand, R., Ramezanpour, M.: An autonomous resource provisioning framework for massively multiplayer online games in cloud environment. J. Netw. Comput. Appl. 142, 76–97 (2019)
13. Gitnux. Cloud Gaming Services: A Look at the Latest Statistics (2023). https://blog.gitnux.com/cloud-gaming-services-statistics/#content. Accessed 26 June 2023
14. Graff, P., Marchal, X., Cholez, T., Mathieu, B., Festor, O.: Efficient identification of cloud gaming traffic at the edge. In: Proceedings of IEEE/IFIP Network Operations and Management Symposium (2023)
15. Han, Y., Guo, D., Cai, W., Wang, X., Leung, V.C.M.: Virtual machine placement optimization in mobile cloud gaming through QoE-oriented resource competition. IEEE Trans. Cloud Comput. 10(3), 2204–2218 (2022)
16. Illahi, G.K., Gemert, T.V., Siekkinen, M., Masala, E., Oulasvirta, A., Ylä-Jääski, A.: Cloud gaming with foveated video encoding. ACM Trans. Multimedia Comput. Commun. Appl. 16, 1 (2020)
17. Iqbal, H., Khalid, A., Shahzad, M.: Dissecting cloud gaming performance with DECAF. In: Proceedings of ACM Measurement and Analysis of Computing Systems (2021)
18. Kämäräinen, T., Siekkinen, M., Ylä-Jääski, A., Zhang, W., Hui, P.: A measurement study on achieving imperceptible latency in mobile cloud gaming. In: Proceedings of ACM MMSys, Taipei, Taiwan (2017)

19. Kinsta. What is a Content Management System (CMS)? (2022). https://kinsta.com/knowledgebase/content-management-system/. Accessed 12 Jan 2023
20. Ky, J., Graff, P., Mathieu, B., Cholez, T.: A hybrid P4/NFV architecture for cloud gaming traffic detection with unsupervised ML. In: Proceedings of IEEE Symposium on Computers and Communications, Los Alamitos, CA, USA (2023)
21. Ky, J.R., Mathieu, B., Lahmadi, A., Boutaba, R.: Assessing unsupervised machine learning solutions for anomaly detection in cloud gaming sessions. In: Proceedings of IEEE International Conference on Network and Service Management, Thessaloniki, Greece (2022)
22. Ky, J.R., Mathieu, B., Lahmadi, A., Boutaba, R.: ML models for detecting QoE degradation in low-latency applications: a cloud-gaming case study. IEEE Trans. Netw. Serv. Manag. (2023)
23. Li, Y., et al.: GAugur: quantifying performance interference of colocated games for improving resource utilization in cloud gaming. In: Proceedings of ACM HPDC, Phoenix, AZ, USA (2019)
24. Liu, S., et al.: AMIR: active multimodal interaction recognition from video and network traffic in connected environments. In: Proceedings of the ACM on Interactive, Mobile, Wearable and Ubiquitous Technologies (2023)
25. Livingood, J.: Comcast Kicks Off Industry's First Low Latency DOCSIS Field Trials (2023). https://corporate.comcast.com/stories/comcast-kicks-off-industrys-first-low-latency-docsis-field-trials. Accessed 26 June 2023
26. Madanapalli, S.C., Gharakheili, H.H., Sivaraman, V.: Know thy lag: in-network game detection and latency measurement. In: Proceedings of PAM (2022)
27. Madanapalli, S.C., Mathai, A., Gharakheili, H.H., Sivaraman, V.: Reclive: real-time classification and QoE inference of live video streaming services. In: Proceedings of IEEE/ACM IWQOS (2021)
28. Marchal, X., et al.: An analysis of cloud gaming platforms behaviour under synthetic network constraints and real cellular networks conditions. J. Netw. Syst. Manag. **31**(2), 39 (2023)
29. Markets and Markets. Cloud Gaming Market by Offering, Device Type, Solution, Game Type, Region - Global Forecast to 2024 (2019). https://bit.ly/3AyEjio. Accessed 27 Apr 2024
30. Microsoft. XBox Cloud Gaming (Beta) (2023). https://www.xbox.com/en-us/play. Accessed 12 Jan 2023
31. News. The Future of Video Games. The Economist (2023)
32. Nvidia. GeForce NOW (2023). https://www.nvidia.com/en-au/geforce-now/. Accessed 12 Jan 2023
33. Nvidia Support. How can i reduce lag or improve streaming quality when using geforce now? (2022). bit.ly/45TOmfR. Accessed 12 Dec 2022
34. Nvidia Support. WebRTC Browser Client (2022). bit.ly/3LhOPAj. Accessed 14 Dec 2022
35. Rietveld, J.: Microsoft and activision: the big questions that will decide whether the US$68 billion deal goes ahead. The Conversation (2023)
36. Roy, S., Shapira, T., Shavitt, Y.: Fast and lean encrypted internet traffic classification. Comput. Commun. **186**, 166–173 (2022)
37. Sabet, S.S., Schmidt, S., Zadtootaghaj, S., Griwodz, C., Möller, S.: Delay sensitivity classification of cloud gaming content. In: Proceedings of the 12th ACM International Workshop on Immersive Mixed and Virtual Environment Systems, Istanbul, Turkey (2020)
38. Schulzrinne, H., Casner, S., Frederick, R., Jacobson, V.: RTP: A Transport Protocol for Real-Time Applications. RFC 3550 (2003)

39. Sharma, T., Mangla, T., Gupta, A., Jiang, J., Feamster, N.: Estimating WebRTC video QoE metrics without using application headers (2023)
40. Shea, R., Liu, J., Ngai, E.C.-H., Cui, Y.: Cloud gaming: architecture and performance. IEEE Network **27**(4), 16–21 (2013)
41. Slivar, I., Suznjevic, M., Skorin-Kapov, L.: Game categorization for deriving QoE-driven video encoding configuration strategies for cloud gaming. ACM Trans. Multimedia Comput. Commun. Appl. **14**, 1–24 (2018)
42. Sony Interactive Entertainment. PlayStation Now (2023). https://www.playstation.com/en-us/ps-now/. Accessed 18 Apr 2023
43. Spang, B., Walsh, B., Huang, T.-Y., Rusnock, T., Lawrence, J., McKeown, N.: Buffer sizing and video QoE measurements at Netflix. In: Proceedings of the 2019 Workshop on Buffer Sizing (2020)
44. Wehner, N., Seufert, M., Schuler, J., Wassermann, S., Casas, P., Hossfeld, T.: Improving web QoE monitoring for encrypted network traffic through time series modeling. SIGMETRICS Perform. Eval. Rev. (2021)
45. Xu, X., Claypool, M.: Measurement of cloud-based game streaming system response to competing TCP cubic or TCP BBR flows. In: Proceedings of ACM Internet Measurement Conference, Nice, France (2022)
46. Zhang, X., et al.: Improving cloud gaming experience through mobile edge computing. IEEE Wirel. Commun. **26**(4), 178–183 (2019)

IPv6

Exploring the Discovery Process of Fresh IPv6 Prefixes: An Analysis of Scanning Behavior in Darknet and Honeynet

Liang Zhao[1]([⊠])(iD), Satoru Kobayashi[2](iD), and Kensuke Fukuda[3](iD)

[1] Sokendai, Tokyo, Japan
`zhaoliang@nii.ac.jp`
[2] Okayama University, Okayama, Japan
`sat@okayama-u.ac.jp`
[3] NII/Sokendai, Tokyo, Japan
`kensuke@nii.ac.jp`

Abstract. Internet-wide scanners can efficiently scan the expansive IPv6 network by targeting the active prefixes and responsive addresses on the hitlists. However, it is not clear enough how scanners discover fresh prefixes, which include newly assigned or deployed prefixes, as well as previously unused ones. This paper studies the whole discovery process of fresh prefixes by scanners. We implement four DNS-based address-exposing methods, analyze the arrival sequence of scans from distinct ASes, and examine the temporal and spatial scan patterns, with darknet and honeynet. Over six months, our custom-made darknet and probabilistic responsive honeynet collected 33 M packets (1.8 M sessions) of scans from 116 distinct ASes and 18.8 K unique source IP addresses. We investigate the whole process of fresh prefix discovery, including address-exposing, initial probing, hitlist registration, and large-scale scan campaigns. Furthermore, we analyze the difference in scanning behavior by ASes, and categorize the scanners into three types, honeynet-exclusive, honeynet-predominant and balanced, based on the respective ratio of scans to darknet and honeynet. Besides, we analyze the intentions of scanners, such as network reconnaissance or scanning responsive targets, and the methods they used to obtain potential targets, such as by sending DNS queries or using public hitlist. These findings bring insights into the process of fresh prefixes attracting scanners and highlight the vital role of responsive honeynet in analyzing scanner behaviors.

Keywords: Network Security · IPv6 scan · Honeynet · Darknet

1 Introduction

The Internet-wide scan is an important tool for benign and malicious activities to collect host and service information. With the recent adoption of IPv6 networks, several studies [10, 22, 28] report that IPv6 scans have been growing. However,

© The Author(s), under exclusive license to Springer Nature Switzerland AG 2024
P. Richter et al. (Eds.): PAM 2024, LNCS 14537, pp. 95–111, 2024.
https://doi.org/10.1007/978-3-031-56249-5_4

unlike the IPv4 network, scanning in the IPv6 network is much more difficult, because scanning the whole IPv6 space is impossible due to its vastness. Thus, the scanning activities in the IPv6 network are still not as prevalent as those in the IPv4 network [2, 6, 20, 21].

The hitlist [7, 11, 12, 15, 23, 30], containing active IPv6 prefixes and responsive addresses, enables scanners to perform scans efficiently across the expansive IPv6 network. A publicly available IPv6 hitlist is maintained by the Technical University of Munich (TUM) [15], though some scanners might rely on their lists. Scanners often target active IPv6 prefixes and responsive addresses on the hitlist. Thus, if a prefix or host is on the hitlist, it is more likely to be scanned. Also, target address generation [5, 9, 18, 24, 26, 29] have been well studied. However, even with the hitlist and target generation methods, it is hard for scanners to discover fresh IPv6 prefixes, which include newly deployed or assigned prefixes, or previously unused ones.

We characterize the whole process of fresh IPv6 prefixes being discovered by scanners. We introduce four DNS-based address-exposing methods to expose the target addresses to the Internet to attract the attention of scanners. We deploy multiple darknets and honeynets to measure the scanning activities associated with various address-exposing methods. A darknet is a network telescope that waits passively for the scans. A honeynet is a deceptive network that is purposely deployed to be scanned, attacked or compromised by the scanner and potential attacker [19, 25]. In this paper, we deploy probabilistic responsive honeynets, in which only a portion of addresses respond to scans, to prevent our honeynets from being recognized as aliased networks. More specifically, we want to answer the following questions. **RQ1:** How do scanners discover fresh IPv6 prefixes and what is the whole process of it? **RQ2:** How does the scanning behavior differ between darknet and honeynet? **RQ3:** What are the possible intentions of the scanners and how did they obtain the potential targets?

The contributions of our paper are as follows:

1. We design and develop an IPv6 scan detection system with darknet and probabilistic responsive honeynet, and deploy four DNS-based address-exposing methods to validate their effectiveness. We collected 33M packets (1.8M sessions) of scans from 116 distinct Autonomous Systems (ASes) and 18.8K unique source IP addresses over six months in 2023.
2. As the addresses of IPv6 fresh prefixes are exposed, it takes around 1–2 weeks before the scan begins to increase after the exposed prefixes are added to the hitlist. We analyze the sequence of arrival of scans from ASes and temporal scan patterns. We clarify the discovery process of fresh IPv6 prefixes as (1) address exposure, (2) DNS queries, (3) initial probes, (4) hitlist registration, and (5) follow-up scans.
3. Despite using the same exposing methods, responsive addresses in the honeynet received a greater amount of scans from a wider variety of source IP addresses and ASes compared to unresponsive addresses in the darknet. We compare the scanning behavior in the darknet and honeynet and categorize the scanners into three types, honeynet-exclusive (hitlist-based), honeynet-

predominant, and balanced (DNS registered-based and/or random), based on the respective ratio of scans to darknet and honeynet.
4. We analyze the intentions of scanners and the methods they use to obtain potential targets. Scanners targeting unregistered addresses probe the target network space with certain strategies for network reconnaissance, while those only targeting the registered addresses scan responsive targets specifically for exploitation. Scanners targeting registered addresses in both the darknet and honeynet are likely to obtain the registered addresses by sending the DNS queries to the auth server, while those only targeting responsive addresses in the honeynet are likely to obtain these addresses from the hitlist.

2 Scan Detection Methods

2.1 System Overview

We design and develop a system to detect the IPv6 scanning activities. We deploy multiple darknets (i.e., blackhole waiting passively for the scans) and honeynets (i.e., deceptive network purposely being deployed to be scanned or attacked [19, 25]) to compare the scanning behaviors within them. The maintainer of the hitlist employs detection algorithms to detect the aliased prefixes, in which all the addresses are responsive. We use probabilistic responsive honeynets, where only a portion of addresses actively respond to scans, to prevent them from being recognized as aliased networks. Our honeynet responds to ICMPv6 Echo, TCP SYN, and UDP requests. The target network in the experiment is a dedicated /56 IPv6 prefix, which is a subnet of a previously announced /32 prefix. Although the /56 prefix was not entirely newly assigned, it was not explicitly announced by BGP and was not used for other purposes. It is expected to experience a minimal level of internet background radiation before the experiment, similar to the unexposed darknet and honeynet (detailed in Table 1). We divide the /56 prefix into non-adjacent /64 s and allocate them as darknets and honeynets, implementing different address-exposing methods in each, as shown in Sect. 2.2.

2.2 Address-Exposing Methods

We design and implement four DNS-based methods to expose addresses to the Internet. The DNS-based methods are proven to be effective in attracting scanners [28]. We conduct experiments to verify the effectiveness of different address-exposing methods and scenarios, comparing scans in darknets and honeynets. For each scenario, we allocate two /64 s for the darknet and honeynet. We utilize the RFC-compliant DNS nameserver Name Server Daemon (NSD) [17] as our authoritative server.

IPv4 Reverse: Some IPv6 Scanners check the PTR records of IPv4 addresses and then use forward lookups to collect the associated IPv6 addresses for targets. We use domains associated with both IPv4 and IPv6 addresses to expose our IPv6 addresses. First, we register IPv4 PTR records to the auth server to return the domain names to IPv4 reverse lookup queries. Then, we register AAAA records to the auth server to return the IPv6 addresses we want to expose to IPv6 forward lookup queries.

We set up two scenarios to verify the effect of the numbers of registered IPv6 addresses: (1) register one randomly chosen IPv6 address for each target subnet. (2) register five randomly chosen IPv6 addresses for each target subnet.

IPv6 Enumeration: Scanners can collect IPv6 addresses by exploiting the "denial of existence" semantics of the DNS (NXDOMAIN) [7]. This method involves iterating over the ip6.arpa zone, and performing a request for each possible child node, ignoring any subtree that returns a NXDOMAIN response. We register the IPv6 PTR records of 100 randomly chosen addresses from the target subnet to the IPv6 reverse lookup zone file so that these IPv6 addresses can be collected by the method in Ref. [7].

Special IPv6 Address: Some special addresses are often set manually and are more likely to be scanned according to RFC7707 [13]. The special addresses include those embedded with the service port of TCP/UDP services (e.g., 2001:db8::80), and addresses embedded with words (e.g., 2001:db8::cafe). We register 118 of these special addresses to the IPv6 reverse lookup zone file.

Popular Service Name: Domain name reconnaissance tools, such as fierce [8], use name dictionaries to scan the domain names of a service. We collect the 100 most popular words from the dictionaries of various domain reconnaissance tools and create domain names with these words, with our domain (in TLD ".com"). We register the IPv6 addresses to these domains so that these addresses are more likely to be scanned by scanners using domain name reconnaissance tools. We also made these domain names publicly available on the Internet so that they can be crawled or accessed by users, thereby increasing the likelihood that they will be discovered by scanners.

The experiment setup is shown in Table 1. As a control experiment, we set up two subnets with no address exposure, dark-unex and honey-unex.

2.3 Acquiring the Hitlist

We analyze the current and historical TUM hitlist [15] to determine whether our subnet and addresses have been included in the hitlist and when they were collected. The hitlist contains three separate lists: aliased prefixes, non-aliased prefixes and responsive addresses. The aliased prefixes list contains prefixes where all addresses are responsive, while non-aliased prefixes are those that are not aliased. The responsive addresses list contains the addresses that respond to ICMPv6, TCP or UDP requests. We discuss how our target network is included in the hitlist in detail in Sect. 3.

Table 1. Configurations and detected scans in each experiment

ID	Exposing Method (Scenario)	#Session	#SIPs	#ASes
dark-unex	No exposing	102	5	4
honey-unex	No exposing	5	1	1
dark-v4rev1	IPv4 reverse (1 random addr.)	23.1k	1.7k	13
honey-v4rev1	IPv4 reverse (1 random addr.)	330.9k	13.9k	37
dark-v4rev5	IPv4 reverse (5 random addr.)	109.4k	2.0k	13
honey-v4rev5	IPv4 reverse (5 random addr.)	1158.0k	16.0k	121
dark-v6enum	IPv6 enumeration (100 random addr.)	91	2	2
honey-v6enum	IPv6 enumeration (100 random addr.)	6	2	2
dark-v6spe	Special IPv6 (90 wordy & 18 port-embed)	8	1	1
honey-v6spe	Special IPv6 (90 wordy & 18 port-embed)	5	1	1
dark-pop	Popular service name (100 random addr.)	111	4	3
honey-pop	Popular service name (100 random addr.)	6	2	2

3 Validation of Methods

3.1 Dataset Overview

We deployed the scan detection system and started the experiment in Apr 2023. Our analysis is based on scan sessions. A scan session for TCP and UDP is defined as a 5-tuple bidirectional flow with a timeout, or maximum packet inter-arrival time, of 3,600 s. Similarly, a scan session of ICMPv6 Echo is a bidirectional flow that shares the same source/destination address, and request ID, with a timeout of 3,600 s. We set the timeout to 1 h regarding Ref. [22]. Over six months, we collected 33 M packets (1.8 M sessions) of scans from 116 distinct ASes and 18.8 K unique source IP addresses.

3.2 Effectiveness of Address-Exposing Methods

Table 1 shows the number of sessions received in each experiment, along with the number of unique source IPs and ASes. We show the information of a sample of ASes of IPv6 scanners in Appendix A.

Comparison in the Four Address-Exposing Methods: The IPv4 reverse method attracted more than 99.99% of the scans, while other methods did not receive any associated DNS queries. Other methods (dark/honey-v6enum, v6spe, pop) only received minimal scans targeting the unregistered addresses, similar to the subnets with no exposure. This result suggests that the NXDOMAIN technique in the IPv6 enumeration method, brutal force dictionary attacks on specific IPv6 addresses or DNS reconnaissance are not yet fully exploited by the IPv6 scanners on a large scale. These methods might not be as straightforward, low-risk or cost-effective in terms of time and computing resources compared to the IPv4 reverse method to discover IPv6 addresses and prefixes. We will discuss the limitations of our address-exposing methods in Sect. 6. Dark-unex, v6enum, and pop received more scans than the others probably because their last nibble of the /64 prefix is 0 (e.g. 2001:db8:1:abc0::/64), which is easier to be selected for a scan. Interestingly, we identified two ASes (CERNET2(AS23910) and Alibaba Advertising(AS37963)) that were engaged in large-scale network reconnaissance spread in our target block (see also Sect. 4).

Scans Attracted by IPv4 Reverse Method: We compare the two scenarios in the IPv4 reverse method: one random IPv6 address mapping from one IPv4 address, and five random IPv6 addresses from one IPv4 address. In general, the honeynet attracted more scans than the darknet, similar to the trend in IPv4 Internet. The source IPs and ASes in the darknet of the two scenarios, dark-v4rev1 and dark-v4rev5, are almost identical, while the sessions of scan in dark-v4rev5 are 4.7 times greater than that in dark-v4rev1. The darknet with five registered addresses attracts more scans than the darknet with a single registered address, but these scans seem to originate from the same ASes and source IPs. On the other hand, the sessions in the honeynet of the two scenarios, honey-v4rev1 and honey-v4rev5, are almost identical, while the number of ASes of honey-v4rev5 is three times greater than that in honey-v4rev1 and the source IPs of honey-v4rev5 are 1.2 times greater than that in honey-v4rev1. The difference in sessions between honeynets of the two scenarios is not as substantial as observed in darknet. In summary, registering multiple IPv6 addresses for one IPv4 address is useful in amplifying sensors' resolution in the honeynet/darknet.

We will focus on the scans attracted by the IPv4 reverse method.

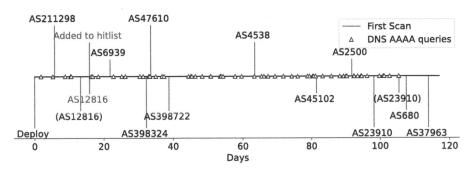

Fig. 1. The arrival sequence of the initial scan from each AS in the Darknet. An AS number enclosed in parentheses (e.g. (AS12816)) indicates the initial scan targeting an unregistered address from this AS. An AS number without parentheses indicates the initial scan targeting a registered address from this AS. See also Table 3 for AS names.

3.3   Arrival Sequence and Hitlist Confirmation

We investigate the arrival sequence of the ASes in the darknet and the honeynet, as shown in Fig. 1 and 2, with DNS AAAA queries shown for reference.

DNS Queries: Regarding the DNS AAAA queries associated with the IPv4 reverse method, we confirmed the arrival of queries for the registered addresses in

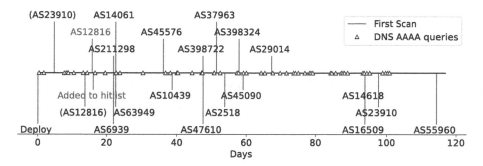

Fig. 2. The arrival sequence of the initial scan from each AS in the Honeynet.

dark/honey-v4rev1/v4rev5 right after exposing them. However, we were unable to establish a correlation between the DNS queries with the initial scans from each AS, since the scanner may use cloud-hosting services for name resolution.

Hitlist Registration: As we noted in Sect. 2.3, the hitlist contains three separate lists, aliased prefixes, non-aliased prefixes and responsive addresses. We confirmed that the target networks associated with IPv4 reverse (dark/honey-v4rev1, v4rev5) are added to the non-aliased *prefixes* lists and the registered honeynet addresses (1 in honey-v4rev1 and 5 in honey-v4rev5) are added to the responsive *address* hitlist about 17 days after deployment. Honeynet addresses responding to scans from Leibniz-Rechenzentrum(AS12816) are added to the responsive addresses list.

Arrival Sequence of ASes: Initially, the scanners probe the target network. Once prefixes are added to the hitlist, more scans originate from a diverse set of ASes. The ASes fall into two categories based on the target of their initial scan. Firstly, the initial scan targets an unregistered address, as seen with CER-NET2 in the honeynet. This suggests that the scanner is conducting network reconnaissance. The registered address was scanned by this AS about 90 days later. Secondly, the initial scan targets the registered addresses, which are supposed to be discovered via hitlist or DNS queries (i.e., an intentional scanning activity). As the hitlist does not include the registered darknet addresses, the scanners targeting these addresses are likely to discover them via DNS queries independently or retrieve them from third parties.

In short, we confirmed the discovery process of fresh IPv6 prefixes: address exposure, DNS queries, initial probes, hitlist registration, and follow-up scans.

4   IPv6 Scan Characteristics

We analyze the scans received over time, and their sources, protocols and ports.

4.1   Scans over Time

Overall Trend: Figure 3 shows the hourly scan sessions over time in each subnet of the IPv4 reverse method since Apr 2023. Some periods of data are missing from

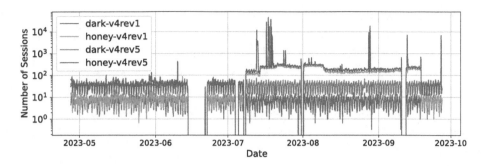

Fig. 3. Number of sessions received in each subnet using IPv4 reverse method

Jun to Sep due to server shutdowns. In May and Jun, the daily scans in both the darknet and honeynet are regular; They are most active from 12am - 4pm UTC (peak 2 pm), though they significantly decreased from 4pm - 12am UTC. There is no significant difference between weekdays and weekends. In both darknet and honeynet, a larger number of scans are observed for a larger number of registered addresses. In Jul, we observed a strong uptick of scans in the honeynets, where a large-scale scan campaign has begun spanning over two months. The average hourly scans in honey-v4rev1 and honey-v4rev5 have increased to a few hundred since Jul. There are also spikes of scans in honey-v4rev5 from Jul to Sep. In the middle of Sep, the large-scale scan campaign ended and the daily scan in the honeynet dropped to the same level as May and Jun. However, the spikes in honey-v4rev5 can still be observed.

Large-Scale Scans: As in Ref. [22], we define a large-scale scan as a source targeting at least 100 destination IPv6 addresses with a timeout of 1 h. According to this definition, we have also observed 28 large-scale scan events from five different sources in our dataset. In a single scan, more than 20,000 unique destination addresses are targeted at most. Most of the destinations of these large-scale scans are in the honeynet, which indicates that the reactive responses might be a triggering factor of large-scale scans.

4.2 Scan Targets

Next, we analyze the scans by their targets: the registered addresses or unregistered addresses. Scans targeting registered addresses account for 97.67% of scans in the darknet and 52.03% of scans in the honeynet. Most of the remaining scans in the honeynet target unregistered addresses near the registered address, accounting for 47.58% of the total scans in the honeynet. However, the remaining scans in the darknet are targeting random unregistered addresses across the /64 subnet, rather than those near the registered address. Table 1 shows the percentage of scans targeting the registered addresses for each AS. Scanners targeting only registered addresses are scanning these addresses specifically for exploitation, while those targeting both registered and unregistered addresses are likely conducting network reconnaissance to discover previously unknown active hosts. Scans targeting the lower byte IID in the /64 subnet (e.g., 2001:db8::2) only account for 0.03% of the total scans.

4.3 Scan Sources

Table 2. Top source ASes targeting Darknet and Honeynet, sorted by #Session.

Darknet					Honeynet				
ASN	#Session	Regist	/128 s	/64 s	ASN	#Session	Regist	/128 s	/64 s
6939	66.9K	100.0%	1.7k	3	23910	685.5k	0.1%	5	2
211298	61.1K	100.0%	231	7	16509	469.3k	100.0%	9.3k	172
12816	3.6k	16.9%	9	1	14618	152.8k	100.0%	2.3k	17
3910	268	62.7%	3	1	6939	67.6k	100.0%	1.7k	4
37963	207	99.0%	2	1	211298	61.4k	100.0%	236	7
398722	199	100.0%	13	1	37963	21.1k	1.4%	14	13
398324	151	100.0%	14	1	10439	13.3k	100.0%	11	1
47610	99	100.0%	1	1	10439	13.3k	100.0%	11	1
2500	35	100.0%	6	2	2637	2.1k	6.4%	1	1
680	24	100.0%	1	1	14061	1.7k	99.9%	579	12

Next, we analyze the intentions of scanners and the methods they use to obtain the potential targets by their sources. Table 2 lists the top source ASes targeting the darknet and honeynet. The top source ASes include R&E networks (CERNET2), ISPs (Hurricane Electric), cloud hosting service (AMAZON-02(AS16509)) and business firms (Alibaba Advertising). The distribution of scan sessions from each AS is long-tailed. The majority of scans originate from a few ASes in both the darknet and honeynet. In the darknet, the scans of the top three ASes account for a combined total of 99% of all scans. In the honeynet, the scans from the top three ASes contribute to a combined total of 88% of all scans. We can only identify two scanners from Censys [3] in an open access acknowledged scanners repository [4].

Scanner Types: There are 13 ASes that simultaneously scan both the darknet and honeynet, 94 ASes exclusively scan the honeynet, while there is no AS that exclusively scans the darknet. Figure 4 shows the scan sessions towards darknet and honeynet for ASes. The ASes can be categorized into three types: honeynet-predominant, honeynet-exclusive and balanced.

Honeynet-Predominant: For ASes above the diagonal such as CERNET2 and Alibaba Advertising, the number of scans in the honeynet is significantly higher than that in the darknet. These ASes probe both the darknet and honeynet initially and then conduct large-scale scans toward the honeynet. As we mentioned

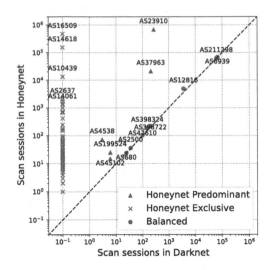

Fig. 4. Scatter plot of Darknet and Honeynet for each AS (10^{-1} indicates no sessions).

in Sect. 3.2, they contribute to the majority of scans to unregistered addresses all across our /56 target network, regardless of the address-exposing method or scenario. Moreover, these scanners mainly target unregistered addresses near the registered address. This indicates that their purpose is to conduct network reconnaissance to find potential targets and then launch large-scale scans targeting these active hosts.

Honeynet-Exclusive: The ASes on the left side of the figure exclusively scan the honeynet. Most of these ASes target the registered addresses exclusively, suggesting they may have learned the registered responsive addresses via the hitlist[1] and were scanning these addresses intentionally. During large-scale scan campaigns, AMAZON-02 and AMAZON-AES(AS14618) conduct scan sessions that last for more than 30 h, generating over 10,000 packets. However, there are still exceptions like GEORGIA-TECH(AS2637), which scans unregistered addresses, suggesting searching for scanning targets.

Balanced: For the ASes along the diagonal, the number of scans is nearly identical for both the darknet and honeynet. The scans are usually stable over time with a fixed periodic cycle. This suggests that the purpose of these ASes scan the network thoroughly without any specific preferences. They mainly target the registered address (e.g., Constantine Cybersecurity(AS211298) and Hurricane Electric), or random unregistered addresses in the /64 subnet (e.g., Leibniz-Rechenzentrum).

In conclusion, honeynet-predominant scanners target the responsive addresses after a probing phase and also search for potential targets near the

---

[1] Recall that the TUM hitlist does not provide registered darknet addresses.

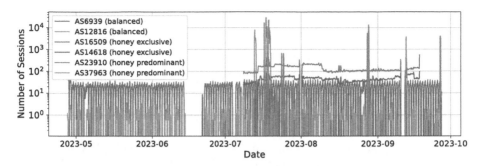

Fig. 5. Number of sessions from each source AS received in honey-v4rev5

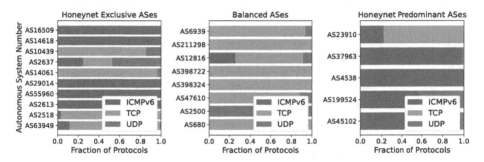

Fig. 6. Fraction of protocols of darknet and honeynet

registered addresses. Balanced scanners probe the entire network space and target the registered addresses or random unregistered addresses. Honeynet-predominant scanners and balanced scanners target registered addresses in both the honeynet and darknet. Therefore, they likely obtain the targets by sending the DNS queries to the authoritative DNS server, since the hitlist only contains responsive addresses. Honeynet-exclusive scanners primarily target the registered addresses in the Honeynet, and they likely obtain these addresses from the hitlist.

Scans over Time by AS in Honeynet: Figure 5 shows the scan over time by AS in honey-v4rev5. Before the uptick in scans in July, the majority of the scans were from security firms and research institutions. These ASes equally scan the darknet and honeynet, showing a periodic fluctuation pattern over time. Scans from Hurricane Electric show a consistent daily pattern, with scanning activities only occurring during the hours of 0am - 3pm UTC, and no scans for the rest of the day. Scans from Leibniz-Rechenzentrum show a notable large surge of scans every four days, with some smaller surges in between. Scans from AMAZON-02 and AMAZON-AES show identical patterns, indicating that they are likely to be carried out by the same entity, while AMAZON-02 has a 4 times/128 s and 10 times/64 s source than AMAZON-AES. In contrast, scans from CERNET2 show significant surges, which mainly target addresses that are not registered on the DNS server. The scans from other ASes only target registered addresses.

4.4   Scan Protocols and Target Ports

Protocols: We analyze the fraction of protocols of scans in each AS and compare the honeynet-exclusive, honeynet-predominant and balanced ASes. Figure 6 shows the fraction of protocols of each type of ASes. In honeynet-exclusive ASes, many scanners use only ICMPv6. On the other hand, balanced ASes use primarily TCP. Most of the honeynet-predominant ASes use primarily ICMPv6, along with TCP or UDP. Interestingly, Leibniz-Rechenzentrum and GEORGIA-TECH, two research institutions, use a combination of TCP, UDP and ICMPv6 to get a whole landscape of the IPv6 network for research proposes.

Ports: Table 4 and 5 in Appendix B show the top destination ports and number of unique ports of the darknet and the honeynet. Some scanners primarily focused on well-known and commonly used ports (i.e., 22, 53, 80, 443 and 8080), such as Leibniz-Rechenzentrum and Hurricane Electric(AS6939). We also observed penetration test behaviors, which scan across a wide range of ports, from some scanners. For example, Constantine Cybersecurity is scanning over 4,000 unique target ports in both darknet and honeynet. Interestingly, both Alibaba Advertising and CERNET2 are targeting the TCP/7547 port, a commonly used target port for the Mirai botnet and its variants [1]. These two ASes are using the same source port, specifically port TCP/37492, for their scanning activities in the darknet, which suggests that these two ASes could either be the same entity or they might use the same scanning software.

5   Related Work

Scan Detection: Scan detection is diligently carried out in the IPv4 network [2,6,20,21]. Darknet and honeynet [16,19,25] are frequently employed to collect information about scanning activities. Recent works [10,14,22,27,28] indicate the increasing prevalence of scanners covering the IPv6 space. Richter et al. [22] investigated the large-scale IPv6 scanning activities on the Internet based on firewall logs captured at a major CDN. They studied the dominant characteristics of scans, including scanner origins and targeted services. Their work focuses more on already existing scan activities in the broad internet space, while we focus on the growth of scan activities in a fresh prefix that is dedicated to our experiments and not used for other purposes. Furthermore, the detected scans in our work are attracted to the target network by address exposing methods, while the scans in Ref. [22] are general scans observed in a CDN. The scans we've detected in our work are supposed to be more specific and exhibit greater similarity. This allows us to analyze their common characteristics and purposes.

Scan Attraction: Tanveer et al. [28] propose to attract potential IPv6 scans by direct/indirect scan attraction methods. Among their indirect (passive) contact approaches, DNS-based (DNS zone) and NTP-based methods (NTP pool/public) are effective in attracting the scans. They studied the relationship between the attraction methods and the scanner attention they evoke. We took a step further and did a more thorough and focused analysis of the scans attracted by the same exposing method. We focused on the DNS-based approach and differentiated the scanner behavior based on their source ASes, targeting (exposed addresses or random addresses), preference on darknet or honeynet, and traffic patterns over time. We show that even the scans attracted by the same exposing method could still vary significantly in their behavior.

Address Discovery: IPv6 hitlist-based scans [7,11,12,15,23,30] have emerged, enabling scanners to perform scans across the vast IPv6 network space. Target generation methods [5,9,18,24,26,29], which generate target addresses based on known addresses, have been proposed to find IPv6 addresses to scan.

6   Limitations

There are still some limitations in this work. First, we mainly focused on DNS-based address exposing methods and the dataset we collected is primarily attracted through the IPv4 reverse method. This dataset allows us to perform a thorough and focused analysis of the scans attracted by the same method. However, address-exposing methods using other services [28], such as NTP-based methods (NTPpool, NTP public), can also attract scans effectively. We plan to implement other methods to retrieve a more complete dataset in future work. Second, we have not observed any DNS queries associated with IPv6 enumeration and special IPv6 methods, possibly due to an insufficient measurement period to fully expose the addresses. Moreover, IPv6 enumeration requires that authoritative DNS servers for parent zones are also RFC-compliant, which is not always guaranteed. Regarding the popular service name method, the URLs we made public are not drawing significant Internet traffic, and are not yet indexed by Google or other search engines. Moreover, we added the name of the experiment as a subdomain to the URLs, which could also make it harder for DNS reconnaissance tools to discover the full URLs. Third, distinguishing whether scans originate from the same user or not can be challenging, especially for multi-tenant cloud networks. However, we find some evidence showing that the scans from some of the ASes are from the same user. For example, both Alibaba Advertising and CERNET2 only use the same source port TCP/37492. AMAZON-02 and AMAZON-AES are sharing a similar scan traffic pattern. Lastly, we confirmed that our prefixes and addresses are added to the TUM hitlist. However, it is uncertain if the scanners are also using other hitlists. To address this issue, we consider intentionally not responding to TUM scans to avoid being included in their hitlist and analyze the effect of other hitlists in future work.

7   Conclusion

This paper studies the whole process of fresh prefixes being discovered by scanners, including address-exposing, initial probing, hitlist registration, and large-

scale scan campaigns. We analyze the difference in scanning behavior by ASes
and categorize the scanners into three types, honeynet-exclusive, honeynet predominant and balanced, based on the respective ratio of scans to darknet and
honeynet. Besides, we analyzed the intentions of scanners, such as network reconnaissance or scanning responsive targets, and the methods they used to obtain
potential targets, such as by sending DNS queries or using the hitlist. These
findings bring insights into the process of fresh prefixes attracting scanners and
highlight the vital role of responsive honeynet in analyzing scanner behaviors.

Acknowledgments. We thank our shepherd, Pawel Foremski, and anonymous
reviewers for their valuable feedback and suggestions, which greatly improved the quality of our manuscript. This work is financially supported by JSPS 21H03438.

A   ASes Information

We list information about a sample of the ASes of IPv6 scanners we confirmed
in Table 3.

Table 3. The Description, ASN Type, Country, and Scanner Type of ASes

ASN	Description	ASN Type	CC	Scanner Type
16509	AMAZON-02	Hosting	US	Honeynet-Exclusive
14618	AMAZON-AES	Hosting	US	Honeynet-Exclusive
55960	Beijing Guanghuan Xinwang Digital	ISP	CN	Honeynet-Exclusive
10439	CARINET	Hosting	US	Honeynet-Exclusive
398324	CENSYS-ARIN-01	Business	US	Balanced
398722	CENSYS-ARIN-03	Business	US	Balanced
4538	China R&E Network Center	Research	CN	Honeynet-Predominant
23910	China Next Gen. Internet CERNET2	Research	CN	Honeynet-Predominant
211298	Constantine Cybersecurity	Business	UK	Balanced
14061	DIGITALOCEAN-ASN	Hosting	US	Honeynet-Exclusive
2637	GEORGIA-TECH	Research	US	Honeynet-Exclusive
6939	HURRICANE	ISP	US	Balanced
37963	Hangzhou Alibaba Advertising	Business	CN	Honeynet-Predominant
12816	Leibniz-Rechenzentrum	Research	DE	Balanced
47610	RWTH Aachen University	Research	DE	Balanced
29014	ScaleUp Technologies	Hosting	DE	Honeynet-Exclusive
680	Verein zur Foerderung eines Deutschen	Research	DE	Balanced
2500	WIDE Project	Research	JP	Balanced

Table 4. Primary ports of scans towards the Darknet. (Percentage) is the portion of scans to a certain port among all scans. Unique is the number of unique dest ports.

ASN	Top 3 Destination Ports						Uniq
6939	8081	(2.5%)	8080	(2.5%)	8001	(2.5%)	82
211298	8443	(0.5%)	21	(0.5%)	135	(0.5%)	4232
12816	80	(85.6%)	443	(10.6%)	161	(1.9%)	4
23910	443	(25.0%)	22	(25.0%)	7547	(25.0%)	4
37963	443	(25.0%)	22	(25.0%)	7547	(25.0%)	4
398722	443	(65.3%)	80	(34.7%)	–	–	2
398324	443	(66.2%)	80	(33.7%)	–	–	2
47610	5671	(30.3%)	8883	(18.2%)	55672	(18.2%)	7
2500	53	(100.0%)	– –	–	–	–	1
680	443	(50.0%)	80	(50.0%)	–	–	2

B   Port Information

Here, we provide the details of destination ports for darknet (Table 4) and honeynet (Table 5).

Table 5. Primary ports of scans towards the Honeynet

ASN	Top 3 Destination Ports						Uniq
23910	443	(25.1%)	7547	(25.1%)	80	(25.1%)	26
6939	8080	(2.5%)	8888	(2.5%)	8001	(2.5%)	82
211298	443	(0.5%)	135	(0.5%)	22	(0.5%)	4171
37963	80	(24.3%)	443	(23.3%)	7547	(23.3%)	5
10439	2152	(2.6%)	2123	(2.1%)	53	(1.4%)	125
12816	80	(69.7%)	443	(22.5%)	161	(3.9%)	4
2637	53	(62.3%)	443	(20.9%)	80	(16.8%)	3
14061	443	(8.5%)	8443	(5.7%)	27017	(3.0%)	224
2518	443	(16.7%)	80	(14.6%)	8080	(13.7%)	7
63949	8443	(14.6%)	443	(11.1%)	5002	(2.4%)	165

References

1. Antonakakis, M., et al.: Understanding the mirai botnet. In: Proceedings of USENIX Security 2017, Vancouver, BC, pp. 1093–1110 (2017)
2. Benson, K., Dainotti, A., Claffy, K., Snoeren, A.C., Kallitsis, M.: Leveraging internet background radiation for opportunistic network analysis. In: Proceedings of ACM IMC 2015, Tokyo, Japan, pp. 423–436 (2015)

3. Censys: OPT out of data collection. https://support.censys.io/hc/en-us/articles/360043177092-Opt-Out-of-Scanning. Accessed Jan 2024
4. Collins, M.P., Hussain, A., Schwab, S.: Identifying and differentiating acknowledged scanners in network traffic. In: 2023 IEEE European Symposium on Security and Privacy Workshops (EuroS&PW), pp. 567–574 (2023). https://doi.org/10.1109/EuroSPW59978.2023.00069
5. Cui, T., Gou, G., Xiong, G.: 6GCVAE: gated convolutional variational autoencoder for IPv6 target generation. In: Proceedings of PAKDD 2020, Singapore (2020)
6. Durumeric, Z., Bailey, M., Halderman, J.A.: An internet-wide view of internet-wide scanning. In: Proceedings of USENIX Security, San Diego, CA, pp. 65–78 (2014)
7. Fiebig, T., Borgolte, K., Hao, S., Kruegel, C., Vigna, G.: Something from nothing (there): collecting global ipv6 datasets from DNS. In: Proceedings of PAM 2018, pp. 30–43 (2018)
8. Fierce: A DNS reconnaissance tool for locating non-contiguous IP space. https://github.com/mschwager/fierce. Accessed Aug 2023
9. Foremski, P., Plonka, D., Berger, A.: Entropy/IP: uncovering structure in IPv6 addresses. In: Proceedings of ACM IMC 2016, Santa Monica, CA, pp. 167–181 (2016)
10. Fukuda, K., Heidemann, J.: Who knocks at the IPv6 door? Detecting IPv6 scanning. In: Proceedings of ACM IMC 2018, Boston, MA, pp. 231–237 (2018)
11. Gasser, O., et al.: Clusters in the expanse: understanding and unbiasing IPv6 hitlists. In: Proceedings of ACM IMC 2018, Boston, MA, pp. 364–378 (2018)
12. Gasser, O., Scheitle, Q., Gebhard, S., Carle, G.: Scanning the IPv6 internet: towards a comprehensive hitlist. CoRR abs/1607.05179 (2016). http://arxiv.org/abs/1607.05179
13. Gont, F., Chown, T.: Network Reconnaissance in IPv6 Networks. Technical report, Internet Engineering Task Force (2015). RFC7707. https://tools.ietf.org/html/rfc7707
14. Hiesgen, R., Nawrocki, M., King, A., Dainotti, A., Schmidt, T.C., Wählisch, M.: Spoki: unveiling a new wave of scanners through a reactive network telescope. In: 31st USENIX Security Symposium (USENIX Security 2022), Boston, MA, pp. 431–448. USENIX Association (2022). https://www.usenix.org/conference/usenixsecurity22/presentation/hiesgen
15. IPv6 Hitlist Service. https://ipv6hitlist.github.io/. Accessed Aug 2023
16. Javadpour, A., Ja'Fari, F., Taleb, T., Benzaid, C.: A mathematical model for analyzing honeynets and their cyber deception techniques. In: Proceedings of ICECCS (2023)
17. NLnet Labs: The NLnet labs name server daemon (NSD) is an authoritative, RFC compliant DNS nameserver. https://github.com/NLnetLabs/nsd. Accessed Jan 2024
18. Murdock, A., Li, F., Bramsen, P., Durumeric, Z., Paxson, V.: Target generation for internet-wide ipv6 scanning. In: Proceedings of ACM IMC 2017, London, UK, pp. 242–253 (2017)
19. Nawrocki, M., Wählisch, M., Schmidt, T.C., Keil, C., Schönfelder, J.: A survey on honeypot software and data analysis (2016). http://arxiv.org/abs/1608.06249
20. Pang, R., Yegneswaran, V., Barford, P., Paxson, V., Peterson, L.: Characteristics of internet background radiation. In: Proceedings of ACM IMC 2004, pp. 27–40 (2004)
21. Richter, P., Berger, A.: Scanning the scanners: sensing the internet from a massively distributed network telescope. In: Proceedings of ACM IMC 2019, Amsterdam, Netherlands, pp. 144–157 (2019)

22. Richter, P., Gasser, O., Berger, A.: Illuminating large-scale ipv6 scanning in the internet. In: Proceedings of ACM IMC 2022, Nice, France, pp. 410–418 (2022)
23. Rye, E., Levin, D.: Ipv6 hitlists at scale: Be careful what you wish for. In: Proceedings of ACM SIGCOMM 2023, pp. 904–916 (2023)
24. Song, G., et al.: DET: enabling efficient probing of ipv6 active addresses. IEEE/ACM Trans. Networking **30**(4), 1629–1643 (2022). https://doi.org/10.1109/TNET.2022.3145040
25. Spitzner, L.: The honeynet project: trapping the hackers. IEEE Secur. Priv. **1**(2), 15–23 (2003)
26. Steger, L., Kuang, L., Zirngibl, J., Carle, G., Gasser, O.: Target acquired? Evaluating target generation algorithms for IPv6. In: Proceedings of TMA 2023 (2023)
27. Strowes, S.D., Aben, E., Wilhelm, R., Obser, F., Stagni, R., Formoso, A.: Debogonising 2a10::/12: analysis of one week's visibility of a new /12. In: Proceedings of TMA 2020 (2020)
28. Tanveer, H.B., Singh, R., Pearce, P., Nithyanand, R.: Glowing in the dark uncovering IPv6 address discovery and scanning strategies in the wild. In: Proceedings of USENIX Security 2023, pp. 6221–6237 (2023)
29. Yang, T., Hou, B., Cai, Z., Wu, K., Zhou, T., Wang, C.: 6Graph: a graph-theoretic approach to address pattern mining for internet-wide IPv6 scanning. Comput. Netw. **203**, 108666 (2022)
30. Zirngibl, J., Steger, L., Sattler, P., Gasser, O., Carle, G.: Rusty clusters? Dusting an IPv6 research foundation. In: Proceedings of ACM IMC 2022, Nice, France, pp. 395–409 (2022)

A First Look at NAT64 Deployment In-The-Wild

Amanda Hsu[1][✉], Frank Li[1], Paul Pearce[1], and Oliver Gasser[2]

[1] Georgia Institute of Technology, Atlanta, Georgia
{ahsu67,frankli,pearce}@gatech.edu
[2] Max Planck Institute for Informatics, Saarbrücken, Germany
oliver.gasser@mpi-inf.mpg.de

Abstract. IPv6 is a fundamentally different Internet Protocol than IPv4, and IPv6-only networks cannot, by default, communicate with the IPv4 Internet. This lack of interoperability necessitates complex mechanisms for incremental deployment and bridging networks so that non-dual-stack systems can interact with the *whole* Internet. NAT64 is one such bridging mechanism by which a network allows IPv6-only clients to connect to the entire Internet, leveraging DNS to identify IPv4-only networks, inject IPv6 response addresses pointing to an internal gateway, and seamlessly translate connections. To date, our understanding of NAT64 deployments is limited; what little information exists is largely qualitative, taken from mailing lists and informal discussions.

In this work, we present a first look at the active measurement of NAT64 deployment on the Internet focused on deployment prevalence, configuration, and security. We seek to measure NAT64 via two distinct large-scale measurements: 1) open resolvers on the Internet, and 2) client measurements from RIPE Atlas. For both datasets, we broadly find that despite substantial anecdotal reports of NAT64 deployment, *measurable* deployments are exceedingly sparse. While our measurements do not preclude the large-scale deployment of NAT64, they do point to substantial challenges in measuring deployments with our existing best-known methods. Finally, we also identify problems in NAT64 deployments, with gateways not following the RFC specification and also posing potential security risks.

1 Introduction

The modern Internet is a mix of both IPv4 and IPv6 hosts. With the exhaustion of the IPv4 address space, network providers are increasingly turning to IPv6 for expansion and new deployments. This increase in IPv6 adoption is measurable and accelerating; as of November 2023, Google estimates that over 40% of its users connect over native IPv6, up from less than 1% a decade ago [17]. However, this migration has been fraught, complex, and slow, and there is no built-in interoperability between IPv4 and IPv6 protocols.

To bridge IPv6-centric networks into the IPv4-only Internet, transition protocols have been proposed [15], deployed [6], and deprecated [33]. The recent

© The Author(s), under exclusive license to Springer Nature Switzerland AG 2024
P. Richter et al. (Eds.): PAM 2024, LNCS 14537, pp. 112–129, 2024.
https://doi.org/10.1007/978-3-031-56249-5_5

acceleration of IPv6 adoption has brought renewed interest in understanding how networks can ease this transition. Among currently deployed tools is NAT64, a mechanism that allows IPv6-only systems to access IPv4-only Internet resources. NAT64 leverages DNS64 resolvers to map IPv4 addresses into IPv6 addresses; when an IPv6-only client issues a DNS request for a domain that only contains an A record, a resolver (implementing the companion DNS64 protocol) will insert synthetic AAAA records mapping to a "gateway" IPv6 address that will proxy the connections from IPv6 to IPv4, in a mechanism akin to traditional Network Address Translation (NAT). This mechanism is economically efficient; it allows operators to keep the edges of their networks, new deployments, and clients, to be IPv6 only; only gateways need to have support for IPv4, without sacrificing customer experience, or needing IPv4 NAT or IPv4 management [2]. Moreover, this technique also enables measurement opportunities, as the synthetic AAAA records can be identified to locate and understand NAT64 deployments.

Anecdotally, substantial NAT64 deployments are reported. The 464XLAT protocol [27] integrates NAT64 and is deployed by T-Mobile in the United States [6], and is reported to be deployed in multiple other networks including Sprint, Telstra, and Deutsche Telekom [18]. Additionally, China Mobile has reported its intention to use it to maintain connectivity to both IPs as it deploys IPv6 [35]. Alongside these deployments, concerns for misconfiguration in transition mechanisms that could impact clients' Internet accessibility arose [38].

To date, NAT64 has not been empirically explored across the Internet. In this work we provide a first look at NAT64 deployment in-the-wild, seeking to understand the prevalence of deployment, configuration issues, and security shortcomings. We achieve this by issuing DNS queries designed to elicit NAT64 responses across both real-world and control IPv4-only domains and explore the responses, and the properties of the machines at the returned addresses.

Our contributions include:

- **NAT64 deployment analysis:** We present the first large-scale NAT64 analysis, finding 2,021 deployments across 262 Autonomous Systems (ASes).
- **Configuration:** We find 60.7–100% of NAT64 configurations are correctly configured when embedding IPv4 addresses within synthetic AAAA records.
- **Security:** Finally, we identify potential security issues, with 1.1–26.6% of NAT64 gateways being publicly accessible.

2   Background and Related Work

In this section, we present an overview of transition mechanisms in general and NAT64 specifically and elaborate on existing work in NAT64 measurements.

Transition mechanisms can be categorized in three ways: single transition, double transition, and tunneling. A single transition mechanism translates IPv4/6 traffic to IPv6/4 traffic, and vice versa. A double transition mechanism translates IPv4/6 to IPv6/4 and then back to IPv4/6. A tunnel encapsulates IPv4/6 in IPv6/4 [7]. NAT64 is an example of a single transition whereby IPv6 traffic is translated to IPv4 on outbound connections, and then back again for responses.

NAT64 Background: NAT64 is a transition mechanism that allows an IPv6-only host to access IPv4-only Internet resources [26]. This mechanism consists of two parts: A DNS64-enabled DNS resolver and a NAT64 gateway. For each domain requested by an IPv6 client, the DNS64 resolver returns a AAAA record. If the requested domain does not have a AAAA record and only an A record, the DNS64 resolver will create a synthetic AAAA record pointing to and designed to be read by a NAT64 gateway. This synthetic AAAA record may use a reserved NAT64 prefix (`64:ff9b::/96` or `64:ff9b:1::/48` [3]), public IPv6 space, or other private address space. The AAAA record embeds the IPv4 address from the A record in the last 32 bits of the IPv6 address, which enables the gateway to translate traffic to and from the IPv4 resource to the IPv6 client. While largely used privately, a number of public NAT64 and DNS64 services are publicly available [10]. Although DNS64 is specifically designed to be used with NAT64, both of these systems do not need to be deployed in the same network (e.g., Google offers a free DNS64 service, but not NAT64 [16]).

NAT64 Deployments: The stateless nature of NAT64 makes it apt and scalable in many networks [25]. Additionally, it may be built into other transition mechanisms such as 464XLAT [27], which allows for IPv4 and IPv6 networks alike to share a part of their infrastructure, again, adding to the network scalability. T-Mobile is known for deploying this mechanism in the United States [6]. In addition to scalability, both of these mechanisms are also more cost-efficient in large networks [2]. Moreover, NAT64 and DNS64 have been reported to be deployed by a number of other large network providers such as Deutsche Telekom in Germany [18]. NAT64 deployment may have also been motivated by Apple's requirement for mobile iOS applications to have IPv6 connectivity to use the app store [4]. App developers report leveraging local NAT64 deployments in their testing [28]. Finally, we highlight the need for NAT64 to be able to access popular domains. Just over 30% of domains in the Cisco Umbrella top list are available via IPv6 [34]. Therefore, to maintain accessibility to a large fraction of the Internet, IPv6 networks must either deploy some form of IPv4 connectivity or use a transition mechanism such as NAT64.

Prior NAT64 Measurements: Prior work on transition mechanisms has focused on performance [1] and classification [24]. Kristoff et al. measured deprecated tunneling transition mechanisms and found many to still exist in ISP backbones [22]. Moreover, Zorz et al. deployed point-wise public testing infrastructure focused on website compatibility [38], which is unfortunately no longer operational. To the best of our knowledge, we present the first measurement study of NAT64 on the public Internet.

3   Methodology

Our methodology (see Fig. 1) is centered around requesting a AAAA record for a domain where we know that the authoritative nameserver only answers with an

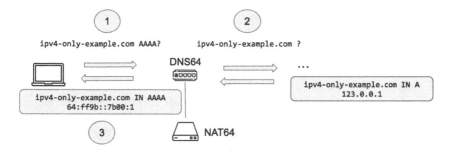

Fig. 1. An overview of our methodology. We request a AAAA record for an IPv4-only domain (1), the DNS64 resolver resolves the domain and only finds an A record (2), and returns a synthetic AAAA record (3).

A record. In step (1) we send AAAA queries for IPv4-only domains to different public resolvers. In step (2) the DNS64 resolver will then try to resolve A and AAAA for the requested domain. In step (3) if only an A record is returned, the DNS64 resolver creates a synthetic AAAA record to be returned to the client. The returned address is usually in the reserved NAT64 prefix (`64:ff9b::/96`). The IPv4 address is embedded in the last 32 bits as required according to the NAT64 RFC [26]. We expand on each part of this method.

Choosing Target Domains: We sample four domains from the Tranco top 1M list [23][1] and measure them for AAAA and A records using ZDNS [21]. We ensure that each domain is online by measuring it for HTTP and HTTPS with ZGrab2 [37] so that we can later perform application-layer measurements of the NAT64 gateways. To avoid censorship, we filter out domains in the Citizenlab global censorship list [8], manually discard domains related to social media or journalism, and ensure that none elicit censorship behavior from China's Great Firewall (GFW) as observed in prior work [32,36]. To avoid overloading authoritative nameservers, we randomly sample from the first 1k domains in Tranco, as these likely expect higher traffic volumes. The domains are: `azure.com`, `cloudflare.net`, `ntp.org`, and `webex.com` We also measure `github.com`, as it is a popular domain that only supports IPv4 and is typically not censored.

Identifying Public Resolvers: To identify public IPv6 resolvers, we use the IPv6 hitlist [14] snapshot from October 18, 2023, containing 279.1k public IPv6 resolvers. To identify public IPv4 resolvers, we use the Censys dataset [11] snapshot from October 16, 2023, containing 1.9M public IPv4 resolvers.

Resolver Measurements: After identifying target domains and public resolvers, we use ZMap [12] and ZMapv6 [14] to request AAAA records for each of our domains. We also request an A record for each domain-resolver pair responding with a valid AAAA record to validate that it correctly embeds the IPv4 address according to the NAT64 RFC [26], as explained in Sect. 2. To avoid

---

[1] We use the Tranco list [23] generated on October 5, 2023, available at https://tranco-list.eu/list/W9P79.

misclassifications that may have arisen due to caching for domains with multiple valid A records, we also check the IPv6 address for embeddings of other valid A records for the domain.

RIPE Atlas Measurements: To understand client DNS64 deployment, we use RIPE Atlas probes [30] to measure AAAA records for our chosen domains using their local resolver. We run measurements from all 5,574 probes that are online and have IPv6 connectivity[2]. In addition, we also run IPv4 measurements on 5,472 probes which are also IPv4-connected[3]. As with our resolver measurements, we issue AAAA as well as A queries to check for valid embeddings of IP addresses.

Application-Layer Measurements Through NAT64 Gateways: With the public IPv6 addresses in DNS answers from the measurements towards our sampled domains, we make HTTPS requests with ZGrab2 [37]. We make these measurements from a university network in Germany. We make these measurements by using SNI to specify the domain name alongside the IPv6 address. From this, we determine whether the gateway operating alongside the DNS64 resolver is publicly accessible. We perform these measurements with all public IPv6 addresses in case the gateway is operating as a NAT64, but keeps some state or uses SNI that is not aligned with the RFC [26].

To determine whether we can access the website content through the gateway, we compare our results to control measurements by measuring the results of HTTP and HTTPS requests to the addresses on the domain's A records. For our HTTPS measurements, we classify a certificate as "correct" if it has the requested domain on it. For our HTTP measurements, we classify a response as "correct" if it matches the response body or the redirect from a control measurement.

Identifying NAT64 Gateways: To identify the "IPv4-side" of NAT64 gateways, we host an authoritative nameserver for an IPv4-only domain. Then, we send AAAA queries for our domain from RIPE Atlas probes to their local resolvers. We then run TCP/80 pings to our domain from the probes to identify the probe's NAT64 gateway by recording the IPv4 address reaching our webserver. Due to platform restrictions, we cannot measure probes that return private addresses outside of the reserved NAT64 prefix. The platform restricts measurements towards arbitrary private IP space besides select special-use prefixes.

Ethical Considerations: We follow ethical scanning guidelines in our measurements [9,12,29]. Specifically, we use a blocklist, maintain public web pages describing our scanning activity, and scan at low rates (less than 100 pps). We additionally ensure we do not request any potentially censored domains. We emphasize that, at most, we are sending 10 DNS requests to each resolver. Finally, we sample our domains from popular Tranco domains (the least popular domain is on rank 132), as these generally expect a higher volume of traffic at the authoritative. During our measurements, we did not receive any complaints.

---

[2] We filter for the probe tag `system-ipv6-works`, which indicates that the RIPE Atlas system confirmed the probe's IPv6 connectivity.

[3] For probes also tagged with `system-ipv4-works`, we run the measurement over IPv4.

Limitations: Our study is limited to publicly available resolvers and RIPE Atlas probes. Due to the nature of the RIPE Atlas measurement platform, our client measurements may not represent NAT64 deployment at large. As described in Sect. 2, NAT64 seems to be predominantly deployed in mobile networks, which are less likely to be in RIPE Atlas, although some are [5]. We also measure for popular domains, but it is possible that resolvers respond differently to less-popular domains. Despite these limitations, our methodology is suitable to provide a lower bound on NAT64 deployment.

4   Datasets

In this section, we describe our data and how we find NAT64 deployments.

Resolver Responses: Out of 1.9M IPv4 resolvers measured, 1.0–1.1M respond to our scans, depending on the domain requested (52.6–57.9%). Out of 279.1k IPv6 resolvers measured, 265.0k-267.2k (94.9–95.7%) respond, also depending on the requested domain. We attribute the lower response rate of IPv4 to a higher churn rate compared to IPv6. Of the responsive IPs, 0.68–0.82% of answering IPv4 resolvers and 0.13–0.15% of answering IPv6 resolvers respond with answers to our AAAA queries, hinting at possible DNS64 deployments. Moreover, 0.016–0.029% of IPv4 resolvers send malformed responses (e.g., uninterpretable hexadecimal characters). Over half of all IPv4 resolvers (52.9–55.5%) respond with DNS responses with no answer (i.e., an `ancount` of 0), showing that these are not DNS64 resolvers, however less than 10% (9.4–9.5%) of IPv6 resolvers respond this way. We find that 6,335 IPv4 resolvers and 309 IPv6 resolvers consistently respond with DNS answers across all domains, the majority of which are of type AAAA (70.3% IPv4, 88.0% IPv6).

Despite requesting a AAAA record, 20.9–24.3% of answering IPv4 resolvers and 1.2–1.3% of answering IPv6 resolvers return an A record, signaling a resolver misconfiguration or perhaps that we reached DNS forwarders in residential gateways that respond with cached values, not actual resolvers [31]. For the remainder of our analysis, we focus on the answers we receive in AAAA responses. Although we see a relatively uniform distribution of the types of responses across resolvers, certain resolvers elicit different quantities of responses from resolvers in certain ASes, especially in requests for `webex.com` in resolvers in China. We expand on the responses of resolvers in more detail in Appendix A.1.

Filtering AAAA Answers: Next, we identify which answers from resolvers are indicators for DNS64 deployments by filtering AAAA answers. Specifically, we filter out resolvers if they (1) answer with the same IP independent of the requested domain, (2) answer with an invalid IPv6 address (e.g., that starts with `::`), or (3) answer with anything other than an IPv6 address in the `answer` field of the DNS response (domains, IPv4 addresses, and miscellaneous values). We characterize the filtered addresses in Appendix A.2.

We filter out these 172 IPv6 resolvers and 2,454 IPv4 resolvers from future analysis. We continue our analysis with the remaining 240 IPv6 and 6,201 IPv4 resolvers that respond consistently to *any* domain query after our filtering.

RIPE Atlas Probes: We find 39 probes that respond across all domains, one of which answers with an NS record that we filter out from our results. 28 have IPv4 and IPv6 connectivity, and 11 are IPv6-only probes. [4] We find that nine probes answer inconsistently across domains.

We note that five of the 39 probes that respond across all domains are from AS 3320, Deutsche Telekom, a Tier-1 ISP from Germany, and one is from AS 2856, British Telecommunications. Both of these ASes have been reported as using 464XLAT and NAT64 [18]. However, we note that ASN 3320 and AS 2856 host a total of 856 and 231 probes, respectively. Therefore, the probes we identify as using NAT64 are a small part of these networks. Overall, these 39 probes cover 32 unique IPv6 ASes and 22 unique IPv4 ASes.

Measurements Towards Our Nameserver: Based on our RIPE Atlas measurements for the five popular domains, we additionally conduct measurements towards our webserver from 47 RIPE Atlas probes that answered with valid NAT64 responses to any domain.

We receive responses from 33 of these probes when requesting AAAA records for our domain. Four respond with public IPv6 addresses, one responds with a private address, and the rest respond with addresses in the special use NAT64 prefix. Due to limitations in RIPE Atlas, we are unable to measure from a probe to private addresses. We do, however, conduct measurements from the remaining probes towards the IPv6 addresses in their respective DNS responses.

As a result, we identify NAT64 gateway addresses on 25 probes. One probe did not participate in our measurement, and the remaining six probes did not complete our measurement successfully. Over all of these probes, we identify 21 unique IPv4 gateway IP addresses in 18 ASes.

5   NAT64 Deployment

In this section, we present the results of our resolver measurements and RIPE Atlas measurements towards our sampled popular domains as well as towards our own nameserver. Specifically, we answer the following questions in this section:
Deployment and demographics:

- What is the prevalence of NAT64 in the wild?
- Where are NAT64 gateways deployed?
- Where are DNS64 resolvers deployed?

Configuration:

- How are NAT64 gateways configured?
- Do NAT64 gateways correctly embed IPv4 addresses in NAT64 addresses?

Security:

- Are NAT64 gateways publicly accessible?

---

[4] We find that in total 102 RIPE Atlas probes are IPv6-only. We leave investigating if and how these probes can reach IPv4-only resources to future work.

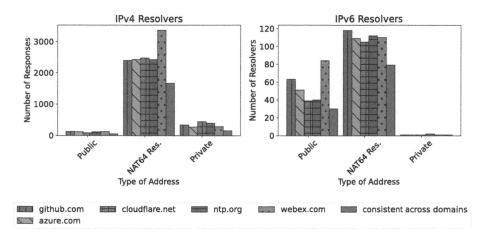

Fig. 2. Resolver responses after filtering out invalid responses. We highlight that the inconsistencies around measurements for webex.com remain.

5.1   Deployment and Demographics

Prevalence: Out of 1.9M public IPv4 resolvers measured, 1,873 deploy NAT64 across all of our domain measurements (0.1%). For IPv6, we identify 110 out of the 279.1k IPv6 resolvers deploying NAT64 across all of our domain measurements (0.04%). Out of 5,574 RIPE Atlas probes measured, 39 deploy NAT64 and consistently respond to our measurements (0.7%).

To summarize: NAT64 is not deployed widely across the Internet in public resolvers and the networks of RIPE Atlas probes.

Gateway Location: Next, we investigate where NAT64 gateways are deployed. We present an overview of the types of addresses returned by DNS64 resolvers in Fig. 2. We highlight that the majority of DNS64 resolvers use NAT64 gateways that use the assigned NAT64 special use prefix. Additionally, in each case, a small number of resolvers use other private IP address space. However, we also find cases in which resolvers return public IPv6 addresses. In these cases, we compare the AS of the returned IPv6 address to that of the resolver. In IPv4, we find that 18 out of the 44 IPv4 resolvers responding with public IPv6 addresses are located in the same respective AS. In IPv6, this is the case for 21 out of the 30 IPv6 resolvers responding with public gateway addresses. We manually confirm that in all but two of these cases across both IPs, the ASes are not siblings, but the gateway AS is a network services provider.

Of the 38 RIPE Atlas probes that respond consistently, 28 of these probes respond with IPv6 addresses in the NAT64 special use prefix, and nine respond with IPv6 addresses that are publicly routable. One probe responds with a private address in the unicast prefix ($fc00::/7$ [19]). These responses are consistent across all domains for all but six probes. When probing our own authoritative nameserver, out of the 33 probes that respond to our AAAA queries, four respond

Table 1. The top 5 ASes of DNS64 resolvers across IPv4 and IPv6 for different domain measurements. Tata Teleservices has two different ASes that both appear in the top 5 ASes in all IPv4 resolver measurements.

	#	github	azure	cloudflare	ntp	webex
IPv4	1	Meditelecom	Tata Tel	Meditelecom	Meditelecom	China Edu
	2	Tata Tel	Meditelecom	China Edu	Tata Tel	Meditelecom
	3	Tata Tel	Tata Tel	Tata Tel	China Edu	Tata Tel
	4	China Telecom	China Edu	Tata Tel	Tata Tel	Tata Tel
	5	Yettel Hun	Yettel Hun	China Tel	China Tel	China Tel.
IPv6	1	China Tel	China Tel	China Tel	China Tel	China Tel
	2	Hurricane El	Hurricane El	Hurricane El	Hurricane El	Akamai
	3	Akamai	Cernet	China Unicom	China Unicom	Hurricane El
	4	Cernet	Giginet	Cernet	Cernet	China Unicom
	5	Giginet	Mythic Beasts	Mythic Beasts	Giginet	Cernet

with public IPv6 addresses, one responds with a private address, and the rest respond with addresses in the NAT64 special use prefix. Out of the 25 probes that complete the measurement towards the gateway, we find that seven gateway IPs are the same as the probe's assigned public IPv4 address. This strongly indicates that the probe is behind a NAT that also acts as a NAT64 gateway. Overall, we find that 20 out of 25 gateway IPs are in the same AS as the probe. Again, we confirm that the disagreeing ASes are not siblings, but the gateway's AS is always from a network services provider.

To summarize: The NAT64 deployment strategy varies, but most are only accessible through private networks that utilize the special use NAT64 prefix. The gateways are likely to exist in the same NAT that the client's IPv4 address is behind, in the same network, or in a different network entirely.

Resolver Location: To understand in which networks DNS64 resolvers are deployed, we analyze the ASes of the resolver IPs. We show the top 5 ASes of NAT64 resolvers that respond to each domain in Table 1. Deployment is relatively concentrated; 49.0–58.3% of IPv4 and 51.1–56.4% of IPv6 resolvers are in the top 5 ASes, despite covering 336–358 and 49–60 ASes, respectively.

Across all IPv4 resolvers, the most common AS of the resolvers is AS 4538 (China Education Network), followed by AS 134540 (Tata Teleservices). Curiously, the top AS that IPv4 DNS64 resolvers are concentrated in varies depending on the domain requested. We attribute this to our hypothesis about caching and prioritization of different domains, as discussed above. Across IPv6 resolvers in all cases except for one domain, the most common AS is AS 4134 (China Telecom), followed by AS 6939 (Hurricane Electric). We can therefore conclude that legitimate NAT64 deployment is most common in China. We manually investigate the *type* of business of each AS and find that out of the 13 unique ASes across all IPv4 and IPv6 resolvers deploying DNS64, four are mobile service providers, four are network service providers, two are Chinese university networks, two are

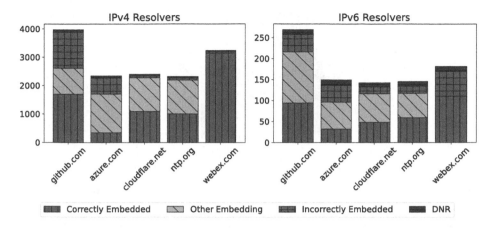

Fig. 3. An overview of the answers for domains that correctly and incorrectly embed the corresponding A record. We note that github.com also has more answers in general than other domains. "Other Embedding" refers to resolvers that respond with a correct embedding for the requested domain, but not the same IPv4 address that the resolver responds with when the domain's A record is requested. "DNR" refers to the resolvers that did not respond to our measurements for A records.

hosting providers, and one is a CDN. For the 39 RIPE Atlas probes, which we identified as using NAT64, five probes are located in AS3320 (Deutsche Telekom, a German ISP) and four are in AS 2027 (MilkyWan, a French ISP).

To summarize: *DNS64 resolvers are concentrated in mobile networks, network service providers, and Chinese networks.*

5.2 NAT64 Gateway Configuration

Next, we analyze the embedding of IPv4 addresses within the returned AAAA records. Figure 3 shows the number of resolvers that correctly and incorrectly embed the respective A record into the AAAA record. When we check other IPv4 addresses from other valid A records for the respective domain, we find that the embeddings are generally correct. For IPv6 resolvers, we find that for all domains except for `webex.com`, 61.3–80.9% of the incorrectly embedded AAAA answers are in this category. For `webex.com`, we find that none of the incorrectly embedded answers fall into this category (i.e., if an answer is incorrectly embedded, it never embeds a different IPv4 address for the domain). For IPv4 resolvers, we find that across all domains except for `webex.com`, 41.2–95.1% of incorrectly embedded answers fall into this category. For `webex.com`, we once again find a much lower rate of this occurring at 2.4%.

We conclude that the majority of our identified resolvers have legitimate NAT64 deployments that follow the specifications in the RFC [26]. Discrepancies in the embeddings are likely due to the caching of different A records at different times. We hypothesize that the differences in measurements for `webex.com` are likely due to it being cached much closer to the resolvers we are measuring.

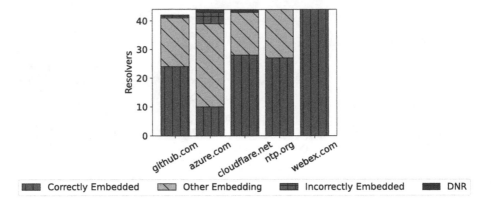

Fig. 4. The results of analyzing the embeddings of the IPv4 addresses in the AAAA records returned by RIPE Atlas probes across domain measurements.

Table 2. Results of our HTTP/S measurements for each domain. We highlight that a low number of NAT64 gateways are open on the Internet.

	Domain	github	azure	cloudflare	ntp	webex
IPv6	**IPs Measured**	65	64	60	61	63
	Correct Certificates	9	10	9	9	7
	HTTP responses	14	17	4	4	13
IPv4	**IPs Measured**	179	187	166	185	174
	Correct Certificates	4	3	1	3	3
	HTTP responses	7	6	3	3	6

For our RIPE Atlas measurements, we compare the IPv6 addresses on AAAA records to the IPv4 addresses on the A records from the same resolver; see Fig. 4. Although we identify in all domains (excluding `webex.com`) that there is a high rate of incorrectly embedded IPv4 addresses, we find that 91.7–100% of these IPv6 addresses embed a valid IPv4 address for an A record of the domain.

To summarize: Overall, DNS64 resolvers correctly embed IPv4 addresses in synthetic AAAA records, but up to 39.2% of resolvers use an incorrect embedding.

5.3   Publicly Reachable NAT64 Gateways

We present the results of our HTTP and HTTPS measurements towards public NAT64 gateways in Table 2. From this analysis, we determine that there are a very low number of open NAT64 gateways on the Internet, though there are slightly more using IPv6 resolvers compared to IPv4. In IPv6, 6.6–26.6% of HTTP responses and 11.1–15.6% of HTTPS responses are "correct." In IPv4, 1.6–3.9% of HTTP responses and 0.6–2.23% of HTTPS responses are "correct."

In our certificate analysis, we find that many of the "incorrect" certificates are from domain name providers, CDN providers, or default certificates for parked

Table 3. The results of our HTTP/S measurements for each domain with the answers from RIPE Atlas probes. We highlight that a low number of NAT64 gateways are open on the Internet.

Domain	github	azure	cloudflare	ntp	webex
IPs Measured	10	15	14	13	10
Correct Certificates	6	8	8	7	6
HTTP responses	6	8	8	7	6

domains. We additionally identify other certificates from websites that have nothing to do with hosting or Internet infrastructure, such as a German medical device company. Finally, we find that one gateway consistently reflects back the certificate that we have on our measurement server. In our analysis of HTTP responses, we similarly find that "incorrect" responses largely consist of redirects to other hosting provider websites, parked domain websites, or other websites that have nothing to do with our measured domains (such as `netflix.com`).

For RIPE Atlas probes that answer with public IPv6 addresses, we once again measure the IPs for HTTP/S to see if the gateway is publicly reachable; see Table 3. Compared to our results presented in Table 2, we are able to access more content through each IP returned by RIPE Atlas probes. We attribute this, the higher rates of correctly embedded addresses, and the stability across measurements to the nature of the RIPE Atlas measurement platform. As these probes are deployed explicitly for measurement, we hypothesize that there is more care around their connectivity. Therefore, if a probe uses NAT64, there is a higher likelihood that is configured correctly and consistently.

To summarize: We find that NAT64 gateways located on public IPs are generally not publicly accessible. The security implications of a gateway being open on the Internet can be severe, depending on whether it is intentional and where it is. We consider it a positive result that we find few open gateways.

6   Concluding Discussion

While IPv6 deployment has certainly increased, IPv4 is not likely to disappear any time soon. Therefore, to maintain Internet connectivity, transition mechanisms will continue to be deployed.

In this work, we presented an overview of NAT64 deployment. We measured public resolvers and included analysis of clients through our use of RIPE Atlas probes. We additionally used the RIPE Atlas probes that deploy NAT64 to measure towards our own web server. Our measurements from three unique perspectives allowed us to understand NAT64 deployment from the resolver, client, and web server perspectives. Specifically, we found that NAT64 resolvers are not deployed publicly at large, but there is notable concentration in China, mobile providers, and other network service providers. Through our measurements of public resolvers and RIPE Atlas probes, we identified several open NAT64 gateways. We emphasized the security implications if this was not purposeful, as they could be used for malicious intent or to access restricted content. Finally, the relative AS of the NAT64 gateway, DNS64 resolver, and client using the transition protocol varies.

Future Work: We recommend that future work uses a variety of domains to measure the upper bound of NAT64 deployment because of the disparity in resolver responses. We note that an IPv6-to-IPv4 transition mechanism has no need to have an IPv4 address for the purposes of DNS64. We therefore hypothesize that the IPv4 resolvers that we find are dual-stack. This additionally implies that there are a substantial number of IPv6 resolvers that have not been found by the IPv6 hitlist [14]. With more robust IPv6 active address discovery techniques, it is possible that more NAT64 deployments could be discovered. Finally, we emphasize the need to understand how these mechanisms are deployed across client networks through the expansion of measurement platforms such as RIPE Atlas. However, we additionally highlight that these transition protocols likely exist largely in private networks that researchers have little vantage into, and therefore our measurements can only be taken as a lower bound.

Acknowledgments. This work was supported in part by National Science Foundation (NSF) Graduate Research Fellowship (GRFP) under Grant No. DGE-2039655, and NSF CNS award 2319315.

A   Appendix

A.1   Details on Resolver Responses

Figure 5 gives an overview of the types of responses the resolvers sent to our queries. We see that the queries get overall similar numbers of response types, independent of the queried domain.

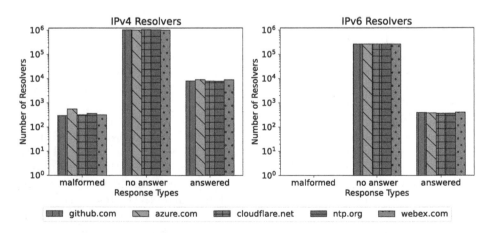

Fig. 5. An overview of the types of DNS responses to our measurements. For DNS responses with no answer, the `rcode` is always NOERROR.

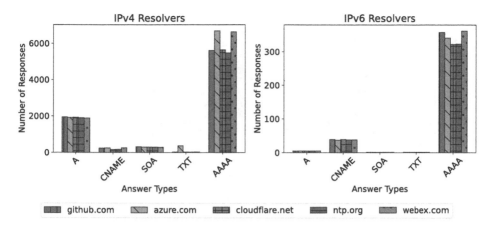

Fig. 6. An overview of the answer types in the resolver responses across domains. We note that from IPv4 resolvers we also receive less than 10 NS records, less than 15 HINFO records, 1 MX record, less than 4 OPT responses, and less than 3 RRSIG responses. From IPv6 resolvers, we also receive one HINFO response. For brevity, we omit these values from the Figure.

Figure 6 shows an overview of the resource record types of answers the resolvers sent for each domain.

A.2   Resolver Answers

Although Fig. 5 shows a relatively uniform distribution in the types of responses across resolvers, we see that certain domains elicit different types of responses across resolvers in Fig. 6. We focus on AAAA answers and the differences in their resolver responses. Figure 7 shows the distribution of the addresses in AAAA answers received from resolvers.

In the left subfigure of Fig. 7 across all domain measurements (the brown bar), 1,663 always respond with a public IPv6 address, 1,664 always respond with an address in a special-use prefix as defined by IANA [19] (e.g., documentation prefix or private address prefix), 141 always respond with an invalid IPv6 address in the answer field (i.e., the ANCOUNT field is 1 but the answer field is populated with ::, or an address that starts with ::), and 635 always respond with an answer in a different private prefix.

In Fig. 7 IPv6 resolvers, 185 always respond with a public IPv6 address, 79 with an address in the special-use prefix, 3 with an empty answer, and 5 with an address in another private prefix.

We highlight the high number of IPv4 resolvers that answer with the special-use prefix for webex.com. There are 895 resolvers that always answer for webex.com that answer inconsistently for the other domains, but when they do, they use the NAT64 prefix. Additionally, there are 118 resolvers that answer for other domains with an 'ancount' of 0 (i.e., with no answer). Finally, 684

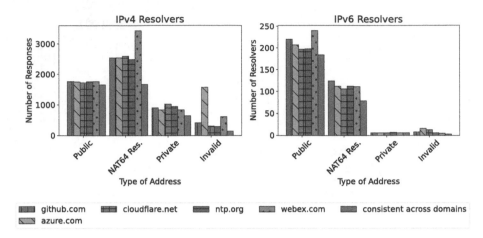

Fig. 7. An overview of the types of IPv6 addresses on the AAAA records returned. We count one response per resolver. "NAT64 Res." exclusively refers to the NAT64 special use prefix. "Private" is other private IPv6 address space. "Invalid" is an IPv6 address that is not in a valid format (i.e., starts with ':::'). The bar labeled "consistent across domains" refers to the resolvers that occur in every domain measurement in the respective address type.

resolvers do not respond at all for other domains. Of the resolvers that respond for webex.com, 92.8% are concentrated in AS 4538, China Education Network. An additional 19.7% are in AS 134540 (Tata Teleservices). We hypothesize that these networks use WebEx as a service and, therefore, this domain over others. There are also higher response rates for azure.com where the answer fields are invalid in IPv4 resolvers. 1,168 of these resolvers only respond to queries for azure.com, 43.0% of which are in AS 9808, China Mobile Network, and 28.9% of which are in AS 4837, China Unicom Backbone. We cannot attribute these abnormalities to any property in particular but note that prior work also finds irregularities in Chinese resolvers on requests for AAAA records [32].

Additionally, more IPv6 resolvers answer with public IPs for webex.com than other domains. All of these are in AS20940, Akamai, and all resolvers answer with IP 2001:4801:7829:105:be76:4eff:fe10:1fc0, an EUI-64 address that encodes a MAC address. The Organizational Unique Identifier (OUI) in this address belongs to Rackspace, US, Inc., a cloud computing company [20].

In our filtering process described in Sect. 4, we find that 2,454 IPv4 resolvers always answer with the same value across different domain measurements. Of these, 991 always respond with 2620:101:9000:53::55, which is used as a redirect address in FortiGuard with DNS over HTTP3 [13]. 449 also always respond with 2607:f740:100:108::1400 and 103 always respond with an invalid IPv6 address in the answer field. 172 IPv6 resolvers always answer with the same value in the AAAA answer field across different domain measurements. In 114 of these cases, the answer is 2607:f740:100:108::1400, an IP address allocated to NetActuate, a network services and infrastructure provider. We hypothesize that this is also a default answer for the resolver software from this company or a redirect.

References

1. Al-hamadani, A., Lencse, G.: A survey on the performance analysis of IPv6 transition technologies. Acta Technica Jaurinensis **14** (2021). https://doi.org/10.14513/actatechjaur.00577
2. Alcatel Lucent: 464XLAT in mobile networks IPv6 migration strategies for mobile networks, January 2017. https://www.apnic.net/wp-content/uploads/2017/01/IPv6_Migration_Strategies_for_Mobile_Networks_Whitepaper.pdf
3. Anderson, T.: Local-Use IPv4/IPv6 translation prefix. RFC 8215, August 2017. https://doi.org/10.17487/RFC8215, https://www.rfc-editor.org/info/rfc8215
4. Apple developer support: IPv6-only networks. https://developer.apple.com/support/ipv6/
5. Atlas, R.: Technical details. https://atlas.ripe.net/docs/faq/technical-details.html
6. Byrne, C.: 464XLAT: Breaking free of IPv4. Presentation (2014). https://conference.apnic.net/data/37/464xlat-apricot-2014_1393236641.pdf
7. Carpenter, B.E., Moore, K.: Connection of IPv6 domains via IPv4 clouds. RFC 3056, February 2001. https://doi.org/10.17487/RFC3056, https://www.rfc-editor.org/info/rfc3056
8. Citizen Lab and Others: URL testing lists intended for discovering website censorship (2014). https://github.com/citizenlab/test-lists
9. Dittrich, D., Kenneally, E.: The menlo report: ethical principles guiding information and communication technology research. SSRN Electron. J. (2012)
10. Dupont, K.: Public NAT64 service (2019). https://nat64.net/
11. Durumeric, Z., Adrian, D., Mirian, A., Bailey, M., Halderman, J.A.: A search engine backed by internet-wide scanning. In: Proceedings of the 22nd ACM SIGSAC Conference on Computer and Communications Security, CCS 2015, pp. 542–553. Association for Computing Machinery, New York, (2015). https://doi.org/10.1145/2810103.2813703
12. Durumeric, Z., Wustrow, E., Halderman, J.A.: ZMap: fast internet-wide scanning and its security applications. In: 22nd USENIX Security Symposium (USENIX Security 13), pp. 605–620 (2013)
13. Fortinet: DNS over QUIC and DNS over HTTP3 for transparent and local-in DNS modes. https://docs.fortinet.com/document/fortigate/7.4.1/administration-guide/8405/dns-over-quic-and-dns-over-https3-for-transparent-and-local-in-dns-modes-new
14. Gasser, O., et al.: Clusters in the expanse: understanding and unbiasing IPv6 hitlists. In: Proceedings of the Internet Measurement Conference 2018, IMC 2018, pp. 364–378. Association for Computing Machinery, New York (2018). https://doi.org/10.1145/3278532.3278564
15. Gilligan, R.E., Nordmark, E.: Basic transition mechanisms for IPv6 hosts and routers. RFC 4213 (Oct 2005). https://doi.org/10.17487/RFC4213, https://www.rfc-editor.org/info/rfc4213
16. Google: google public DNS64. https://developers.google.com/speed/public-dns/docs/dns64
17. Google: IPv6 statistics (2023). https://www.google.com/intl/en/ipv6/statistics.html

18. Howard, L.: [v6ops] Transition mechanisms in use, March 2018. https://mailarchive.ietf.org/arch/msg/v6ops/_8SKyRon_tbZb4l1F9Ysly5ZGSM/
19. IANA: IANA IPv6 special-purpose address registry, March 2023. https://www.iana.org/assignments/iana-ipv6-special-registry/iana-ipv6-special-registry.xhtml
20. IEEE: IEEE OUI (2023). https://standards-oui.ieee.org/oui/oui.txt
21. Izhikevich, L., et al.: ZDNS: a fast DNS toolkit for internet measurement. In: Proceedings of the 22nd ACM Internet Measurement Conference, IMC 2022, pp. 33–43. Association for Computing Machinery, New York (2022). https://doi.org/10.1145/3517745.3561434
22. Kristoff, J., Ghasemisharif, M., Kanich, C., Polakis, J.: Plight at the end of the tunnel. In: Hohlfeld, O., Lutu, A., Levin, D. (eds.) PAM 2021. LNCS, vol. 12671, pp. 390–405. Springer, Cham (2021). https://doi.org/10.1007/978-3-030-72582-2_23
23. Le Pochat, V., Van Goethem, T., Tajalizadehkhoob, S., Korczyński, M., Joosen, W.: Tranco: a research-oriented top sites ranking hardened against manipulation. In: Proceedings of the 26th Annual Network and Distributed System Security Symposium, NDSS 2019, February 2019. https://doi.org/10.14722/ndss.2019.23386
24. Lencse, G., Kadobayashi, Y.: Comprehensive survey of IPv6 transition technologies: a subjective classification for security analysis. IEICE Trans. Commun. E102.B, April 2019. https://doi.org/10.1587/transcom.2018EBR0002
25. Li, X., Baker, F., Yin, K., Bao, C.: Framework for IPv4/IPv6 translation. RFC 6144, April 2011. https://doi.org/10.17487/RFC6144, https://www.rfc-editor.org/info/rfc6144
26. Matthews, P., van Beijnum, I., Bagnulo, M.: Stateful NAT64: network address and protocol translation from IPv6 Clients to IPv4 servers. RFC 6146, April 2011. https://doi.org/10.17487/RFC6146, https://www.rfc-editor.org/info/rfc6146
27. Mawatari, M., Kawashima, M., Byrne, C.: 464XLAT: combination of stateful and stateless translation. RFC 6877, April 2013. https://doi.org/10.17487/RFC6877, https://www.rfc-editor.org/info/rfc6877
28. Opredelennov, E.: NAT64 setup using tayga, August 2016. https://packetpushers.net/nat64-setup-using-tayga/
29. Partridge, C., Allman, M.: Ethical considerations in network measurement papers. Commun. ACM 59(10), 58–64 (2016)
30. RIPE NCC: RIPE Atlas (2023). https://atlas.ripe.net/
31. Schomp, K., Callahan, T., Rabinovich, M., Allman, M.: On measuring the client-side DNS infrastructure. In: Proceedings of the 2013 Conference on Internet Measurement Conference, IMC 2013, pp. 77–90. Association for Computing Machinery, New York (2013). https://doi.org/10.1145/2504730.2504734
32. Steger, L., Kuang, L., Zirngibl, J., Carle, G., Gasser, O.: Target acquired? Evaluating target generation algorithms for IPv6. In: Proceedings of the Network Traffic Measurement and Analysis Conference (TMA), June 2023
33. Tróan, O., Carpenter, B.E.: Deprecating the anycast prefix for 6to4 relay routers. RFC 7526, May 2015. https://doi.org/10.17487/RFC7526, https://www.rfc-editor.org/info/rfc7526
34. Wing, D.: AAAA and IPv6 connectivity statistics, October 2023. https://www.employees.org/~dwing/aaaa-stats/
35. Wu, J., Zhang, H., Li, X., Chen, M., Bao, C.: The China education and research network (CERNET) IVI translation design and deployment for the IPv4/IPv6 coexistence and transition. RFC 6219, May 2011. https://doi.org/10.17487/RFC6219, https://www.rfc-editor.org/info/rfc6219

36. Zirngibl, J., Steger, L., Sattler, P., Gasser, O., Carle, G.: Rusty clusters? Dusting an IPv6 research foundation. In: ACM Internet Measurement Conference 2022, October 2022. https://doi.org/10.1145/3517745.3561440
37. ZMap: ZGrab2 (2023). https://github.com/zmap/zgrab2
38. Zorz, J.: August 2017. https://labs.ripe.net/author/janzorz/introducing-nat64-checker/

Machine Leaning

Dom-BERT: Detecting Malicious Domains with Pre-training Model

Yu Tian[1,2] and Zhenyu Li[1,2(✉)]

[1] Institute of Computing Technology, Chinese Academy of Sciences, Beijing, China
{tianyu21b,zyli}@ict.ac.cn
[2] University of Chinese Academy of Sciences, Beijing, China

Abstract. Domain Name System (DNS) is widely abused by attackers, which thus makes malicious domain detection a crucial routine task for operators to combat cyber crimes. Existing classification-based models often struggle to achieve high accuracy in practical settings due to the class imbalance of the task. Moreover, inference-based models, which hinge upon the resolution similarity between domains, often fail to harness the full potential of linguistic associations among domains. This paper first conducts a detailed analysis of the characteristics of malicious domains and contrasts them with those of benign ones, using a real-life passive DNS dataset obtained from several major ISPs (Internet Service Providers). With this basis, we then propose an efficient solution for the detection of malicious domains, called *Dom-BERT*. To adeptly capture the resolution associations among domains, Dom-BERT constructs a heterogeneous graph and incorporates a pruning module, facilitating the modeling of relationships among domains, clients, and hosting servers. Building upon this graph, we employ techniques such as random walks with restart and a domain association prediction downstream task to compute similarity scores for domains. These scores are then used to fine-tune the pre-trained BERT model. The performance of Dom-BERT is evaluated using our passive DNS logs. The results notably illustrate that Dom-BERT surpasses the state-of-the-art solutions, achieving higher F1 scores and demonstrating resilience to class imbalance. (The implementation of Dom-BERT is publicly available at https://github.com/yutian99/Dom-BERT).

Keywords: malicious domain analysis · malicious domain detection · pre-training models

1 Introduction

The Domain Name System (DNS) is an essential component of most Internet applications and services. It provides the crucial function of mapping domain names to IP addresses that host the services of the domain names. However, DNS is also vulnerable to malicious attacks, as the naming scheme is isolated

© The Author(s), under exclusive license to Springer Nature Switzerland AG 2024
P. Richter et al. (Eds.): PAM 2024, LNCS 14537, pp. 133–158, 2024.
https://doi.org/10.1007/978-3-031-56249-5_6

from underlying network changes, making it an essential resource for attackers. Malicious domains have been widely used in phishing, botnet, spam, and other network attacks. Therefore, detecting malicious domains accurately and effectively is of great importance for networks operation.

Malicious domain detection requires processing datasets where domains are labeled as either malicious or benign, with the former class being significantly smaller than the latter in terms of the number of domains. The dataset can be processed in multiple ways to construct the detector. For instance, one approach is to build classification-based models that capture either the linguistic structure of domain names [5,8,17,21,27,30] or the correlations between domains in terms of client IPs or hosting infrastructures [16,23,24]. However, the quandary of class imbalance continues to pose a formidable obstacle, as the number of malicious domains constitutes a minor fraction relative to their benign counterparts. Existing models demonstrate efficacy under controlled circumstances, assuming the ratio of malicious domain names to benign ones ranging from 1:1 to 1:5 while they often grapple with suboptimal performance when confronting with real-world scenarios characterized by a disproportionate distribution of malicious domains, such as a 1:25 ratio as observed in our empirical dataset collected from major ISPs. An alternative approach is to use inference-based models where malicious domains are identified based on their correlation or similarity with known malicious domains [14,15,18,22]. However, the performance of inference-based approaches can be further boosted by leveraging external text resources for language representation and effectively combining linguistic and infrastructural information. For example, with external text resources, one can take the tokens *ali*, *taobao*, and *youku* as associated ones, as these tokens are all related to Alibaba.

Motivated by these observations, this paper first conducts a detailed analysis of the characteristics of malicious domains and contrasts them with those of benign ones, using a real-life passive DNS dataset obtained from several major ISPs. We then propose Dom-BERT, a malicious domain detection system that incorporates both the linguistic and resolution associations of domains and successfully mitigates the class imbalance problem. To achieve this, Dom-BERT first constructs a heterogeneous graph consisting of three types of nodes: client IPs, domains, and resolved addresses for individual domains. It then leverages random walks on the graph and a domain association prediction downstream task to compute the correlation of domains through three types of meta paths. We use the above resolution association information as input and fine-tune BERT to obtain the inference model. Domains whose association prediction with any known malicious domain name exceeds a pre-defined threshold are labeled as malicious.

In summary, the contributions of this paper are as follows:

– We investigate the characteristics of malicious domains and propose Dom-BERT. Dom-BERT is a malicious domain detection model that captures both the linguistic and resolution associations of domains and facilitates the efficacious identification of malicious domains within the fact of class imbalance, a formidable challenge pervading the field.

- We propose several solutions for capturing the association of domains accurately and quickly, including employing random walk algorithms on the heterogeneous graph and fine-tuning a pre-training model to avoid training from scratch.
- We demonstrate through extensive experiments with real-life datasets that Dom-BERT outperforms the state-of-the-art solutions in terms of F1 score (which is as high as 0.9177). Moreover, its performance is consistent with different ratios of malicious domains, demonstrating its robustness under the class-imbalance scheme.

The rest of this paper is organized as follows. We introduce the background and our motivation in Sect. 2 and the design of Dom-BERT is presented in Sect. 3. Section 4 introduces our dataset and evaluates the performance of Dom-BERT compared with several state-of-the-art solutions. Related work is reviewed in Sect. 6 and we conclude this paper in Sect. 7.

2 Dataset and Motivation

2.1 Dataset Description

Our dataset comprises passive DNS logs generated by Deep Packet Inspection (DPI) appliances deployed within three prominent ISPs. It is noteworthy that each DPI appliance within these ISPs provides comprehensive nationwide coverage. These DPI appliances are responsible for the meticulous parsing of DNS response traffic, originating from recursive resolvers and directed towards end users. Subsequently, they generate a dedicated log entry for each such DNS response. Each log entry encompasses two distinct categories of information:

- DNS Query Information: DNS query information includes the anonymized IP address of the end client, the specific domains that were queried, and the type of query made.
- DNS Response Information: The logs also provide information regarding the resource records present in the answer section. These records encompass various types such as CNAME, A, and AAAA records.

The dataset was collected in the last ten days of December, 2020. On each day, we collected DNS query logs for 10 min. Failed DNS queries were removed from the dataset before processing. Our paper used the samples of two days. As we focus on identifying malicious domains, we further filtered out the queries from famous benign domains (*i.e.* the top 1k domains from the Alexa list [1]). In order to classify domains as either malicious or benign, we employed external threat intelligence sources that are widely used in the related works [14,22,23,31] in terms of malicious domains detection, *i.e.* VirusTotal [4] and Qihoo 360 [3]. VirusTotal examines a given domain against over 60 well-known blacklists. Given that our dataset was collected from China, we also used Qihoo 360 that has a better coverage of Chinese domain names. Qihoo 360 labels a given domain based on its threat intelligence database and AI-based models. We submitted each domain under consideration to VirusTotal and Qihoo 360 using their public API; those listed by at least one of the blacklists form our ground truth of malicious domains. In the entirety of our dataset, we identified a total of 433 malicious domains and 11,118 benign domains.

Ethical Issues. The ISPs collected the DNS logs for the purpose of improving their service quality and security. The end users' IP addresses were anonymized and we are not allowed to link queries to users. Users are notified when subscribing that the ISPs may collect this information, and may share it with academics for research. Our study has not triggered the collection of any new data.

2.2   Linguistic Structure Patterns

Table 1. Examples for malicious domain groups

Kraken [21]	bknllsnbfzqr.net
	cdzogoexis.tv
	hdozpcycom
Corebot [21]	3lgrupwdivsfm2w4kng2iha.ddns.net
	ojyvips6klsnqpy.in
	af5fmb78sbuno4c.ws
A pharmaceutical domain group [10]	pill-erectionmeds.ru
	rxpill-medstore.ru
	medspill-erection.ru
	online-drugstoremen.ru
	onlinepharmacydrugs.ru
	pillcheap-med.ru

A widely adopted approach in the field involves classification-based models that capture the linguistic structure of the domain names. Malicious domains often exhibit substantial disparities compared to their benign counterparts concerning the distribution of alphanumeric characters as this discrepancy is primarily attributable to the utilization of Domain Generation Algorithms (DGAs) in the creation of malicious domains. Notably, certain DGAs, such as Kraken and Corebot shown in Table 1, produce domain names with character sequences that appear to be entirely random, while benign domains typically display a more heterogeneous character distribution. This critical observation has been employed in previous studies [7,8,17,19,21] to formulate classification models aimed at effectively distinguishing malicious domains from their benign counterparts.

To evaluate the performance of these models with respect to character distribution, we conducted an analysis by calculating the Shannon entropy of both

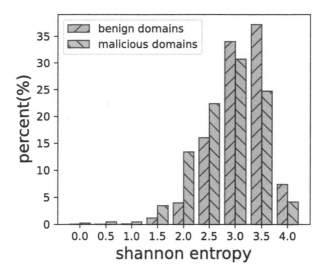

Fig. 1. The distribution of Shannon entropy.

malicious and benign domain names within the dataset. The Shannon entropy quantifies the uncertainty or randomness of a given domain name (d) and is calculated as follows [21]:

$$-\sum_{c\in d} p_c \cdot \log_2(p_c)$$

, where p_c is the relative frequency of character c. As illustrated in Fig. 1, the Shannon entropy of malicious and benign domains manifests a similar distribution pattern, with both tending to concentrate within the range of 2 to 4.

Furthermore, we conducted an in-depth analysis of several linguistic features commonly employed in the detection of malicious domain names [7,17,21]. These features are designed to capture deviations from conventional linguistic patterns typically observed in domain names and include:

- Ratio of repeated characters. This metric is calculated by determining the number of characters that occur more than once in the domain name and dividing it by the cardinality of the alphabet.
- Ratio of consecutive consonants. Defined as the sum of the lengths of sequences containing more than one consonant, divided by the overall length of the domain name.
- Ratio of vowels. This feature is represented as the number of vowels divided by the length of the domain name.
- Ratio of digits. Calculated by determining the number of digits within the domain name and dividing it by the total length of the domain name.

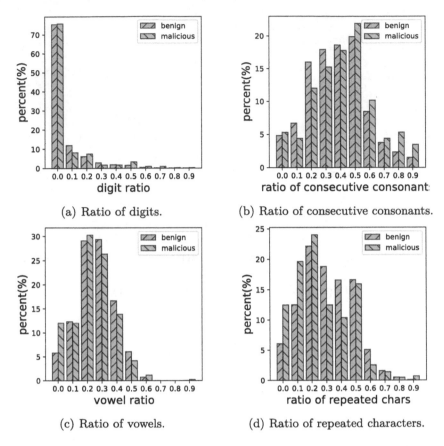

(a) Ratio of digits.   (b) Ratio of consecutive consonants.

(c) Ratio of vowels.   (d) Ratio of repeated characters.

Fig. 2. Distribution of malicious domains and benign domains in terms of different features.

As depicted in Fig. 2, it becomes evident that the task of effectively discriminating between malicious domain names and their benign counterparts encounters considerable challenges when relying solely on manually engineered linguistic features. This predicament arises from the evolving tactics employed by attackers, who increasingly employ sophisticated techniques such as the concatenation of DGA domains with legitimate words or the construction of domain names closely resembling well-established and popular domain names. A noteworthy example of the latter is illustrated in Table 1, wherein a group of pharmaceutical domain names exhibits these resemblances.

2.3   Passive DNS Patterns

In addition to linguistic features of domain names, passive DNS data is frequently harnessed to assess the relationships between domain names. Notably, several prior works [14,15,18,20] have employed inference-based models for the detection of malicious domains. These models identify malicious domains based on their correlations or similarities with known malicious domains, often referred to as 'seeds' or 'anchors'. The computation of similarity hinges on various factors, including correlations in terms of client IP addresses and hosting infrastructures.

The underlying rationale for this approach is twofold. Firstly, it is found on the observation that infected clients tend to issue queries for the same or partially overlapping set of malicious domains, whereas uninfected clients infrequently interact with these domains. Secondly, attackers often resort to reusing IP addresses and other infrastructure elements for different malicious domains due to economic constraints [31]. Consequently, [16] quantifies the association between two domains based on the number of IP addresses they share in hosting or the number of clients who query both domains within a defined time window.

Our study delves into the assessment of relationships between malicious domain names from three distinct perspectives: being queried by the same client, resolved to the same IP address, and functioning as CNAME aliases for one another. When two domain names are queried by the same client (a similar definition applies when they are resolved to the same IP address or share a CNAME record), we mark these two domain names as being connected by one edge and thus the distance between them is one hop. Furthermore, if two domain names are both one hop away from the same target domain, their distance is two hops, and so forth for additional hops. Taking the example in which client C_1 queries both domain d_1 and domain d_2 within the same time window while client C_2 queries both domain d_2 and domain d_3 within the same time window, starting from domain d_1, we can find domain d_2 within one hop and domain d_3 within two hops. Figure 3 illustrates the ratio of malicious domains found within 5 hops to all domains found starting from malicious and benign domains respectively.

Our results illustrate that malicious domains and benign domains exhibit distinct patterns. On one hand, client query behavior and domain resolution patterns indeed serve as reflective indicators of associations between malicious domain names. This is substantiated by the fact that a single hop can establish connections between numerous pairs of malicious domain names. Simultaneously, the presence of CNAME records also contributes to this understanding. On the other hand, as cyberattack techniques become increasingly sophisticated and concealed, it may necessitate multiple hops to uncover the connections between malicious domain names.

2.4   Class Imbalance Problem

Some researchers have proposed the application of deep neural networks (DNNs) to acquire linguistic and semantic features of domain names, given DNNs' capacity to unveil latent information within domain data. An illustrative example is the HAGDetector approach [17], which employs multiple heterogeneous neural networks for the detection of malicious domains, classifying them based on the length of their respective domain names. Other studies have ventured into the utilization of graph convolutional networks (GCNs). These GCNs are constructed by establishing graphs that represent the correlations between domains

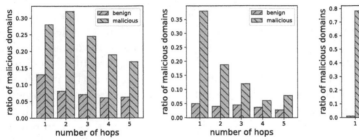

(a) Resolved to the same IP. (b) Being queried by the   (c) CNAME records.
                              same client.

Fig. 3. The relationship between the number of malicious domain pairs and their distance distribution.

Table 2. Description of the selected malicious domains.

Name	Number	Description
track-like [a]	7	Malicious domains containing `track`, such as `retrack`, `track`, `tracker`, etc
log-like [b]	3	Malicious domains containing `log`
pirate-like[c]	2	Malicious domains containing `pirate`, such as `pirateparty`
involving coupon [d]	2	Malicious domains containing description involving coupon, such as `youhui` and `bill`.

[a] tracker.mg64.net, track.mediav.com, popcorn-tracker.org, tracker.kamigami.org, tracker.msm8916.com, atrack.pow7.com, bt.xxx-tracker.com.
[b] mobilelog.upqzfile.com, ios.pclog.i4.cn.cdn20.com, xui.ptlogin2.qq.com.
[c] thepiratebays.com, thepiratebay2.to.
[d] down.tantanyouhui.cn, paypalticket91661.info.

in terms of client IP addresses or hosting infrastructures, thus deriving domain representations. To assess the efficacy of these methodologies, we have employed a real-time domain name classification method utilizing Long Short-Term Memory (LSTM) networks as proposed in [30] and the HAGDetector on our dataset, with the objective of identifying malicious domains.

Interestingly, the results have unveiled a striking phenomenon, where both the LSTM and HAGDetector models exhibit high accuracy, exceeding 90%, but suffer from low recall rates, falling below 20%. It is important to clarify that accuracy denotes the proportion of correctly labeled domains, while in this specific context, recall measures the ability to correctly predict malicious domains. To further illustrate this phenomenon, we have selected a set of 14 malicious domain names that exhibit overt semantic characteristics; the detailed descriptions of these domains are presented in Table 2. The experimental outcomes reveal that the LSTM model and the HAGDetector can only identify only 2 and

3 of the 14 domains, respectively. This limitation can be attributed to inherent issues associated with existing classification methods based on neural networks:

- Limited Text Corpora: Existing models designed for the acquisition of linguistic features from domain names are trained exclusively on domain datasets. These models often overlook the potential benefits of incorporating external text corpora. Furthermore, among the domain dataset, malicious domain names constitute a notably minor proportion. Consequently, neural networks face challenges in comprehending the true semantic meanings of these words when trained on limited datasets.
- Class Imbalance: Comparable to other classification tasks, models such as the ones mentioned above grapple with an inherent class imbalance problem. In this context, malicious domains represent a minor fraction of the dataset, resulting in a substantial class imbalance. Under the circumstance that malicious domains only account for a small part of all domains, a high accuracy can be obtained even if all malicious domains are predicted as benign which instead leads to a small recall. In our dataset from three prominent ISPs, the ratio of malicious domain names to benign ones approximates 1:25. In contrast, existing classification-based models frequently assume class ratios ranging from 1:1 to 1:5. This often entails the utilization of under-sampling strategies for benign domains or over-sampling for malicious domains. Consequently, these models may yield suboptimal performance, as corroborated by our findings presented in Sect. 4.

2.5 Summary

In summary, our experimental results and statistical analyses reveal the following key observations:

- Ineffectiveness of Manual Feature Engineering. Traditional approaches that rely on manually crafted linguistic features have become less effective, primarily due to the evolving sophistication of malicious domain generation techniques. Additionally, models based on neural networks face challenges in achieving high accuracy, as they often overlook the potential benefits of incorporating external text resources for improved language representation.
- Relevance of Client Query Behavior and Domain Resolution Patterns. Client query behavior and domain resolution patterns serve as valuable indicators of associations between malicious domain names. These behaviors offer insights into the connections between domains and their interactions with various network resources.
- Class Imbalance Challenge. Malicious domain names represent only a minor fraction of the total domain names. Addressing the class imbalance problem is essential to effectively identify malicious domains in this context.

In response to these observations, we introduce Dom-BERT as a novel solution. Dom-BERT harnesses the power of the BERT (Bidirectional Encoder Representations from Transformer) model, which has been pre-trained on extensive unlabeled data sources with rich semantics. A novel domain association prediction task is then proposed, which involves fine-tuning the BERT model, to incorporate passive DNS features. The fine-tuning process is specifically designed to effectively alleviate the class imbalance problem, ultimately enhancing the overall robustness of our approach.

3   Dom-BERT Design

Our proposed model for detecting malicious domains, called Dom-BERT, consists of two main stages: *neighbor sampling* and *BERT fine-tuning*. In the neighbor sampling stage, we construct a heterogeneous graph that captures the relationships among domains, clients, and IP addresses. To reduce the graph size, we apply a pruning module before performing random walks on the graph, which samples a limited number of neighbors for each domain node. In the fine-tuning stage, we design a downstream task to compute the correlation of domains based on the result of sampling. We then leverage the pre-trained parameters of BERT and fine-tune them on this task to obtain a specialized model for domain similarity prediction. Finally, we classify domains based on the model's results. In what follows, we first provide some definitions that are essential to understand the proposed approach, and then present each stage in detail.

3.1   Preliminaries

Heterogeneous Graph. Recently, researchers have paid attention to the diversity among different types of components and relations in a graph. Instead of simply modeling the real-world systems as homogeneous networks, they begin to use heterogeneous information networks (HIN) to fully represent the semantic information. The following are some basic concepts of HIN.

Definition1: Heterogeneous Information Network (HIN). As mentioned in [26], information network is defined as a directed graph $G = (V, E)$ with an object type mapping function $\Phi : V \to A$ and a link type mapping function $\Psi : E \to R$, where each object $v \in V$ belongs to one particular object type $\Phi(v) \in A$, and each link $e \in E$ belongs to a particular relation $\Psi(e) \in R$. Note that, ARB means there is an existing relation R from type A to type B. When the types of objects $|A| > 1$ or the types of relations $|R| > 1$, the network is called a heterogeneous information network.

Definition2: Meta Path [25]. A meta path P is denoted in the form of $A_1 R_1 A_2 R_2 \cdots R_l A_{l+1}$, which defines a composite relation $R = R1 \circ R2 \circ \cdots \circ R_l$ between type A_1 and A_{l+1}, where $\circ$ denotes the composition operator on relations.

Pre-trained Model. Pre-training models have had a significant impact on natural language processing (NLP), computer vision, and various other fields [9,28]. In the domain of NLP, a pre-trained model that is trained on a large corpus of text can acquire a comprehensive understanding of common language representations, which can be advantageous for downstream NLP tasks. Moreover, pre-training models can significantly reduce the requirement for training new models from scratch. BERT is a pre-trained transformer network [28] that performs exceptionally well on diverse NLP tasks, including question answering, sentence classification, and sentence-pair regression.

3.2   Neighbor Sampling on HIN

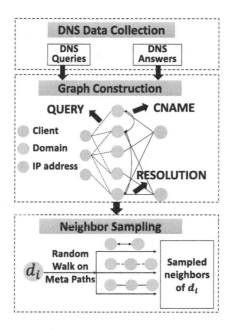

Fig. 4. Dom-Bert Stage 1: Neighbor Sampling on HIN.

Figure 4 illustrates the process of neighbor sampling over the heterogeneous information network that is constructed using the alias between domains, query relationship between domains and clients and the resolution relationship between domains and hosting servers.

Heterogeneous Graph Construction. We employ A records, AAAA records, and CNAME records in DNS traffic to construct a heterogeneous graph consisting of three types of nodes: clients, domains, and IP addresses, as well as three types of edges: QUERY, RESOLUTION, and CNAME. The QUERY relationship exists between domains and clients, the RESOLUTION relationship exists between domains and IP addresses, and the CNAME relationship exists between different domains. Specifically, we add a QUERY edge between the client and the domain it queried for each DNS query whose query type is A or AAAA. Records in the Answers field of DNS response are analyzed. For each A record or AAAA record, we add a RESOLUTION edge between the queried domain and the returned IP address. Likewise, for each CNAME record, we add a CNAME edge between the queried domain and the returned domain.

It is noteworthy that Dom-BERT operates as an association-based method, detecting domains based on their relationships with other (malicious) domains. Therefore, a large number of inactive IP addresses and domains indeed introduce noise. Dom-BERT then uses a pruning module, similar to [22] to reduce the impact of noise from benign domains and public IPs. Graph pruning is conducted following these rules:

- Inactive clients. They seldom query domains and cannot provide useful information for the query relationship. Client nodes that query fewer than two domain names are removed.
- Popular domains. Popular domains tend to be known domains, such as baidu.com and google.com. Domain nodes queried by more than 10% of clients are removed.
- Inactive (resolved) IPs. Considering that attackers always try to make full use of IP resources, IPs that host a limited number of domains tend to be benign. IP nodes resolved by only one domain name are removed.

We design 3 meta-paths (shown in Fig. 4) to describe the neighborhood relationship between domains and measure the association between the two domains. The first meta-path is based on the intuition that a domain often belongs to the same category as its CNAME domain. The second meta-path describes clients' query behaviors, where the malicious domain set queried by infected clients of the same attackers tends to be the same or partially overlapped, while normal clients have no reasons to reach out to them. The third meta-path represents the mapping relationship between IP addresses and domains. Domains resolved to the same set of IPs in the same time period are likely to belong to the same category.

Random Walk with Restart. To sample several neighbors for every domain node on each meta-path, we use random walks with a restart strategy. First, for each domain node $\omega \in W$, we call it a starting node and initiate a random walk from itself. At each step, the random walker moves to one of the current node's direct neighbor nodes on the meta-path, or returns to the starting node with probability q. All nodes reached during the random walk process, except the starting node, are added to the sampling list. The random walk process ends when the size of the sampling list reaches Nei_n, and this process is repeated $Walk_n$ times. In this study, we set Nei_n to 50 and $Walk_n$ to 10.

The strategy we employ is based on the intuition that attackers tend to reuse domain names or IP resources due to financial constraints, leading to a covert relationship between domain names and their corresponding network resources. To address this challenge, we utilize random walks with a restart strategy that aggregates more network topology information than the methods that only consider direct neighbor nodes. The restart strategy ensures that nearer neighbor nodes are more likely to be sampled, thereby capturing important relationships that may be missed by simpler sampling methods.

To leverage both domain embedding features and entity relationships, we introduce a domain association prediction task that fine-tunes a pre-trained BERT model. The goal of this task is to predict the relationship between pairs of domains based on their embedding features and their neighborhood relationships in the graph.

3.3   Fine-Tuning

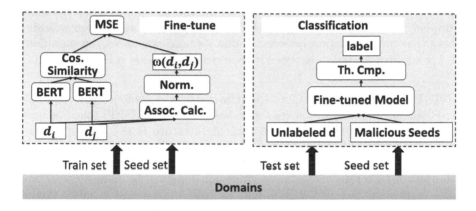

Fig. 5. Dom-Bert Stage 2: BERT fine-tuning.

To jointly take advantage of domain embedding features and the relationship between entities, we design a domain association prediction task to fine-tune pre-trained BERT and then classify domains based on prediction results.

Downstream Task Design. BERT may not perform well when linguistic patterns are not easily distinguishable, as it relies solely on text features and ignores the latent connection among domains, client IPs, and hosting infrastructures. As we shall see in Sect. 4.5, BERT performance drops significantly without a fine-tuning stage. Like other classification-based models, the domain classification task is facing the class-imbalance problem since malicious domains only account for a very small proportion. In our dataset that was captured from three major ISPs in China, the ratio of malicious domain names to benign ones is around 1:25, while existing classification-based models often assume a ratio ranging from 1:2 to 1:5 through under-sampling benign domains or over-sampling malicious domains. As such, they would perform poorly in practice as shown in Sect. 4.

To address these limitations, we propose a domain association prediction task that fine-tunes the network to learn how similar domains behave when they are queried and resolved.

As shown in Fig. 5, we divide domain nodes into three groups called D_{seed}, D_{test} and D_{train}. D_{seed} is a set of labeled malicious domain names and D_{test} contains domains that need to be classified. The training domain set D_{train} is used to build training set to fine-tune the BERT model. Specifically, the training set consists of records in the form of $< d_1, d_2, \omega(d_1, d_2) >$, where $d_1, d_2 \in D_{train} \cup D_{seed}$. $\omega(d_1, d_2)$ is defined as follows and we use it as the label of input data$< d_1, d_2 >$:

$$\omega(d_1, d_2) = \begin{cases} \frac{c_i}{\omega_{max} - \alpha} + \beta & d_2 \in Nei(d_1) \\ 0 & d_2 \notin Nei(d_1) \end{cases} \tag{1}$$

where $\omega_{max} = max\left\{c_1, c_2, ..c_{Nei(d_1)}\right\}$, $Nei(d_1)$ refers to the neighbor nodes of domain d_1 based on random walk and c_i represents how many times domain d_i is sampled. α and β are used to adjust the distribution of association weights. β ensures that the association between d_i and its neighbor nodes can be differentiated from the association between its non-neighbor nodes. α ensures $\omega \in [0, 1]$.

BERT Fine-Tuning and Classification. For the sentence-pair regression task, BERT utilizes two sentences separated by a special [SEP] token as input. One disadvantage of the BERT network architecture is the lack of independent sentence embeddings since the output of BERT provides embeddings for each token, including the [CLS] and [SEP] tokens. We add a mean operation to the output of BERT to derive embeddings for domains. In doing so, individual domain names are fed into BERT, and we take the average value of the output layer of BERT as domain embeddings. Then we calculate cosine similarity between two domain embeddings and use the mean square error (MSE) of label and cosine similarity as the loss function to fine-tune BERT.

Finally, for each domain $d \in D_{test}$, we construct its test dataset:

$$\{(d, d_1), (d, d_2), ..., (d, d_n)\}$$

where $d_i \in D_{seed}$. After feeding domain name pairs into the fine-tuned Dom-BERT model, we obtain a set of corresponding predictions $\{p_1, p_2, ...p_n\}$. Specifically, Domain d will then be labeled as malicious if $min\{p_1, p_2, ...p_n\} \geq \theta$, where θ is a designated threshold that aims to balance between precision and recall, and its value is critical in determining the effectiveness of the model. We conduct a parameter sensitivity test in Sect. 4.3 to determine the optimal value for θ.

4   Experiment

4.1   Experimental Setup

Dataset. Our dataset consists of passive DNS logs that were generated by DPI appliances in 3 large ISPs. Each DPI appliance parses the DNS response traffic from recursive resolvers to end users and generates a log entry for each response. We use a sample of total data, including 433 malicious domains and 11,118 benign domains. We randomly choose 1/4 of malicious domains as seeds that constitute D_{seed}.

Baseline. We compare Dom-BERT with several state-of-the-art malicious domain detection methods and their detailed descriptions are listed as follows:

- LSTM [30]. This is a real-time classification method for domain names using the LSTM network. It directly operates on the original domain name (such as `google.com`) without other context information.
- FANCI [21]. FANCI extracts 21 features of domain names and employs supervised learning approaches to classify domains.
- GAT [29]. GAT is a representative graph neural network algorithm based on homogeneous graphs. We employ GAT to obtain domain embeddings that can fully represent the resolution relationship.
- DeepDom [23]. DeepDom constructs a heterogeneous graph based on passive DNS traffic data and classifies domains using convolution networks.
- HAGDetector [17]. HAGDetector constructs 3 different classifiers according to the length of the domain name.
- G-resolution1 [14] and G-resolution2 [20]. They construct the domain resolution graph using passive DNS data and measure the strength of associations between domains based on the number of IP addresses they are co-hosted at.

Implementation Details. For Dom-BERT, we construct the heterogeneous graph on the entire dataset and perform random walks. Then we divide the domains other than D_{seed} into training domain set D_{train}, validation set, and test domain set D_{test} according to 6:2:2. Then we construct training set, validation set, and test set for the downstream task in the way described in Sect. 3.3.

Dom-BERT and baseline methods are all implemented using Python 3.8, and the deep learning methods are implemented on Pytorch. We use BERT-Base, uncased (12-layer, 768-hidden, 12-heads, 110M parameters) as our BERT Model [2]. We used one NVIDIA GeForce RTX 3080Ti in our evaluation. Since we only need to finetune the model by training dozens of epochs, the training process takes only a few minutes while inference requires only a few seconds.

Metrics. Table 3 lists the evaluation metrics used in the experiments. Precision refers to the proportion of domains labeled as malicious in all predicted malicious domains and recall indicates how many of the domains labeled as malicious can be predicted correctly. F1 score is defined as the harmonic average of precision and recall.

Table 3. List of metrics

Metric	Description
TP	malicious domains predicted as malicious
FP	benign domains predicted as malicious
TN	benign domains predicted as benign
FN	malicious domains predicted as benign
accuracy	(TP + TN) / (TP + FP + TN + FN)
precision	TP / (TP + FP)
recall	TP / (TP + FN)
F1	2 * precision * recall / (precision + recall)

4.2   Performance Comparison

To assess the effectiveness of Dom-BERT, we conducted a comprehensive comparative analysis against seven notable malicious domain detection methods mentioned previously, and the results are meticulously detailed in Table 4.

On one hand, classification-based methods, which encompass FANCI, LSTM, HAGDetector, and GAT, tend to exhibit good accuracy but suboptimal recall, primarily due to the inherent class imbalance problem. In situations where malicious domains constitute only a fraction of the overall dataset, these methods often prioritize accuracy by designating all malicious domains as benign, inadvertently leading to a reduced recall.

On the other hand, inference-based techniques, notably G-resolution1 and G-resolution2, have showcased a better recall. Their effectiveness stems from the fundamental principles of maximizing the identification of malicious domains and leveraging extensive domain associations that encompass domains, IP addresses, and clients. These methods involve computing the correlation between the target domain and each seed domain within the malicious seed set, followed by sorting and weighted summing. To illustrate, if a domain name has a correlation of 0.5 with two known malicious domains, its final malicious value would exceed 0.625 $(0.5 + (1 - 0.5) \times \frac{1}{2} \times 0.5)$. This approach facilitates the detection of more malicious domains.

However, it is worth noting that such methodologies might increase the risk of misclassifying benign domains as malicious. In contrast, our approach opts for a different strategy by selecting the maximum similarity value for comparison. Notably, this similarity already incorporates multi-hop similarity, eliminating the need to sum up the entire seed set and thereby avoiding the introduction of irrelevant noise. As a result, Dom-BERT effectively sidesteps the issue of labeling a substantial number of benign domains as malicious.

Overall, our proposed approach, Dom-BERT, emerges as the frontrunner in terms of performance by integrating local domain features with the complex information in passive DNS data. Moreover, Dom-BERT effectively mitigates the class imbalance issue, ultimately achieving a harmonious balance between high accuracy and recall.

Table 4. Performance of Comparison

Method	accuracy	precision	recall	F1
FANCI	0.9644	0.8261	0.0491	0.0927
LSTM	0.9325	1.0000	0.2018	0.3359
HAGDetector	0.9865	0.9815	0.5146	0.6752
GAT	0.9526	0.8571	0.1200	0.2105
DeepDom	0.9588	1.0000	0.0400	0.0769
G-resolution1	0.9678	0.4679	0.8027	0.5912
G-resolution2	0.9709	0.4987	**0.9082**	0.6439
Dom-BERT	**0.9968**	**1.0000**	0.8479	**0.9177**

4.3 Parameter Sensitivity

We conducted a sensitivity analysis on two pivotal parameters in the Dom-BERT model, namely the number of neighbors sampled on each meta-path in the random walk, denoted as Nei_n, and the association threshold, denoted as θ. We adopted a hold-out cross-validation approach and divided the validation set and test set in accordance with the methodology outlined in Sect. 4.1. The results of the analysis are summarized in Table 5 and Table 6.

Table 5 illustrates the impact of varying Nei_n values on the performance metrics, including accuracy, precision, recall, and F1. Notably, as Nei_n increases from 10 to 50, Dom-BERT exhibits improved performance, indicating a positive correlation between the neighbor size and model efficacy. Beyond a Nei_n value of 50, the model's performance experiences a marginal fluctuation. On one hand, too many sampled neighbor nodes may introduce noises into our model. On the other hand, the runtime rises sharply with Nei_n increasing. As such, we set $Nei_n = 50$ as the optimal parameter value for our experiments.

Table 5. Accuracy, precision, recall and F1 with different Nei_n

Nei_n	accuracy	precision	recall	F1
10	0.9956	0.9882	0.7962	0.8819
20	0.9957	1.0000	0.7926	0.8843
50	0.9968	1.0000	0.8479	**0.9177**
100	0.9908	0.9926	0.8297	0.9039
200	0.9978	1.0000	0.8391	0.9125

Table 6 delves into the impact of the association threshold θ on model performance. Dom-BERT attains its optimal performance when the threshold is set at $\theta = 0.6$. A notable observation is that as the threshold exceeds 0.6, model performance, specifically in terms of recall and F1 score, starts to deteriorate with an increasing threshold value. This decline is primarily attributed to the elevated threshold, which results in a greater number of malicious domains being incorrectly labeled as benign. In light of the severe consequences associated with malicious domains, our aim is to maximize the identification of malicious domains while maintaining high precision levels for benign domains. Hence, we opt to set the association threshold θ at 0.6.

Table 6. Accuracy, precision, recall and F1 under different θ

θ	accuracy	precision	recall	F1
0.5	0.9895	0.9813	0.8142	0.8900
0.6	0.9968	1.0000	0.8479	**0.9177**
0.7	0.9884	1.0000	0.7838	0.8788
0.8	0.9777	1.0000	0.5697	0.7258
0.9	0.9516	1.0000	0.0681	0.1275

4.4 Robustness Analysis

Table 7. Accuracy, precision, recall and F1 under different ratios between malicious domains and benign domains

ratio	accuracy	precision	recall	F1
1:2	0.7694	1.0000	0.6097	0.7575
1:5	0.9602	1.0000	0.8222	0.9024
1:10	0.9787	1.0000	0.8314	0.9079
all data	0.9968	1.0000	0.8479	0.9177

To assess the robustness of Dom-BERT, we employed under-sampling techniques on the benign domain subset, enabling us to control the ratio of malicious domains to benign domains in the dataset. The findings of this evaluation are summarized in Table 7.

A notable observation is that Dom-BERT's performance diminishes notably when subjected to a dataset with a 1:2 ratio of malicious to benign domains. This outcome can be attributed to the challenge posed by the limited dataset size, where the associations among domains and other network resources become less discernible.

Conversely, when evaluated on datasets with more balanced ratios, such as 1:5 or 1:10, and across the entire dataset, Dom-BERT demonstrates consistent and stable performance. Furthermore, we conducted a comparative analysis of Dom-BERT, DeepDom, and HAGDetector under various class imbalance ratios. The results, depicted in Fig. 6, serve to underscore the robustness of Dom-BERT in effectively handling class imbalance challenges. Moreover, the findings underscore the effectiveness of our model in practical scenarios, where malicious domains represent a marginal fraction of the total domain landscape.

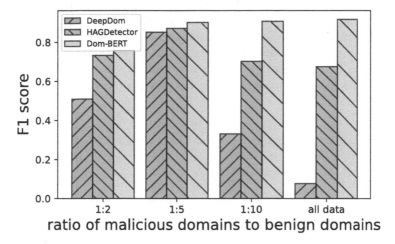

Fig. 6. Performance of Dom-BERT, DeepDom, and HAGDetector under different ratios between malicious domains and benign domains

4.5 Ablation Study

In this set of experiments, we first verify the necessity of random walks on multiple meta paths. In the random walk, we sample neighbor nodes on the three meta paths, named DD (domain-domain), DID (domain-IP-domain), and DCD (domain-CNAME-domain) respectively. The results shown in Table 8 report the contribution of each meta path and also prove that each meta path is indispensable. (1) In model '1–3', we evaluate the impact of each meta path. The respective decrease of 2.10%, 1.23%, and 5.75% on F1 for '1', '2', and '3' indicates that the lack of any meta path will lead to the degradation of model performance. The lack of the DCD meta path has the greatest impact on model performance, which shows that the query relationship between clients and domains can reflect the potential relationship between malicious domains and is crucial for malicious domain detection. (2) Models '4–6' only sample neighbor nodes on a single meta path and the results show that the performance of the model utilizing the DD meta path decreases more than utilizing the DCD or DID meta path. It might be attributed to the fact that CNAME records are fewer than A and AAAA records.

We finally remove the fine-tuning phase and directly add a fully connected layer after the output of BERT to evaluate the effectiveness of downstream task design (model '7'). The ablation study's results show the need for BERT's fine-tuning and emphasize the importance of domain knowledge. While BERT may initially struggle with domain-specific characteristics, the fine-tuning process allows the model to adapt and specialize in capturing features relevant to the particular task at hand, namely, domain classification. Training a new model from scratch would necessitate significant amounts of labeled domain-specific data, which may not always be readily available. By adopting a transfer learning approach with BERT, we make efficient use of pre-existing knowledge, requiring less labeled data for fine-tuning while still achieving competitive performance. While BERT may initially underperform without fine-tuning, the subsequent adaptation process allows the model to excel in understanding domain-specific characteristics. This approach provides a practical and effective means of leveraging transfer learning for domain classification tasks, optimizing both performance and resource utilization.

Table 8. Ablation study of different meta path in Dom-BERT (w/o represents *without*)

Method		Accuracy	Precision	Recall	F1
Dom-BERT		0.9968	1.0000	0.8479	0.9177
1	w/o DD	0.9950	1.0000	0.8155	0.8984
2	w/o DID	0.9963	0.9946	0.8326	0.9064
3	w/o DCD	0.9954	0.9931	0.7660	0.8649
4	w/o DD & DID	0.9958	0.9946	0.7742	0.8727
5	w/o DD & DCD	0.9937	1.0000	0.8106	0.8932
6	w/o DID & DCD	0.9952	1.0000	0.7337	0.8464
7	w/o fine-tune	0.3620	0.0213	0.6605	0.0412

4.6 Case Study

Dom-BERT has the ability to detect malicious domains that have not been identified yet and Fig. 7 shows an example. Among them, red nodes represent IP addresses, blue nodes are domains, and the green node represents a client node. The black dotted line represents the CNAME relationship between domains, and the orange and blue dashed lines represent the query relationship between clients and domains. The red domains are malicious domains identified through the same data labeling method mentioned earlier, namely VirusTotal and Qihoo 360. By extracting the latent association with known malicious domain *p0.itc.cn*, Dom-BERT identifies *jzsxzmdkpr.xjtlu.edu.cn* as malicious and discovers other suspicious DGA-generated domains (red font ones) by their similarity with *jzsxzmdkpr.xjtlu.edu.cn* in terms of linguistic association as well as query relationship. Note that among the newly identified domains, only the one with a red italic label has been identified as malicious before.

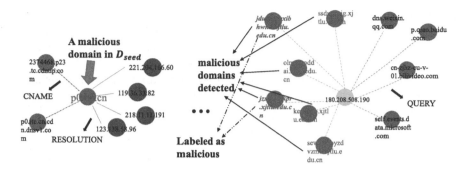

Fig. 7. An example for malicious domain detection. (Color figure online)

5 Discussion

5.1 Real-World Deployment

Dom-BERT offers practical utility for real-time malicious domain detection within operational networks. The deployment process is streamlined and efficient, characterized by constant-time operations for adding or reducing nodes in the initialized heterogeneous graph. Additionally, the execution time of random walks is inherently constrained by the length of the walk sequence, ensuring that it scales linearly with the size of the graph, preventing any undue computational burden. The integration of the pre-trained BERT model, with fine-tuning performed solely on downstream tasks, further expedites the real-world deployment process.

In a real-world deployment scenario, the system continually aggregates DNS logs and dynamically updates the heterogeneous graph in real time. Concurrently, the system conducts random walks on newly introduced domain nodes, appending their sequences to the corpus, and executes the detection of potential malicious domains. The identified malicious domains are subsequently incorporated into the seed set, contributing to the ongoing refinement of the detection process.

5.2 Impact of the Number of the Seeds

The size of the seed set (D_{seed}) is intuitively expected to influence the accuracy of the Dom-BERT model. However, in practical applications, the number of seeds remains outside our direct control. To systematically evaluate the influence of the number of seeds on performance, we vary the proportion of seeds, denoted as γ, relative to the total number of malicious domains. The results are presented in Table 9.

It is noteworthy that Dom-BERT operates as an association-based method, detecting domains based on their relationships with other domains. The model's inherent high precision facilitates the expansion of the D_{seed}. Due to the fact that Dom-BERT does require a domain seed set to achieve malicious domain name recognition, there exists the cold start issue. But with the continuous discovery of malicious domains, identified malicious domains can iteratively be added to the seed set, while mature domain blacklists can also be introduced to the seed set, thereby enhancing the overall detection capability and ensuring the effectiveness of the model. The outcomes corroborate this intuitive observation, underscoring the model's capacity for ongoing improvement and adaptability.

5.3   Open Questions

Encrypted DNS, DoT, DoH, DoQ and other technologies are gradually becoming popular, which has to some extent removed the visibility used in the paper. The encryption of DNS traffic obscures the details of domain queries and responses, making it more challenging to gather the necessary data for domain classification. We envision that the methods aimed to recognize malicious domains at early stage based on registration information may help us solve these problems [11–13].

Another pertinent concern is the dynamic behavior of domain information and its potential impact on our results, particularly in the context of botnets utilizing flux techniques. The dynamic behavior of domain information can potentially influence the constructed graph and, subsequently, the performance of Dom-BERT. In scenarios where there are rapid changes in domain resolution patterns, the graph structure may evolve over time, affecting the relationships captured by Dom-BERT.

Table 9. Accuracy, precision, recall and F1 under different proportion of D_{seed}

γ	accuracy	precision	recall	F1
1/2	0.9977	1.0000	0.8563	0.9226
1/4	0.9968	1.0000	0.8479	0.9177
1/5	0.9841	1.0000	0.7130	0.8325
1/10	0.9668	1.0000	0.4627	0.6327
1/20	0.9547	1.0000	0.3041	0.4664

6   Related Work

Linguistic Pattern Based Classification. Malicious domains generated by DGAs often have similar character distributions or text patterns that are different from those of benign ones. This difference is wildly leveraged for malicious domain detection. For example, FANCI [21] extracts several types of features of domain names and classifies domains using supervised learning. Moreover, detectors based on deep learning models are constructed to capture implicit features of malicious domains. LSTM is applied on domain names [5] and HAGDetector [17] constructs 3 deep models respectively for short domain names, moderate-length domain names and extra-long domain names. These methods only consider the text structure of domains, which can be further improved by using the language representation models that include external text resources. In addition, researchers began to focus on the issue of inaccurate identification of malicious domain names in practical scenarios. Some approaches struggle to achieve high accuracy by solving the problem of class imbalance [27,32] while another approach is to automatically solve the problem of inaccurate classification caused by feature miss [7].

DNS Behavior Based Classification. Malicious domains and benign ones may also exhibit different DNS resolution behavior. EXPOSURE [8] employs several sets of resolution features (*e.g.* time-based features and DNS-answer-based features) to distinguish malicious domains from benign ones; Pleiades [6], on the other hand, focuses on NXDomain responses based on the observation that a host under the same attack will generate a large number of DNS queries, while most of them will return NXDomain response. Capturing this DNS behavior may further improve the detection accuracy of Dom-BERT, we will investigate this in future work.

Graph-Based Classification. Graphs can be abstracted from the relationships of query originators (*i.e.* client IPs), queried domains as well as the resolved IPs [16]. HGDom [24] and DeepDom [23] construct heterogeneous graphs in which nodes can be client IPs, domains and resolved IPs. Specifically, HGDom leverages graph convolution network with attention mechanism to generate the final embedding for each domain; DeepDom further utilizes WHOIS to get external information about domains, such as registrant and registrar, for better embedding. The embeddings are then used as the input for classification. A major concern of the classification-based solutions is that they often assume a less imbalanced distribution of malicious domains and benign ones. Nevertheless, in practice, the proportion of malicious domains are far less than the benign ones. Besides, as the domains, originator IPs as well as the resolved IPs grow, the graphs will be too large to obtain the embeddings efficiently.

Inference-Based Models. These models aim to assign a malicious score to domains based on their correlation between labeled malicious domains. Some methods construct the domain-IP graph based on the resolution relationship between domains and IP addresses [14,15], while others construct the client-domain graph based on the query behaviors of clients [18]; HinDom [22] constructs a heterogeneous information network. The association scores between any two domains are then extracted from these graphs. Existing inference-based solutions ignore the linguistic characteristics of malicious domains.

7   Conclusion and Future Work

In order to solve the class-imbalance problem, which remains an endemic quandary in malicious domain detection, this paper proposes a malicious domain detection model named Dom-BERT which can fully excavate both the local features of the domains themselves through BERT and the interactive behaviors among clients, domains and IP addresses by random walks on the heterogeneous graph. We use DNS-related data from ISPs and validate the effectiveness of our method. For future work, we hope to introduce local features of IP addresses and clients such as AS numbers and BGP prefixes. We also intend to assign different probabilities to different neighbor nodes in random walks based on interactive features such as query times and resolution times.

Acknowledgement. This work is supported by National Key R&D Program of China (Grant No. 2022YFB3103000), by the National Natural Science Foundation of China (Grant No. U20A20180 and 62072437).

References

1. Alexa top domains. http://www.alexa.com
2. BERT. https://github.com/google-research/bert
3. Qihoo 360. https://www.360.cn
4. VirusTotal. http://www.virustotal.com
5. Anderson, H.S., Woodbridge, J., Filar, B.: DeepDGA: adversarially-tuned domain generation and detection. In: Proceedings of the 2016 ACM Workshop on Artificial Intelligence and Security (2016)
6. Antonakakis, M., et al.: From throw-away traffic to bots: detecting the rise of DGA-based malware. In: Kohno, T. (ed.) Proceedings of the 21th USENIX Security Symposium (2012). https://www.usenix.org/conference/usenixsecurity12/technical-sessions/presentation/antonakakis
7. Bayer, J., et al.: Operational domain name classification: from automatic ground truth generation to adaptation to missing values. In: Brunstrom, A., Flores, M., Fiore, M. (eds.) International Conference on Passive and Active Network Measurement, vol. 13882, pp. 564–591. Springer, Cham (2023). https://doi.org/10.1007/978-3-031-28486-1_24
8. Bilge, L., Sen, S., Balzarotti, D., Kirda, E., Kruegel, C.: Exposure: a passive DNS analysis service to detect and report malicious domains. ACM Trans. Inf. Syst. Secur. (2014). https://doi.org/10.1145/2584679
9. Dosovitskiy, A., et al.: An image is worth 16x16 words: transformers for image recognition at scale. In: International Conference on Learning Representations (2021)
10. Gao, H., et al.: An empirical reexamination of global DNS behavior. In: Chiu, D.M., Wang, J., Barford, P., Seshan, S. (eds.) ACM SIGCOMM 2013 Conference, SIGCOMM 2013, Hong Kong, 12–16 August 2013, pp. 267–278. ACM (2013). https://doi.org/10.1145/2486001.2486018
11. Hao, S., Feamster, N., Pandrangi, R.: Monitoring the initial DNS behavior of malicious domains. In: Proceedings of the 2011 ACM SIGCOMM Conference on Internet Measurement Conference, pp. 269–278 (2011)
12. Hao, S., Kantchelian, A., Miller, B., Paxson, V., Feamster, N.: PREDATOR: proactive recognition and elimination of domain abuse at time-of-registration. In: The 2016 ACM SIGSAC Conference (2016)

13. Hao, S., Thomas, M., Paxson, V., Feamster, N., Hollenbeck, S.: Understanding the domain registration behavior of spammers. In: Conference on Internet Measurement Conference (2013)
14. Khalil, I., Yu, T., Guan, B.: Discovering malicious domains through passive DNS data graph analysis. In: Chen, X., Wang, X., Huang, X. (eds.) AsiaCCS (2016). https://doi.org/10.1145/2897845.2897877
15. Khalil, I.M., Guan, B., Nabeel, M., Yu, T.: A domain is only as good as its buddies: detecting stealthy malicious domains via graph inference. In: Zhao, Z., Ahn, G., Krishnan, R., Ghinita, G. (eds.) CODASPY (2018). https://doi.org/10.1145/3176258.3176329
16. Lei, K., Fu, Q., Ni, J., Wang, F., Yang, M., Xu, K.: Detecting malicious domains with behavioral modeling and graph embedding. In: ICDCS (2019). https://doi.org/10.1109/ICDCS.2019.00066
17. Liang, J., Chen, S., Wei, Z., Zhao, S., Zhao, W.: HAGDetector: heterogeneous DGA domain name detection model. Comput. Secur. (2022). https://doi.org/10.1016/j.cose.2022.102803
18. Manadhata, P.K., Yadav, S., Rao, P., Horne, W.: Detecting malicious domains via graph inference. In: Kutyłowski, M., Vaidya, J. (eds.) ESORICS 2014. LNCS, vol. 8712, pp. 1–18. Springer, Cham (2014). https://doi.org/10.1007/978-3-319-11203-9_1
19. Maroofi, S., Korczyński, M., Hesselman, C., Ampeau, B., Duda, A.: COMAR: classification of compromised versus maliciously registered domains. In: 2020 IEEE European Symposium on Security and Privacy (EuroS&P), pp. 607–623. IEEE (2020)
20. Nabeel, M., Khalil, I.M., Guan, B., Yu, T.: Following passive DNS traces to detect stealthy malicious domains via graph inference. ACM Trans. Priv. Secur. (2020). https://doi.org/10.1145/3401897
21. Schüppen, S., Teubert, D., Herrmann, P., Meyer, U.: FANCI: feature-based automated NXDomain classification and intelligence. In: 27th USENIX Security Symposium (2018). https://www.usenix.org/conference/usenixsecurity18/presentation/schuppen
22. Sun, X., Tong, M., Yang, J., Liu, X., Liu, H.: HinDom: a robust malicious domain detection system based on heterogeneous information network with transductive classification. In: RAID (2019). https://www.usenix.org/conference/raid2019/presentation/sun
23. Sun, X., Wang, Z., Yang, J., Liu, X.: DeepDom: malicious domain detection with scalable and heterogeneous graph convolutional networks. Comput. Secur. (2020). https://doi.org/10.1016/j.cose.2020.102057
24. Sun, X., Yang, J., Wang, Z., Liu, H.: HGDom: heterogeneous graph convolutional networks for malicious domain detection. In: NOMS (2020). https://doi.org/10.1109/NOMS47738.2020.9110462
25. Sun, Y., Han, J., Yan, X., Yu, P.S., Wu, T.: PathSim: meta path-based top-K similarity search in heterogeneous information networks. Proc. VLDB Endow. (2011). http://www.vldb.org/pvldb/vol4/p992-sun.pdf
26. Sun, Y., Yu, Y., Han, J.: Ranking-based clustering of heterogeneous information networks with star network schema. In: Elder, J., Fogelman-Soulié, F., Flach, P.A., Zaki, M. (eds.) SIGKDD (2009). https://doi.org/10.1145/1557019.1557107
27. Tran, D., Mac, H., Tong, V., Tran, H.A., Nguyen, L.G.: A LSTM based framework for handling multiclass imbalance in DGA botnet detection. Neurocomputing (2018). https://doi.org/10.1016/j.neucom.2017.11.018

28. Vaswani, A., et al.: Attention is all you need. In: Advances in Neural Information Processing Systems (2017). https://proceedings.neurips.cc/paper/2017/hash/3f5ee243547dee91fbd053c1c4a845aa-Abstract.html

29. Velickovic, P., Cucurull, G., Casanova, A., Romero, A., Liò, P., Bengio, Y.: Graph attention networks. In: ICLR (2018). https://openreview.net/forum?id=rJXMpikCZ

30. Woodbridge, J., Anderson, H.S., Ahuja, A., Grant, D.: Predicting domain generation algorithms with long short-term memory networks. CoRR abs/1611.00791 (2016). http://arxiv.org/abs/1611.00791

31. Yang, D., Li, Z., Tyson, G.: A deep dive into DNS query failures. In: USENIX ATC 20. USENIX Association, July 2020. https://www.usenix.org/conference/atc20/presentation/yang

32. Yilmaz, I., Siraj, A., Ulybyshev, D.A.: Improving DGA-based malicious domain classifiers for malware defense with adversarial machine learning. CoRR abs/2101.00521 (2021). https://arxiv.org/abs/2101.00521

Data Augmentation for Traffic Classification

Chao Wang[1,2] , Alessandro Finamore[1(✉)] , Pietro Michiardi[2] ,
Massimo Gallo[1] , and Dario Rossi[1]

[1] Huawei Technologies SASU, Boulogne-Billancourt, France
`alessandro.finamore@huawei.com`
[2] EURECOM, Biot Sophia Antipolis, France

Abstract. Data Augmentation (DA)—enriching training data by
adding synthetic samples—is a technique widely adopted in Computer
Vision (CV) and Natural Language Processing (NLP) tasks to improve
models performance. Yet, DA has struggled to gain traction in networking contexts, particularly in Traffic Classification (TC) tasks. In this
work, we fulfill this gap by benchmarking 18 augmentation functions
applied to 3 TC datasets using packet time series as input representation and considering a variety of training conditions. Our results show
that (*i*) DA can reap benefits previously unexplored, (*ii*) augmentations
acting on time series sequence order and masking are better suited for
TC than amplitude augmentations and (*iii*) basic models latent space
analysis can help understanding the positive/negative effects of augmentations on classification performance.

1 Introduction

Network monitoring is at the core of network operations with Traffic Classification (TC) being key for traffic management. Traditional Deep Packet
Inspection (DPI) techniques, i.e., classifying traffic with rules related to packets content, is nowadays more and more challenged by the growth in adoption
of TLS/DNSSEC/HTTPS. Despite the quest for alternative solutions to DPI
already sparked about two decades ago with the first Machine Learning (ML)
models based on packet and flow features, a renewed thrust in addressing TC
via data-driven modeling is fueled today by the rise of Deep Learning (DL),
with abundant TC literature, periodically surveyed [29,34], reusing/adapting
Computer Vision (CV) training algorithms and model architectures.

Despite the existing literature, we argue that *opportunities laying in the data
itself are still unexplored* based on three observations. First, CV and Natural Language Processing (NLP) methods usually leverage "cheap" Data Augmentation
(DA) strategies (e.g., image rotation or synonym replacement) to complement
training data by increasing samples variety. Empirical studies show that this
leads to improved classification accuracy. Yet to the best of our knowledge, only
a handful of TC studies considered DA [20,32,46] and multiple aspects of DA
design space remain unexplored. Second, network traffic datasets are imbalanced

P. Richter et al. (Eds.): PAM 2024, LNCS 14537, pp. 159–186, 2024.
https://doi.org/10.1007/978-3-031-56249-5_7

due to the natural skew of app/service popularity and traffic dynamics. In turn, this calls for training strategies emphasizing classification performance improvement for classes with fewer samples. However, the interplay between imbalance and model performance is typically ignored in TC literature. Last, the pursuit of better model generalization and robustness necessitates large-scale datasets with high-quality labeling resulting in expensive data collection processes. In this context, the extent to which DA can alleviate this burden remains unexplored.

In this paper, we fill these gaps by providing a comprehensive evaluation of "hand-crafted" augmentations—transformations designed based on domain knowledge—applied to packets time series typically used as input in TC. Given the broad design space, we defined research goals across multiple dimensions. First of all, we selected a large pool of 18 augmentations across 3 families (amplitude, masking, and sequence) which we benchmark both when used in isolation as well as when multiple augmentations are combined (e.g., via stacking or ensembling). Augmentations are combined with original training data via different batching policies (e.g., replacing training data with augmentation, adding augmented data to each training step, or pre-augmenting the dataset before training). We also included scenarios where imbalanced datasets are rebalanced during training to give more importance to minority classes. Last, we dissected augmentations performance by exploring their geometry in the classifiers latent space to pinpoint root causes driving performance. Our experimental campaigns were carried over 2 mid-sized public datasets, namely MIRAGE-19 and MIRAGE-22 (up to 20 classes, 64k flows), and a larger private dataset (100 classes, 2.9M flows). We summarize our major findings as follows:

– We confirm that augmentations improve performance (up to +4.4% weighted F1) and expanding training batches during training (i.e., the Injection policy) is the most effective policy to introduce augmentations. Yet, improvements are dataset dependent and not necessarily linearly related to dataset size or number of classes to model;
– Sequence ordering and masking are more effective augmentation families for TC tasks. Yet, no single augmentation is found consistently superior across datasets, nor domain knowledge suffice to craft effective augmentations, i.e., the quest for effective augmentations is an intrinsic trial-and-error process;
– Effective augmentations introduce good sample variety, i.e., they synthesize samples that are neither too close nor too far from the original training data.

To the best of our knowledge, a broad and systematic study of hand-crafted DA techniques in TC as the one performed in our study is unprecedented. Ultimately, our analysis confirms that DA is currently suffering from a single pain point—exploring the design space via brute force. However, our results suggest a possible road map to achieve better augmentations via generative models which might render obsolete the use of brute force.

In the remainder, we start by introducing DA basic concepts and reviewing relevant ML and TC literature (Sect. 2). We then introduce and discuss our research goals (Sect. 3) and the experimental setting used to address them (Sect. 4). Last, we present our results (Sect. 5) before closing with final remarks (Sect. 6).

2   Background and Related Work

Data augmentation consists in adding synthetic samples (typically derived from real ones) to the training set to increase its variety. DA has been popularized across many ML disciplines [26,36,44] with a large number of variants which we can be broadly grouped into two categories [26]: hand-crafted DA and data synthesis. Hand-crafted DA (also known as data transformations) involves creating new samples by applying predefined rules to existing samples. Instead, data synthesis relates to generating new samples via generative models, e.g., Variational AutoEncoders (VAE), Generative Adversarial Neural networks (GAN), Diffusion Models (DM), etc., trained on existing and typically large datasets.

In this section, we overview the existing DA literature with an emphasis on hand-crafted DA and methods closer to the scope of our work. We begin by introducing relevant CV and time series ML literature. Then, we review TC literature using DA and close with a discussion about general design principles/requirements that we used for defining our research goals outlined in Sect. 3.

2.1   Data Augmentation in Traditional Machine Learning Tasks

To ground the discussion of different methods merits, we start by revisiting the internal mechanisms of supervised ML/DL models.

Supervised Modeling and DA. In a nutshell, a supervised model is a function $\varphi : \mathbf{x} \in \mathcal{X} \to y \in \mathcal{Y}$ mapping an input $\mathbf{x}$ to its label y. Training such models corresponds to discover a good function $\varphi(\cdot)$ based on a training set. When performing DA, the training set is enlarged by adding new samples $\mathbf{x}' = \text{Aug}(\mathbf{x})$ created by altering original samples $\mathbf{x}$—these transformations act directly in the input space $\mathcal{X}$ and the additional synthetic samples contribute in defining $\varphi(\cdot)$ as much as the original ones. It follows that having a comprehensive understanding of samples/classes properties and their contribution to models training is beneficial for designing *effective* augmentations, i.e., transformations enabling higher classification performance.

Beside operating in the input space, DL models offer also a latent space. In fact, DL models are typically a composition of two functions $\varphi(\mathbf{x_i}) = h(f(\mathbf{x_i})) = y_i$: a feature extractor $f(\cdot)$ and a classifier $h(\cdot)$, normally a single fully connected layer (i.e., a linear classifier) in TC. In other words, an input sample $f(\mathbf{x_i}) = \mathbf{z_i}$ is first projected into an intermediate space, namely the *latent space*, where different classes are expected to occupy different regions. The better such separation, the easier is for the classifier $h(\mathbf{z_i}) = y_i$ to identify the correct label. It follows that this design enables a second form of augmentations based on altering samples in the latent space rather than in the input space.

Last, differently from DA, generative models aims to learn the training set data distribution. In this way generating new synthetic data corresponds to sampling from the learned distribution. In the following we expand on each of these three methodologies.

Input Space Transformations. In traditional ML, Synthetic Minority Oversampling TEchnique (SMOTE) [7] is a popular augmentation technique. This approach generates new samples by interpolating the nearest neighbors of a given training sample. To address class imbalance, SMOTE is often employed with a sampling mechanism that prioritizes minority classes [16, 17].

In CV, several image transformations have been proposed to improve samples variety while preserving classes semantics. These transformations operate on colors (e.g., contrast and brightness changes, gray scaling) and geometry (e.g., rotation, flipping, and zooming), or via filters (e.g., blurring with Gaussian kernel) and masks (e.g., randomly set to zero a patch of pixels). Furthermore, transformations like CutMix [51] and Mixup [52] not only increase samples variety but also increase *classes variety* by creating synthetic classes from a linear combination of existing ones. The rationale behind this approach is that by introducing new artificial classes sharing similarities with the true classes the classification task becomes intentionally more complex, thereby pushing the training process to extract better data representations. Empirical validations of DA techniques in CV have consistently demonstrated their effectiveness across a diverse range of datasets, tasks, and training paradigms [8, 18, 31]. As a result, DA has become a ubiquitous component in the CV models training pipelines.

Considering time series instead, input transformations can either modify data *amplitude* (e.g., additive Gaussian noise) or manipulate *time* (e.g., composing new time series by combining different segments of existing ones). Similarly to CV, the research community has provided empirical evidence supporting the effectiveness of these transformations in biobehavioral [47] and health [49] domains. However, contrarily to CV, these transformations are less diverse and have been less widely adopted, possibly due to the stronger reliance on domain knowledge—an amplitude change on an electrocardiogram can be more difficult to properly tune compared to simply rotating an image.

Latent Space Transformations. Differently from traditional ML, DL models offer the ability to shape the feature extractor to create more "abstract" features. For example, Implicit Semantic Data Augmentation (ISDA) [42] first computes class-conditional covariance matrices based on intra-class feature variety; then, it augments features by translating real features along random directions sampled from a Gaussian distribution defined by the class-conditional covariance matrix. To avoid computational inefficiencies caused by explicitly augmenting each sample many times, ISDA computes an upper bound of the expected cross entropy loss on an enlarged feature set and takes this upper bound as the new loss function. Based on ISDA, and focused on data imbalance, Sample-Adaptive Feature Augmentation (SAFA) [19] extracts transferable features from the majority classes and translates features from the minority classes in accordance with the extracted semantic directions for augmentation.

Generative Models. In addition to traditional hand-crafted data augmentation techniques, generative models offer an alternative solution to generate samples variety. For instance, [6, 40] use a multi-modal diffusion model trained on an Internet-scale dataset composed of (image, text) pairs. Then, the model is used to synthesize new samples—text prompts tailored to specific downstream classification tasks are used as conditioning signal to create task-specific samples—to enlarge the training set for a classification task. While these types of generative models can provide high-quality samples variety, their design and application still requires a considerable amount of domain knowledge to be effective.

2.2   Data Augmentation in Traffic Classification

TC tasks usually rely on either packet time series (e.g., packet size, direction, Inter Arrival Time (IAT), etc., of the first 10–30 packets of a flow) or payload bytes (e.g., the first 784 bytes of a flow, possibly gathered by concatenating payload across different packets) arranged as 2d matrices. Recent literature also considers combining both input types into multi-modal architectures [2,4,24].

Such input representations and datasets exhibit three notable distinctions when compared to data from other ML/DL disciplines. First, TC datasets show *significant class imbalance*—this is a "native" property of network traffic as different applications enjoy different popularity and traffic dynamics while, for instance, many CV datasets are balanced. Second, TC input representation is typically *"small"* to adhere to desirable system design properties—network traffic should be (*i*) *early classified*, i.e., the application associated to a flow should be identified within the first few packets of a flow, and (*ii*) computational/memory resources required to represent a flow should be minimal as an in-network TC systems need to cope with hundreds of thousands of flow per second. Last, TC input data has *weak semantics*—the underlying application protocols (which may or not be known a priori) may not be easy to interpret even for domain experts when visually inspecting packet time series.

Hand-crafted DA. The combination of the above observations leads to have only a handful of studies adopting DA in TC. Rezaei et al. [32] created synthetic input samples by means of three hand-crafted DA strategies based on sampling multiple short sequences across the duration of a complete flow. Horowicz et al. [20] instead focused on a *flowpic* input representation—a 2d summary of the evolution of packets size throughout the duration of a flow—augmented by first altering the time series collected from the first 15 s of a flow and used to compute the flowpic. While both studies show the benefit of DA, these strategies violate the early classification principle as they both consider multiple seconds of traffic, thus they are better suited for post-mortem analysis only. Conversely, Xie et al. [1,46] recently proposed some packet series hand-crafted DA to tackle data shifts arising when applying a model on network traffic gathered from networks different from the ones used to collect the training dataset. Specifically, inspired by TCP protocol dynamics, authors proposed five packets time series augmentations (e.g., to mimic a packet lost/retransmission one can replicate a value at a later position in the time series) showing that they help to mitigate data shifts. Yet, differently from [20,32], the study in [46] lacks from an ablation of each individual augmentation's performance.

Generative Models. Last, [41,43,48] investigate augmentations based on GAN methods when using payload bytes as input for intrusion detection scenarios, i.e., a very special case of TC where the classification task is binary. More recently, [22] compared GAN and diffusion model for generating raw payload bytes traces while [37,38] instead leveraged GAN or diffusion models to generate 2D representations (namely GASF) of longer traffic flow signals for downstream traffic fingerprinting, anomaly detection, and TC.

2.3   Design Space

Search Space. Independently from the methodology and application discipline, DA performance can only be assessed via empirical studies, i.e., results are bound to the scenarios and the datasets used. Moreover, to find an efficient strategy one should consider an array of options, each likely subject to a different parametrization. In the case of hand-crafted DA, one can also opt for using *stacking* (i.e., applying a sequence of transformations) or *ensembling* (i.e., applying augmentations by selecting from a pool of candidates according to some sampling logic)— an exhaustive grid search is unfeasible given the large search space. Besides following guidelines to reduce the number of options [10], some studies suggest the use of reinforcement learning to guide the search space exploration [9]. Yet, no standard practice has emerged.

Quantifying Good Variety. As observed in TC literature [20,32,46], domain knowledge is key to design efficient augmentations. Yet, ingenuity might not be enough as models are commonly used as "black boxes", making it extremely challenging to establish a direct link between an augmentation technique and its impact on the final classification performance. For instance, rotation is considered a good image transformation as result of empirical studies. Likewise, generative models are trained on large image datasets but without an explicit connection to a classification task [33]—the design of the augmentation method itself is part of a trial-and-error approach and the definition of metrics quantifying the augmentation quality is still an open question.

One of the aspects to be considered when formulating such metrics is the *variety* introduced by the augmentations. Gontijo-Lopes et al. [11] propose metrics quantifying the distribution shift and diversity introduced by DA contrasting models performance with and without augmentations. Other literature instead focuses on mechanisms that can help defining desirable properties for augmentations. For instance, from the feature learning literature, [35,53] find that DA induces models to better learn rare/less popular but good features by altering their importance, thus improving model generalization performance. Samyak et al. [21] find that optimization trajectories are different when training on different augmentations and propose to aggregate the weights of models trained on different augmentations to obtain a more uniform distribution of feature patches, encouraging the learning of diverse and robust features.

Training Loss. Self-supervision and contrastive learning are DL training strategies that take advantage of augmentations by design. In a nutshell, contrastive learning consists of a 2-steps training process. First, a feature extractor is trained in a *self-supervised* manner with a contrastive loss function that pulls together different augmented "views" of a given sample while distancing them from views of other samples. Then, a classifier head is trained on top of the learned representation in a *supervised* manner using a few labeled samples—the better the feature representation, the lower the number of labeled samples required for training the head. Empirical studies have demonstrated the robustness of the feature representations learned with contrastive learning [8,13,30,50] and a few recent studies investigated contrastive learning also in TC [15,20,39,46].

Linking Generative Models to Classifiers. When we consider the specific case of using generative models to augment training data, we face a major challenge—generative models are not designed to target a specific downstream task [37,38,43]. While studies like [28] integrated a classifier in GAN training in the pursuit of improving the reliability the model, how to properly link and train a generative model to be sensitive to a downstream classification task is still an open question even in CV literature.

3   Our Goals and Methodology

Drawing insights from the literature reviewed in Sect. 2, we undertake a set of empirical campaigns to better understand hand-crafted DA when applied in the input space for TC task and address the following research goals:

G1. How to compare the performance of different augmentations? This includes investigating augmentations sensitivity to their hyper-parametrization and dataset properties (e.g., number of samples and classes).
G2. How augmented samples should be added to the training set and how many samples should be added? Is augmenting minority classes beneficial to mitigate class imbalance?
G3. Why some augmentations are more effective than others?
G4. Does combining multiple augmentations provide extra performance improvement?

   In the remainder of this section, we motivate each goal and introduce the methodology we adopted to address them.

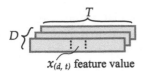

D   Number of packet features

T   Number of packets per feature

$\sigma_{(d,t)}^y$ Standard deviation of a generic coordinate (d, t) for class y

$\overline{\sigma_{(d,:)}^y}$ Average standard deviation for dimension d for class y

Fig. 1. Input sample **x** shape and related notation.

Table 1. Amplitude augmentations.

Name	Pkts Feat. Size Dir IAT	Description	Example magnitude $\alpha=0.5$
Gaussian Noise	◑ ○ ◑	Add independently sampled Gaussian noise to Size or IAT *Details:* Sample a feature $d\in\{Size, IAT\}$ and add Gaussian noise to its values $x_{(d,t)}+\varepsilon_t$ where $\varepsilon_t\sim\mathcal{N}(0,\alpha\{\sigma_{(d,t)}^y\}^2)$ px	
Spike Noise [44]	◑ ○ ◑	Add independently sampled Gaussian noise to Size or IAT *Details:* Sample a feature $d\in\{Size, IAT\}$ and add Gaussian noise to up to 3 of its non-zero values $x_{(d,t)}+|\varepsilon_t|$ where $\varepsilon_t\sim\mathcal{N}(0,\alpha\{\sigma_{(d,t)}^y\}^2)$	
Gaussian WrapUp [13]	◑ ○ ◑	Scale Size or IAT by independently sampled Gaussian values *Details:* Sample a feature $d\in\{Size, IAT\}$ and multiply Gaussian noise to its values $x_{(d,t)}\cdot\varepsilon_t$ with $\varepsilon_t\sim\mathcal{N}(1+0.01\alpha,0.02\alpha\{\sigma_{(d,t)}^y\}^2)$	
Sine WrapUp [30]	◑ ○ ◑	Scale Size or IAT by sinusoidal noise *Details:* Sample a feature $d\in\{Size, IAT\}$ and multiply its values by a sine-like noise $x_{(d,t)}\cdot\varepsilon_t$ with $\varepsilon_t=[1+0.02\alpha\cdot\overline{\sigma_{(d,:)}^y}\cdot\sin(\frac{4\pi t}{T}+\theta)]$ and $\theta\sim U[0,2\pi[$	
Constant WrapUp [20]	○ ○ ●	Scale IAT by a single randomly sampled value *Details:* Sample a single uniformly sampled value $\epsilon\sim U[a,b]$ and perform $x_t\cdot\epsilon$ to all x_t of IAT with $a=1+\overline{\sigma_{(d,:)}^y}\cdot(0.06-0.02\alpha);\ b=1+\overline{\sigma_{(d,:)}^y}\cdot(0.14+0.02\alpha)$	

○ feature never used; ◑ feature selected randomly; ● feature always used.
In the figures, black solid lines ■ for original samples, red ● lines for augmented samples; x-axis for time series index and y-axis the feature value (either packet size or IAT).

Table 2. Masking augmentations

All three features (Size, DIR and IAT) are affected by all transformations.

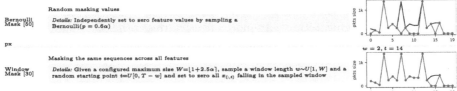

Name	Description	Example magnitude $\alpha=0.5$
Bernoulli Mask [50] px	Random masking values *Details:* Independently set to zero feature values by sampling a Bernoulli($p=0.6\alpha$)	
Window Mask [30]	Masking the same sequences across all features *Details:* Given a configured maximum size $W=\lfloor 1+2.5\alpha\rceil$, sample a window length $w\sim U[1,W]$ and a random starting point $t=U[0,T-w]$ and set to zero all $x_{(:,t)}$ falling in the sampled window	$w=2, t=14$

In the figures, black solid lines ■ for original samples, red ● lines for augmented samples.

Table 3. Sequence order augmentations.

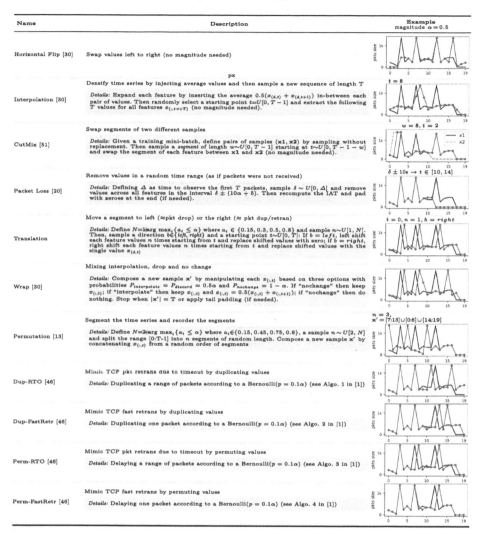

Name	Description	Example magnitude $\alpha = 0.5$
Horizontal Flip [30]	Swap values left to right (no magnitude needed)	
Interpolation [30]	Densify time series by injecting average values and then sample a new sequence of length T *Details:* Expand each feature by inserting the average $0.5(x_{(d,t)} + x_{(d,t+1)})$ in-between each pair of values. Then randomly select a starting point $t{\sim}U[0, T-1]$ and extract the following T values for all features $x_{(:,t:t+T)}$ (no magnitude needed).	
CutMix [51]	Swap segments of two different samples *Details:* Given a training mini-batch, define pairs of samples (**x1**, **x2**) by sampling without replacement. Then sample a *segment* of length $w{\sim}U[0, T-1]$ starting at $t{\sim}U[0, T-1-w]$ and swap the segment of each feature between **x1** and **x2** (no magnitude needed).	
Packet Loss [20]	Remove values in a random time range (as if packets were not received) *Details:* Defining Δ as time to observe the first T packets, sample $\delta \sim U[0, \Delta]$ and remove values across all features in the interval $\delta \pm (10\alpha + 5)$. Then recompute the IAT and pad with zeroes at the end (if needed).	
Translation	Move a segment to left ($\approx$pkt drop) or the right ($\approx$ pkt dup/retran) *Details:* Define $N=\frac{1}{2}\arg\max_i\{a_i \leq \alpha\}$ where $a_i \in \{0.15, 0.3, 0.5, 0.8\}$ and sample $n{\sim}U[1, N]$. Then, sample a direction $b{\in}\{left, right\}$ and a starting point $t{\sim}U[0, T]$; If $b = left$, left shift each feature values n times starting from t and replace shifted values with zero; if $b = right$, right shift each feature values n times starting from t and replace shifted values with the single value $x_{(d,t)}$	
Wrap [30]	Mixing interpolation, drop and no change *Details:* Compose a new sample x' by manipulating each $x_{(:,t)}$ based on three options with probabilities $P_{interpolate} = P_{discard} = 0.5\alpha$ and $P_{nochange} = 1 - \alpha$. If "nochange" then keep $x_{(:,t)}$; if "interpolate" then keep $x_{(:,t)}$ and $x_{(:,t)} = 0.5(x_{(:,t)} + x_{(:,t+1)})$; if "nochange" then do nothing. Stop when $|x'| = T$ or apply tail padding (if needed).	
Permutation [13]	Segment the time series and reorder the segments *Details:* Define $N=2\arg\max_i\{a_i \leq \alpha\}$ where $a_i{\in}\{0.15, 0.45, 0.75, 0.9\}$, a sample $n \sim U[2, N]$ and split the range $[0;T-1]$ into n segments of random length. Compose a new sample x' by concatenating $x_{(:,t)}$ from a random order of segments.	
Dup-RTO [46]	Mimic TCP pkt retrans due to timeout by duplicating values *Details:* Duplicating a range of packets according to a Bernoulli($p = 0.1\alpha$) (see Algo. 1 in [1])	
Dup-FastRetr [46]	Mimic TCP fast retrans by duplicating values *Details:* Duplicating one packet according to a Bernoulli($p = 0.1\alpha$) (see Algo. 2 in [1])	
Perm-RTO [46]	Mimic TCP pkt retrans due to timeout by permuting values *Details:* Delaying a range of packets according to a Bernoulli($p = 0.1\alpha$) (see Algo. 3 in [1])	
Perm-FastRetr [46]	Mimic TCP fast retrans by permuting values *Details:* Delaying one packet according to a Bernoulli($p = 0.1\alpha$) (see Algo. 4 in [1])	

In the figures, black solid lines ■ for original samples, red ● lines for augmented samples.

3.1 Benchmarking Hand-Crafted DA (G1)

Figure 1 sketches a typical TC input **x**, i.e., a multivariate time series with D dimensions (one for each packet feature) each having T values (one for each packet) while $x_{(d,t)}$ is the value of **x** at coordinates (d,t) where $d \in \{0..D-1\}$ and $t \in \{0..T-1\}$. In particular, in this work, we consider $D = 3$ packet features, namely packet size, direction, and Inter Arrival Time (IAT), and the first $T = 20$ packets of a flow. We also define $\mathbf{x}' = \text{Aug}(\mathbf{x}, \alpha)$ as an augmentation, i.e., the transformation $\mathbf{x}'$ of sample $\mathbf{x}$ is subject to a *magnitude* $\alpha \in]0,1[$ controlling the intensity of the transformation (1 = maximum modification).

Augmentations Pool. In this study, we considered a set $\mathcal{A}$ of 18 augmentation functions. These functions can be categorized into 3 families: 5 *amplitude* transformations, which introduce different type of jittering to the feature values (Table 1); 2 *masking* transformations, which force certain feature values to zero (Table 2); and 11 *sequence* transformations, which modify the order of feature values (Table 3). It is important to note that, given a sample $\mathbf{x}$, amplitude augmentations are solely applied to either packet size or IAT while packet direction is never altered since the latter is a binary feature and does not have amplitude (i.e., it can be -1 or 1). On the contrary, masking and sequence augmentations are applied to all features in parallel (e.g., if a transformation requires to swap $t = 1$ with $t = 6$, all features are swapped accordingly $x_{(i,1)} \leftrightarrow x_{(i,6)}$ for $\forall i \in \{0..D-1\}$). For each augmentation, Tables 1-3 report a reference example annotating its parametrization (if any).

By adopting such a large pool of augmentations our empirical campaign offers several advantages. First, we are able to investigate a broader range of design possibilities compared to previous studies. Second, it enables us to contrast different families and assess if any of them is more prone to disrupt class semantics. Considering the latter, TC literature [20,32,46] predominantly investigate sequence transformations (typically acting only on packet timestamp) with only [46] experimenting with masking and amplitude variation, yet targeting scenarios where models are exposed to data shifts due to maximum segment size (MSS) changes, i.e., the network properties related to the training set are different from the ones of the test set.

Augmentations Magnitude. As described in Tables 1-3, each augmentation has some predefined static parameters[1] while the magnitude α is the single hyper-parameter controlling random sampling mechanisms contributing to defining the final transformed samples. To quantify augmentations sensitivity to α, we contrast two scenarios following CV literature practice: a static value of $\alpha = 0.5$ and a uniformly sampled value $\alpha \sim U[0,1]$ extracted for each augmented sample.

Datasets Size and Task Complexity. Supervised tasks, especially when modeled via DL, benefit from large datasets. For instance, as previously mentioned, some CV literature pretrains generative models on large datasets and use those models to obtain auxiliary training data for classification tasks. While data availability clearly plays a role, at the same time the task complexity is equivalently important—a task with just a few classes but a lot of data does not necessarily yield higher accuracy than a task with more classes and less data. To understand how augmentations interplay with these dynamics, it is relevant to evaluate augmentations across datasets of different sizes and number of classes.

---

[1] These parameters are tuned via preliminary investigations.

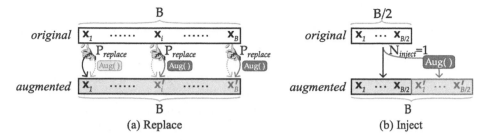

Fig. 2. Training batch creation policies.

3.2 Training Batches Composition (G2)

In order to mitigate any undesirable shifts introduced by artificial samples, it is necessary to balance original and augmented samples. Yet, the way original and augmented samples are combined to form the augmented training set is a design choice. For instance, in TC literature, [20, 32] augment the data before starting the training, while [46] augments mini-batches during the training process. In this work, we apply augmentation samples to a training mini-batch of size B, with the two policies sketched in Fig. 2. *Replace* substitutes an original sample x_i with its augmentation by sampling from a Bernoulli (P = $P_{replace}$) random variable—during one training epoch, approximately a $P_{replace}$ fraction of the original data is "hidden". Instead, *Inject* increases the batch size by augmenting each sample N_{inject} times (e.g., in Fig. 2 the original batch size is doubled by setting $N_{inject} = 1$).

3.3 Latent Space Geometry (G3)

Augmented samples play a crucial role in model training, just like the original training samples from which they are derived. To understand the impact of augmentations on the improvement or detriment of classification performance, we propose to examine the latent space of the classifier. In order to conduct a comprehensive analysis, we need to consider two aspects applicable to any supervised classification task.

Augmentation-vs-Test. ML methods operate on the assumption that training data serves as a "proxy" for test samples, i.e., the patterns learned on training data "generalize" to testing data as the two sets of data resemble each other properties. In this context, augmentations can be considered as a means for fostering data generalization by incorporating samples that resemble even more testing data compared to what is available in training data. However, it is important to empirically quantify this effect by measuring, for instance, the distance between augmented and test samples. In other words, we aim to quantify up to which extent augmented samples are better at mimicking test samples compared to the original data.

Augmentation-vs-Train. The performance of a feature extractor greatly depends on how well the feature extractor separates different classes in the latent space. Data augmentations play a role in shaping intra/inter-class relationships created by the feature extractor in the latent space. For instance, an augmentation that generates samples far away from the region of a class can *disrupt class semantics*—the augmentation is introducing a new behavior/mode making it hard for the classifier to be effective. At the same time, however, expanding the region of a class can be a beneficial design choice—augmentations that enable a better definition of class boundaries simplify the task of the classifier. Understanding such dynamics requires empirical observations, for instance, by comparing the distance between original training data and augmented data. In other words, we aim to verify if augmentations yielding good performance are in a "sweet spot": they create samples that are neither too close (i.e., introduce too little variety) nor too far (i.e., disrupt class semantics) from original samples.

3.4   Combining Augmentations (G4)

To address **G1**, each trained model is associated to an individual augmentation. However, in CV it is very common to combine multiple augmentations [8]. Hence, we aim to complement **G1** by measuring the performance of three different policies augmenting mini-batches based on a set $\mathcal{A}' \subset \mathcal{A}$ composed of top-performing augmentations based on the **G1** benchmark: the *Ensemble* policy uniformly samples one of the augmentations in $\mathcal{A}'$ independently for each mini-batch sample; the *RandomStack* policy randomly shuffles $\mathcal{A}'$ independently for each mini-batch sample before applying all augmentations; finally, the *MaskedStack* policy uses a predefined order for $\mathcal{A}'$ but each augmentation is associated to a masking probability, i.e., each sample in the mini-batch independently selects a subset of augmentations of the predefined order.

4   Experimental Settings

4.1   Datasets

To address our research goals we considered the datasets summarized in Table 4. MIRAGE-19 [3] is a *public* dataset gathering traffic logs from 20 popular Android apps[2] collected at the ARCLAB laboratory of the University of Napoli Federico II. Multiple measurement campaigns were operated by instrumenting 3 Android devices handed off to ≈300 volunteers (students and researchers) for interacting with the selected apps for short sessions. Each session resulted in a pcap file and an strace log mapping each socket to the corresponding Android application name. Pcaps were then post-processed to obtain bidirectional flow logs by grouping all packets belonging to the same 5-tuple (srcIP, srcPort, dstIP, dst-Port, L4proto) and extracting both aggregate metrics (e.g., total bytes, packets,

---

[2] Despite being advertised with having traffic from 40 apps, the *public* version of the dataset only contains 20 apps.

Table 4. Summary of datasets properties.

Name	Classes	Curation	Flows per-class				Pkts
			all	*min*	*max*	*ρ*	*mean*
MIRAGE-19 [3]	20	none	122 k	1,986	11,737	5.9	23
		>10pkts	64 k	1,013	7,505	7.4	17
MIRAGE-22 [14]	9	none	59 k	2,252	18,882	8.4	3,068
		>10pkts	26 k	970	4,437	4.6	6,598
Enterprise	100	none	2.9 M	501,221	5,715	87.7	2,312

ρ : ratio between max and min number of flows per-class—the larger the value, the higher the imbalance;

etc.), per-packet time series (packet size, direction, TCP flags, etc.), raw packets payload bytes (encoded as a list of integer values) and mapping a ground-truth label by means of the `strace` logs.

MIRAGE-22 [14] is another *public* dataset collected by the same research team and with the same instrumentation as MIRAGE-19 which targets 9 video meeting applications used to perform webinars (i.e., meetings with multiple attendees and a single broadcaster), audio calls (i.e., meetings with two participants using audio-only), video calls (i.e., meetings with two participants using both audio and video), and video conferences, (i.e., meetings involving more than two participants broadcasting audio and video).

Enterprise is instead a *private*[3] dataset collected by monitoring network flows from vantage points deployed in residential access and enterprise campus networks. For each flow, the logs report multiple aggregate metrics (number of bytes, packets, TCP flags counters, round trip time statistics, etc.), and the packet time series of packet size, direction and IAT for the first 50 packets of each flow. Moreover, each flow record is also enriched with an application label provided by a commercial DPI software directly integrated into the monitoring solution and supporting hundreds of applications and services.

Data Curation. Table 4 compares different dataset properties. For instance, MIRAGE-19 and MIRAGE-22 are quite different from each other despite being obtained via the same platform. Specifically, MIRAGE-19 gathers around 2× more flows than MIRAGE-22 but those are 100× shorter. As expected, all datasets are subject to class imbalance measured by ρ, i.e., the ratio between maximum and minimum number of samples per class. However, Enterprise exhibits a larger class imbalance with respect to the other two datasets. Last, while Enterprise did not require specific pre-processing, both MIRAGE-19 and MIRAGE-22 required a curation to remove *background traffic*—flows created by netd deamon, SSDP, Android google management services and other services unrelated to the target Android apps—and flows having less than 10 packets.

---

[3] Due to NDA we are not allowed to share the dataset.

Data Folds and Normalization. As described in Sect. 3.1, each flow is modeled via a multivariate time series $\mathbf{x}$ consisting of $D = 3$ features (packets size, direction, and IAT) related to the first $T = 20$ packets (applying zero padding in the tail where needed). From the curated datasets we created 80 random 70/15/15 train/validation/test folds. We then processed each train+val split to extract statistics that we used for normalizing the data and to drive the augmentation process. Specifically, we computed both per-coordinate (d, t) and global (i.e., flattening all flows time series into a single array) mean and standard deviation for each class—these statistics provided us the $\sigma^y_{(d,t)}$ and $\sigma^y_{(:,t)}$ needed for the augmentations (see Fig. 1 and Tables 1-3). For IAT, we also computed the global 99th percentile across all classes q^{99}_{iat}. Given a multi-variate input $\mathbf{x}$, we first clip packet size values in the range $[0, 1460]$ and IAT values in the range $[1e\text{-}7, q^{99}_{iat}]$. Due to high skew of IAT distributions, we also log10-scaled the IAT feature values.[4] Last, all features are standardized to provide values $x_{(d,t)} \in [0, 1]$.

Model Architecture and Training. We rely on a 1d-CNN based neural network architecture with a backbone including 2 ResNet blocks followed by a linear head resulting in a compact architecture of $\approx$100k parameters. (see Fig. 7 and Listing 1.1 in the appendix for details). Models are trained for a maximum of 500 epochs with a batch size B = 1,024 via an AdamW optimizer with a weight decay of 0.0001 and a cosine annealing learning rate scheduler initialized at 0.001. Training is subject to early stopping by monitoring if the validation accuracy does not improve by 0.02 within 20 epochs. We coded our modeling framework using PyTorch and PyTorch Lightning and ran our modeling campaigns on Linux servers equipped with multiple NVIDIA Tesla V100 GPUs. We measured the classification performance via the weighted F1 score considering a reference baseline where training is not subject to augmentations.

5   Results

In this section, we discuss the results of our modeling campaigns closely following the research goals introduced in Sect. 3.

5.1   Augmentations Benchmark (G1)

We start by presenting the overall performance of the selected augmentations. Specifically, Table 5 collects results obtained by applying augmentations via Inject with $N_{inject} = 1$ (i.e., each original sample is augmented once)[5] and sampling uniformly the magnitude $\alpha \sim U[0, 1]$. Table 5 shows the average weighted F1 score across 80 runs and related 95th-percentile confidence intervals.

---

[4] We did not log-scale packet sizes values as we found this can reduce accuracy based on preliminary empirical assessments.

[5] Since we train the reference baseline with a batch size B = 1024, when adding augmentations we instead adopt B = 512 (which doubles via injection).

Table 5. Augmentations benchmark (**G1**).

	Augmentation	MIRAGE-19	MIRAGE-22	Enterprise
Baseline	None	75.43±.10	94.92±.07	92.43±.33
Amplitude	Constant WrapUp	0.61±.12	0.36±.09	−0.02±.15
	Gaussian Noise	0.89±.11	0.24±.09	0.15±.14
	Gaussian WrapUp	1.01±.13	0.74±.09	0.24±.12
	Spike Noise	1.66±.12	0.91±.09	0.93±.13
	Sine WrapUp	0.63±.11	0.25±.09	−0.06±.16
Masking	Bernoulli Mask	2.55±.12	1.29±.09	1.25±.16
	Window Mask	2.37±.13	1.08±.09	1.18±.16
Sequence	CutMix	2.65±.13	1.40±.10	−0.21±.10
	Dup-FastRetr	3.23±.13	1.56±.09	0.83±.15
	Dup-RTO	2.89±.13	1.33±.09	0.91±.15
	Horizontal Flip	−0.71±.11	−0.52±.09	−0.88±.15
	Interpolation	0.44±.12	0.53±.10	−0.61±.14
	Packet Loss	0.88±.12	0.66±.09	0.60±.22
	Permutation	3.67±.13	1.97±.09	0.89±.08
	Perm-RTO	3.15±.12	1.54±.09	0.88±.12
	Perm-FastRetr	2.11±.12	1.00±.09	0.74±.26
	Translation	4.40±.13	2.02±.09	0.95±.15
	Wrap	4.11±.13	2.09±.08	0.57±.12

The top-3 best and worst augmentations are color-coded.

Reference Baseline. We highlight that our reference baseline performance for MIRAGE-19 and MIRAGE-22 are *qualitatively* aligned with previous literature that used those datasets. For instance, Table 1 in [14] reports a weighted F1 of 97.89 for a 1d-CNN model when using the first 2,048 payload bytes as input for MIRAGE-22; Fig. 1 in [5] instead shows a weighted F1 of ≈75% for 100 packets time series input for MIRAGE-19. Notice however that since these studies use training configurations not exactly identical to ours, a direct comparison with our results should be taken with caution. Yet, despite these differences, we confirm MIRAGE-19 to be a more challenging classification task compared to MIRAGE-22. However, we argue that such a difference is unlikely depending only on the different number of classes (MIRAGE-19 has 20 classes while MIRAGE-22 only 9). This is evident by observing that Enterprise yields very high performance despite having 10× more classes than the other two datasets. We conjecture instead the presence of "cross-app traffic" such as flows generated by libraries/services common across multiple apps from the same provider (e.g., apps or services provided by Google

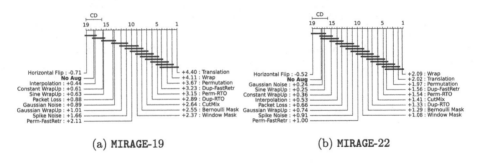

(a) MIRAGE-19   (b) MIRAGE-22

Fig. 3. Augmentations rank and critical distance **(G1)**.

or Facebook) and/or the presence of ads traffic,[6] but the datasets raw data is not sufficiently detailed to investigate our hypothesis.

Takeaways. *While the classification tasks complexity is well captured by models performance, it does not necessarily relate to the number of classes or dataset size. These effects are visible only when studying multiple datasets at once, but unfortunately a lot of TC studies focus on individual datasets.*

Augmentations Rank. Overall, all augmentations are beneficial except for Horizontal Flip which, as we shall see in Sect. 5.3, breaks class semantics. As expected, not all augmentations provide the same gain and their effectiveness may vary across datasets. Specifically, *sequence* and *masking* better suit our TC tasks.

For a more fine-grained performance comparison, we complement Table 5 results by analyzing augmentations rank via a critical distance by following the procedure described in [12]. Specifically, for each of the 80 modeling runs we first ranked the augmentations from best to worst (e.g., if augmentations A, B, and C yield a weighted F1 of 0.9, 0.7, and 0.8, their associated rankings would be 1, 3, and 2) splitting ties using the average ranking of the group (e.g., if augmentations A, B, and C yield a weighted F1 of 0.9, 0.9 and 0.8, their associated rankings would be 1.5, 1.5, and 3). This process is then repeated across the 80 runs and a global rank is obtained by computing the mean rank for each augmentation. Last, these averages are compared pairwise using a post-hoc Nemenyi test to identify which groups of augmentations are statistically equivalent. This decision is made using a Critical Distance $CD = q_\alpha \sqrt{k(k+1)/6N}$, where q_α is based on the Studentized range statistic divided by $\sqrt{2}$, k is equal to the number of augmentations compared and N is equal to the number of samples used. Results are then collected in Fig. 3 where each augmentation is highlighted with its average rank (the lower the better) and horizontal bars connect augmentations that are statistically equivalent. For instance, while Table 5 shows that Translate is the best on average, Fig. 3 shows that {Translate, Wrap, Permutation,

---

[6] MIRAGE-22 focuses on video meeting apps which are all from different providers and ads free by design.

Dup-FastRetr} are statistically equivalent. We remark that Fig. 3 refers to MIRAGE-19 and MIRAGE-22 but similar considerations hold for Enterprise as well.

Recall that our training process is subject to an early stop mechanism. Interestingly, we observed that augmentations yielding better performance also present a longer number of training epochs (see Fig. 8 in Appendix). This hints that effective augmentations foster better data representations extraction, although some CV studies also show that early stopping might not necessarily be the best option to achieve high accuracy in some scenarios. An in-depth investigation of these training mechanisms is however out of scope for this paper.

Takeaways. Augmentations bring benefits that, in absolute scale, are comparable to what is observed in CV literature [27]. Our benchmark shows that TC sequencing and masking augmentations are better options than amplitude augmentations. This confirms previous literature that implicitly discarded amplitude augmentations. Finally, despite performance ranks can suggest more performant augmentations (e.g., Translation or Bernoulli mask), agreement between datasets seems more qualitative than punctual (e.g., masking is preferred to sequencing for Enterprise , but the reverse is true for the other two datasets).

Sensitivity to Magnitude. Most of the augmentations we analyzed are subject to a magnitude α hyper-parameter (see Tables 1-3) that is randomly selected for the results in Table 5. To investigate the relationship between classification performance and augmentation magnitude we selected 3 augmentations among the top performing ones {Translation, Wrap, Permutation} and three among the worst performing {Gaussian Noise, Sine WrapUp, Constant WrapUp}.[7] For each augmentation, we performed 10 modeling runs using magnitude $\alpha = 0.5$ and we contrasted these results with the related runs from the previous modeling campaign. Specifically, by grouping all results we obtained a binary random-vs-static performance comparison which we investigated through a Wilcoxon signed rank sum test that indicated *no statistical difference*, i.e., the selection of magnitude is not a distinctive factor to drive the augmentation performance. The same conclusion holds true when repeating the analysis for each individual augmentation rather than grouping them together.

Takeaways. Although we do not observe any dependency on the augmentation magnitude α, augmentations performance can still be affected by their tuning (as will be discussed further in Sect. 5.3). Unfortunately, this tuning process often relies on a trial-and-error process, making it challenging to operate manually.

5.2   Training Batches Composition (G2)

Correctly mixing original with augmented data is an important design choice.

Batching Policies. To show this, we considered the three policies introduced in Sect. 3.2: Replace (which randomly substitutes training samples with augmented ones), Inject (which expands batches by adding augmented samples),

---

[7] We excluded HorizontalFlip as it hurt performance and Interpolation since it does not depend from a magnitude.

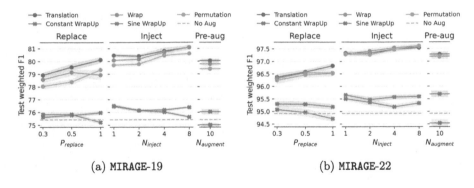

(a) MIRAGE-19   (b) MIRAGE-22

Fig. 4. Comparing *Replace*, *Inject* and *Pre-augment* batch creation policies **(G2)**.

and Pre-augment (which expands the whole training set before the training start).[8] Batching policies are compared against training without augmentations making sure that each training step has the same batch size $B = 1{,}204$.[9] Based on Sect. 5.1 results, we limited our comparison to {Translation, Wrap, Permutation} against {Sine WrapUp, Constant WrapUp} as representative of good and poor augmentations across the three datasets under study. We configured Replace with $P_{replace} \in \{0.3, 0.5, 1\}$, Inject with $N_{inject} \in \{1, 2, 4, 8\}$ and augmented each training sample 10 times for Pre-augment. Figure 4 collects the results with lines showing the average performance while shaded areas correspond to 95th percentile confidence intervals. Overall, top-performing augmentations (● marker) show a positive trend—the higher the volume of augmentations the better the performance—while poor-performing augmentations (× marker) have small deviations from the baseline (dashed line). Based on performance, we can order *Replace* < *Pre-augment* < *Inject*, i.e., the computationally cheaper Pre-augment is on par with the more expensive Replace when $P_{replace} = 1$ but Inject is superior to both alternatives.

Takeaways. *On the one hand, Inject shows a positive trend that perhaps continues beyond $N_{inject} > 8$.[10] On the other hand, the performance gain may be too little compared to the computational cost when using many augmentations. For instance, $N_{inject} = 8$ requires 3× longer training compared to $N_{inject} = 1$.*

Class-weighted Sampling. TC datasets are typically imbalanced (see Table 4). It is then natural to wonder if/how augmentations can help improve performance for classes with fewer samples, namely *minority classes*. While the batching policies discussed do not alter the natural distribution of the number of samples

---

[8] Based on our experience on using code-bases related to publications, we were unable to pinpoint if any of those techniques is preferred in CV literature.

[9] For instance, when $N_{inject} = 1$, a training run needs to be configured with $B = 512$ as the mini-batches size doubles via augmentation.

[10] The limit of our experimental campaigns were just bounded by training time and servers availability so it is feasible to go beyond the considered scenarios.

Table 6. Impact of class-weighted sampler on MIRAGE-19 (**G2**).

	Cls samp.	Majority classes			Minority classes		
		Pre	*Rec*	*weight F1*	*Pre*	*Rec*	*weight F1*
No Aug	with	83.90±.21	81.01±.21	82.36±.14	56.63±.38	60.78±.26	58.18±.21
	without	81.60±.23	82.93±.19	82.16±.12	62.29±.48	58.02±.38	59.78±.27
	diff	2.30±.32	−1.92±.28	0.20±.20	−5.66±.60	2.76±.46	−1.60±.35
Translation	with	89.12±.09	84.26±.11	86.43±.08	60.71±.24	68.64±.17	63.65±.10
	without	85.36±.14	86.73±.10	85.86±.09	69.69±.25	64.14±.25	66.20±.22
	diff	3.77±.06	−2.48±.02	0.57±.02	−8.98±.04	4.50±.09	−2.55±.05

per class, alternative techniques like Random Over Sampling (ROS) and Random Under Sampling (RUS) allow to replicate/drop samples for minority/majority classes [23]. A *class-weighted sampler* embodies a more refined version of those mechanisms and composes training mini-batches by selecting samples with a probability inversely proportional to the classes size—each training epoch results in a balanced dataset. When combined with augmentations, this further enhance minority classes variety.

The adoption of a class-weighted sampler seems a good idea in principle. Yet, the enforced balancing in our experience leads to conflicting results. We showcase this in Table 6 where we show Precision, Recall, and weighted F1 for 20 runs trained with/without a weighted sampler and with/without Translation (selected as representative of a good augmentation across datasets). We break down the performance between majority and minority classes and report per-metric differences when using or not the weighted sampler. The table refers to MIRAGE-19 but similar results can be obtained for the other datasets. Ideally, one would hope to observe only positive differences with larger benefits for minority classes. In practice, only the Recall for minority classes improves and overall we observe a poorer weighted F1 (−0.26 across all classes). By investigating misclassifications, we found that majority classes are more confused with minority classes and when introducing augmentations those effects are further magnified.

Takeaways. *Paying too much attention to minority classes can perturb the overall classifier balance, so we discourage the use of class-weighted samplers.*

5.3 Latent Space Geometry (G3)

Table 5 allows to identify effective augmentations bringing significant benefits in terms of model performance. However, to understand the causes behind the performance gaps we need to investigate how original, augmented, and test samples relate to each other.

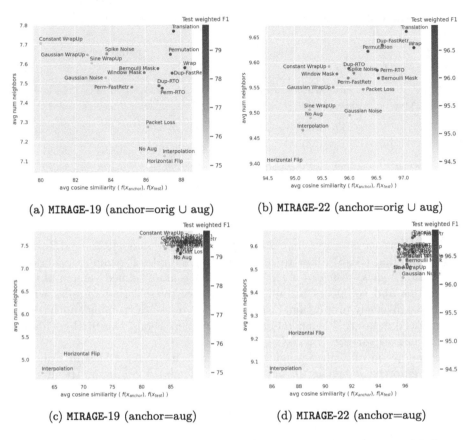

(a) MIRAGE-19 (anchor=orig ∪ aug)   (b) MIRAGE-22 (anchor=orig ∪ aug)

(c) MIRAGE-19 (anchor=aug)   (d) MIRAGE-22 (anchor=aug)

Fig. 5. Investigating train, augmented and test samples relationships **(G3)**.

Augmented-vs-Test Samples. We start our analysis by taking the point of view of the test samples. Specifically, we investigated which type of points are found in the "neighbourhood" of a test sample. To do so, we started creating "true anchors" by projecting both the original training data and 5 augmentations of each training sample—these anchors are "proxy" of what is presented to the model during training. Then we projected the test samples and looked for the closest 10 anchors (based on cosine similarity) of each test sample. Finally, we counted how many of the 10 anchors share the same label as the test samples. Results for each augmentation are reported in Fig. 5 for MIRAGE-19 and MIRAGE-22 (similar results holds for Enterprise) as a scatter plot where the coordinates of each point correspond to the average number of anchors with the correct label found and their average cosine similarity with respect to the test sample. Each augmentation is color-coded with respect to its weighted F1 score.

Despite both metrics vary in a subtle range, such variations suffice to capture multiple effects. First of all, considering the layout of the scatter plot, we expected good transformations to be placed in the top-right corner. This is

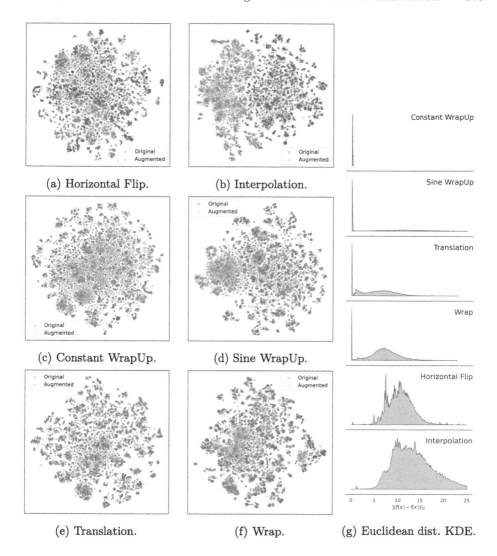

(a) Horizontal Flip.   (b) Interpolation.

(c) Constant WrapUp.   (d) Sine WrapUp.

(e) Translation.   (f) Wrap.   (g) Euclidean dist. KDE.

Fig. 6. Comparing original and augmented samples in the latent space **(G3)**.

indeed the case as presented in Fig. 5 (a-b) where darker colors (higher weighted F1) concentrate in the top-right corner. However, while MIRAGE-22 (Fig. 5(a)) shows a linear correlation between the two metrics, MIRAGE-19 (Fig. 5(a)) shows outliers, most notably Horizontal Flip, Interpolation, and Constant Wrapup.

Figure 5 (c-d) complement the analysis by showing results when considering only augmented samples as anchors. Differently from before, now Horizontal Flip and Interpolation are found to be the most dissimilar to the test samples—this is signaling that augmentations are possibly disrupting class semantics, i.e., they are introducing unnecessary high variety.

Last, for each test sample we looked at the closest augmented anchor and the closest original sample anchor with the same label. The average ratio of those pairwise distances is centered around 1—augmented samples "mimic" test samples as much as the original samples do.

Takeaways. *Top-performing augmentations do not better mimic test samples compared to original samples. Rather, they help training the feature extractor* $f(\cdot)$ *so that projected test samples are found in neighborhood of points likely to have the expected label.*

Augmented-vs-Original Samples. We complement the previous analysis by investigating original $\mathbf{x}$ and augmented $\mathbf{x}'$ samples relationships. Differently from before, for this analysis original samples are augmented once. Then all points are projected in the latent space $f(\mathbf{x})$ and $f(\mathbf{x}')$ and visualized by means of a 2d t-SNE projection.[11] We also compute the Kernel Density Estimation (KDE) of the Euclidean distance across all pairs. Figure 6 presents the results for 2 top-performing (Translate, Wrap) and 4 poor-performing (Constant Wrapup, Interpolation, Sine Wrapup, Horizontal Flip) augmentations for MIRAGE-19. Points in the t-SNE charts are plotted with alpha transparency, hence color saturation highlights prevalence of either augmented or original samples.

Linking back to the previous observations about Horizontal Flip and Interpolation, results now show the more "aggressive" nature of Interpolation—the t-SNE chart is split vertically with the left (right) side occupied by augmented (original) samples only and the Euclidean distance KDEs show heavier tails. By recalling their definition, while it might be easy to realize why Horizontal Flip is a poor choice—a client will never observe the end of the flow before seeing the beginning, hence they are too artificious—it is difficult to assess a priori the effect of Interpolation. Overall, both augmentations break class semantics.

At the opposite side of the performance range we find augmentations like Sine WrapUp and Constant WrapUp. From Fig. 6 we can see that both introduce little-to-no variety—the Euclidean distance distributions are centered around zero. That said, comparing their t-SNE charts we can still observe a major difference between the two transformations which relates to their design. Specifically, Constant WrapUp is applied only to IAT and introduces negligible modifications to the original samples. Conversely, Sine WrapUp is applied on either packet size or IAT. As for Constant WrapUP, the changes to IAT are subtle, while variations of packet size lead to generating an extra "mode" (notice the saturated cluster of points on the left side of the t-SNE plot). In other words, besides the design of the augmentation itself, identifying a good parametrization is very challenging and in this case is also feature-dependent.

Compared to the previous, Translate and Wrap have an in-between behavior—the body of the KDEs show distances neither too far nor too close and the t-SNE charts show a non-perfect overlap with respect to the original samples. Overall, both these augmentations show positive signs of good sample variety.

---

[11] Our model architecture uses a latent space of 256 dimensions (see Listing 1.1) which the t-SNE representation compresses into a 2d space.

Table 7. Combining augmentations **(G4)**.

	Augmentation	MIRAGE-19	MIRAGE-22
Baseline	No Aug	75.43±.10	94.92±.07
Single	Translation	4.40±.13	2.02±.09
	Wrap	4.11±.13	2.09±.08
	Permutation	3.67±.13	1.97±.09
Combined	Ensemble	4.44±.12	2.18±.09
	RandomStack	4.17±.12	2.18±.09
	MaskedStack ($p = 0.3$)	4.45±.13	2.26±.09
	MaskedStack ($p = 0.5$)	4.60±.15	2.24±.09
	MaskedStack ($p = 0.7$)	4.63±.14	2.18±.10

Takeaways. *Effective transformations operate in a "sweet spot": they neither introduce too little variety—traditional policies like Random Over Sampling (ROS) and Random Under Sampling (RUS) [23] are ineffective—nor they break classes semantic by introducing artificial "modes".*

5.4 Combining Augmentations (G4)

We conclude our analysis by analyzing the impact of combining different augmentations. For this analysis, we selected 3 top-performing augmentations and compared their performance when used in isolation against relying on *Ensemble*, *RandomStack* and *MaskedStack* (see Sect. 3.4). Table 7 collects results obtained from 80 modeling runs for each configuration. Overall, mixing multiple augmentations is beneficial but gains are small, i.e., <1%.

Takeaways. *While one would expect that mixing good augmentations can only improve performance, we note that also CV literature is split on the subject. If on the one hand combining augmentations is commonly done in training pipelines, recent literature shows that such combinations bring marginal benefits [27].*

6 Discussion and Conclusions

In this work we presented a benchmark of hand-crafted DA for TC covering multiple dimensions: a total of 18 augmentations across 3 families, with 3 policies for introducing augmentations during training, investigating the classification performance sensitivity with respect to augmentations magnitude and class-weighted sampling across 3 datasets with different sizes and number of classes. Overall, our results confirm what previously observed in CV literature—*augmentations are beneficial even for large datasets, but in absolute terms the gains are dataset-dependent.* While from a qualitative standpoint, sequence and mask augmentations are better suited for TC tasks than amplitude augmentations, no single augmentation is found superior to alternatives and combining them (via stacking or ensembling), even when selecting top-performing ones, marginally improves performance compared to using augmentations in isolation. Last, by investigating the models latent space geometry, we confirm that *effective augmentations provide good sample variety* by creating samples that are neither too similar nor too different from the original ones which fosters better data representations extraction (as suggested by the longer training time).

Despite the multiple dimensions covered, our work suffers from some limitations. Most notably, it would be desirable to include the larger and more recent CESNET-TLS22 [25] and CESNET-QUIC23 [24] datasets but such expansion requires large computational power.[12] Still related to using large datasets, we can also envision more experiments tailored to investigate the relationship between datasets size and augmentations. For instance, one could sample down a large dataset (e.g., by randomly selecting 1% or 10% of the available samples) and investigate if augmentations result more effective with the reduced datasets. In particular, since Inject shows a positive trend with respect to its intensity N_{inject} we hypothesize that by augmenting a small dataset one can achieve the same performance as using larger datasets—showing these effects are clearly relevant for TC as collecting and releasing large datasets is currently a pain point. Last, our campaigns rely only a CNN-based architecture while assessing DA with other architectures (e.g., Transformer-based for time series [45]) is also relevant.

Ultimately, DA modeling campaigns as the one we performed require operating with a grid of configurations and parameters—it is daunting to explore the design space by means of brute forcing all possible scenarios. While domain knowledge can help in pruning the search space, it can also prevent from considering valuable alternatives. For instance, recall that Xie et al. [46] suggest to use augmentations inspired by TCP protocol dynamics. According to our benchmark, these augmentations are indeed among the top performing ones, yet not necessarily the best ones—navigating the search space results in a balancing act between aiming for qualitative and quantitative results.

We identify two viable options to simplify the design space exploration. On the one hand, re-engineering the augmentations so that their parametrization is discovered during training might resolve issues similar to what observed for Sine Wrap (see Sect. 5.3). On the other hand, a more efficient solution would be to rely on generative models avoiding the burden of designing hand-crafted augmentations. More specifically, we envision a first exploration based on conditioning the generative models on the latent space properties learned via hand-crafted DA (e.g., the distance between original and augmented samples should be in the "sweet spot"). Then, we could target the more challenging scenario of training unconditionally and verify if effective representations are automatically learned.

Overall, we believe that the performance observed in our experimental campaigns might still represent a lower bound and extra performance improvements could be achieved via generative models. We call for the research community to join us in our quest for integrating DA and improve TC performance.

---

[12] For reference, models trained on Enterprise can take up to 6 h. Since CESNET datasets contains 100× the number of samples of Enterprise, performing a thorough exploration of the DA design space is extremely resource demanding.

Appendix

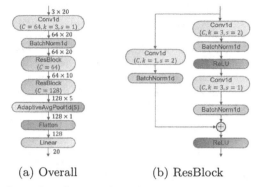

(a) Overall   (b) ResBlock

C: number of output channels, k: kernel size; s: stride

Fig. 7. Model architecture.

Listing 1.1. Model architecture printout (MIRAGE-19, 20 classes)

```
----------------------------------------------------------------
          Layer (type)          Output Shape          Param #
================================================================
            Conv1d-1            [-1, 64, 20]              576
       BatchNorm1d-2            [-1, 64, 20]              128
            Conv1d-3            [-1, 64, 10]           12,288
       BatchNorm1d-4            [-1, 64, 10]              128
            Conv1d-5            [-1, 64, 10]           12,288
       BatchNorm1d-6            [-1, 64, 10]              128
            Conv1d-7            [-1, 64, 10]            4,096
       BatchNorm1d-8            [-1, 64, 10]              128
            Conv1d-9            [-1, 128, 5]           24,576
      BatchNorm1d-10            [-1, 128, 5]              256
           Conv1d-11            [-1, 128, 5]           49,152
      BatchNorm1d-12            [-1, 128, 5]              256
           Conv1d-13            [-1, 128, 5]            8,192
      BatchNorm1d-14            [-1, 128, 5]              256
 AdaptiveAvgPool1d-15           [-1, 128, 1]                0
           Linear-16               [-1, 20]            2,580
================================================================
Total params: 115,028
Trainable params: 115,028
Non-trainable params: 0
----------------------------------------------------------------
Input size (MB): 0.00
Forward/backward pass size (MB): 0.09
Params size (MB): 0.44
Estimated Total Size (MB): 0.53
----------------------------------------------------------------
```

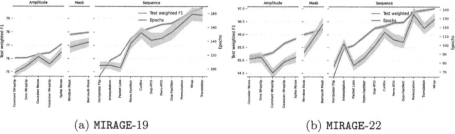

(a) MIRAGE-19   (b) MIRAGE-22

Fig. 8. Comparing performance improvement and training length.

References

1. Additional material for the paper: Rosetta: Enabling Robust TLS Encrypted Traffic Classification in Diverse Network Environments with TCP-Aware Traffic Augmentation. https://cloud.tsinghua.edu.cn/f/7f250d2ffce8404b845e/?dl=1
2. Aceto, G., Ciuonzo, D., Montieri, A., Pescapè, A.: Mimetic: mobile encrypted traffic classification using multimodal deep learning. Comput. Netw. **165**, 106944 (2019)
3. Aceto, G., Ciuonzo, D., Montieri, A., Persico, V., Pescapè, A.: Mirage: mobile-app traffic capture and ground-truth creation. In: IEEE International Conference on Computing, Communication and Security (ICCCS) (2019)
4. Akbari, I., et al.: A look behind the curtain: traffic classification in an increasingly encrypted web. ACM Measur. Anal. Comput. Syst. **5**(1), 1–26 (2021)
5. Bovenzi, G., et al.: A first look at class incremental learning in deep learning mobile traffic classification. In: IFIP Traffic Measurement and Analysis (TMA) (2021)
6. Burg, M.F., et al.: A data augmentation perspective on diffusion models and retrieval. arXiv:2304.10253 (2023)
7. Chawla, N.V., Bowyer, K.W., Hall, L.O., Kegelmeyer, W.P.: SMOTE: synthetic minority over-sampling technique. J. Artif. Intell. Res. **16**, 321–357 (2002)
8. Chen, T., Kornblith, S., Norouzi, M., Hinton, G.: A simple framework for contrastive learning of visual representations. arXiv:2002.05709 (2020)
9. Cubuk, E.D., Zoph, B., Mane, D., Vasudevan, V., Le, Q.V.: Autoaugment: learning augmentation policies from data. arXiv:1805.09501 (2019)
10. Cubuk, E.D., Zoph, B., Shlens, J., Le, Q.V.: Randaugment: practical automated data augmentation with a reduced search space. arXiv:1909.13719 (2019)
11. Cubuk, E.D., Dyer, E.S., Lopes, R.G., Smullin, S.: Tradeoffs in data augmentation: an empirical study. In: International Conference on Learning Representations (ICLR) (2021)
12. Demšar, J.: Statistical comparisons of classifiers over multiple data sets. J. Mach. Learn. Res. **7**, 1–30 (2006)
13. Eldele, E., et al.: Time-series representation learning via temporal and contextual contrasting. arXiv:2106.14112 (2021)
14. Guarino, I., Aceto, G., Ciuonzo, D., Montieri, A., Persico, V., Pescapé, A.: Classification of communication and collaboration apps via advanced deep-learning approaches. In: IEEE International Workshop on Computer Aided Modeling and Design of Communication Links and Networks (CAMAD) (2021)
15. Guarino, I., Wang, C., Finamore, A., Pescapé, A., Rossi, D.: Many or few samples? Comparing transfer, contrastive and meta-learning in encrypted traffic classification. In: IFIP Traffic Measurement and Analysis (TMA) (2023)
16. Han, H., Wang, W.-Y., Mao, B.-H.: Borderline-SMOTE: a new over-sampling method in imbalanced data sets learning. In: Huang, D.-S., Zhang, X.-P., Huang, G.-B. (eds.) ICIC 2005. LNCS, vol. 3644, pp. 878–887. Springer, Heidelberg (2005). https://doi.org/10.1007/11538059_91
17. He, H., Bai, Y., Garcia, E.A., Li, S.: ADASYN: adaptive synthetic sampling approach for imbalanced learning. In: International Joint Conference on Neural Networks (IJCNN) (2008)
18. He, K., Zhang, X., Ren, S., Sun, J.: Deep residual learning for image recognition. arXiv:1512.03385 (2015)
19. Hong, Y., Zhang, J., Sun, Z., Yan, K.: SAFA: sample-adaptive feature augmentation for long-tailed image classification. In: Avidan, S., Brostow, G., Cissé, M., Farinella, G.M., Hassner, T. (eds) Computer Vision. ECCV 2022. LNCS, vol. 13684, pp. 587–603. Springer, Cham (2022). https://doi.org/10.1007/978-3-031-20053-3_34

20. Horowicz, E., Shapira, T., Shavitt, Y.: A few shots traffic classification with mini-flowpic augmentations. In: ACM Internet Measurement Conference (IMC) (2022)
21. Jain, S., Addepalli, S., Sahu, P.K., Dey, P., Babu, R.V.: Dart: diversify-aggregate-repeat training improves generalization of neural networks. In: Computer Vision and Pattern Recognition (CVPR) (2023)
22. Jiang, X., Liu, S., Gember-Jacobson, A., Schmitt, P., Bronzino, F., Feamster, N.: Generative, high-fidelity network traces. In: ACM Workshop on Hot Topics in Networks (HotNets) (2023)
23. Johnson, J.M., Khoshgoftaar, T.M.: Survey on deep learning with class imbalance. J. Big Data **6**, 1–54 (2019)
24. Luxemburk, J., Hynek, K., Cejka, T.: Encrypted traffic classification: the QUIC case. In: IFIP Traffic Measument and Analysis (TMA) (2023)
25. Luxemburk, J., Čejka, T.: Fine-grained TLS services classification with reject option. Comput. Netw. **220**, 109467 (2023)
26. Mumuni, A., Mumuni, F.: Data augmentation: a comprehensive survey of modern approaches. Array **16**, 100258 (2022)
27. Müller, S.G., Hutter, F.: Trivialaugment: tuning-free yet state-of-the-art data augmentation. In: International Conference on Computer Vision (ICCV) (2021)
28. Odena, A., Olah, C., Shlens, J.: Conditional image synthesis with auxiliary classifier gans. arXiv:1610.09585 (2017)
29. Pacheco, F., Exposito, E., Gineste, M., Baudoin, C., Aguilar, J.: Towards the deployment of machine learning solutions in network traffic classification: a systematic survey. IEEE Commun. Surv. Tutor. **21**(2), 1988–2014 (2019)
30. Pöppelbaum, J., Chadha, G.S., Schwung, A.: Contrastive learning based self-supervised time series analysis. Appl. Soft Comput. **117**, 108397 (2022)
31. Redmon, J., Divvala, S., Girshick, R., Farhadi, A.: You only look once: Unified, real-time object detection. arXiv:1506.02640 (2016)
32. Rezaei, S., Liu, X.: How to achieve high classification accuracy with just a few labels: a semi-supervised approach using sampled packets. In: IEEE Industrial Conference Advances in Data Mining - Applications and Theoretical Aspects (ICDM) (2019)
33. Schuhmann, C., et al.: LAION-5b: an open large-scale dataset for training next generation image-text models. In: Neural Information Processing Systems (NeurIPS) - Datasets and Benchmarks Track (2022)
34. Shen, M., et al.: Machine learning-powered encrypted network traffic analysis: a comprehensive survey. IEEE Commun. Surv. Tutor. **25**(1), 791–824 (2023)
35. Shen, R., Bubeck, S., Gunasekar, S.: Data augmentation as feature manipulation. arXiv:2203.01572 (2022)
36. Shorten, C., Khoshgoftaar, T.M.: A survey on image data augmentation for deep learning. J. Big Data **6**(1), 1–48 (2019)
37. Sivaroopan, N., Madarasingha, C., Muramudalige, S., Jourjon, G., Jayasumana, A., Thilakarathna, K.: SyNIG: synthetic network traffic generation through time series imaging. In: IEEE Local Computer Networks (LCN) (2023)
38. Sivaroopan, N., Bandara, D., Madarasingha, C., Jourjon, G., Jayasumana, A., Thilakarathna, K.: Netdiffus: network traffic generation by diffusion models through time-series imaging. arXiv:2310.04429 (2023)
39. Towhid, M.S., Shahriar, N.: Encrypted network traffic classification using self-supervised learning. In: IEEE International Conference on Network Softwarization (NetSoft) (2022)
40. Trabucco, B., Doherty, K., Gurinas, M., Salakhutdinov, R.: Effective data augmentation with diffusion models. arXiv:2302.07944 (2023)

41. Wang, P., Li, S., Ye, F., Wang, Z., Zhang, M.: PacketCGAN: exploratory study of class imbalance for encrypted traffic classification using CGAN. In: International Conference on Communications (ICC) (2020)
42. Wang, Y., Pan, X., Song, S., Zhang, H., Wu, C., Huang, G.: Implicit semantic data augmentation for deep networks. arXiv:1909.12220 (2020)
43. Wang, Z., Wang, P., Zhou, X., Li, S., Zhang, M.: FlowGAN: unbalanced network encrypted traffic identification method based on GAN. In: Conference on Parallel and Distributed Processing with Applications, Big Data and Cloud Computing, Sustainable Computing and Communications, Social Computing and Networking (ISPA/BDCloud/SocialCom/SustainCom) (2019)
44. Wen, Q., et al.: Time series data augmentation for deep learning: a survey. In: International Joint Conference on Artificial Intelligence (IJCAI) (2021)
45. Wen, Q., et al.: Transformers in time series: a survey. arXiv:2202.07125 (2023)
46. Xie, R., et al.: Rosetta: enabling robust TLS encrypted traffic classification in diverse network environments with TCP-Aware traffic augmentation. In: USENIX Security Symposium (Security) (2023)
47. Yang, H., Yu, H., Sano, A.: Empirical evaluation of data augmentations for biobehavioral time series data with deep learning. arXiv:2210.06701 (2022)
48. Yin, C., Zhu, Y., Liu, S., Fei, J., Zhang, H.: An enhancing framework for botnet detection using generative adversarial networks. In: IEEE International Conference on Artificial Intelligence and Big Data (ICAIBD) (2018)
49. Yu, H., Sano, A.: Semi-supervised learning and data augmentation in wearable-based momentary stress detection in the wild. arXiv:2202.12935 (2022)
50. Yue, Z., et al.: Ts2vec: towards universal representation of time series. In: Proceedings of the Association for the Advancement of Artificial Intelligence Conference (AAAI) (2022)
51. Yun, S., Han, D., Oh, S.J., Chun, S., Choe, J., Yoo, Y.: Cutmix: regularization strategy to train strong classifiers with localizable features. arXiv:1905.04899 (2019)
52. Zhang, H., Cisse, M., Dauphin, Y.N., Lopez-Paz, D.: mixup: Beyond empirical risk minimization. arXiv:1710.09412 (2018)
53. Zou, D., Cao, Y., Li, Y., Gu, Q.: The benefits of mixup for feature learning. arXiv:2303.08433 (2023)

Measurement Tools

Towards Improving Outage Detection with Multiple Probing Protocols

Manasvini Sethuraman$^{(\boxtimes)}$, Zachary S. Bischof, and Alberto Dainotti

Georgia Institute of Technology, Atlanta, USA
msethuraman3@gatech.edu

Abstract. Multiple systems actively monitor the IPv4 address space for outages, often through ICMP probing. In this work, we explore the potential benefits (in terms of increased coverage) of leveraging additional protocols for probing by analyzing Internet-wide scans conducted using transport layer (TCP/UDP) probes. Using several existing Internet-wide scan snapshots, we show that between 531k to 606k additional /24 blocks, which were originally too sparse to be monitored via ICMP probing alone, now have the potential to be monitored for outages. We also find that it is possible to improve the probing efficiency for 850k–970k blocks, of which, 106k–125k blocks were not observed in the previous two years of ICMP-based scans. We observe that the average percent of /24 blocks per AS that could potentially be reliably monitored for outages increases from 65% to 83%, spanning 28k ASes.

1 Introduction

The Internet is critical communications infrastructure. As such, the ability to monitor connectivity and detect outages is of exceptional importance. An effective approach to detecting Internet outages requires broad coverage (i.e., not limited to a particular ISP or protocol), accuracy (i.e., few false positives and false negatives) and speed (i.e., rapid identification of outages). Active probing techniques have been demonstrated to be particularly successful in meeting some of these requirements and are currently deployed in various operational outage detection systems [2,18]. However their coverage of the address space is in some cases limited, and—as we show in this study—this is partially due to their exclusive use of ICMP probes.

This paper studies the potential for improving active measurement based outage detection coverage by supplementing ICMP measurements with transport layer (TCP, UDP) probing. In the context of network discovery and scanning, previous work has shown that leveraging multiple protocols (e.g., ICMP, UDP, TCP) allows for discovering the largest number of active addresses in use [6]. In this paper, we explore if and to what extent this property applies in the context of outage detection, where certain prerequisites—such as stability over time of address block responsiveness—are fundamental.

To estimate the potential benefits of a multi-protocol approach in practice, we use Trinocular as a reference outage detection method [5,18]. Trinocular is a well-studied active probing methodology that uses ICMP probes to detect outages at

© The Author(s), under exclusive license to Springer Nature Switzerland AG 2024
P. Richter et al. (Eds.): PAM 2024, LNCS 14537, pp. 189–205, 2024.
https://doi.org/10.1007/978-3-031-56249-5_8

the /24 block granularity using Bayesian inference. The methodology is currently deployed in operational outage detection systems, including IODA [2].

In order to determine which address blocks can be monitored for outages with active probes, Trinocular analyzes historical full Internet scan data over the preceding three years to identify responsive hosts and calculate the average availability for each /24 block. To simulate augmenting the calculation of /24 block availability to include the results of transport layer measurements, our analysis incorporates two existing datasets: ICMP probing results from ISI ANT's Internet history dataset [13] and snapshots of Internet-wide transport layer (TCP/UDP) scans from Censys [8]. By leveraging both of these datasets, we are able to quantify temporal variations in host responsiveness for each protocol individually as well as the resulting combined set of hosts. Analyzing two years of data on host responsiveness from both datasets, we calculate the potential improvements for outage detection coverage in terms of /24 block discovery and host availability that can be obtained by supplementing ICMP probes with transport layer probing.

The contributions of our analysis[1] can be summarized as follows:

- Hosts that respond to a combination of transport layer and ICMP probes have, on average, 10% higher availability than hosts that respond only to ICMP probes.
- Incorporating transport layer probing can improve coverage in various ways: (i) 845k blocks defined "unreliable" in Trinocular (i.e., with availability <30%) experience an increase in availability from an average of 13% to 48%; (ii) an additional 320k blocks that were not seen at all via ICMP, of which, between 106k–125k are "reliable". As a baseline for comparison, note that with ICMP only, Trinocular finds 3.5M reliable blocks.
- We find that such a non-negligible improvement – i.e., a relatively small percentage but over a very large set (i.e., the Internet) – is particularly pronounced in certain ASes, thus illuminating portions of the Internet where outage visibility would otherwise be limited. E.g., the blocks discovered only through transport layer scans span 14k ASes, of which 1.8k ASes are newly discovered through the additional probes.
- Improvements in outage detection coverage are exceptionally notable in certain geographic regions, often in the Global South. For example, Ethiopia, Suriname and French Polynesia all have a relatively small number of blocks that can be reliably monitored via ICMP-only probing (26, 25 and 37 blocks respectively). In each case, the addition of transport layer probes increases the number of blocks that can be reliably monitored to over 200 blocks.

2   Related Work

Detecting network outages via active measurements has received significant focus from the networking research community. Prior work, such as Fan and Heidemann, studied the use IPv4 hit lists to make scanning more efficient for surveying

---

[1] Repository: https://github.com/InetIntel/ioda-censys-isi

the topology of the Internet [10]. The authors demonstrate that selecting appropriate representative hosts can improve traceroute-based coverage of edge hosts. Later efforts used this idea, such as in the Trinocular methodology [18], which proposed techniques for outage detection probing hitlists with active ICMP measurements in 11-min cycles. However, /24 blocks that contained a small number of hosts (i.e., blocks with less than 15 hosts responding to probes) were difficult to accurately monitor. In subsequent work that aimed to reduce the impact of sparse blocks in identifying outages, Baltra and Heidemann proposed full-block scanning (FBS) as an extension to Trinocular [5]. However, FBS involves probing every address in the /24 block and may take several probing cycles to complete.

In addition to Trinocular, there are a number of efforts that aim to detect Internet outages. Long-running TCP probes within the RIPE infrastructure [4] are used to infer outages in DISCO [22]. Thunderping examines outages due to adverse weather conditions in residential networks by probing against a sample of hosts in a geographical area, before and after adverse weather [17,21].

Passive measurement techniques using various data sources for inferring outages have been proposed in literature—including Internet Background Radiation [11], NTP server events [23], and HTTP logs [19]. However, they are more commonly used in conjunction with other approaches. IODA uses several signals (active ICMP probes, passive monitoring of BGP prefix announcements, and passive monitoring of Internet background radiation) to detect outages across the world [2]. Hubble uses a combination of active measurements (ICMP probing) and passive monitoring (BGP prefixes) to infer connectivity problems on the Internet [14].

With regards to enumerating hosts and identifying liveness in the address space, Bano et al. use a combination of TCP, UDP, and ICMP probes to create a point-in-time snapshot of the Internet and analyze host activity that is visible via different protocols [6]. They investigate the liveness of hosts, under different protocol probes and the correlation in responses between different protocols. However, they do not investigate the implications of TCP/UDP probes on a block's availability and do not analyze the longitudinal trends in availability of a host or a block. On a similar vein, IRLScanner investigates host liveness and service discovery via Internet-wide scans comprised of different protocols (DNS, HTTP, SMTP, EPMAP, ICMP, and UDP ECHO) [15].

3   Datasets and Methodology

In this section, we first briefly describe the datasets that we use in our analysis. We then provide a high level summary of our findings (Sect. 3.1) and discuss metrics for comparing the coverage of the datasets (Sect. 3.2).

Our analysis in this paper primarily relies on data from two sources: IPv4 censuses collected by the ANT Lab at ISI [1] and IPv4 scans conducted by Censys [8] using Zmap [9]. For both datasets, we use scans collected between November 2020 and December 2022. We do not consider specific vantage points which elicited a response, since we are primarily interested in whether or not measurements elicit a response from a particular IP, rather than the route to a specific host. Further, while IP address churn is possible, we are interested in knowing which hosts consistently respond to probes across multiple surveys, and are likely to respond in future measurement cycles, and may be informative for detecting outages.

ANT Dataset (ANT): As part of the ANT Censuses of the Internet Address Space project [12], researchers at ISI conduct periodic surveys of the IPv4 address space, recording responses from each host. Hosts are probed using ICMP and the response is recorded as a 0 or a 1. A zero could indicate either error, not probed or not responded, and a 1 represents an echo response. Historical data of host responses is made available through the IP history dataset. This dataset contains responses from every address from all previous surveys, starting in 2011. Surveys are typically about 2–3 months apart with each survey taking several weeks to complete [12].

Censys Internet-Wide Scan Data (Censys): Censys provides researchers access to its Internet scan data. Snapshots in this dataset contain Internet-wide scan data at roughly one week intervals. The scanning method is based on ZMap [9], with each scan taking about 45 min to complete. Entries in a snapshot contain information about the responding IP address, the services running on the host, and other information (exposed ports etc.) that are identified using a variety of handshakes such as TLS, HTTP, SSH and TELNET. A host could respond to several protocol handshakes, and we see this quite often in the snapshots. We record the list of protocols for which a response was received to aid us in constructing our dataset.

Censys scans contain the results from more than 30 protocol handshakes. For designing a probing system that is fast, making multiple protocol handshakes is time consuming. Instead we consider those protocols which produce responses from the maximum number of hosts. We narrowed down this list of protocols to HTTP, SSH, FTP, NTP, SMTP and DNS. For each host, we then find the protocol which yields the most number of responses across the nine scans. The full set of protocols in Censys produces responses from 467M across nine scans. This number drops to 440M hosts, or 94% of the original set of Censys hosts when we limit the number of probing protocols to one per host. From Fig. 1(a), we see that HTTP probes elicit responses from well over 300M hosts, followed by SSH with 45M hosts, and the remaining protocols with fewer than 10M hosts, across all nine snapshots. In Fig. 1(b) we see that there is a decrease in the number of hosts responding to two or more surveys up until 8 surveys, and then an increase in the number of hosts responding across all nine surveys.

For our analysis, using the ANT and Censys scans to which we had access at the time we conducted our analysis, we match each ANT survey to a Censys scan such that the difference between the two start dates is as small as possible. We use nine matched ANT and Censys scans between November 2020 and December 2022. While there are sometimes differences between the start dates of the corresponding ANT and Censys snapshots, these differences are relatively small in comparison to the long time frames of the ANT censuses. Additional details on these scans are available in Appendix A.

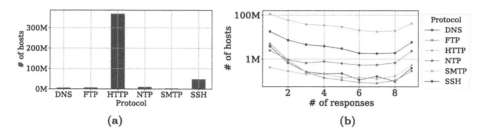

Fig. 1. (a) Distribution of best protocol responses across hosts across all nine snapshots (b) Variation of number of hosts responding to a protocol handshake with number of surveys.

3.1 High Level Observations

We first investigate how many additional blocks can be discovered via Censys' probing methodology and if existing (and new) blocks can be reliably probed using other protocols by collating the ANT and Censys datasets. On average, over nine surveys, we find that ANT covers 660M hosts across 5.8M /24 blocks, Censys covers 467M hosts spanning 5.78M /24 blocks, and the combination of the two datasets covers 820M hosts spanning 6.21M /24 blocks, if we consider probing every host using 30 different protocols. We will refer to this dataset as "Censys-any". If we only consider the best protocol for each individual host, which we call "Censys-best", we get 440M hosts, spanning 5.72M /24 blocks. When we consider ANT and Censys-best together, we get 810M hosts spanning 6.21M /24 blocks.

Over time, we noticed that the number of ASes covered by ANT went from roughly 64k in November 2020 to over 69k in December 2022. The combination of the two datasets yielded 67k ASes in November 2020 and 71k ASes in December 2022. More information on these summary statistics can be found in Appendix A.

3.2 Key Terms and Metrics for Comparison

In our analysis, we compare the coverage of ANT and of the combined "ANT + Censys" datasets using metrics such as block availability and sparsity, as defined in the Trinocular [18] work. We will add -any or -best to Censys to indicate which method was used to elicit responses from hosts. In this section, we first define these and other related terms.

Availability. In the outage-centric model of the Internet proposed in the Trinocular, historical block availability is used to seed the outage detection model. Block availability, or $A(E(b))$ is defined as the response rate of the block averaged over the last four surveys, for all the hosts that ever responded in that block in the last three years. This metric is used as an initial estimate to seed the calculation of a block's status (up/down). $E(b)$ represents the number of hosts in a block that ever responded to any probe. As a simplified example, consider two probing cycles. In the first cycle, only one host from the block responded, and in the next cycle, a different set with nine hosts responded. In this case, over the two cycles, $E(b)$ would be 10. $A(E(b))$ for the block would then be 0.5, since all of the hosts that were ever observed in any cycle responded in one of the two probing cycles. Since we only had access to approximately two years of Censys snapshot data (from November 2020 to December 2022), we modify the definition of $A(E(b))$ to only consider hosts which responded to any probe over the approximately two year period for both datasets. We used all the snapshots we collected for computing availability scores. Trinocular computes $A(E(b))$ from ICMP probes in ANT censuses (lasting several weeks) to generate initial probabilities for block statuses. We extend this methodology to incorporate TCP/UDP probes from Censys in addition to ICMP probes.

Sparse Block. A block that has fewer than 15 responding hosts in a particular survey is labeled as a sparse block. Blocks with 15 or more responding hosts are referred to as nonsparse blocks.

Reliable Block. Among non-sparse blocks, there are blocks that require fewer rounds of probing to infer their status. Specifically, when a block's availability $A(E(b))$ is at least 0.3, Trinocular is able to *always* detect an outage which lasts longer than one round of probing ($\approx$11 min). We refer to the blocks with $A(E(b)) \geq 0.3$ as reliable blocks. Blocks with $A(E(b)) < 0.3$ are referred to as unreliable blocks, and it may take several rounds of probing to establish the status of such blocks.

Upper/Lower Bounds on Sparsity. ANT surveys and Censys scans do not typically start on precisely the same day and take different periods of time to complete. This makes a direct comparison of sparse blocks difficult, as differences could be due to DHCP, hosts being restarted, etc. In order to avoid over-estimating the reduction in the number of sparse blocks by adding Censys probing techniques, we calculate a lower and upper bounds for the number of sparse /24 blocks when combining the two data sources.

For each matched survey, we consider the combined set of hosts in each block from both ANT and Censys. We then compute the number of sparse blocks from the combined data to get an optimistic lower bound on the number of sparse blocks. To calculate an upper bound, we compute the list of sparse blocks from the ANT dataset and then locate these blocks in the Censys data, checking for sparsity in the Censys dataset. If the blocks would be considered nonsparse using only the Censys data, we exclude these blocks from the list of sparse blocks. The final list of sparse blocks in either scenario is expected to be smaller than the original list of sparse blocks in ANT.

4   Impact at the Host Level

We first investigate if incorporating Censys' probing techniques could help identify hosts that can be reliably probed. Such hosts can be used when building hit lists, potentially allowing for easier and more rapid detection of outages.

Table 1. Average number of responses for hosts across 9 surveys. Combining datasets increases the number of responses.

Metric	IPs unique to ANT		Common IPs/ ANT		Common IPs/ ANT + Censys	
	Censys-Any	Censys-Best	Censys-Any	Censys-Best	Censys-Any	Censys-Best
Avg. response count	5.29	5.24	5.20	5.25	6.12	6.02
Prob. of low response count	0.17	0.17	0.15	0.15	0.03	0.04
Prob. of high response count	0.25	0.24	0.22	0.22	0.27	0.28

We calculate the number of responses of each host across 9 surveys as the number of times it responded to a probe, meaning each host has a response count between 1 and 9. We summarize host responses for different views of the data: *(i)* the average number of responses using ANT data for IP addresses that were unique to ANT (i.e., did not appear in any Censys scan); *(ii)* the average number of responses using only ANT data for IP addresses that appeared in both the ANT and Censys scans (though not necessarily in the same matched survey); and *iii)* the combined average number of responses for the IPs common to both datasets, with each IP considered responsive for a survey if the IP appeared in a corresponding ANT or Censys scan. For each category, we also calculated the fraction of hosts with a low response count (i.e., only appeared in 1 of the 9 surveys) and high response rate (i.e., appears in all 9 surveys). We consider two cases for Censys: using the dataset constructed from using any protocol to probe an address (Censys-any), and using only one protocol per address that yielded the most number of responses across the surveys (Censys-best).

Table 1 summarizes our findings related to host responses. On average, a host that is present in either dataset provides a response in 6 surveys (for both the Censys-Any and Censys-Best subsets), compared to 5.2–5.3 surveys for a host when only considering the ANT dataset. More importantly, the fraction of hosts that appear in both datasets with a low response rate, decreases from 15% to 3–4% when Censys data is added. Finally, adding Censys data also increases the fraction of highly available hosts from 22% to 27–28% for the hosts that are common to both datasets.

Takeaway. Hosts present in both datasets are likely to appear in more surveys than hosts present in only one of the datasets.

5   Impact at the /24 Block Level

In this section, we study how adding Censys data can impact sparsity and reliability at the /24 block level.

5.1   Sparsity

We classify blocks as sparse (or nonsparse) based on the number of hosts found in the block (as defined in Sect. 3). For blocks that appear in the Censys dataset but not in the ANT dataset, we denote the block as absent. Using the most recent snapshot of the data, we calculate the number of sparse, nonsparse, and absent blocks for both the ANT and combined (ANT and Censys) datasets. Figure 2a shows that 58k (18%) of the 328k blocks that are completely missing in the ANT dataset become nonsparse by adding Censys-best. Further, 532k (21%) blocks which were sparse in the ANT dataset are no longer sparse after adding Censys-best.

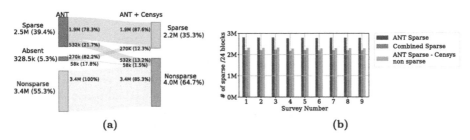

(a)   (b)

Fig. 2. (a) In the most recent snapshot, adding hosts from Censys reduces the number of sparse blocks. (b) ANT sparse (blue bars) shows the number of sparse blocks in the ANT dataset in each survey. Combined sparse (purple bars) shows the lower bound on number of sparse blocks in the combined dataset (Censys-best). The pink bars show the upper bound on the number of sparse blocks in the combined dataset (Censys-best). (Color figure online)

For each snapshot, we compute the upper and lower bounds (defined in Sect. 3) for the number of sparse blocks after the addition of Censys-best data (Fig. 2b). We observe that sparsity decreases somewhere between 17% and 21%. The upper and lower bounds on the reduction in the number of sparse blocks are within 4% of the total number of sparse blocks originally found in the ANT data.

Takeaway. Combining the two datasets yields between 488k to 600k fewer sparse blocks in comparison to the ANT dataset, or 17–21% reduction in the number of sparse blocks. Using Censys probing techniques has potential to increase the number of blocks that can be monitored for outage detection and may improve the accuracy and rapidness for other blocks.

5.2   Reliability

We consider the universe of hosts H to be the set of hosts discovered through either probing method. We then compute $A(E(b))$ using only ANT and again using the combined dataset, for each /24 block, where the elements of b are members of H. We classify the blocks as reliable or unreliable based on $A(E(b))$. We denote blocks with zero availability, or blocks not found in the ANT dataset as absent. Figure 3 shows the Sankey diagram before and after combining the two datasets. It shows that 720k, or 31% of the blocks which were unreliable in ANT (2.3M) can now be efficiently probed for outages after adding hosts from Censys-best. Another 106k (32%) of 328.5k blocks which were missing in ANT, now can be probed efficiently for outages in the combined dataset.

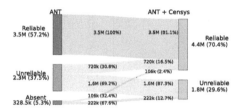

Fig. 3. Adding hosts from Censys improves representation and block availability.

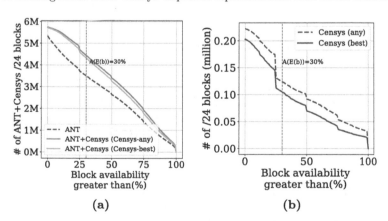

Fig. 4. (a) Number of /24 blocks in either dataset with an availability score above a particular percentage for the ANT and combined datasets. (b) Block availability for /24 blocks found only in the Censys data. The vertical red dashed line in each plot represents the $(A(E(b)) = 0.3)$ threshold for reliable outage detection. (Color figure online)

Improvement in Reliability of Existing Blocks. Figure 4a illustrates the improvement in block availability as a consequence of adding Censys-any/Censys-best data for all blocks (appeared in either dataset). Using only ICMP probing, 56.5% (3.5M) of all (6.2M) /24 blocks are reliable. Incorporating Censys data, increases the percent of reliable blocks to 70% using Censys-best (4.37M blocks) to 72% in Censys-any (4.48M blocks). Figure 5a illustrates the block availability for only the blocks that appeared in the ANT dataset (5.8M blocks). As expected, the gains from Censys-any are slightly higher than Censys-best, since we use only one additional probe per host in Censys-best.

For the blocks which originally were not reliable in ANT, and are reliable in the combined dataset, we compute the change in availability. On average, we see an increase in availability from 13% to 50% across 845k /24 blocks, with Censys-any. With Censys-best, we get an increase in availability from 13% to 49% across 720k /24 blocks. Figure 5b shows that about 25% of /24 blocks see at least a 50% increase in $(A(E(b)))$.

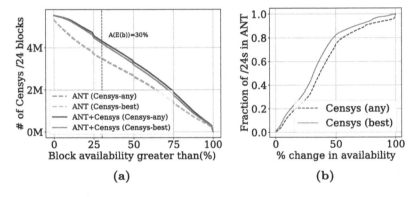

(a)   **(b)**

Fig. 5. (a) Block availability for /24 blocks discovered in ANT (b) Change in availability of previously unreliable blocks in the ANT ISI dataset upon addition of hosts from Censys scans.

Discovery of New Blocks. Adding Censys data also increases the number of blocks that we discover. After computing $A(E(b))$ for the newly discovered blocks, we find that 106k (Censys-best) to 125k (Censys-any) can be reliably probed for outages as shown in Fig. 4b. These blocks were previously unresponsive and make up 2–3% of the final set of all reliable blocks.

Takeaway. On average, $A(E(b))$ for a block b increases from 0.45 to between 0.51 (Censys-best) and 0.54 (Censys-any) when we consider host probing when we use a combination of probing methods. Furthermore, an additional 857k to 974k /24 blocks can now be reliably monitored for outages in a single Trinocular probing cycle and do not require full scanning (e.g., via FBS). Finally, 100–125k previously unseen blocks can now be probed reliably.

6   Impact at the AS Level

In this section, we explore the impact of combining the ANT and Censys datasets at the level of autonomous systems. We look up the AS associated with a /24 through CAIDA's pyipmeta [7]. We find 71k ASes, from both data sources combined, making up 76% of the 94,935 assigned AS numbers from NRO's extended delegation file published on April 14, 2023 [16].

6.1   AS-Level Reduction in Sparsity

For the most recent snapshot of ANT and combined datasets, we group /24 blocks by their origin AS. We then find the number of nonsparse blocks per AS for the ANT dataset. For the combined dataset, we find the upper bound of the number of sparse blocks per AS and subtract these from the total number of blocks associated with the AS. Figure 6a shows the number of ASes that have a particular percentage of nonsparse blocks for the ANT and combined dataset. We find that 60%(Censys-best) to 62% (Censys-any) of ASNs have at least 50% nonsparse blocks, in comparison to 50% of ASNs when using only the ANT dataset. Figure 6b shows the CDF of the percentage of nonsparse blocks grouped by AS for the blocks unique to Censys. On average, 48% (Censys-best) to 51% (Censys-any) of the blocks per AS are nonsparse.

Takeaway. On average, 53%(Censys-best) to 55% (Censys-any) of the blocks belonging to an AS are nonsparse in the combined dataset, in comparison to 44% of blocks per AS in the ANT dataset in the most recent snapshot of the datasets.

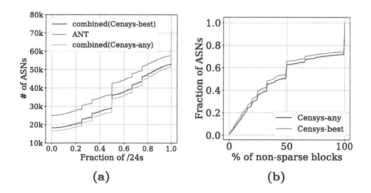

(a)   (b)

Fig. 6. (a) CDF of % of non sparse /24 blocks per AS for blocks originally in ANT versus blocks that are non sparse in at least one of the datasets (ANT or Censys) for two cases: when using any protocol in Censys (pink line) and when using only the best protocol for the fiven host (blue line) (b) CDF of % of non sparse /24 blocks per AS for blocks discovered uniquely through Censys (Color figure online)

6.2   Availability at the AS Level

We consider the effect of increased availability at the AS level on blocks already covered by ANT, and new blocks discovered by Censys.

Existing Blocks. We compare the number of reliable blocks within an AS, when only ICMP probing is used and when a combination of probing methods is considered. ASes vary widely in size, so we plot the CDF of relative increase in the number of reliable /24 blocks per AS, for those ASes already discovered by ANT (Fig. 7a). We find that within an AS, 83% (Censys-best) to 86% (Censys-any) of /24s are reliable on average, when we consider both ICMP probing and internet scanning, in comparison to 66% of reliable /24 blocks per AS if we only consider ICMP probing. Out of the 12,559 ASes which did not have any reliable /24 block originally in the ANT dataset, 8,908 (Censys-best) to 9,732 (Censys-any) of the ASes have at least one reliable block when Censys hosts are added.

New Blocks. The CDF of the number of reliable /24 blocks per ASN from Censys is shown in Fig. 7b. 9,849 to 10,404 ASes are covered by 0.106M to 0.125M reliable blocks unique to Censys-best and Censys-any respectively. Of these, 1,854 ASes were unique to Censys-any, covering 4,767 reliable /24 blocks, and 1,838 ASes were unique to Censys-best, covering 4,647 reliable /24 blocks.

Takeaway. Combining the two datasets results in an increase in the number of reliable blocks per AS from 65% to 83–86% on average.

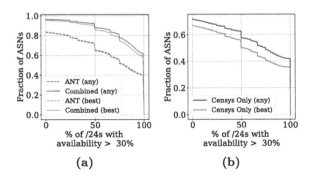

Fig. 7. (a) CDF of % reliable /24 blocks per AS for all ASes discovered through combination of ANT ISI and combination of ICMP and other protocols for the same blocks (b) CDF of % of reliable /24 blocks per AS for all blocks discovered uniquely through Censys.

7   Block Geolocation

We investigate which countries and continents experience reduction in sparsity and improvements to reliability. We used the commercial version of the IpInfo [3] data to geolocate /24 blocks found in ANT and in the combined dataset.

Geolocating Sparse Blocks. For the most recent snapshot of ANT and the combined (Censys-best) dataset, we compute the number of sparse blocks by country. For the combined dataset, we consider the lower bound on the number of sparse blocks. We first filter out all sparse blocks both datasets. We then geolocate the blocks and plot the percentage increase in the number of non-sparse blocks per country (Fig. 8a). The number of nonsparse blocks in Yemen, Suriname and Ethiopia increase from 17 each to, 713, 221, and 81 respectively. While the countries with the largest percent increase in number of nonsparse blocks lie outside of North America and Europe, US, France, UK, Australia and Brazil see the largest improvement in the raw number of nonsparse blocks.

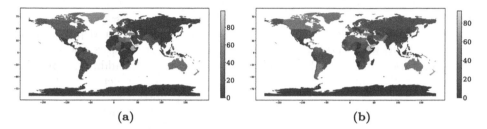

(a)   (b)

Fig. 8. (a) Improvement percentage in nonsparse block coverage over ANT by country. (b) Improvement percentage in reliable /24 block coverage over ANT by country.

Geolocating Reliable Blocks. We geolocate each /24 block in the combined dataset and then group the blocks by country. We then filter out the blocks with $A(E(b)) < 0.3$. Figure 8b shows the per country percentage increase in the number of reliable /24 blocks in the combined dataset. The number of reliable blocks mapped to French Polynesia, Suriname and Ethiopia increase from 37, 25 and 26, to 237, 230 and 208 respectively (Table 3). The baseline coverage in these countries however varies widely. For example, coverage in Ethiopia increased by 184 /24 blocks, and in Ireland by 19k /24 blocks.

Takeaway. Combining the two datasets produces relative increase in nonsparse and reliable /24 blocks in some countries outside North America and Europe.

8 Limitations and Future Work

This work is a step towards incorporating TCP and UDP-based probing into outage detection systems. We investigated the potential improvement in the coverage of /24 blocks for outage detection when using a combination of ICMP probes and other protocols. Specifically, we demonstrated that it is possible to reduce the number of sparse blocks and improve block availability for outage detection. Our method uses snapshots of data collected on different days and therefore, there might be some turnaround of hosts. We note that the initial availability scores in Trinocular are derived in a similar manner.

IP churn has been reported to be as high as 25% (observed from CDN logs) [20], and our analysis is based on point-in-time estimates of /24 block

202   M. Sethuraman et al.

availability. We have merely shown that the initial estimation of block availability can improve with the addition of Censys data. There is still work to do in order to realize the actual gains in active monitoring of the IPv4 address space.

In this work, we consider probing a host using the protocol that yields the most responses for each IP. However, hosts may change IP addresses or change which services they are running. In such cases, probing via multiple protocols could potentially increase the likelihood of eliciting a response. Further analysis of our dataset could shed additional light on the most effective, yet practical, probing policies.

Based on the potential benefits described in this work, in future work, we plan to integrate TCP/UDP scanning techniques into the active probing signal of an operational outage detection system (IODA). Integrating these techniques into an operational outage detection system will also allow for more in-depth analysis of the degree to which additional probing techniques can improve the system's ability to outage detection. Extending IODA to support the additional probing techniques will require: getting consistent access to or conducting TCP/UDP scans of the full IPv4 address space across many ports (e.g., using ZMap), automating the analysis these scans to create a hit list of IPs and ports to monitor (i.e., applying the methodology of this work), integrating these hit lists into IODA's active measurement infrastructure, adding supporting for launching TCP/UDP probes, and integrating the results into IODA's dashboards.

Acknowledgements. We thank the anonymous reviewers for their thoughtful feedback and our shepherd, Dr. Kyle Schomp, for helping improve the presentation of this paper.

A   Appendix 1

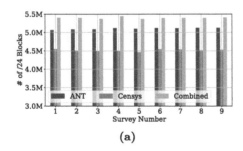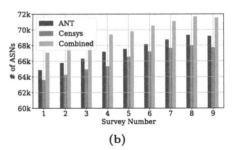

(a)   (b)

Fig. 9. (a) /24 coverage across surveys from both datasets. On average, ANT covers 5.1 million /24 blocks and Censys-best covers 4.5 million /24 blocks. The combination of the two datasets yields about 5.39 million /24 blocks on average per survey (b) Autonomous systems identified in the two datasets. On average ANT scans span over 67k ASes and Censys over 66k ASes. The combination of the two datasets yields 69k ASes

/24 blocks covered in the datasets. We count the number of active /24 blocks (/24 block with at least one responding host) in every snapshot, for both datasets and find the union of /24 blocks (Fig. 9a). On average, the coverage of /24 blocks increases by 293k when the ICMP probing is supplemented with scan data from Censys.

ASes Covered in the Datasets. We look at the number of ASes found in each snapshot by both methods in Fig. 9b. On average, we find a 91% overlap in the ASNs between the two datasets. The set of ASes covered by Censys is slightly more than those covered by ICMP probing in the more recent surveys.

Survey Dates for the Datasets. The scan/survey dates for ANT and Censys datasets are listed in Table 2.

Table 2. Snapshot dates for ANT ISI and Censys datasets

Snapshot	ANT date	Censys date	Difference (days)
1	2020-11-10	2020-11-10	0
2	2021-03-06	2021-03-09	3
3	2021-06-19	2021-06-22	3
4	2021-08-27	2021-08-23	4
5	2022-01-28	2022-01-25	3
6	2022-04-19	2022-04-19	0
7	2022-06-29	2022-06-28	1
8	2022-09-09	2022-09-06	3
9	2022-12-03	2022-12-06	3

Table 3. Countries with the largest increase in % of reliable /24 blocks.

Country	% increase in no. of reliable /24 blocks	Increase in number of blocks
Suriname	89.1	205
Ethiopia	87.5	182
French Polynesia	84.38	200
Andorra	80.55	145
Ireland	73.95	26,450

Geolocation of Reliable Blocks. While countries like Yemen and Suriname see relative improvements in /24 coverage (Table 3), a large fraction of improvement in the number of reliable blocks are observed in North America and Europe. Table 4 lists the countries with the largest improvement to the number of reliable blocks. Table 4 shows the countries with the biggest percentage increase in number of reliable /24 blocks, for each continent.

Table 4. Countries with the largest increase in number of reliable /24 blocks.

Country	% increase in no. of reliable /24 blocks	Increase in number of blocks
United States	19.95	235071
Japan	22.05	42,679
Germany	21.38	39,718
France	34.97	391,12
Brazil	24.87	37,051

References

1. Ant datasets (2022). https://ant.isi.edu/datasets/index.html
2. IODA (2022). https://ioda.live
3. IPInfo (2022). https://ipinfo.io/products/ip-database-download
4. RIPE Atlas (2022). https://atlas.ripe.net/
5. Baltra, G., Heidemann, J.: Improving coverage of internet outage detection in sparse blocks. In: Sperotto, A., Dainotti, A., Stiller, B. (eds.) PAM 2020. LNCS, vol. 12048, pp. 19–36. Springer, Cham (2020). https://doi.org/10.1007/978-3-030-44081-7_2
6. Bano, S., et al.: Scanning the internet for liveness. ACM SIGCOMM Comput. Commun. Rev. **48**(2), 2–9 (2018)
7. CAIDA: pyipmeta (2022). https://github.com/CAIDA/pyipmeta
8. Durumeric, Z., Adrian, D., Mirian, A., Bailey, M., Halderman, J.A.: A search engine backed by internet-wide scanning. In: Proceedings of the 22nd ACM SIGSAC Conference on Computer and Communications Security, pp. 542–553 (2015)
9. Durumeric, Z., Wustrow, E., Halderman, J.A.: ZMap: fast internet-wide scanning and its security applications. In: 22nd USENIX Security Symposium (USENIX Security 13), pp. 605–620 (2013)
10. Fan, X., Heidemann, J.: Selecting representative IP addresses for internet topology studies. In: Proceedings of the 10th ACM SIGCOMM Conference on Internet Measurement, IMC 2010, Melbourne, Australia, pp. 411–423. Association for Computing Machinery, New York, NY, USA (2010)
11. Guillot, A., et al.: Chocolatine: outage detection for internet background radiation. In: 2019 Network Traffic Measurement and Analysis Conference (TMA), pp. 1–8 (2019). https://doi.org/10.23919/TMA.2019.8784607
12. Heidemann, J., Pradkin, Y., Govindan, R., Papadopoulos, C., Bartlett, G., Bannister, J.: Census and survey of the visible internet. In: Proceedings of the 8th ACM SIGCOMM Conference on Internet Measurement, pp. 169–182 (2008)
13. Internet Addresses IPv4 Response History Dataset: Dataset, PREDICT ID: USC-LANDER/internet_address_history_it95w-20210727/rev12156. Provided by the USC/LANDER project (2022). http://www.isi.edu/ant/lander
14. Katz-Bassett, E., Madhyastha, H.V., John, J.P., Wetherall, D., Anderson, T.: Studying black holes in the internet with Hubble. In: 5th USENIX Symposium on Networked Systems Design and Implementation (NSDI 08). USENIX Association, San Francisco, CA, April 2008. https://www.usenix.org/conference/nsdi-08/studying-black-holes-internet-hubble

15. Leonard, D., Loguinov, D.: Demystifying service discovery: implementing an internet-wide scanner. In: Proceedings of the 10th ACM SIGCOMM Conference on Internet Measurement, pp. 109–122 (2010)
16. NRO: RIR Statistics (2023). https://www.nro.net/about/rirs/statistics/
17. Padmanabhan, R., Schulman, A., Dainotti, A., Levin, D., Spring, N.: How to find correlated internet failures. In: Choffnes, D., Barcellos, M. (eds.) PAM 2019. LNCS, vol. 11419, pp. 210–227. Springer, Cham (2019). https://doi.org/10.1007/978-3-030-15986-3_14
18. Quan, L., Heidemann, J., Pradkin, Y.: Trinocular: understanding internet reliability through adaptive probing. SIGCOMM Comput. Commun. Rev. **43**(4), 255–266 (2013)
19. Richter, P., Padmanabhan, R., Spring, N., Berger, A., Clark, D.: Advancing the art of internet edge outage detection. In: Proceedings of the Internet Measurement Conference 2018, IMC 2018, pp. 350–363. Association for Computing Machinery, New York, NY, USA (2018). https://doi.org/10.1145/3278532.3278563
20. Richter, P., Smaragdakis, G., Plonka, D., Berger, A.: Beyond counting: new perspectives on the active IPv4 address space. In: Proceedings of the 2016 Internet Measurement Conference, IMC 2016, Santa Monica, California, USA, pp. 135–149. Association for Computing Machinery, New York, NY, USA (2016)
21. Schulman, A., Spring, N.: Pingin' in the rain. In: Proceedings of the 2011 ACM SIGCOMM Conference on Internet Measurement Conference, pp. 19–28 (2011)
22. Shah, A., Fontugne, R., Aben, E., Pelsser, C., Bush, R.: Disco: fast, good, and cheap outage detection. In: 2017 Network Traffic Measurement and Analysis Conference (TMA), pp. 1–9. IEEE (2017)
23. Syamkumar, M., Gullapalli, Y., Tang, W., Barford, P., Sommers, J.: Bigben: telemetry processing for internet-wide event monitoring. IEEE Trans. Netw. Serv. Manage. **19**(3), 2625–2638 (2022)

WHOIS Right? An Analysis of WHOIS and RDAP Consistency

Simon Fernandez[✉], Olivier Hureau, Andrzej Duda, and Maciej Korczynski

Univ. Grenoble Alpes, Grenoble INP, LIG, Saint-Martin-d'Hères, France
{simon.fernandez,olivier.hureau,andrzej.duda,
maciej.korczynski}@univ-grenoble-alpes.fr

Abstract. Public registration information on domain names, such as the accredited registrar, the domain name expiration date, or the abuse contact is crucial for many security tasks, from automated abuse notifications to botnet or phishing detection and classification systems. Various domain registration data is usually accessible through the WHOIS or RDAP protocols—*a priori* they provide the same data but use distinct formats and communication protocols. While WHOIS aims to provide human-readable data, RDAP uses a machine-readable format. Therefore, deciding which protocol to use is generally considered a straightforward technical choice, depending on the use case and the required automation and security level. In this paper, we examine the core assumption that WHOIS and RDAP offer the same data and that users can query them interchangeably. By collecting, processing, and comparing 164 million WHOIS and RDAP records for a sample of 55 million domain names, we reveal that while the data obtained through WHOIS and RDAP is generally consistent, 7.6% of the observed domains still present inconsistent data on important fields like IANA ID, creation date, or nameservers. Such variances should receive careful consideration from security stakeholders reliant on the accuracy of these fields.

Keywords: WHOIS · RDAP · DNS · domain names · registration data · measurements

1 Introduction

Malicious activities such as phishing scams, botnet operations, or malware distribution often involve the use of domain names. To investigate these activities and mitigate their impact, it is crucial to have access to specific information about domain registration. Essential information for investigating malicious activities related to domain names encompasses details such as the domain creation date, the registrant name, the sponsoring registrar, the domain status, the expiration date, email addresses designated for reporting domain name abuse, and other relevant data. However, in compliance with the European General Data Protection Regulation (GDPR) [37] and the Temporary Specification of the Internet Corporation for Assigned Names and Numbers (ICANN) for generic Top-Level

P. Richter et al. (Eds.): PAM 2024, LNCS 14537, pp. 206–231, 2024.
https://doi.org/10.1007/978-3-031-56249-5_9

Domain (gTLD) registration data [20], personal information pertaining to registrants is typically obscured or hidden.

Different entities involved in the domain registration process typically provide registration information through two protocols: WHOIS [6] and RDAP (Registration Data Access Protocol) [15]. Despite the historical reasons for the coexistence of two protocols, each having its own specific format, and theoretically providing access to the same data, numerous studies [10,25,29,30] raised valid concern about the effectiveness and drawbacks of both protocols.

While both protocols were designed to provide registration information, there are no formal requirements mandating consistent results across different data sources. In practice, the registration data may vary between TLD registries, and registrars, as well as between the responses obtained from WHOIS and RDAP. This variability introduces an element of unpredictability with respect to the consistency and accuracy of the provided information.

Furthermore, studies that use registration data tend to favor one protocol over the other without providing explicit justification, and they base their preference on factors such as data retrieval speed, parsing capabilities, the presence of WHOIS and RDAP records for each domain, and other convenience-related considerations. Hence, an important issue emerges: to what degree do both protocols offer consistent information? Addressing this question requires a thorough and comprehensive analysis of how the data provided by the WHOIS and RDAP protocols align with each other.

To our knowledge, no previous research examined the assumption that information provided by WHOIS and RDAP is consistent. Nevertheless, many articles put forth classification algorithms, conducted studies on the domain behavior, or initiated abuse and vulnerability notification campaigns relying on data obtained through these protocols. In doing so, they implicitly depend on the accuracy and consistency of the information provided by WHOIS and RDAP.

Our paper makes the following contributions:

- We provide an overview of the disparities between WHOIS and RDAP, shedding light on the rationale behind the coexistence of multiple servers and protocols for accessing registration data. Delving into the historical and technical aspects, we highlight the intricate choices that have led to the current state of uncertainty surrounding the assurance of data consistency.
- We undertake a comprehensive data collection encompassing WHOIS and RDAP records for more than 55 million domains. Our focus is on parsing the fields commonly used in security and privacy studies. We will contribute all the collected registration data to the research community.
- We perform a thorough analysis of the parsed fields evaluating their consistency and deliberating over potential factors contributing to content variations. By doing so, we aim to raise awareness within the community about the importance of exercising caution with trust in registration data as 7.6% of the observed domains presented inconsistencies in fields used by security and privacy studies.
- We conduct a comprehensive analysis of the nameservers field, cross-referencing the gathered data with the results obtained from active DNS

measurements. Our aim is to determine which data source, whether WHOIS or RDAP, is more likely to provide accurate and trustful information.

2 Background

We begin by providing background information on the administration of domain names and the collaborative processes within the DNS ecosystem. Delving into the history of WHOIS and RDAP, we explore the reasons for their coexistence. Furthermore, we explain how to access registration data through both protocols, providing a clear outline of their respective procedures. Lastly, we elaborate on diverse approaches and challenges related to parsing WHOIS and RDAP.

2.1 The Ecosystem of Domain Management and Registration

The administration of a domain name entails the collaboration of multiple actors who collectively ensure the provision of all the necessary technical and administrative records vital for its operational use. At the top of the Domain Name System (DNS), the Internet Assigned Numbers Authority (IANA) manages the root nameservers and delegates the management of each top-level domain (TLD) to different registries. Country-code top-level domains (ccTLDs) such as .uk and .fr are managed by country-specific organizations (registries) like Nominet (for .uk) or AFNIC (for .fr). In contrast, generic top-level domains (gTLDs) such as .com and .business can be managed by any organization that meets the necessary requirements [19] and obtains authorization from the Internet Corporation for Assigned Names and Numbers (ICANN), like VeriSign Inc. (for .com) or Identity Digital (for .business). Registries are responsible for managing their top-level domain zones and have the authority to create new domains under their TLD. Each registry delegates the task of registering new domains to registrars, responsible for selling domains to users, referred to as registrants. When contacted by users, registrars collect and centralize user information, and communicate with the registry. In the interaction between registrars and registries, a variety of protocols may be used with the Extensible Provisioning Protocol (EPP) [12] commonly used for seamless communication. The registry then generates the required records such as DNS ones and administrative details to create the domain. For gTLDs under the ICANN agreement [19] and the majority of ccTLDs, both the registry and the registrar make the registration information available to the public. This information is typically accessible through the WHOIS and/or RDAP protocols.

2.2 Why Two Different Systems?

The existing WHOIS protocol as defined in RFC 3912 [6] published in 2004 formalized a practice in use since 1982 [21]. RFC 3912 established the guidelines on how a server could offer the information about various Internet entities, including users, servers, domains, and IP addresses with a straightforward query/response protocol. However, it recognized that the WHOIS protocol had certain deficiencies in terms of crucial design goals like internationalization and robust security, typically expected of IETF protocols. RFC 3912 explicitly stated that it did not address these shortcomings and only required the content to be presented in a human-readable format. The decision to retain the original design flaws in the WHOIS protocol can be attributed to historical reasons. The original WHOIS system in use since the early 80 s was already implemented on numerous servers. To maintain backward compatibility and prevent disruption to existing systems and practices, the IETF chose to accept the original design flaws rather than mandating widespread changes. This approach aimed to mitigate the risk of a new protocol facing low adoption rates, similar to what occurred with the SPF DNS record [24].

After several years, the IETF initiated efforts to design a new protocol aimed at providing domain registration information while addressing the limitations of WHOIS. This endeavor culminated in 2015 in the publication of RFC 7482 [33] that specified RDAP. RFC 7482 [33], along with subsequent extensions [3,15,16,28,34], specifies the protocol emphasizing the provision of machine-readable data in the JSON format. It defines data types, keys, and encoding to ensure structured information. Despite the introduction of RDAP, the WHOIS protocol has not been replaced, and both protocols continue to coexist, offering comparable data.

2.3   Data Access and Availability

RFC 3912 [6] and RFC 8521 [14] define the WHOIS and RDAP data access protocols, respectively. The RDAP protocol operates over HTTP(s) using the REST paradigm and returns data in JSON format, while a WHOIS user needs to connect to a server over TCP on port 43 and receive a plain text response.

The registration data may be incomplete, and some registries may only offer minimal information—in this case, they are called "thin", in opposition to "thick" registries that directly provide the full registration data. This difference in the completeness of registration data remains valid for both WHOIS and RDAP. For instance, the .com registry provides minimal information and does not include the registrant organization data. To obtain complete information (with respect to GDPR), the user of both protocols may need to follow referrals to one or several servers (see Fig. 1): they first need to locate the registry server (①), then submit a query to the registry to obtain the registration information (②), and optionally, retrieve more detailed data from the registrar (③).

For WHOIS queries, users can rely on command line tools provided by their system to bundle most steps and referrals, like the Debian *whois* package. On the contrary, there is no widely deployed command line tool to query RDAP databases.

The user needs to follow the steps below to retrieve registration information of google.com using RDAP:

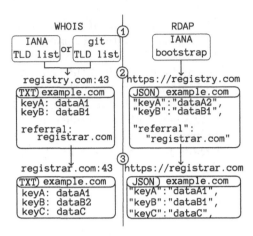

Fig. 1. Referral system to obtain complete registration data

① The user begins by retrieving the bootstrap configuration file from IANA,[1] as specified in RFC 9224. From this file, they obtain the URI of the .com RDAP server.

② The user appends the string `domain/google.com` to the server URI obtained in step ①, and forms the query to retrieve the registry RDAP answer at https://rdap.verisign.com/com/v1/domain/google.com. (an illustration of the result can be found in Appendix A, Fig. 7)

③ The returned JSON object contains a referral to the registrar server (in this example, MarkMonitor, Inc). The user can access this information at https://rdap.markmonitor.com/rdap/domain/google.com.

For WHOIS, RFC 3912 [6] does not provide a bootstrap file for step ①. Instead, users can query the IANA WHOIS server at `whois.iana.org` to retrieve TLD-related information. The response includes the details about the TLD registry, in particular, the domain name of the WHOIS server for that zone. As an example, let us examine the procedure involved in retrieving the registration information for the domain `google.com` using the WHOIS protocol:

① The user proceeds by querying the IANA WHOIS server for the .com TLD and locates the record `whois: whois.verisign-grs.com`. This information directs them to the VeriSign server.

② Next, the user queries this server that provides registry WHOIS information for the domain `google.com` (the result is presented in Appendix A, Fig. 6).

③ Within this record, there is a referral to the registrar server `WHOIS Server: whois.markmonitor.com`. The user can retrieve the most detailed registration data by querying this registrar WHOIS server.

Nevertheless, users may encounter problems when following this approach:

---

[1] https://data.iana.org/rdap/dns.json.

Table 1. Number of active TLDs providing RDAP and WHOIS servers

Source	RDAP	WHOIS	
	Boostrap	IANA	GitHub
ccTLD (309)	27 (9%)	222 (72%)	231 (75%)
gTLD (1152)	1152 (100%)	999 (86%)	1147 (99%)

– Certain WHOIS servers may require specific query flags. For example, the WHOIS server for the .de TLD expects the flags "-T dn,ace".
– The IANA database may not always be up to date, resulting in inaccurate information about certain TLDs. For example, it does not provide a WHOIS server for the .cm TLD.
– In some cases, the TLD registry may not handle the registration information for domain names associated with public suffixes. For instance, the registry server whois.nic.uk for the .uk TLD does not manage the .ac.uk TLD, managed instead by whois.nic.ac.uk.

For these reasons, the Debian *whois* package[2] adopts a different approach. It uses a dedicated database that specifies servers responsible for the public suffixes and the corresponding flags to be used. The source code for this package is accessible in a collaborative GitHub repository.[3] While the repository allows anyone to propose modifications, it has been mainly maintained by Marco d'Itri since 1999. This repository serves as a valuable alternative to the IANA WHOIS server, acting as a reliable starting point for retrieving WHOIS information (referred to as the git TLD list in Fig. 1, step ①).

We have retrieved the information from the RDAP bootstrap file, the GitHub repository of the *whois* package, and queried the server whois.iana.org for all active gTLD and ccTLD listed on the IANA website. Table 1 shows that the GitHub repository provides 148 additional WHOIS servers compared to the IANA list. For instance, it includes a WHOIS server for the .cm TLD, not available on whois.iana.org. The table also highlights the proportion of active gTLDs and ccTLDs that offer WHOIS and RDAP services. It is important to highlight that ccTLDs provide relatively less access to registration data than gTLDs. In particular, the adoption of the RDAP protocol among ccTLDs is significantly low, accounting for only 9%. We can attribute the disparity between ccTLDs and gTLDs to the agreement established between gTLDs and ICANN [19]. As per this agreement, registries have to offer access to registration data through the RDAP protocol. However, it does not require gTLDs to maintain WHOIS servers, and it does not apply to ccTLDs. Contrarily, the deployment of RDAP by ccTLD registries is influenced by various factors such as voluntary adoption, local regulations, and technical considerations.

---

[2] https://tracker.debian.org/pkg/whois.
[3] https://github.com/rfc1036/whois.

2.4   Parsing Registration Data

One of the primary motivations behind the design of RDAP is to address the inherent limitations of the WHOIS system, in particular, its vague and loosely defined "human-readable" format for data. By incorporating the JSON-structured response format and well-defined data element features, among others, RDAP provides a more standardized, machine-readable approach to accessing registration data. This enhancement significantly improves the efficiency and reliability of parsing and extracting information from RDAP responses when compared to the traditional WHOIS system.

WHOIS data has been presented in various formats, undergone frequent changes, and may even be expressed in the local language of the registrar or TLD registry (e.g., the Bolivian ccTLD .bo WHOIS records are written in Spanish). The absence of normalization or implicit conventions raises a significant challenge when parsing WHOIS records, as highlighted in the studies that use WHOIS data [11,25,27,29,30,38].

We can categorize traditional algorithms for parsing WHOIS data into two distinct approaches: templates and rules. The template-based approaches, such as Net::Whois[4] (Perl), whoisrb[5] (Ruby), and PHPWhois[6] (PHP), offer regular expression templates specifically tailored to each registry or registrar. When using this approach, the user obtains WHOIS data from the registry, parses it using the relevant template for the TLD and registry, extracts any potential referral link to a registrar WHOIS server, and then retrieves and parses the registrar WHOIS data using the corresponding template. This approach is effective when the templates are available and regularly maintained. However, it becomes challenging when no template is available for a specific entity or if the format undergoes changes. Therefore, its success heavily relies on the quantity and quality of the templates, necessitating manual updates for each template.

Rule-based approaches such as python-whois[7] use a collection of predefined rules, regular expressions, and Natural Language Processing techniques to identify prevalent formats found in WHOIS records such as Key: Value, and extract as many fields as feasible. This approach is versatile and can be applied to any registrar without the need for dedicated templates. It may also accommodate format changes over time. However, it is generally less efficient compared to the use of custom-made templates [27].

Previous work explored existing parsers to train machine-learning algorithms based on Natural Language Processing or used techniques like Conditional Random Field [31] to automatically deduce the data structure and enhance the accuracy of field extraction. This approach demonstrated improved capabilities in extracting various fields from data.

While the template-based and rule-based approaches offer some potential for obtaining registration data through WHOIS, they require regular maintenance

---

[4] https://metacpan.org/pod/Net::Whois.
[5] https://whoisrb.org/.
[6] https://github.com/SimpleUpdates/phpwhois.
[7] https://pypi.org/project/python-whois/.

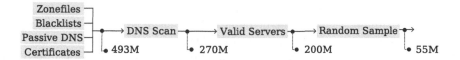

Fig. 2. The stages of domain selection with the number of domains at each step

and may be less efficient than RDAP. The introduction of RDAP offers a promising alternative for enhanced parsing efficiency and accuracy.

3 Methodology

In this section, we outline our methodology for collecting and parsing WHOIS and RDAP records. Considering the significant volume of data, we have meticulously designed our scheme to efficiently collect and parse registration data for a large number of domains within a reasonable time frame. All this is achieved while ensuring that WHOIS and RDAP servers experience minimal strain. We begin by explaining the process of domain selection, as illustrated in Fig. 2, followed by a comprehensive description of the WHOIS and RDAP parsing process. Lastly, we provide an overview of how we have identified and analyzed discrepancies among the records.

3.1 Domain Data Collection and Filtering

Compilation of Registered Domain Names. First, we gathered an extensive list of domains by consolidating multiple data sources:

- gTLD zone files obtained from ICANN Centralized Zone Data Service (CZDS)[8],
- ccTLD zone files accessible via `AXFR` zone transfers (`.se`, `.nu`, `.li`, `.ch`),
- Passive DNS feed from SIE Europe[9],
- Domain blacklists including SpamHaus[10], APWG[11], OpenPhish[12], URL-Haus[13], ThreatFox[14], and SURBL[15],
- Google Certificate Transparency Logs[16], which we continuously monitored to identify newly issued Transport Layer Security (TLS) certificates and extract the corresponding domain names.

---

[8] https://czds.icann.org.
[9] http://sie-europe.net.
[10] https://www.spamhaus.org.
[11] https://apwg.org.
[12] https://openphish.com.
[13] https://urlhaus.abuse.ch.
[14] https://threatfox.abuse.ch.
[15] https://surbl.org.
[16] https://certstream.calidog.io.

All the collected domains are aggregated and deduplicated, resulting in a list of 493 million unique domain names. To guarantee the inclusion of only registered domains, we performed an active DNS scan on each domain, querying for A resource records using zdns [23], and exclude those for which the response is NXDOMAIN (non-existent domain).

Filtering Domains with Valid WHOIS and RDAP Servers. To study the inconsistencies between WHOIS and RDAP records, we carefully filtered out domains that lacked a recognized WHOIS or RDAP server. This filtering process involved cross-referencing the official IANA list [17] and the GitHub repository, as detailed in Sect. 2.3. After this filtering step, our dataset comprised 200 million domain names.

Scanning all 200M domains would be a time-consuming process spanning several months, along with significant storage challenges. To address this, we opted to work with a representative subset of domains. This subset was randomly chosen from the pool of 200 million domains, with a sample size of 55 million domains carefully determined to facilitate the collection and parsing of WHOIS and RDAP records within a one-month time frame.

3.2 Gathering and Parsing Resgistration Data

Data Collection. After identifying WHOIS and RDAP servers for the sampled domain names, we proceeded with the collection of the corresponding records. We gathered the registration data of the selected domains between December 6th and December 31st, 2022. During the collection process, we parsed each record to determine if it belonged to a "thin" registry that delegated a part of the data to a referral server, and follow the eventual referral. This step was iteratively repeated to ensure we obtained all versions of the registration data, following all referrals. At the end, we successfully collected a total of 164 million unique records, covering information from over 55 million distinct domains.

To ensure accurate comparisons, we collected WHOIS and RDAP records of each domain within a narrow time window, typically under 1 min. This prevents the comparison of records collected at different times and reduces discrepancies resulting from domain updates during the scanning process. Moreover, some registrars impose query limits on IP addresses and enforce timeouts or blacklist IP addresses that exceed these limits. To ensure compliance and prevent any disruptions, we adjusted our data collection speed accordingly.

After the collection process, we carefully examined the gathered WHOIS and RDAP records. Any malformed responses (like invalid HTTP packets or JSON objects for RDAP) or timeouts were discarded, while valid responses underwent parsing for further analysis.

Parsing WHOIS. Parsing WHOIS data and extracting all pertinent fields presents a challenge, as detailed in Sect. 2. Consequently, this study focuses on specific fields used in previous research (see Table 2), using custom templates

Table 2. Fields extracted from WHOIS and RDAP records

Field	Data type	Missing rate		Domain inconsistency	Used by
		Records	Domains		
Nameservers	Text	3.2%	6.6%	573,790 (1%)	[5,9,13]
IANA ID	Integer	5.9%	13.7%	106,813 (0.2%)	[1,5,8,26]
Creation date	Date	0.8%	2.2%	3,138,024 (5.7%)	[1,8,11,26]
Expiration date	Date	1.0%	2.7%	2,424,951 (4.4%)	[25,26]
Emails	Email	7.9%	14.8%	18,958,821 (34.5%)	[4,8,29,38]
					[5,11,26,30]

designed to accurately parse various formats. We developed 242 custom templates comprising regular expressions that outline the extraction process for selected fields from WHOIS records across numerous registrars. The templates are designed to handle multiple languages and formats, maximizing the comparability of records.

Parsing RDAP. Contrasted with WHOIS, parsing RDAP records is typically more straightforward, primarily due to the JSON format. Nevertheless, despite the data format being defined in RFC 9083 [15], there might be ambiguity regarding the correct placement of information within the data structure. Consequently, different registries and registrars may have varying interpretations of where specific information should be located.

We gathered the designated fields from all locations allowed by the RFC. We considered malformed fields, those containing incorrect data types, or located in the wrong place within the data structure as missing. For instance, there are two primary representations of domain names in RDAP: as a string object (e.g., ns.example.com) or as an array of labels (e.g., [ns, example, com]). However, according to RFC 9083 [15], when listing domain nameservers, they must be in the string format. Therefore, if we encountered a nameserver in the array format instead of the expected string format, we considered it as missing. This decision was based on the assumption that most automated systems would adhere to the RFC and disregard the field due to its invalid type.

Field Selection. To compare different data sources, it is important to note that not all registration data records share the same set of fields. As a result, we selected a limited number of fields, which have been commonly used in previous security studies and are consistently present in both WHOIS and RDAP records, whether at the registry or registrar levels. Table 2 presents the selected fields, along with the type of data they hold and the articles that have used them. For this research, we have chosen the following fields:

- **Nameservers**: this field indicates the name servers that have the authority over a particular domain.

- IANA ID and Registrar: the sponsoring registrar responsible for managing the domain is captured in the Registrar text field. Additionally, the IANA ID is an integer field that typically represents the unique identifier assigned by IANA [18] to each ICANN-accredited registrar (if applicable).
- Creation date and Expiration date: these fields denote the date of the initial registration for the domain and the subsequent expiration date. Once the registration expires, the domain becomes available for purchase again unless the owner renews it.
- Emails: This field contains a range of contact email addresses that can be used, for instance, for reporting domain-related abuse.

We deliberately omitted selecting fields associated with a registrant, despite their use in several studies, due to their absence in many registries. Furthermore, the implementation of the European General Data Protection Regulation (GDPR) resulted in the removal or redaction of the field content by most servers. The impact of GDPR on the content of these fields falls outside the scope of this paper and has already been analyzed in prior research [29].

When a field is absent from a record, or the content could not be parsed, the data is marked as missing. Table 2 shows the proportion of records missing each field. The record missing rate indicates the proportion of records with missing data, whereas the domain missing rate represents the percentage of domains that have at least one record with missing data. This considers that each domain has multiple records (i.e., WHOIS and RDAP, including records collected by following referrals).

The missing rates for all fields, except for the IANA ID and Emails fields, are relatively low. This result was expected since the IANA ID solely pertains to domains under generic TLDs and ICANN-accredited registrars. Furthermore, each field presented its own set of parsing challenges, particularly in the case of WHOIS records, but also for RDAP. In RDAP, certain records, such as email contact addresses, can be located in different parts of the JSON structure as defined by RFC 7483 [34].

3.3 Analyzing Data Consistency

After collecting, parsing, and cleaning the registration data for all studied domains, we analyzed the consistency among various WHOIS and RDAP records.

For a given domain, if we were able to collect registration data from multiple sources and if these records have common fields, we evaluated the consistency of the data. If the formatted data in same fields is identical, we considered them to be matching fields. On the other hand, if there is a discrepancy between the data, it results in a mismatch. We consider two types of mismatches: the first one involves two records from the same protocol, such as the registry WHOIS not aligning with the registrar WHOIS. The second type involves two records from different protocols, for instance, the registrar WHOIS not corresponding to the registrar RDAP.

3.4 Ethical Consideration

We adhered to the best practices recommended by the measurement community to ensure reliable results with minimal disruption to the servers [7,35]. When gathering various data sources, including WHOIS, RDAP, and DNS records, we meticulously adhered to server rate limits [23]. Additionally, upon visiting the scanner's source IP address, users are presented with a webpage that provides information about our identity, work, and instructions for adding a scanned server to our opt-out lists, allowing them to cease receiving requests from us. Throughout the study, we did not receive any opt-out requests via email.

The raw data we collected may include information about registrants. However, after the implementation of GDPR, most registrars provide options for their customers to choose which fields are visible or automatically redact personal information. In practice, most fields that could potentially contain personal data were redacted by default.

4 Results

In this section, we present the analysis of inconsistencies and explore the root causes of the disparities observed in specific fields. Table 2 provides a breakdown, field by field, indicating the count of records where the field was missing, the number of domains in which at least one mismatch was identified, or if the field was entirely absent from the records. Excluding the `emails` field, which raises its unique challenges discussed in Scct. 4.3, we observed that 7.6% of all examined domains exhibited at least one inconsistency in the remaining fields.

4.1 Nameservers

The typical method to obtain a list of authoritative nameservers for a given domain involves sending recursive queries within the DNS tree, starting from the root zone and progressing toward the registry nameserver, which then provides the relevant information [8]. However, in certain prior studies that had a primary focus on detecting malicious domains [5,9,13], the nameserver information used in the analysis was obtained from WHOIS.

The primary purpose of the nameserver fields was either to cluster domains with identical nameservers [5,9] or to conduct further analysis on the nameserver itself. For instance, investigations could involve verifying whether the nameserver is self-hosted, such as `ns.example.com` being authoritative for `example.com`, determining if it is managed by well-kown DNS service operators, or identifying if the apex domain of the nameserver is newly registered [13].

In the subsequent part of this section, we begin by examining the various types of nameserver mismatches and their frequency. Then, we use DNS as a reference point to ascertain the accuracy of the data sources involved in cases of mismatches.

Table 3. Number of records and domains with mismatching nameservers

Case	Records	Domains
All	1,044,268	576,204
Inclusion	314,633 (30.1%)	224,833 (39.1%)
Intersection	48,693 (4.6%)	23,934 (4.1%)
Disjoint	680,942 (65.2%)	343,994 (60.0%)

Mismatch Types. We identified a total of 1,044,268 mismatches between two registration records of the same domain, encompassing 576,204 unique domain names. This accounts for approximately 1% of the overall collected domains; hence 99% of the measured domains did not have mismatching nameservers records.

When the nameservers of two records (referred to as A and B) are found to be inconsistent, three potential scenarios may arise:

Inclusion. $A \subset B$ or $A \supset B$: one set is a subset of the other one.
Intersection. No inclusion but $A \cap B \neq \emptyset$: A and B do not match but they have at least one server in common.
Disjoint. $A \cap B = \emptyset$: A and B have no nameserver in common.

Table 3 presents the number of mismatches detected in each scenario. As described in Sect. 3.3, a given domain may have multiple records for each protocol, as each registration record may contain a referral field. As a result, each domain can exhibit multiple types of mismatches. For example, the nameservers extracted from the registrar's WHOIS record could be included in the list of nameservers found in the registrar's RDAP record, and additionally, the nameservers listed in the registry's WHOIS record could entirely differ from the servers in the registry's RDAP record. In such cases, a domain would be counted in both the inclusion and disjoint categories. Consequently, the values in the Domains column may exceed 100%.

When using DNS to fetch a domain's resource records, if the client (e.g., a recursive resolver) has multiple nameservers to choose from, it can use any of them interchangeably or query all and process the first received answer [22]. This means that the inclusion and intersection cases may be less worrisome, as both records share at least one nameserver, potentially indicating that all nameservers serve the same data. Conversely, the disjoint case, in which both records have no servers in common, is concerning as it raises suspicion that the nameservers may not serve the same data or be authoritative for the domain name. This situation concerns 65% of the studied mismatches and 60% of the domains with mismatching records. The mismatch often involves records from different protocols. We have observed that 67.6% of the nameserver mismatches were between a WHOIS record and an RDAP record, whereas 17% were between two RDAP records (registry RDAP and registrar RDAP) and 15.4% were between two WHOIS records of the same domain.

In summary, while affecting only 1% of domains, nameserver mismatches, especially the 67.6% involving disparities between WHOIS and RDAP, raise concerns. In 60% of such cases, both sources lack any common nameservers, making the choice between WHOIS and RDAP for gathering nameserver information non-neutral and yielding incompatible results.

Who is Right? To successfully collect any DNS record for a domain it is essential to have an NS record in the parent zone file, specifying the authoritative nameserver for the domain. To gather the nameserver information, we actively queried the DNS infrastructure and performed a comparison with the nameservers listed in the WHOIS and RDAP records.

Methodology. To find the example.com nameservers, the client (e.g., a recursive resolver) first sends an NS query to the DNS root servers and receives the name of the servers that have authority over the .com zone. The client then sends another NS query to one of these servers and receives the NS record of example.com. This last answer comes from the registry in charge of the .com zone. The client can then either return the result because it retrieved the NS record of example.com from the authoritative nameservers of the parent (nameserver of .com) or perform additional NS queries to the nameservers received at the previous step and get the nameservers configured by the administrator of the domain. RFC 1034 [32] states that the nameservers returned by the registry and the nameservers configured by the administrator must be identical, but previous study [36] revealed that around 10% of the domains in the .com, .org and .not zones had differences between the nameservers provided by the parent registry servers and the nameservers provided by the child domain servers. If a domain is active, it must have an NS record at the registry level, as it is a part of the resolution chain. On the contrary, some domain owners do not put NS records in the child nameservers. To maximize the number of collected domains, we queried the NS resource records for each domain at the registry level.

Scans. To determine the consistency between registration data sources and DNS data, we used zdns [23] to retrieve the NS resource records of each domain where a mismatch was detected. Additionally, we collected their WHOIS and RDAP records for a second time, specifically between January 24th and January 27th, 2023. This ensured that all three data sources (DNS, WHOIS, and RDAP) were collected simultaneously, eliminating cases where domain configurations were altered during our scans.

While some domains had expired between our initial scan and this supplementary analysis, approximately 90% of the domains remained active and produced a NOERROR DNS response with non-empty results during the scan.

Results. The second data collection unveiled 365,521 distinct domains exhibiting nameserver mismatches.

After the collection of the new registration data and the NS records from the authoritative DNS servers, the resulting data falls into two categories: the mismatch can be between two records from the same protocol (two WHOIS records or two RDAP records), or between two records of different protocols.

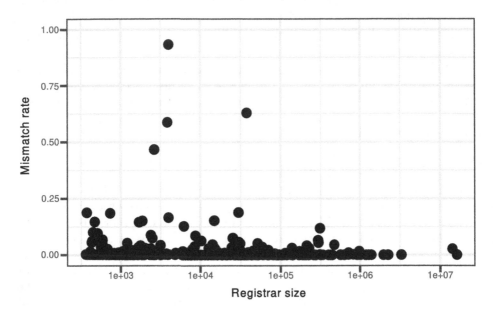

Fig. 3. Nameserver mismatch rate per registrar

WHOIS-RDAP Mismatches. In 74.9% of the identified mismatch cases, the disparity exists between a record gathered through WHOIS and a record collected through RDAP. As previously described, the nameservers obtained from DNS may constitute a subset, superset, or have a non-empty intersection with each record. Upon examining all possible scenarios, we found that in 99.5% of cases, the DNS record corresponded to either the WHOIS or RDAP record. The remaining 0.5% involved intermediate situations where the DNS result only partially matched one of the records. Due to the limited number of domains affected by this situation, we opted for concentrating our analysis on cases where the DNS matched one of the records.

In 78.5% of cases, the DNS data corresponded to the nameservers provided by the RDAP record. This underscores the fact that, although nameservers obtained from DNS typically align with data from RDAP, there are still 21% of mismatch instances where the DNS results match the WHOIS record. Interestingly, Fig. 3 highlights that a few registrars exhibit a notably high mismatch rate compared to others. We observed that only four registrars have a mismatch rate exceeding 25%, while the largest registrars, representing the majority of domains, maintain a very low mismatch rate.

Registry-Registrar Mismatches. The remaining 25.1% of cases represent the situations in which the mismatch is between two records from the same protocol but collected from different servers. In this case, the collector queried the registry server, got a referral to another server, and recursively called it, gathering an additional record. If two records are inconsistent, we checked if the nameservers provided by the DNS matched the records collected at the registry server or at the referral servers. In 99.2% of the cases, the DNS data matched the registry record, and in the remaining 0.8% of the cases, it did not match either records. The DNS data matched the registrar record in only 0.008% of the cases.

As described in Sect. 4.1, we decided to collect the NS records at the DNS authoritative nameservers of the registry. Consequently, we expected the record provided by the registry to be consistent with the DNS data from the same registry. Hence, the mismatches between two records from the same protocol almost always come from invalid data from the referral server.

The main takeaway is that when both sets of nameservers have no common elements, and the discrepancy lies between an RDAP and a WHOIS record, the RDAP record is accurate and aligns with the NS records from DNS in 78% of the cases.

4.2   IANA ID, Creation and Expiration Dates

When it comes to obtaining the IANA ID, creation date or registrar name of a domain, research primarily relies on the WHOIS and RDAP protocols. Unlike nameservers, which can also be retrieved from DNS, there is no third-party service that offers direct access to this data. Consequently, when two sources diverge in these fields, there is no simple method to determine which record contains the accurate information.

In this section, we outline the types of mismatches identified in IANA ID, creation and expiration dates, and highlight a few cases where we can ascertain the correct record.

Creation and Expiration Dates. The creation date represents the domain's initial registration instant, providing insight into its age. In domain-related research, the domain age is a pivotal factor as older domains, active for multiple years, are generally deemed more trustworthy than newly registered ones. The extensive analyses of the domain registration behavior [1,13] have shown that malicious domains tend to have shorter lifespans and are used in attacks shortly after registration. Other studies [8,9] have used the creation date to detect bulk registrations of malicious domains.

The domain age is also frequently combined with other parameters to distinguish between benign and malicious domains [11,26]. While some approaches [1] attempt to estimate the domain activity period by monitoring its appearance and disappearance in publicly accessible zone files, this method is contingent on zone file accessibility and the availability of historical data for the domain. Consequently, most studies depend on WHOIS or RDAP to acquire the creation date.

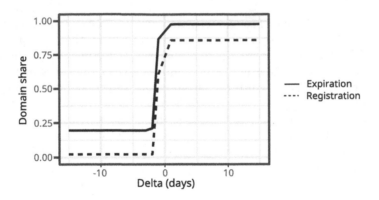

Fig. 4. Cumulative distribution of creation and expiration date mismatches

The expiration date also provides insights into the domain behavior and can shed light on various scenarios. For instance, if a domain is removed from its zone file before its expiration date, it may suggest actions taken by the registrar or seizure by authorities [1]. Additionally, parking and drop-catching entities use the expiration date to identify when a domain will become available for re-registration [38].

Both creation and expiration dates are usually found in the majority of WHOIS and RDAP records. However, in the case of WHOIS, they may be listed under various names, such as `Creation Date`, `Registration Date`, `Created at`, `Valid until`, and more.

After filtering out dates that were not possible to parse and dates lower or equal to the UNIX Epoch (which may indicate a default value or a configuration error), we observed that 5.7% (for creation dates) and 4.4% (for expiration dates) of the domains exhibited inconsistencies across their records. Figure 4 illustrates the distribution of time differences between these records.

We can observe that in 84% of the cases for creation dates and 78% of the cases for expiration dates, the differences are less than 2 days. These discrepancies have minimal impact on the analyses relying on creation dates to gauge the domain age [13] or on the speed of domain re-registration after expiration [1].

Previous studies [25] highlighted common misunderstanding of the different expiration steps before the deletion of a domain and pointed out that these steps can account for a mismatch of up to 30 days, as a confusion could be made between the expiration date, the deletion date and how the grace and redemption periods should be accounted for, but the collected data shows no specific mismatch proportion at 30 days. However, our analysis points out that several records present an expiration date difference of exactly one year, which corresponds to the minimal duration of a registration, so the difference could come from the fact that the renewal of the domain was taken into account in one of the records and not in the other. Then, 98% of expiration date mismatches are either under 2 days or exactly 1 year, leaving only a few domains with unexplained expiration date mismatches.

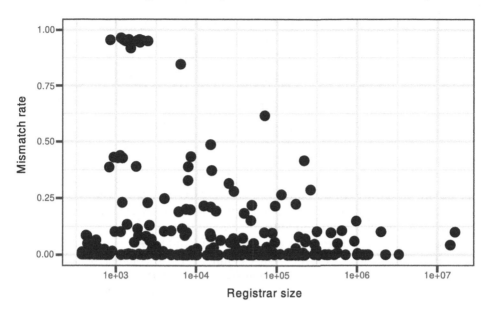

Fig. 5. Creation date mismatch rate per registrar

Approximately 16% of the creation date mismatches extend beyond 2 days. In contrast to expiration date mismatches, creation date mismatches are more evenly distributed. One possible explanation for these discrepancies is that different entities may have distinct definitions of the `Creation Date`. While RFC 9083 [15] clearly defines keywords to describe creation events in RDAP, such as `registration`, `reregistration`, `reinstantiation`, and `transfer`, WHOIS lacks such precision. Consequently, the `Creation Date` recorded in the WHOIS record may not correspond to the same events in the domain life cycle as the `registration` event in the RDAP record.

The `Creation Date` mismatch rate for each registrar, as shown in Fig. 5, highlights that while many registrars have over 10% of their domains with creation date mismatches, a few registrars exhibit nearly 100% of their domains with mismatched creation dates. This observation supports our hypothesis that some of these mismatches may result from registrar misinterpretations, custom registration processes or systematic configuration errors. For example, the vast majority of domains presenting a `Creation Date` mismatch of 30 or 31 days are under the .com TLD and share the same registrar, `FastDomain Inc`. For these domains, the registrar record `Creation Date` is always one month earlier that the one in the registry record. After investigation, we found that this registrar allows their customers to cancel their domain order up to 30 days after payment, while the ICANN Agreement [19] only imposes a 5-day refund window. Consequently, we can hypothesize that the creation of the registry record was delayed until the end of the 30-days period, while the registrar record was created when the customer first ordered the domain.

Table 4. Number of records and domains with mismatching emails

Case	Records	Domains
All	50.1M	19.0M
Inclusion	37.1M (74%)	15.1M (79.8%)
Intersection	0.59M (1.2%)	0.56M (2.9%)
Disjoint	12.4M (24.8%)	4.9M (26%)

IANA ID and Registrars. ICANN-accredited registrars play a crucial role in domain registration and management. The IANA ID associated with each registrar is a unique identifier, often found in WHOIS and RDAP records, helping to trace domain ownership and authority.

The content of the `Registrar` field in WHOIS and RDAP may differ from the name listed in the IANA registry. For example, 2.4% of domains with IANA ID 146 (GoDaddy.com, LLC) have different `Registrar` entries, including GoDaddy LLC, GoDaddy.com, Inc., GODADDY or Go Daddy, LLC. Therefore, parsing the `Registrar` field to identify registrars can be challenging, and users often rely on the IANA ID for accuracy. However, in certain ccTLDs, registrars receive local accreditation, and the corresponding IANA IDs are not assigned or displayed in the public WHOIS and RDAP. In these cases, extracting registrar information relies solely on the `Registrar` field.

Our analysis uncovered that a mere 0.2% of domain names had records with inconsistent `IANA ID`. The analysis of IANA IDs reveals that the majority of mismatches occur between specific pairs of IDs. Approximately 91% of these detected mismatches involve a record with IANA ID 1556 (`Chengdu West Dimension Digital Technology Co., Ltd.`) and another record with IANA ID 1915 (`West263 International Limited`). Additionally, 4% of the mismatches involve IANA ID 3951 (`Webempresa Europa, S.L.`) and ID 5555555, which is an invalid ID. This pattern may suggest misconfiguration issues by particular entities, resulting in consistent mismatches across all the domains they manage.

In the second case, we confirmed the issue by registering a domain name with the registrar `Webempresa Europa, S.L.` and examining its records. While the registry WHOIS record correctly indicated the valid IANA ID 3951, the registrar WHOIS record contained an IANA ID field with the value 5555555, which does not correspond to any valid registrar number. The registrar's WHOIS record also displayed place-holder values for various fields, including the abuse contact phone number and the reseller name. We verified that all domains registered with this registrar had inconsistent records. We reported the issue to the registrar, and over several months, we noticed that all the domains they managed were updated with correct registration data, resolving the inconsistencies. We suspect that the mismatches between ID 1556 and ID 1915 share the same origin. However, we were unable to test this hypothesis, as both registrars exclusively serve users in China and Hong Kong.

4.3   Email Addresses

Various types of email addresses are included in registration data, serving different purposes. These addresses are associated with the registry, registrar, or registrant, as well as for technical, administrative, and abuse-related functions. RFC 9083 [15] provides specific keywords in RDAP for describing the role of each email address, such as administrative, abuse, billing, or technical. This allows for easy identification of the address role, a capability that WHOIS lacks. For these reasons, we chose to collect all addresses in each record without distinguishing their roles. We then compared the records based on the sets of addresses they contain. Mismatches can occur due to protocol-specific contact addresses; for instance, the technical contact email for RDAP records may differ from that in WHOIS records if a registrar delegates technical administration to a third party. However, we anticipate that some addresses will be common across multiple records for the same domain, such as the abuse contact email for reporting domain-related abuse.

To analyze email mismatches, we applied the techniques described in Sect. 4.1. Initially, email addresses were parsed and duplicates were removed. Subsequently, we compared the various possible inclusion and intersection cases. The results of this analysis are presented in Table 4.

We identified 50 million mismatches on 19 million unique domains, encompassing 34.5% of the domains in this study. Among them, 74% of mismatches and 79.8% of domains featured one set of email addresses included in the other. About 75.2% of mismatches were either inclusions or intersections, potentially arising from shared addresses (e.g., abuse or registrant emails) while the addition of server or protocol-specific addresses by different entities (e.g., contact addresses for WHOIS or RDAP servers) may result in differences. However, nearly 5 million domains (8.8% of all analyzed domains) had a pair of records with no common email addresses.

The disjoint cases may be attributed to the GDPR implementation. Previous research [29] explored the impact of GDPR on the availability of personal information fields before and after its enactment. Following the GDPR implementation, many registrars and registries replaced the registrants' personal details like the name, the phone number, and the email address in WHOIS and RDAP records with entries such as 'REDACTED FOR PRIVACY', effectively concealing this information. However, some entities introduced proxy email addresses to safeguard the registrants' actual addresses. These proxy servers mediate communication between proxy addresses and registrant emails. For example, in an RDAP record under the registrant role, one might encounter the address b4ebaf9bfeba@withheld forprivacy.com. While this conceals the registrants' personal data from the public, a valid contact address remains accessible. Protecting user privacy by redacting or using proxy email addresses can create discrepancies between WHOIS and RDAP records, as the registrant's address, which should be consistent in all records, may be redacted or hidden behind proxies.

Email mismatches can also occur when registrars or registries use distinct addresses for WHOIS and RDAP, even though both email addresses are administered by the same organization, such as `abuse.whois@registrar.com` and `abuse.rdap@registrar.com`.

To address these discrepancies, we conducted a new analysis by extracting and comparing only the domain names from email addresses, discarding the local parts. This approach considered email addresses within the same domain as consistent. The results are presented in Table 5. We found that this approach resolved 18.6% of the mismatches and reduced the rate of disjoint email addresses from 24.8% to 9.7%. This suggests that in many cases where email addresses appeared disjoint, they actually originated from records with different email addresses hosted under the same domain.

Table 5. Number of records and domains with email domain mismatches after removing the local part of the address, retaining only the base domain name

Case	Records	Domains
All	50.1M	19M
Equality	9.3M (18.6%)	4.0M (21.4%)
Inclusion	35.7M (71.3%)	14.5M (76.7%)
Intersection	0.24M (0.5%)	0.23M (1.2%)
Disjoint	4.8M (9.7%)	2M (10.6%)

In conclusion, this analysis underscores the need for caution when gathering email addresses, especially for notification campaigns [30]. The choice of data source significantly affects the collected email addresses for 34.5% of domains. Additionally, in 10% of cases where email records mismatch, the domains hosting these addresses are unrelated, suggesting that email servers may be managed by different entities, potentially leading to varying effectiveness in notification campaigns.

5   Related Work

Table 2 provides an overview of prior research that used WHOIS and RDAP data for domain name registration information. Nevertheless, the accuracy of the collected data has not been thoroughly investigated. Some earlier studies [5, 8,9,25] relied on WHOIS data prior to the introduction of RDAP. However, as discussed in Sect. 2, inconsistencies are also present in WHOIS data obtained from servers managed by registries and registrars.

Challenges in processing WHOIS records have been identified, particularly concerning the reliability of extracted data such as AS numbers for IP WHOIS [2] and domain status [25]. In a previous in-depth analysis of the .com zone [27], the authors developed a machine-learning algorithm to address the multiple formats used in WHOIS records, demonstrating the difficulties in consistently parsing relevant fields.

The performance analysis of WHOIS and RDAP [10] focused on the speed but lacked the examination of data consistency across different servers and protocols.

In our work, we observed that 7.6% of the scanned domains exhibited mismatching records, raising concerns about the reliability of security metrics relying on such data. Notably, metrics that use the Creation Date field [26] or the bulk registration status [1] may be impacted, especially for registrars with high mismatch rates as presented in Fig. 5. Obtaining accurate creation dates for domains under these registrars may require alternative data sources.

The Emails field exhibited the highest mismatch rates, even with a conservative parsing approach. Previous studies on notification campaigns [4,30] reported difficulties in extracting valid email addresses from WHOIS records, with email bounce rates exceeding 50%. These findings raise concerns about the effectiveness of notification campaigns due to the challenges associated with obtaining consistent and valid abuse emails from different entities.

6 Conclusions

Registration data plays a crucial role in the development of detection systems and gaining insights into the domain name behavior and entity management. However, obtaining this information may require interacting with various servers (either registries or registrars) and protocols (either WHOIS or RDAP). Our extensive analysis of 164 million records from 55 million domains unveiled that the data obtained through WHOIS and RDAP is generally consistent. Nonetheless, 7.6% of the analyzed domains displayed discrepancies in one or more of the following fields: IANA ID, creation and expiration dates, or nameservers. In cases related to the nameserver field, we used active DNS measurements to determine the accurate record. When disparities involved RDAP and WHOIS records, our findings showed that RDAP records were correct in 78% of instances where mismatches occurred.

The principal insight underscores the importance of studies reliant on dependable registration data to diversify their data sources by collecting it from various servers and protocols. Although larger registrars generally display lower mismatch rates, this observation does not inherently guarantee the accuracy of the data. Smaller registrars present a wide range of outcomes, with some demonstrating minimal discrepancies, while others exhibit higher rates. The potential risk exists for malicious actors to exploit registrars with inconsistent data, allowing them to evade detection systems that rely on the availability and reliability of registration data. An analysis of the extent of malicious domains managed by such inconsistent registrars could offer valuable insights into evasion strategies.

To facilitate future research, we will provide the collected records (both raw and parsed) and the associated data analysis as resources linked to this publication.

A   Examples of Records

```
Domain Name: GOOGLE.COM
Registry Domain ID: 2138514_DOMAIN_COM-VRSN
Registrar WHOIS Server: whois.markmonitor.com
Registrar URL: http://www.markmonitor.com
Updated Date: 2019-09-09T15:39:04Z
Creation Date: 1997-09-15T04:00:00Z
Registry Expiry Date: 2028-09-14T04:00:00Z
Registrar: MarkMonitor Inc.
Registrar IANA ID: 292
Registrar Abuse Contact Email: abusecomplaints@markmonitor.com
Registrar Abuse Contact Phone: +1.2086851750
Domain Status: clientDeleteProhibited https://icann.org/epp#clientDeleteProhibited
Domain Status: clientTransferProhibited https://icann.org/epp#clientTransferProhibited
Domain Status: clientUpdateProhibited https://icann.org/epp#clientUpdateProhibited
Domain Status: serverDeleteProhibited https://icann.org/epp#serverDeleteProhibited
Domain Status: serverTransferProhibited https://icann.org/epp#serverTransferProhibited
Domain Status: serverUpdateProhibited https://icann.org/epp#serverUpdateProhibited
Name Server: NS1.GOOGLE.COM
Name Server: NS2.GOOGLE.COM
Name Server: NS3.GOOGLE.COM
Name Server: NS4.GOOGLE.COM
DNSSEC: unsigned
URL of the ICANN Whois Inaccuracy Complaint Form: https://www.icann.org/wicf/
```

Fig. 6. Registry WHOIS record of `google.com` obtained from the VeriSign server

```
{
 "objectClassName": "domain",
 "ldhName": "GOOGLE.COM",
 "links": [{
     "value": "https://rdap.verisign.com/com/v1/domain/GOOGLE.COM",
     "rel": "self",
     "href": "https://rdap.verisign.com/com/v1/domain/GOOGLE.COM",
     "type": "application/rdap+json"
   },{
     "value": "https://rdap.markmonitor.com/rdap/domain/GOOGLE.COM",
     "rel": "related",
     "href": "https://rdap.markmonitor.com/rdap/domain/GOOGLE.COM",
     "type": "application/rdap+json"}],
 "entities": [{
     "objectClassName": "entity",
     "handle": "292",
     "roles": ["registrar"],
     "publicIds": [{"type": "IANA Registrar ID","identifier": "292"}],
     "vcardArray": [
       "vcard", [
         ["version",{},"text","4.0"],
         ["fn",{},"text","MarkMonitor Inc."]]],
     "entities": [{
         "objectClassName": "entity",
         "roles": ["abuse"],
         "vcardArray": ["vcard",[
             ["version",{},"text","4.0"],
             ["fn",{},"text",""],
             ["tel",{"type": "voice"},"uri","tel:+1.2086851750"],
             ["email",{},"text","abusecomplaints@markmonitor.com"]]]}]}],
 "events": [
   {"eventAction": "registration", "eventDate": "1997-09-15T04:00:00Z"},
   {"eventAction": "expiration", "eventDate": "2028-09-14T04:00:00Z"},
   {"eventAction": "last changed", "eventDate": "2019-09-09T15:39:04Z"},
   {"eventAction": "last update of RDAP database", "eventDate": "2023-05-26T13:57:10Z"}],
 "nameservers": [
   {"objectClassName": "nameserver","ldhName": "NS1.GOOGLE.COM"},
   {"objectClassName": "nameserver","ldhName": "NS2.GOOGLE.COM"},
   {"objectClassName": "nameserver","ldhName": "NS3.GOOGLE.COM"},
   {"objectClassName": "nameserver","ldhName": "NS4.GOOGLE.COM"}],
}
```

Fig. 7. Part of the Registry RDAP record of `google.com` obtained from the VeriSign server

References

1. Affinito, A., et al.: Domain name lifetimes: baseline and threats. In: 6th Network Traffic Measurement and Analysis Conference, TMA 2022. IFIP (2022). https://dl.ifip.org/db/conf/tma/tma2022/tma2022-paper32.pdf

2. Bianzino, A.P., Pezzuolo, D., Mazzini, G.: Who is whois? An analysis of results consistence. In: 2014 22nd International Conference on Software, Telecommunications and Computer Networks (SoftCOM), pp. 289–292. IEEE (2014). https://doi.org/10.1109/SOFTCOM.2014.7039137

3. Blanchet, M.: Finding the Authoritative Registration Data Access Protocol (RDAP) Service. Request for Comments RFC 9224, Internet Engineering Task Force (2022). https://doi.org/10.17487/RFC9224

4. Çetin, O., Hanif Jhaveri, M., Gañán, C., van Eeten, M., Moore, T.: Understanding the role of sender reputation in abuse reporting and cleanup. J. Cybersecur. **2**(1), 83–98 (2016). https://doi.org/10.1093/cybsec/tyw005
5. Christin, N., Yanagihara, S.S., Kamataki, K.: Dissecting one click frauds. In: Proceedings of the 17th ACM Conference on Computer and Communications Security - CCS 2010, p. 15. ACM Press (2010). https://doi.org/10.1145/1866307.1866310
6. Daigle, L.: WHOIS Protocol Specification. Request for Comments RFC 3912, Internet Engineering Task Force (2004). https://doi.org/10.17487/RFC3912
7. Dittrich, D., Kenneally, E.: The Menlo Report: Ethical Principles Guiding Information and Communication Technology Research (2012)
8. Du, K., Yang, H., Li, Z.: The ever-changing labyrinth: a large-scale analysis of wildcard DNS powered blackhat SEO. In: USENIX Security 2016, p. 19 (2016)
9. Felegyhazi, M., Kreibich, C., Paxson, V.: On the potential of proactive domain blacklisting. In: LEET 2010 (2010)
10. Ganan, C.: WHOIS sunset? A primer in registration data access protocol (RDAP) performance. In: TMA, p. 8 (2021)
11. Ghaleb, F.A., Alsaedi, M., Saeed, F., Ahmad, J., Alasli, M.: Cyber threat intelligence-based malicious URL detection model using ensemble learning. Sensors **22**(9), 3373 (2022). https://doi.org/10.3390/s22093373
12. Gould, J.: Extensible Provisioning Protocol (EPP) and Registration Data Access Protocol (RDAP) Status Mapping. Request for Comments RFC 8056, Internet Engineering Task Force (2017). https://doi.org/10.17487/RFC8056
13. Hao, S., Kantchelian, A., Miller, B., Paxson, V., Feamster, N.: PREDATOR: proactive recognition and elimination of domain abuse at time-of-registration. In: Proceedings of the 2016 ACM SIGSAC Conference on Computer and Communications Security, pp. 1568–1579. ACM (2016). https://doi.org/10.1145/2976749.2978317
14. Hollenbeck, S., Newton, A.: Registration data access protocol (RDAP) object tagging. Request for Comments RFC 8521, Internet Engineering Task Force (2018). https://doi.org/10.17487/RFC8521
15. Hollenbeck, S., Newton, A.: JSON Responses for the Registration Data Access Protocol (RDAP). Request for Comments RFC 9083, Internet Engineering Task Force (2021). https://doi.org/10.17487/RFC9083
16. Hollenbeck, S., Newton, A.: Registration Data Access Protocol (RDAP) Query Format. Request for Comments RFC 9082, Internet Engineering Task Force (2021). https://doi.org/10.17487/RFC9082
17. IANA: List of TLDS (2023). https://www.iana.org/domains/root/db
18. IANA: Registrar IDS (2023). https://www.iana.org/assignments/registrar-ids/registrar-ids.xhtml
19. ICANN: ICANN registrar agreement. https://www.icann.org/resources/pages/registrars-0d-2012-02-25-en
20. ICANN: ICANN temporary agreement for GTLDS to comply with GDPR. https://www.icann.org/resources/pages/gtld-registration-data-specs-en
21. ICANN: ICANN whois history. https://whois.icann.org/en/history-whois
22. IETF: Domain names - implementation and specification. Request for Comments RFC 1035, Internet Engineering Task Force (1987). https://doi.org/10.17487/RFC1035
23. Izhikevich, L., et al.: ZDNS: a fast DNS toolkit for internet measurement. In: Proceedings of the 22nd ACM Internet Measurement Conference, pp. 33–43. ACM (2022). https://doi.org/10.1145/3517745.3561434

24. Kitterman, S.: Sender Policy Framework (SPF) for Authorizing Use of Domains in Email, Version 1. Request for Comments RFC 7208, Internet Engineering Task Force (2014). https://doi.org/10.17487/RFC7208

25. Lauinger, T., Onarlioglu, K., Chaabane, A., Robertson, W., Kirda, E.: WHOIS lost in translation: (mis)understanding domain name expiration and re-registration. In: Proceedings of the 2016 Internet Measurement Conference, pp. 247–253. ACM (2016). https://doi.org/10.1145/2987443.2987463

26. Le Pochat, V., et al.: A practical approach for taking down avalanche botnets under real-world constraints. In: Proceedings 2020 Network and Distributed System Security Symposium. Internet Society (2020). https://doi.org/10.14722/ndss. 2020.24161

27. Liu, S., Foster, I., Savage, S., Voelker, G.M., Saul, L.K.: Who is.com?: learning to parse WHOIS records. In: Proceedings of the 2015 Internet Measurement Conference, pp. 369–380. ACM (2015). https://doi.org/10.1145/2815675.2815693

28. Loffredo, M., Martinelli, M.: Registration Data Access Protocol (RDAP) Partial Response. Request for Comments RFC 8982, Internet Engineering Task Force (2021). https://doi.org/10.17487/RFC8982

29. Lu, C., et al.: From WHOIS to WHOWAS: a large-scale measurement study of domain registration privacy under the GDPR. In: Proceedings 2021 Network and Distributed System Security Symposium. Internet Society, Virtual (2021). https:// doi.org/10.14722/ndss.2021.23134

30. Maass, M., et al.: Effective notification campaigns on the web: a matter of trust, framing, and support. In: USENIX Security 2021 (2021). https://doi.org/10.48550/ ARXIV.2011.06260

31. McCallum, A., Li, W.: Early results for named entity recognition with conditional random fields, feature induction and web-enhanced lexicons. In: Proceedings of the Seventh Conference on Natural Language Learning at HLT-NAACL 2003, Edmonton, Canada, vol. 4, pp. 188–191. Association for Computational Linguistics (2003). https://doi.org/10.3115/1119176.1119206

32. Mockapetris: Domain names - concepts and facilities. Request for Comments RFC 1034, Internet Engineering Task Force (1987). https://doi.org/10.17487/RFC1034

33. Newton, A., Hollenbeck, S.: Registration Data Access Protocol (RDAP) Query Format. Request for Comments RFC 7482, Internet Engineering Task Force (2015). https://doi.org/10.17487/RFC7482

34. Newton, A., Hollenbeck, S.: JSON Responses for the Registration Data Access Protocol (RDAP). Request for Comments RFC 7483, Internet Engineering Task Force (2015). https://doi.org/10.17487/RFC7483

35. Partridge, C., Allman, M.: Ethical considerations in network measurement papers. Commun. ACM **59**(10), 58–64 (2016)

36. Sommese, R., et al.: When parents and children disagree: diving into DNS delegation inconsistency. In: Sperotto, A., Dainotti, A., Stiller, B. (eds.) PAM 2020. LNCS, vol. 12048, pp. 175–189. Springer, Cham (2020). https://doi.org/10.1007/ 978-3-030-44081-7_11

37. European Union: General data protection regulation. https://eur-lex.europa.eu/ eli/reg/2016/679/oj

38. Vissers, T., Joosen, W., Nikiforakis, N.: Parking sensors: analyzing and detecting parked domains. In: Proceedings 2015 Network and Distributed System Security Symposium. Internet Society (2015). https://doi.org/10.14722/ndss.2015.23053

Spoofed Emails: An Analysis of the Issues Hindering a Larger Deployment of DMARC

Olivier Hureau[1]([envelope]), Jan Bayer[1,2], Andrzej Duda[1], and Maciej Korczyński[1]

[1] Université Grenoble Alpes, CNRS, Grenoble INP, LIG, Grenoble, France
{olivier.hureau,jan.bayer,andrzej.duda,
maciej.korczynski}@univ-grenoble-alpes.fr
[2] KOR Labs Cybersecurity, Saint-Martin-d'Hères, France
jan.bayer@korlabs.io

Abstract. In 2015, the IETF released an informational specification for the DMARC protocol, not establishing it as an Internet standard. DMARC is designed to fight against email spoofing, on top of SPF and DKIM. Given that these anti-spoofing measures could lead to the loss of legitimate emails, DMARC embedded a reporting system enabling domain owners to monitor rejected messages and enhance their configurations. Research communities have extensively examined various aspects of DMARC, including adoption rates, misuse, and integration into early spam detection systems while overlooking other vital aspects, potentially impeding its broader use and adoption.

This paper sheds light on a widespread lack of comprehension of the standard and unexpected behavior regarding DMARC among various groups, including professionals, open-source libraries, and domain owners. We propose measurement and analysis approaches that include a DMARC record parser, a methodology for dataset collection, and an analysis of the domain name landscape. We provide insights for fostering a deeper understanding of the DMARC ecosystem.

We also identify email addresses in DMARC records belonging to 9,121 unregistered domain names, which unintended users could register, leading to potential data leakage from the email systems of domain owners.

Keywords: Email anti-spoofing mechanisms · DMARC · SPF · DKIM

1 Introduction

In the current email distribution system based on the Simple Mail Transfer Protocol (SMTP) [25], it is relatively easy to spoof messages: a malicious actor just sends a message with a forged sender address and other parts of the email header to appear as sent from a legitimate source.

Internet Engineering Task Force (IETF) specified several email anti-spoofing schemes in *security extensions* such as the Sender Policy Framework (SPF) [24], the DomainKeys Identified Mail (DKIM) [7], and Domain-based Message

P. Richter et al. (Eds.): PAM 2024, LNCS 14537, pp. 232–261, 2024.
https://doi.org/10.1007/978-3-031-56249-5_10

Authentication, Reporting, and Conformance (DMARC) [28]. They aim at authenticating the sender and deciding what to do with suspicious emails. The extensions define a set of rules that specify the servers allowed to send emails on behalf of a domain name and provide strategies for dealing with spoofed messages. If properly configured, the anti-spoofing mechanisms allow the recipient of an email to verify that the sender domain name is legitimate.

However, some legitimate emails may get rejected because of misconfigured or too tight anti-spoofing mechanisms. Thus, domain administrators must precisely set up the SPF/DKIM parameters of their domains to avoid the loss of legitimate emails. Although the email receiver can apply their own policies and actions regarding the SPF and DKIM results, a domain owner, through her DMARC record, can provide the expected behavior the email receiver should undertake when receiving a message failing the DMARC check mechanism.

Several studies considered the operation of the anti-spoofing mechanisms via active and passive measurements [2,8,10,13,18,21,34,36,39,44,46,48,49,51]. Much effort focused on active scans and the analysis of DMARC deployment across popular domain names [8,13,18,21,44,46,51] as well as for the overall population of domain names [2,34,36,39]. The studies concluded that the adoption of DMARC is still low and subject to misconfigurations and vulnerabilities [2,3,5,35].

In this paper, we present a large-scale study of DMARC to observe the user habits and preferences, consider the evolution of DMARC adoption in time, and understand how popular domains use DMARC. Our measurements indicate that DMARC is frequently not well understood or effectively used. There are several reasons for this state of affairs—we identify four main problems:

- Specifications are complex, occasionally ambiguous, and at times contradictory, with a multitude of over thirty RFCs interlinked with intricate dependencies in the realm of anti-spoofing mechanisms. Some of these RFCs have been abandoned, updated, or rendered obsolete, potentially resulting in diminished understanding, suboptimal configurations, or possibly misapplications.
- Although DMARC checker tools are designed to help users create and configure their DMARC records, they can generate false positives and false negatives, potentially resulting in inaccurate evaluations of the records' validity and effectiveness.
- Progressive improvement of configurations is tedious due to a suboptimal, at times incorrect, or delegated use of DMARC reporting.
- Some domain owners may choose not to adopt DMARC, either due to a perceived lack of added value or skepticism about its effectiveness. For cases with limited benefits of using DMARC, they might not allocate resources to its deployment.

In summary, the paper brings the following contributions:

- We propose a methodology for gathering DMARC-related data: parsing DMARC records, analyzing protective means used by domain owners and the prevalence of various DMARC tags, URIs specified in `rua` or `ruf` tags, and collecting statistics on popular domain names. We also report on the time evolution of DMARC policies. Our analysis suggests that DMARC is not well understood by domain owners.

- We gather statistics on DMARC report receivers to identify the main stakeholders involved in report processing: we show that three the most important third-party services (Proofpoint, Mailinblue, and Agari) represent 21% of those present in DMARC records.
- We discover a vulnerability related to email addresses in DMARC records that may allow attackers to retrieve DMARC reports.
- We assess the compliance of online DMARC checkers and open source libraries with RFC 7489 and observe that none of them fully comply with the standard. To improve this situation, we have developed a Python-based DMARC parser based on the Augmented Backus-Naur Form (ABNF) that adheres to the syntactic rules of RFC 7489 and RFC 6376, to be shared with the community.
- We analyze the collected statistics and formulate recommendations aiming at simplifying the DMARC specifications and making them more clear to enable their larger adoption and deployment.

2   Related Work

Over the years, IETF strived to enhance email security by proposing, refining, and updating SPF, DKIM, and DMARC anti-spoofing mechanisms with many RFCs. The protocols have already demonstrated their effectiveness as a means for securing the email distribution system [19, 32, 45]. However, previous work also revealed vulnerabilities in their implementation [3, 5], and explored possible misuse [2, 35]. SPF, DKIM, and DMARC records and email reception logs have been used to study other vulnerabilities [41], or they were integrated into early spam detection systems [9, 15, 26, 43].

Previous research extensively investigated their adoption through both active and passive measurements [2, 8, 10, 13, 18, 21, 34, 36, 39, 44, 48, 49, 51], with a particular focus on analyzing DMARC deployment across popular domain names [8, 13, 18, 21, 44, 46, 51] and the broader population of domain names [2, 33, 34, 36, 39]. Only Czybik et al. [8] indicated which software and methodology they used to parse DMARC records.

Hu et al. [20] aimed at understanding the reasons behind their limited adoption. They concluded that significant effort is needed to address technical issues and create incentives for widespread adoption within the community. The studies by Portier et al. [39] and Ishtiaq et al. [2] are the only ones that present the statistics regarding the prevalence of `rua` and `ruf` tags in DMARC records.

Our analysis involves inspecting the domain name part of the email addresses specified in the DMARC record (`rua` and `ruf` tags) to identify domains available for registration that can be set up by attackers to receive DMARC reports. Moreover, our results are consistent with prior studies demonstrating how misspelled or expired domains can compromise the security of both users and systems [13, 29–31, 42, 47].

We propose measurement and analysis approaches that include a DMARC record parser and a methodology for dataset collection and analysis. Our findings highlight the lack of understanding among various stakeholders and software, offering valuable insights for its improvement.

3 Background

In this section, we provide an introduction to the email ecosystem followed by an overview of three key mechanisms that help ensuring email integrity and prevent domain name spoofing: SPF, DKIM, and DMARC. In this context, we discuss DMARC reporting, the mechanism that provides administrators with information on email activity related to their domains including SPF, DKIM, and DMARC authentication checks.

3.1 Simple Mail Transfer Protocol (SMTP)

SMTP is a protocol for sending and receiving email messages, specified first in 1982 by RFC 821 [40] and further refined by the current standard RFC 5321 [25]. Despite being widely used, SMTP is inherently insecure because it lacks built-in mechanisms for authentication and encryption, making it vulnerable to eavesdropping, domain name spoofing, and other forms of email abuse. As a result, modern email systems often use additional security protocols such as Transport Layer Security (TLS) and anti-spoofing mechanisms: SPF, DKIM, and DMARC to mitigate its design flaws.

Emails are sent using a Mail Transfer Agent (MTA) from the sender to the recipient MTA. Then, the Mail Delivery Agent (MDA), referred to as the receiver, queries the name server of the sender domain to check the SPF, DKIM, and DMARC records of the sender domain. If the checks are successful, the email is delivered to the recipient inbox.

3.2 Sender Policy Framework (SPF)

RFC 4408 [50] defined SPF as an experimental protocol in 2006 and it was further refined in RFC 7208 [24]. The purpose of SPF is to enable an email receiver to identify the hosts authorized to send emails on behalf of a domain name based on the information published in the DNS TXT Resource Records (RRs) of the domain (called SPF records). An SPF record needs to start with the version string v=spf1 and provides the specification of the authorized email senders for the domain by the following SPF mechanisms: a, ip4, mx, all, include, exists, redirect. For instance, if there is the A record example.com A 198.51.100.1 in DNS for the domain example.com, the following SPF record v=spf1 a ip4:192.0.2.0/24 -all indicates that only hosts with the IP address of 198.51.100.0 (the a mechanism), or with the IP address in the 192.0.2.0/24 prefix (the ip4 mechanism) are permitted senders, all others are forbidden (the -all mechanism).

Upon the reception of an email, the mail receiver executes the `check_host()` function on the domain name specified in the `Mail From` address [24] that checks the SPF record for the domain to determine whether the host sending the email is authorized. The validation result can be `neutral`, `pass`, `fail`, `soft fail`, `temperror`, or `permerror`. If the result is `fail`, `permerror`, or `temperror`, the mail receiver may reject the email, depending on its anti-spoofing procedures.

3.3   DomainKeys Identified Mail (DKIM)

RFC 4871 [1] defined DKIM in 2007 and it was obsoleted by RFC 6376 in 2011 [7]. DKIM specifies the authentication and integrity verification of email messages using public-key cryptography according to the principles stated in RFC 4870 [11]. The sender of an email uses its private key to generate a digital signature for the email, adds a header that includes a hash of the signature and the selector of the associated public key. The `TXT` record of `<selector>._domainkey.example.com` contains the public key used for the signature. The mail receiver can verify the digital signature, which gives one of the following results: `success`, `permfail`, or `tempfail`. An email can contain multiple DKIM signatures. If at least one of them is valid, the evaluation is successful.

3.4   Domain-Based Message Authentication, Reporting, and Conformance (DMARC)

DMARC [28] builds on top of SPF and DKIM to specify how mail receivers should treat the emails that fail authentication checks.

For a given domain name, a `TXT` RR stored in the `_dmarc` subdomain (called a DMARC record) specifies the DMARC handling policy. When an email receiver receives a message, it performs the DMARC check. If the check fails, the handling policy specifies the actions that the email receiver should undertake. DMARC also provides reporting capabilities that allow domain owners to receive feedback on how their emails are treated. In the following, we review the DMARC format and its most common rules.

DMARC Check Mechanism. DMARC associates the names verified by SPF and DKIM with the content of the `FROM:` field in the email header (referred to as the `Author Domain` [28]). This association is established through the concept of *alignment*, meaning that these domain names must match (or partially match in the case of a relaxed configuration). The evaluation results in a 'success' for DKIM and a 'pass' for SPF. Both the DKIM evaluation and the SPF `check_host()` functions are executed on the `Author Domain`. An email is deemed to satisfy the DMARC check mechanism if either SPF **or** DKIM are *aligned*. The DMARC check mechanism fails if and only if both SPF **and** DKIM are not aligned (this conjunction is usually not well understood).

Figure 1 provides an overview of the DMARC check mechanism involving Alice and Mallory sending an email to the Bob's email address: `bob@example.com`

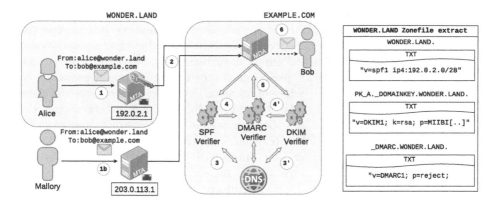

Fig. 1. DMARC check mechanism overview

(①, ①b). In this scenario, Alice is a legitimate user of `wonder.land`,[1] while Mallory attempts to spoof the Alice's email address, `alice@wonder.land`. Both Mallory's and Alice's MTAs connect to the Bob's `example.com` MDA and transfer the email starting with the command `MAIL FROM: wonder.land` (②). The MDA runs the SPF `check_host()` function on the `wonder.land` domain name. Since the SPF records for `wonder.land`, as retrieved by the Bob's MDA (④), specify permission for the `192.0.2.0/28` IPv4 range, the Alice's MDA SPF check is successfully passed because `192.0.2.1` is designated as a permitted sender. In this context, the Alice's SPF is considered *aligned*, while the Mallory's SPF is not aligned.

In the Alice's email, there is a `DKIM-Signature` with the `pk_a` selector. The Bob's MDA retrieves the `TXT` records at `pk_a._domainkey.wonder.land` (③). The signature in the email matches the public key in the DKIM records. The result of the DKIM check is `success`. In this scenario, the Alice's DKIM is considered *aligned*.

The Bob's MDA retrieves the `wonder.land` DMARC record at `_dmarc.wonder.land`. It specifies the `p=reject` handling policy (⑤). Since the Alice's email DKIM or SPF are aligned, the DMARC check (⑤) passes, and the email is successfully delivered to Bob (⑥). However, in the case of Mallory, whose DKIM and SPF are not aligned, the DMARC check fails. According to the `wonder.land` DMARC record, the domain owner wants the rejection of the Mallory's email.

DMARC Record Format. A valid DMARC record must start with `v=DMARC1` and be unique. Domain name owners may specify multiple policies represented as tags separated by semicolons (the `p` tag is mandatory, other tags are optional, and some of them have default values). Any tag that does not conform to RFC must be ignored. The tags are defined as follows:

- `p`: requested handling policy with three possible options:

---

[1] A fictional domain name.

reject, quarantine, or none. When an email fails the DMARC check, indicating that both SPF and DKIM are not aligned, the email receiver is expected to take one of the following actions based on the value of the p tag: reject the email if p=reject, flag the email as suspicious (e.g., by directing it to a quarantine or spam folder) if p=quarantine, or take no action if p=none.

- sp: requested handling policy for subdomains. The options for sp are the same as for p, and by default, sp takes the same value as p. For instance, when the domain owner of example.com specifies p=none and sp=reject, she requests that the email failing the DMARC check with the example.com Author Domain should be accepted. However, any email with a subdomain of example.com (e.g., email.example.com) as the Author Domain should be rejected.
- adkim and aspf: DKIM, and SPF alignment modes with the following values: s meaning strict and r relaxed (default). In strict mode, the authenticated domain and the Author Domain must be the same. The relaxed mode accepts that both names are in the same organizational domain. For instance, if the policy is aspf=r, and if an email with the Author Domain example.com is sent from the host email.example.com passing the SPF checks for email.example.com, the email will be aligned because example.com and email.example.com are within the same organizational domain.
- rua and ruf: specify one or several URIs (e.g., an email address) for receiving the aggregate (rua) and failure (also called forensic) (ruf) reports. While email receivers are expected to send reports, it is not an obligation (as per RFC 2119, which uses SHOULD to indicate a recommended action [4]). Nonetheless, these reports can provide valuable insights into email management and serve as a monitoring instrument for uncovering domain name abuse.
- ri: aggregate reporting interval. By default set to 86400 s, aggregate reports are generated on a daily basis. However, a domain name owner can specify the time frame for which she wants to receive aggregated reports.
- fo: failure reporting options. By default '0', it indicates which anti-spoofing mechanism triggers the event of sending a failure report to the URIs specified in the ruf tag:
  - 0: generate a DMARC failure report if SPF *and* DKIM are not aligned (default option),
  - 1: generate a DMARC failure report if SPF *or* DKIM are not aligned,
  - d: generate a DKIM failure report if DKIM is not aligned,
  - s: generate an SPF failure report if SPF is not aligned.
  Note that the requested handling policy is not affected by the fo tag.
- pct: sampling rate. The pct tag accepts an integer between 0 and 100 (default) that indicates the percentage of emails subject to the DMARC handling policy. However, it does not have any impact on the reporting system. The DMARC check procedure is still executed, and the outcome of the check is reported [28].

DMARC Feedback. While both SPF and DKIM have their own reporting mechanisms defined in their respective RFCs [23,27], DMARC is the primary email authentication protocol that leverages both SPF and DKIM to provide a unified and aggregated reporting mechanism and has become a *de facto* industry standard for reporting on email processing. We provide more information on aggregate and failure reports below.

- *Aggregate Reports*: an aggregate report contains statistical data on the authentication results of emails received by DMARC-compliant mail receivers during a specific period, usually 24 h. The data includes both emails that passed the DMARC check and those that failed. The report helps domain owners to monitor and evaluate the effectiveness of their DMARC policy, identify issues with their email authentication setup, and stop any unauthorized use of their domain for malicious purposes. Aggregate reports are generated and automatically sent to the email address specified in the `rua` tag of the DMARC record for the domain.
- *Failure Reports*: a failure report is a feedback mechanism that provides information about email messages that failed SPF and/or DKIM checks. The report is sent to the email address specified in the `ruf` tag of the DMARC record for the domain according to the failure reporting options (`fo` tag). It includes detailed information about the failed message, such as the message headers and the reasons for the failure. The failure report may include the email that did not pass the authentication mechanism as an attachment. The purpose of failure reports is to help domain owners identify and stop any unauthorized use of their domain for malicious purposes or determine any misconfiguration. Failure reports are in a standard, machine-readable format called ARF (Abuse Reporting Format) defined by RFC 6591 [17].

External Destination Verification. A potential vulnerability exists regarding URIs specified in `rua` and `ruf` tags. An attacker can specify the email address of their victim in the `rua` or `ruf` tags and cause email receivers to send reports. This may result in unsolicited emails flooding the mailbox of the victim. By design, DMARC is immune to such a scenario because the email receiver is requested to perform an *external destination verification*. Let us assume that an external domain name in the `rua` or `ruf` tag of a given monitored domain name is not within the same organizational domain. The external destination verification involves checking if the domain name has a specific `TXT` record that can be queried at the domain name formed by appending the monitored domain name, the string `._report._dmarc.`, and the external domain name.

```
v=DMARC1;p=none;sp=reject;fo=1:d;ruf=mailto:ruf@security.example.com;
rua=mailto:rua@example.com,mailto:dmarc@help.example.org;ri=43200
```

Fig. 2. Example of DMARC record found for the `example.com` domain name

As an example, the record at Fig. 2 contains three email addresses: `ruf@security.example.com`, `rua@example.com`, and `drua@example.com`. Given that `dmarc-ag@example.com` and `ruf@security.example.com` are part of the `example.com` organizational domain name, the external destination verification are not performed for these URI. However, an email receiver should retrieve the DNS `TXT` record of `example.com._report._dmarc.help.example.org`. Given the result `"v=DMARC1;"`, the domain owner of `help.example.org` permits email receiver to send the DMARC report towards `example.com` and from any email address `'@help.example.org'`.

4 DMARC Large Scale Measurements

In this section, we begin with an overview of our measurement platform and the raw data obtained from DNS queries. Then, we delve into the protective measures selected by domain owners and analyze the data regarding the prevalence of various DMARC tags to gain insights into different behaviors. Subsequently, we present statistics related to URIs specified in `rua` or `ruf` tags. Finally, we focus on popular domain names (Fig. 3).

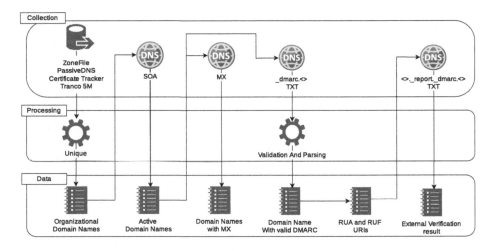

Fig. 3. Overview of the methodology for collecting DMARC data

We have used `zdns` [22] to conduct a large-scale data collection campaign to analyze the feedback information expected from DMARC reports.

First, we have created a list of domain names by collecting data from various feeds: the generic Top-Level Domain (gTLD) zone files from the ICANN Centralized Zone Data Service (CZDS),[2] passive DNS data from the SIE Europe,[3]

---

[2] https://czds.icann.org.

[3] https://www.sie-europe.net.

domain names from the Google certificate transparency logs,[4] and the Tranco 5 M list[5] [38].

We have used the Mozilla public suffix list[6] to extract only the *organizational domain names*. The aggregation of the domain names extracted from our feeds results in 513 M unique domain names. Since the list contains unregistered domain names, we have queried the SOA (Start of Authority) RR for each domain and excluded those with an NXDOMAIN response.

We then have queried the TXT records for the subdomain _dmarc to obtain DMARC records [28] and parse them using our parser described later. As they may include an external address in the rua or ruf tags, we have carried out the external destination verification of the addresses.

We scanned the SOA, TXT (DMARC) records, and performed the external destination verification both in September 2022 and October 2023.

Table 1. DNS scan results

	Name	Record Type	Domain Prefix	Dataset Size	Noerror	Nxdomain	Other	Empty Records	Successfully Retrieved
	Dataset description				**Measurements Numbers**				
09/2022	M_1	SOA	∅	287.9 M	273 M	12.6 M	2.1 M	15.2 M	257.7 M
	M_2	MX	∅	257.7 M	257.3 M	155 K	317 K	145.2 M	112.1 M
	M_3	TXT	_dmarc.	257.7 M	87.6 M	168.6 M	1.5 M	65.4 M	11.6 M
	M_4	TXT	<>._report._dmarc.	7,9 M	4,4 M	3,4 M	23 K	205 K	4,2 M
10/2023	M_5	SOA	∅	513.7 M	286.5 M	212.0 M	15.1 M	6.2 M	280.3 M
	M_6	MX	∅	280.3 M	273 M	12.7 M	2,145 K	119.4 M	153.6 M
	M_7	TXT	_dmarc.	280.3 M	95.5 M	182.4 M	2.3 M	68.8 M	15.9 M
	M_8	TXT	<>._report._dmarc.	5.4 M	4.26 M	1.1 M	13 K	126 K	4.13 M

Table 1 shows the results of active DNS measurements related to DMARC. We get the status and the content of each DNS response and parse the records to keep only the valid ones. For each measurement denoted by $M_{[1-8]}$, we provide the requested RR type, the prefix of the domain, the size of the collected dataset, the DNS status and the numbers of each status type, the number of empty records, and the number of valid (according to the related RFC) records after parsing it.

A DNS query returns different DNS error codes: i) NOERROR when the query was successful, ii) NXDOMAIN for the domain name not present in the DNS zone file of the queried name server, and iii) OTHER for all remaining error codes such as TIMEOUT, SERVFAIL, or REFUSED.

Even if the returned DNS error code is NOERROR, it does not imply that the answer contains any Resource Record. The "Empty records" column in Table 1 corresponds to the answers with NOERROR and no data inside. The "Successfully retrieved" column contains the number of domain names for which we have

---

[4] https://googlechrome.github.io/CertificateTransparency.
[5] https://tranco-list.eu.
[6] https://publicsuffix.org/.

obtained valid data in response to a given query. For instance, when looking for the DMARC record in M_3, we query the TXT record of the _dmarc subdomain and parse it to validate its content.

To begin our scans, we have collected and parsed the SOA records for the 513 M (M_1) domains from our aggregated list to exclude unsuitable domain names. We kept only domain names with the SOA records with status NOERROR and excluded those with empty records. As a result, our dataset contains 280.3 M (286.5 M–6.2 M) domain names. This dataset is used to perform measurements M_6 and M_7.

Measurements M_7 involve querying the TXT record for the domain name with the prefix '_dmarc.'. The DNS answer, the RRset, may contain multiple records. We have then parsed all RRs and excluded the invalid strings: either because the content was invalid[7] or because the domain had more than one valid record (a record is a valid DMARC record if only one RR is syntactically correct). Around 150 K domain names had an RR containing the 'dmarc' string but were not syntactically correct, and 68 K contained multiple valid RRs. Thus, for the 16.7 M (95.5 M–68.8 M) domain with a non-empty answer, the RRset contained in total 295 M RRs. Only 15.9 M domain names had a valid DMARC record.

Measurements M_8 is the External Destination Verification. We have found 3.3 M domain names and a total of 5.4 M email addresses for which the External Destination Verification should be processed. 20% of these requests result in either NXDOMAIN, SERVFAIL, REFUSED or TIMEOUT. Finally, 4.1 M (75%) verifications succeeded.

4.1   DMARC as a Domain Name Protection Mechanism

Table 2. DMARC handling policies according to MX and rua/ruf

	p = none	p = quarantine	p = reject	total
NO MX, DMARC with rua/ruf	204,376	229,777	836,199	1,270,352
NO MX, DMARC without rua/ruf	149,498	35,420	724,429	909,347
MX, DMARC with rua/ruf	3,129,176	1,050,756	1,255,646	5,435,578
MX, DMARC without rua/ruf	5,375,281	1,529,969	1,449,045	8,354,295
Total	8,858,331	2,845,922	4,265,319	15,969,572

DMARC has two main features to protect a domain name against spoofing attacks:

- By configuring DMARC with restrictive handling policies (i.e., p=quarantine or p=reject), emails failing the DMARC check mechanism may not reach the destination. Table 2 shows that 7,111,241 (44.5%) domain names having DMARC choose this type of protection.

---

[7] https://dmarc.org/2016/07/common-problems-with-dmarc-records/.

- By configuring a DMARC policy with reporting options (i.e., `rua` and/or `ruf`), domain owners can receive alerts regarding any attempt to spoof their domains. 6705930 (42%) domain names having DMARC (see Table 2) opt-in for receiving aggregate and/or failure reports.

When a domain name has no `MX` record (no mail server), it means that no legitimate emails are expected to be sent on behalf of that domain. As a result, it may not be effective for the domain owners to have a DMARC record with `p=none`, which would be less restrictive than `p=reject`.

While domains without `MX` records represent 16.6% of active domains with valid DMARC, 41.7% of them do not use the reporting system, and 149,498 domains choose the handling policy `p=none` (see Table 2). If the domain owners aim to monitor the distribution of malicious emails and have no `MX` records, they can achieve this goal by employing the `rua` or `ruf` mechanisms (204,376 domain names).

For example, the Google domain names `googletagmanager.com` and `goo.gl` do not have `MX`, and contain the SPF record `"v=spf1 -all"` indicating that no server is authorized to send emails on behalf of that domain name. It also contains the following DMARC record:

`"v=DMARC1; p=reject; rua=mailto:mailauth-reports@google.com"`

that specifies the policy of `p=reject` and an aggregate reports to be sent to `mailauth-reports@google.com`.

4.2 Application of DMARC Tags

We next analyze the occurrence frequency of DMARC tags and their content, which provides insight into the behavior of email receivers expected by domain owners with respect to spoofed emails.

Figure 4 shows that domain owners tend to specify tags with default values, even if there is no need to state them explicitly. For instance, most domain owners specify the `pct` tag to 100 (default value), indicating the percentage of emails that should be subject to the DMARC handling policy.

The `fo` tag has a default value of '0' that requests the receiver generate a DMARC failure report when SPF and DKIM are not aligned. As shown in Fig. 4, when it is present, 75% of the `fo` values differ from '0'. It is important to note that the `fo` tag is only useful when a `ruf` tag is present. However, our analysis shows that 33.45% of the DMARC records with an explicit `fo` tag do not have a corresponding `ruf` tag, which may indicate that their domain owners have misunderstood the meaning of `fo` tag and its relationship with `ruf`.

Similarly, the `pct` tag, whose default value is 100, is unnecessary when the domain owner specifies `p=none` since no action (contrary to `reject` or `quarantine`) needs to be taken if DMARC check fails.

However, about 42% of domain owners who use the `pct` tag also set `p=none`. This error may stem from misunderstanding the DMARC mechanism, but it does not interfere with the DMARC check mechanism.

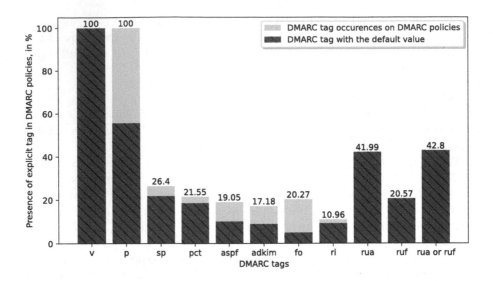

Fig. 4. Occurrence frequency of DMARC tags

In contrast, the `adkim` and `aspf` tags are only present in 16.91% of all DMARC records. However, when considering only the domains with `p=quarantine` or `p=reject`, over 28.63% of domain names specify either `adkim` or `aspf`, which suggests that the administrators of the domains with `p!=none` have more DMARC expertise because the risks of misconfiguration are not negligible.

Lastly, as many as 42% and 21% of domain names have at least one URI in the `rua` and `ruf` tags, respectively, which shows that domain owners with DMARC enabled want to receive DMARC reports. In the following section, we analyze the recipients of aggregate and failure reports as specified in the `ruf` and `rua` tags.

4.3 Statistics on DMARC Report Receivers

We have gathered statistics on DMARC report receivers to identify the main stakeholders involved in report processing. Over 6.8 M domain name owners have expressed interest in receiving at least one type of reports, with a combined total of 11.7 M email addresses, 4.0 M of which are unique. Figure 5 presents the proportion of the registered domain names in the email addresses. We can observe that the first five domain names alone represent 30% of all email addresses present in the DMARC records. We identify three distinct categories of report receivers:

- Third-party email security services such as Proofpoint,[8] Agari,[9] or Mime-cast.[10]
- Individuals or organizations who receive DMARC reports to their personal email addresses (e.g., `gmail.com` or `163.com`).
- Hosting providers and domain registrars that provide email systems for their clients such as `dhosting.pl`.

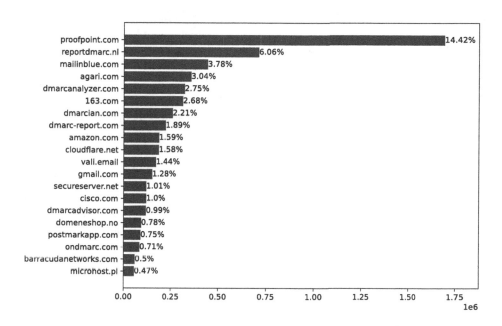

Fig. 5. Registered domain names in the `rua` and `ruf` tags

As Table 1 indicates, M_4 results show that 25% of external verifications failed. Due to this misconfiguration, one million domain names have at least one URI that is not supposed to receive any report as per the RFC specification [28]. Upon aggregating the email addresses specified in the tags `rua` or `ruf` that failed external verification, we have identified approximately 195 K domain names in this category.

We have noticed that some DMARC third-party services choose to accept reports from any domain. For instance, Agari returns `"v=DMARC1;"` for any DNS `TXT` query for any domain name under the `*._report._dmarc.agari.com` wildcard. When querying the `TXT` record for domains such as `example.tld._report.` `_dmarc.agari.com` or `jhdgvr3zt4wcsa._report._dmarc.agari.com` (where `example.tld` is not a valid domain and `jhdgvr3zt4wcsa` is a random string), the

---

[8] https://www.proofpoint.com/.
[9] https://www.agari.com/.
[10] https://dmarcanalyzer.com/.

returned result is `"v=DMARC1;"`. This result does not seem to be true for Proof-point, the largest third-party email security services provider (see Fig. 5).

We have also observed that three invalid email addresses: `address@yourdomain.com`, `me@example.com`, and `youremailaddress@yourdomain.com` appear in more than 29 K records, and each of them is included in the guide for setting up DMARC.[11][12][13]

It is interesting to see the distribution of email addresses used for receiving DMARC reports and the dominance of a few third-party email security services, ESPs, and hosting providers/domain registrars. An issue of concern is the significant number of domains incorrectly set up, which should not receive reports due to failing email verification processes.

4.4 Popular Domains

The owners of popular domains have more resources for securing systems and are more susceptible to email spoofing. Therefore, it is reasonable to expect that they deploy DMARC to a larger extent than other domains.

To explore this hypothesis, we have analyzed the DMARC deployment of 1 M most popular domains in the Tranco top site ranking [38]. Figure 6 presents the proportion of the following features characterizing DMARC deployment: a `TXT` record for `_dmarc`, a valid DMARC record, the presence of the `rue/ruf` tag, strict (`p=reject`) handling policy, and external email verification errors for all domains.

As expected, as domain popularity increases, the proportion of valid DMARC records also tends to rise. This trend is accompanied by an increase in the number of domains with the `p=reject` policy, which suggests that more popular domains tend to have a higher confidence level in their DMARC deployment and stricter policies in place.

Nevertheless, the proportion of invalid DMARC records (a `TXT` record present for `_dmarc` but with an invalid DMARC record) remains stable regardless of the popularity rank. Figure 6 indicates that among the most popular domains, there are fewer domain names with active email addresses (no `MX` records). This outcome suggests that large companies may use different domain names for their web presence, which are more popular, and other domain names for email communication.

Although the `ruf` reporting tag is less commonly used than `rua`, it is more prevalent among popular domains. On average, 75% of domain names with DMARC in the top 1 million have at least one reporting tag. In contrast, 42.8% of all domain names have it. This percentage decreases as the domain rank decreases, and the number of email verification errors tends to increase for less popular domain names. The deployment of DMARC, stringent handling policies, the presence of reporting tags, and external destination errors appear to be

---

[11] https://proton.me/support/custom-domain-google.

[12] https://help.elasticemail.com/en/articles/2303947-the-dmarc-generator-tool.

[13] https://wpmailsmtp.com/how-to-create-dmarc-record/.

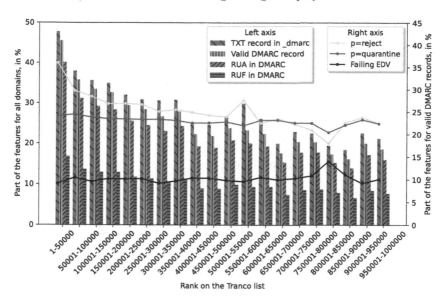

Fig. 6. Features of DMARC deployment for popular domains in Tranco

correlated with the importance of a domain name, which suggests that popular domains allocate more resources to DMARC, as they have greater incentives to implement DMARC rigorously, given that their domain names are at higher risk of spoofing attacks.

5   Time Evolution of the DMARC Use and Deployment

Table 3 presents the DMARC statistics from related work and the summary of our measurements. The first section of this table, with the measurements based on domain ranking lists (such as Alexa or Tranco), illustrates the trends in DMARC adoption and handling policies since 2014. The results indicate a rising trend in DMARC adoption, with over 25% of popular domains currently having valid DMARC records. The second part of Table 3, which includes a broad sample of the overall domain population, supports similar conclusions with caution due to differences in sample sizes and domain coverage.

As shown in Table 3, our two measurements reveal a decline in p=none policies from 67.7% to 55.5%. To understand the changes over a year, we have proceeded with a comparative analysis of our two sets of measurements. Figure 7 illustrates the differences in reporting policies between the two years, allowing us to gain insights into how DMARC adoption and handling policies have evolved.

While the domains included in the measurement M_7 conducted in 2023 (refer to Fig. 7 and Table 1) but not present in the measurement M_3 from 2022 constitute 41% of the 2023 datasets, they contribute to 48% of quarantine or reject policies. Therefore, the adoption of more restrictive policies can be attributed to the new DMARC domain names.

Table 3. DMARC related data (related work and our measurements)

	Dataset			DMARC Statistics				
Source	Study	Date	Size	Adoption Rate	none	p tag value quarantine	reject	RUA or RUF
Popularity list	Gojmerac et al. [18]	2014-08	677K	0.5%	71.6%	8.0%	20.5%	-
	Tatang et al. [46]	2015-01	1M	1.0%	75.2%	8.2%	16.5%	-
	Durumeric et al. [13]	2015-04	792K	1.1%	72.6%	8.0%	19.4%	-
	Szalachowski et al. [44]	2016-08	100K	7.4%	-	-	-	-
	Hu et al. [21]	2017-10	1M	4.6%	77.6%	10.1%	12.3%	-
	Tatang et al. [46]	2018-12	1M	7.2%	76.1%	11.0%	12.9%	-
	Tatang et al. [46]	2020-05	1M	11.5%	68.5%	15.9%	15.6%	-
	Yajima et al. [51]	2022-02	1M	19.4%	-	-	-	-
	Our parser	2022-09	1M	21.4%	55.3%	21.2%	23.5%	74.6%
	Czybik et al. [8]	2023-05	1M	22.6%	-	-	-	-
	Our parser	2023-10	1M	25.1%	50.9%	23.0%	26.1%	74.9%
Broader source	Portier et al. [39]	2018-01	336M	0.0%	75.2%	7.2%	14.4%	48.9%
	Maroofi et al. [34]	2020-09	236M	0.1%	39.6%	9.3%	41.0%	-
	Nosyk et al. [36]	2022-01	251M	3.3%	49.7%	11.2%	37.1%	-
	DMARC.org [a]	2022-06	-	-	68.2%	12.1%	19.6%	-
	Our parser	2022-09	257M	4.5%	67.7%	14.0%	24.3%	43.4%
	Ashiq et al. [2]	2023-01	89M	6.6%	39.6%	9.3%	41.0%	49.0%
	Our parser	2023-10	280M	5.4%	55.5%	17.8%	26.7%	42.9%

[a] https://dmarc.org/stats/dmarc/.

Fig. 7. DMARC evolution between 2022 and 2023

Ovrall, the DMARC population is growing and the trend towards adopting more restrictive handling policies primarily stems from new DMARC domains. However, the influence of aggregate reports on policy modifications remains an open question.

The Parallel Sets Chart in Fig. 8 visually illustrates the modifications made to the p and rua tags within a one-year timeframe. The two colors represent the presence or absence of rua tags in DMARC records in 2023. To ensure consistent data in both sets, we undertook specific steps when dealing with domain names in M_7 that were not present in M_3. For these domain names, we collected the registration information and then excluded those that had been registered prior to the previous scans.

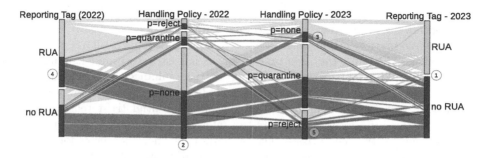

Fig. 8. DMARC evolution between 2022 and 2023. Domains with modified p or rua tags.

In the past, 59% of domain names had rua tags, but this proportion decreased to 47% (①). Almost 80% of the modifications occurred when domain names had the p=none handling policy in 2022 (②). Among them, 64.1% changed to p=quarantine, 21.8% moved to p=reject, and 14.1% maintained p=none while modifying the rua tag. When only the rua tags is modified (③), 39.2% names added the tag and 60.3% removed them.

Notably, 28.4% of domains with rua tags (④) removed the tag while adopting a more restrictive handling policy.

Surprisingly, 54.7% of the domain name that had p=none and move to p=reject, did not have rua tags (⑤). Globally, 35.8% of domain names that have toughened their policies did not have a rua tag, which is contradictory to the hypothesis that domain names use the reporting system to transition to more strict policies.

In total, 48.2% of all domain names displayed unexpected behavior: they removed the rua tag without adopting more restrictive policies or have adopted more strict policies without having rua tags.

When looking at global measurements and related work, it becomes evident that DMARC adoption is on the rise, and restrictive policies such as p=quarantine and p=reject are becoming more prevalent. However, this growth in handling policies is largely driven by newcomers to the DMARC ecosystem. Older DMARC domains do not appear to be inclined to change their handling policies, suggesting that the reporting system may be ineffective.

6   Vulnerability Notification Campaign

During the analysis of the M_4 external verification process, we have found email addresses specified in rua or ruf tags belonging to unregistered domain names. So, a malicious actor can register such domain names and configure the support for receiving DMARC reports.

Having unauthorized access to DMARC reports raises several significant threats to an organization. The primary concern is the potential compromise of user communication. If an attacker successfully acquires forensic reports, it may contain the original messages exchanged among users, potentially exposing sensitive information. Additionally, access to aggregate reports allows attackers to gather insights into the organization email infrastructure and communication patterns. This information can be exploited to enhance the effectiveness of impersonation. Lastly, aggregate reports include details about the entities with whom the organization communicates, revealing potential trust relationships. Exploiting this information, attackers can pinpoint weaknesses in anti-spoofing protocols among trusted entities, thereby optimizing their strategies for targeting the organization. This section presents the details on how we have detected vulnerable domain names and how we have contacted their owners. We also present the results of our notification campaign.

The measurement M_4 results in 150 K domain names for which the external verification query returns NXDOMAIN, which indicates that the domain name parts of the emails in rua or ruf do not exist. However, a non-existing subdomain is not enough to decide whether the domain is not registered. Therefore, we have performed an SOA query for all organizational domain names. 7,462 of the queries have returned NXDOMAIN or empty SOA. Then, we have used the WHOIS and RDAP protocols to retrieve the registration information of these domain names. Since certain TLDs, like .es, do not offer public WHOIS information, we cannot determine the availability of a given domain name for registration. To avoid sending unsolicited emails, we have selected only the domains for which the WHOIS or RDAP query succeeded. In total, we have found 7,286 domains available for registration, leading to 9,142 vulnerable domain names.

Next, we needed to find a way to contact the owners of the domain names. First, the DMARC record may contain several email addresses in rua and ruf. Even if the email addresses are used to monitor DMARC reports, they can be an adequate means of contact. Out of 2,458 email addresses in the DMARC record, 799 of them belong to the same organizational domain (which we label as *direct contact*) of the vulnerable domain and 1,659 did not (which we label as *indirect contact*). Second, the WHOIS or RDAP answers may contain the email addresses of the domain registrant or administrator. Even if Ferrante et al. showed that GDPR makes this process less relevant [16], we have obtained the email addresses form WHOIS or RDAP for 1,674 domain names (which we label as *WHOIS contact*). Finally, the email addresses from DMARC and WHOIS or RDAP only represent 3,584 domains. As a consequence, we have also generated email addresses according to the RFC 2142 [6] for the remaining 5,558 domains without WHOIS/RDAP contact, direct, or indirect contact. RFC 2142 specifies the email addresses to be used for contacting common services of an organization such as common-services@domain. We have chosen to contact security@domain and admin@domain (which we label as *RFC contact*).

We have grouped the recipients according to our labels: *direct, indirect, WHOIS*, and *RFC contacts*, and send emails based on the corresponding templates. As indirect contacts (any email address not directly related to the organizational domain name) may appear in multiple DMARC records, instead of

```
dmarc-version    = "v" *WSP "=" *WSP %x44 %x4d %x41 %x52 %x43 %x31
dmarc-request    = "p" *WSP "=" *WSP ("none" / "quarantine" / "reject" )
```

Fig. 9. Extract of the DMARC record ABNF definition from RFC 7489

sending an email for each vulnerable domain name, we have sent a list of the vulnerable domains. For multiple WHOIS contacts, we only send a single email. If the emails appear in the same mailbox, they will be shown as one email because of the unique email id. However, a domain owner might have been contacted through multiple channels (WHOIS, direct, and indirect).

We have sent 9,218 emails in October 2022. 4,540 emails bounced back, and among them, 4,098 lack any existing recipient. Specifically, 57 WHOIS, 632 direct, 52 indirect, and 3357 RFC. Additionally, 263 messages sent to WHOIS contacts faced delivery challenges and generated automated responses as they were protected by GDPR masking. As a result, we managed to deliver the email to at least one of the contacts for 4,582 domain names. 89 administrators have responded regarding the notifications.

Two weeks after sending the notifications, we re-scanned the vulnerable domain names. The owners of 185 domains removed their DMARC records, 519 modified their DMARC records but 19 were still vulnerable, and 11 added new DMARC records resulting in an invalid DMARC record. Our notification campaign resulted in 685 no longer vulnerable domain names, which makes the remediation rate of 7.5% for the total vulnerable domain names and 15% for the domain names that received an email.

7   Parsing DMARC Records

The DMARC record specification and its grammar are outlined in RFC 7489, described using both Augmented Backus-Naur Form (ABNF) and the RFC itself (see Fig. 9). However, the general public may not be familiar with the ABNF specification or all the finer details presented in the RFC. To address this issue, numerous documentation and services have been created to assist users in creating and verifying their DMARC records. Nevertheless, we have encountered instances for which certain services do not adhere to all the specifications or potentially making them susceptible to Cross-Site Scripting (XSS) vulnerabilities.[14] To investigate this aspect further, we have tested various checkers with different corner cases presented below:

- space: in the ABNF rule for dmarc-version, the '=' character is surrounded by "*WSP" (white-space or tab), allowing "v = DMARC1; p=none" to be a valid DMARC record.

---

[14] https://6point6.co.uk/insights/xss-bugs-on-dmarc-checking-sites/.

- **case**: in contrast to the `dmarc-version` rule, where every character in the string 'DMARC1' is considered a terminal value, the `dmarc-request` is not case-sensitive. Therefore, `"v=DMARC1; p=ReJeCt"` is recognized as a valid DMARC record.
- **case-tag**: similar to the `case` scenario, all tags are not case-sensitive, making `"V=DMARC1; p=none"` a valid DMARC record.
- **xss**: while some DMARC tools assist users in verifying their records, certain tools display the content of the record. If this record is not correctly escaped, it can potentially enable attackers to execute XSS. For example, the record `"v=DMARC1;p=<script>alert('This is an XSS test')</script>;"` will show an alert box in the vulnerable websites.
- **dup**: RFC 6376 specifies that duplicate tags are not allowed in a `tag-list` (see Appendix, Fig. 16). However, the handling of this corner case is not clearly defined in RFC 7489. We have brought this issue to the attention of the IETF and it is under consideration.
- **u-tag**: RFC 7489 states that any unknown tags must be ignored. For instance, the record `'v=DMARC1; p=reject; foo=bar;'` is considered a valid DMARC record.
- **p-down**: the 6th bullet in the policy discovery section of RFC 7489 specifies that a record with an invalid `p` or `sp` tag, but with a `rua` containing at least one valid URI, should be interpreted as a record with `p=none` (see Appendix, Fig. 13). Therefore, the record `"v=DMARC1;p=reject;sp=error;rua=mailto:rua@example.com"` should be interpreted as `'v=DMARC1;p=none;rua=mailto:rua@example.com'`.

Our experiments involved publishing various DMARC records, as defined earlier, and manually using the DMARC checkers provided by 16 different companies. In the first round of measurements in S1-2022, we identified non-conforming organizations and reached out to them when possible. Four organizations responded and made the necessary changes. As shown in Table 4, four of these organizations were found to be susceptible to XSS vulnerabilities.

During this period, Agari, Dmarcian, and SimpleDmarc did not reply to us and have changed their checker. In October 2023, we re-ran the measurements with the newly discovered corner case `dup`, `u-tag`, and `p-down`. SimpleDmarc has changed its implementation and is vulnerable to XSS. We have contacted the founder of SimpleDmarc and they have fixed the vulnerability. Dmarc360 does not provide a freely accessible DMARC checker anymore.

While it is true that none of the organizations fully adhere to all the RFC 7489 specifications, the `space`, `case`, and `case-tag` rules rely on ABNF knowledge that may not be commonly known by DMARC users. These rules serve to provide relaxed standards to accommodate a wider range of DMARC records. On the other hand, the `dup` and `u-tag` tags hold more significant importance. The `dup` corner case, when not respected, corresponds to a situation in which the email receiver must choose between two handling policies, leading to an undefined behavior. We have contacted the DMARC working group regarding our concerns. The group has indicated that the record should be disregarded.

Table 4. Compliancy of DMARC parsers. ✓: compliant, ✗: not compliant, ⊗ fixed the issue after our contact, ?: Behavior cannot be defined.

	2022				2023						
	space	case	case-tag	xss	space	case	case-tag	xss	dup	u-tag	p-down
Online DMARC checker											
Agari	✓	✓	✗	✗	✓	✓	✗	✓	✗	✓	✗
Dmarc360	✗	✓	✓	✓	?	?	?	?	?	?	?
Dmarcadvisor	✓	✗	⊗	✓	✓	✗	✓	✓	✗	✓	✗
Dmarcanalyzer	✗	✗	✗	✓	✗	✗	✗	✓	✓	✗	✗
Dmarcian	✓	✗	✗	✓	✓	✓	✓	✓	✓	✓	?
Dmarcly	✗	✗	✗	✗	✗	✗	✗	✗	✗	✗	✗
Dnschecker	✗	✗	✓	✓	✗	✗	✓	✓	✗	✓	✗
EasyDmarc	✗	✗	✗	✓	✗	✗	✗	✓	✓	✗	✗
Google	✗	✓	✗	✓	✗	✓	✗	✓	✗	✓	✗
Kdmarc	✓	✓	✓	✓	✓	✓	✓	✓	✗	✗	✗
Merox	✓	✓	⊗	✓	✓	✓	✓	✓	✓	✗	✗
Mxtoolbox	✗	✗	✗	✓	✗	✗	✗	✓	✓	✓	✗
PowerDmarc	⊗	✓	⊗	⊗	✓	✓	✓	✓	✓	✗	✗
Proofpoint	✓	✗	⊗	⊗	✓	✗	✓	✓	✓	✓	✗
SimpleDmarc	✗	✓	✗	✓	?	?	?	⊗	?	?	?
Valimail	✗	✗	✗	✓	✗	✗	✗	✓	✗	✗	?
Libraries											
Checkdmarc	⊗	⊗	⊗	-	✓	✓	✓	-	✗	✗	✗
OpenDmarc	-	-	-	-	✓	✓	✓	-	✗	✓	✗
Rspamd	-	-	-	-	✓	✓	✗	-	✗	✓	✗
Our parser	-	-	-	-	✓	✓	✓	-	✓	✓	✓

The u-tag tag is particularly vital. If the tag list is updated, and the checker is not, the introduction of new tags may cause the checker to reject the records. However, it is noteworthy that none of the checkers adhere to the downgrade corner case. It is essential to consider that the downgrade feature may be seen as somewhat far-fetched, and email receivers might not necessarily need to account for this corner case. We have brought up our concerns about these issues to the DMARC working group (details not provided for anonymity reasons).

Table 4 also presents the measurements we conducted on three popular DMARC libraries: OpenDmarc, Rspamd, and checkdmarc. Notably, in related work, only Czybik et al. [8] have disclosed the software they used to parse DMARC records (checkdmarc). In their survey, Ashiq et al. [2] found that one-third of DMARC operators use OpenDMARC. However, none of these libraries met our requirements, particularly for parsing. Consequently, we have developed our own Python ABNF-based DMARC parser, accessible at:

https://github.com/drakkar-lig/abnf-dmarc-parser

RFC 7489 provides four different resources for parsing DMARC records (see Appendix, Figs. 10, 11, 12, and 13). These resources outline specific rules for parsing DMARC records. The first statement regarding parsing specifies that DMARC records follow the "tag-value" syntax defined in DKIM, and any unknown tags must be ignored. The second statement highlights that a DMARC policy record must adhere to the ABNF, with the 'v' and 'p' tags appearing first and second, respectively. Unknown tags must be ignored, and certain syntax errors should be discarded. The third statement provides the ABNF rules for DMARC records, while the last statement addresses the 'p-down' corner case. To ensure proper parsing, we initially apply the rules outlined in RFC 6376 (see Appendix, Figs. 14, 15, and 16) to ensure that the strings match the 'tag-list' ABNF, without duplicate. Subsequently, we apply the RFC 7489 ABNF, ignoring any unknown tags, Finally, we verify that the 'v' and 'p' tags are in the correct order, 'sp' inherit from 'p' if not provided, and verify the `pct` value. This three-step process helps ensure the compliance with the specified parsing rules. As a default behavior, the parser does not apply the 'p-downgrade' corner case, as it is considered optional ('should') rather than mandatory ('must'). This approach aligns with the flexibility provided in the DMARC specifications and ensures that the parser does not enforce this corner case by default.

Ashiq et al. [2] provided their measurement data. We have run our parser with the `follow_dowgrade` option on their data. We have observed slight differences of 1.5% less valid DMARC records according to the value provided in their paper. Unfortunately, we cannot make a direct comparison as they did not provide the parsed data nor their code.

8   Ethical Considerations

To obtain reliable results with minimal interference on the tested systems, we followed the best practices recommended by the measurement community [12,14, 37]. We used Google and Cloudflare public resolvers for active measurements and respected the default DNS rate limits. We also randomized our input lists across the IP space and TLDs to avoid sending bulk DNS requests to any single entity, even though most responses are expected to come from Google and Cloudflare DNS caches. Finally, we distributed our scanning activities over several days.

We have enforced contacting each organization having a DMARC checker which was vulnerable to XSS vulnerability before the publication of the article. The only organization that is still vulnerable at the publication time has acknowledged the vulnerability in May 2022. They replied to us that they would 'take a look shortly'. Furthermore, the XSS is performed when a user specifically queries a domain name, not any URL can result directly in an XSS.

Finally, we alerted the domain owners or associated intermediaries about the unregistered domain names we found in the `rua` and `ruf` URIs, to prevent malicious actors from registering them and receiving DMARC reports. Instead of sending multiple emails to the same recipients for each vulnerable domain name, we sent single emails informing each responsible party of all the vulnerable domains.

9   Conclusion

Our measurements reveal potential shortcomings in the understanding and interpretation of the DMARC protocol, as outlined in RFC 7489. None of the organizations we evaluated managed to successfully pass all of our test scenarios. Our analysis of various corner cases reveals that, despite DMARC being a fundamental service, some organizations and open-source projects have either implemented DMARC record parsing tools incorrectly or taken initiatives that deviate from the standards.

Our analysis, which covered 280 million domain names, reveals the following findings regarding the DMARC adoption:

– Out of the 16.4 M domain names containing at least the case-insensitive string 'dmarc' in their TXT record, 150 K were found to be syntactically invalid. Additional 68 K had multiple syntactically valid records, rendering their DMARC invalid.
– Approximately 15.9 million domain names were identified as having valid DMARC records.
– Within this group, one million domain names failed the Email Destination Verification.
– 5.5 million domain names had DMARC records but lacked protections, including reporting options and restrictive handling policies.
– Notably, 35% of domain names that specified an fo tag did not have a ruf tag (equivalent to 1.1 M domain names).
– Furthermore, 268 K domain names had a pct value different from '100' while the p tag was set to none.

Within the realm of popular domains, our observations suggest that administrators of top-ranked domain names demonstrate a better understanding, implementation, and stricter handling policies, potentially linked to the resources dedicated to DMARC. Notably, we have observed that while 42% of domain names with valid DMARC record express a preference for receiving reports, more than 30% opt for the five biggest third-party services to handle these reports, highlighting the complexity of self-management.

To offer a comprehensive overview, our temporal analysis has unveiled that the use of aggregate reports does not display a clear correlation with the changes in handling policies, which indicates that the adjustments in handling policies might not always be directly influenced by the analysis of aggregate reports.

The complexity of standards hinders DMARC deployment and its correct configuration. Improving specifications is an on-going work, for instance, RFC 7489 was published as an informational document and the IETF DMARC working group currently works on an Internet Standards Track for DMARC.[15] The latest accessed version (28) includes modifications to the current DMARC protocol such as the addition or updating of terms and definitions, the introduction

---

[15] https://datatracker.ietf.org/doc/draft-ietf-dmarc-dmarcbis/.

of a new process of policy discovery, the removal of the `pct`, `rf`, and `ri` tags, the addition of three new tags, and new RFCs for aggregate and forensic reports.

Nevertheless, it is unlikely that the DMARC version will change, and email receivers will need to ensure backward compatibility between two RFCs. We suggest that a more effective approach would be to define a new DMARC version (`v=DMARC2`) in the new RFC. Specifying DMARC v2 could be an opportunity to deeply redesign the protocol to simplify and clarify its operation. A common belief on DMARC is that the check mechanism would fail if DKIM **or** SPF: Yajima et al. [51] and Ashiq et al. [2] have embraced this misconception. Additionally, the `fo` tag is often misunderstood: as it is often thought to allow the domain owner to indicate the logical operators for the DMARC check mechanism and not the generation of failure reports. Our measurements show that 35% of the DMARC records with `fo` do not have the `ruf` tag, which reveals a misunderstanding of this feature. We think that it is necessary to have more verbal tags and be able to choose the logical operator of the DMARC check mechanism.

Acknowledgments. We thank the reviewers for their valuable and constructive feedback. This work has been partially supported by the French Ministry of Research projects PERSYVAL Lab under contract ANR-11-LABX-0025-01 and DiNS under contract ANR-19-CE25-0009-01.

10   Appendix

```
DMARC records follow the extensible "tag-value" syntax for
DNS-based key records defined in DKIM [DKIM].
Section 11 creates a registry for known DMARC tags and registers
the initial set defined in this document.  Only tags defined in
this document or in later extensions, and thus added to that
registry, are to be processed; unknown tags MUST be ignored.
```

Fig. 10. RFC 7489 Extract - 6.3. General Record Format

```
A DMARC policy record MUST comply with the formal specification
found in Section 6.4 in that the "v" and "p" tags MUST be present
and MUST  appear in that order.  Unknown tags MUST be ignored.
Syntax errors in the remainder of the record SHOULD be discarded
in favor of default values (if any) or ignored outright.
```

Fig. 11. RFC 7489 Extract - 6.3. General Record Format

```
dmarc-record    = dmarc-version dmarc-sep  [dmarc-request]
[dmarc-sep dmarc-srequest] [dmarc-sep dmarc-auri]
[dmarc-sep dmarc-furi] [dmarc-sep dmarc-adkim]
[dmarc-sep dmarc-aspf] [dmarc-sep dmarc-ainterval]
[dmarc-sep dmarc-fo] [dmarc-sep dmarc-rfmt]
[dmarc-sep dmarc-percent] [dmarc-sep]
; components other than dmarc-version and
; dmarc-request may appear in any order
```

Fig. 12. RFC 7489 Extract - 6.3. General Record Format

```
6.  If a retrieved policy record does not contain a valid "p" tag
    , or contains an "sp" tag that is not valid, then:
    1.  if a "rua" tag is present and contains at least one
        syntactically valid reporting URI, the Mail Receiver SHOULD
        act as if a record containing a valid "v" tag and "p=none"
        was retrieved, and continue processing;
    2.  otherwise, the Mail Receiver applies no DMARC processing to
        this message.
```

Fig. 13. RFC 7489 Extract - 6.6.3. Policy Discovery

```
DKIM uses a simple "tag=value" syntax in several contexts,
including in messages and domain signature records.
Values are a series of strings containing either plain text,
"base64" text (as defined in [RFC2045], Section 6.8),
"qp-section" (ibid, Section 6.7), or "dkim-quoted-printable"
(as defined in Section 2.11). The name of the tag will
determine the encoding of each value.  Unencoded semicolon
(";") characters MUST NOT occur in the tag value, since that
separates tag-specs.
```

Fig. 14. RFC 6376 Extract - 3.2. Tag=Value Lists

```
tag-list   =  tag-spec *( ";" tag-spec ) [ ";" ]
tag-spec   =  [FWS] tag-name [FWS] "=" [FWS] tag-value [FWS]
tag-name   =  ALPHA *ALNUMPUNC
tag-value  =  [ tval *( 1*(WSP / FWS) tval ) ]
              ; Prohibits WSP and FWS at beginning and end
tval       =  1*VALCHAR
VALCHAR    =  %x21-3A / %x3C-7E
              ; EXCLAMATION to TILDE except SEMICOLON
ALNUMPUNC  =  ALPHA / DIGIT / "_"
```

Fig. 15. RFC 6376 Extract - 3.2. Tag=Value Lists

```
Tags MUST be interpreted in a case-sensitive manner.  Values MUST
be processed as case sensitive unless the specific tag
description of semantics specifies case insensitivity.
Tags with duplicate names MUST NOT occur within a single tag-list
; if a tag name does occur more than once, the entire tag-list is
invalid.
Whitespace within a value MUST be retained unless explicitly
excluded by the specific tag description.
Tag=value pairs that represent the default value MAY be included
to aid legibility.
Unrecognized tags MUST be ignored.
```

Fig. 16. RFC 6376 Extract - 3.2. Tag=Value Lists

References

1. Allman, E., Callas, J., Delany, M., Libbey, M., Fenton, J., Thomas, M.: Domainkeys identified mail (DKIM) signatures. RFC 4871, RFC Editor, May 2007
2. Ashiq, M.I., Li, W., Fiebig, T., Chung, T.: You've got report: measurement and security implications of DMARC reporting. In: USENIX Security Symposium (2023)
3. Bennett, N., Sowards, R., Deccio, C.: SPFail: discovering, measuring, and remediating vulnerabilities in email sender validation. In: ACM Internet Measurement Conference, pp. 633–646. ACM (2022)
4. Bradner, S.: Key words for use in RFCs to indicate requirement levels. BCP 14, RFC Editor, March 1997
5. Chen, J., Paxson, V., Jiang, J.: Composition kills: a case study of email sender authentication. In: USENIX Security Symposium, pp. 2183–2199 (2020)
6. Crocker, D.: Mailbox names for common services, roles and functions. RFC 2142, RFC Editor, May 1997
7. Crocker, D., Hansen, T., Kucherawy, M.: Domainkeys identified mail (DKIM) signatures. STD 76, RFC Editor, September 2011
8. Czybik, S., Horlboge, M., Rieck, K.: Lazy gatekeepers: a large-scale study on SPF configuration in the wild. In: ACM Internet Measurement Conference, pp. 344–355. ACM (2023)
9. Dan, K., Kitagawa, N., Sakuraba, S., Yamai, N.: Spam domain detection method using active DNS data and e-mail reception log. In: Computer Software and Applications Conference (COMPSAC), vol. 1, pp. 896–899 (2019)
10. Deccio, C., et al.: Measuring email sender validation in the wild. In: ACM International Conference on Emerging Networking EXperiments and Technologies (CoNEXT), pp. 230–242. ACM (2021)
11. Delany, M.: Domain-based email authentication using public keys advertised in the DNS (domainkeys). RFC 4870, RFC Editor, May 2007
12. Dittrich, D., Kenneally, E.: The Menlo Report: Ethical Principles Guiding Information and Communication Technology Research (2012)
13. Durumeric, Z., et al.: Neither snow nor rain nor MITM...: an empirical analysis of email delivery security. In: ACM Internet Measurement Conference (IMC), pp. 27–39. ACM (2015)

14. Durumeric, Z., Wustrow, E., Halderman, J.A.: ZMap: fast internet-wide scanning and its security applications. In: USENIX Security Symposium (2013)
15. Fernandez, S., Korczyński, M., Duda, A.: Early detection of spam domains with passive DNS and SPF. In: Hohlfeld, O., Moura, G., Pelsser, C. (eds.) PAM 2022. LNCS, vol. 13210, pp. 30–49. Springer, Cham (2022). https://doi.org/10.1007/978-3-030-98785-5_2
16. Ferrante, A.J.: The impact of GDPR on WHOIS: implications for businesses facing cybercrime. Cyber Secur. Peer-Rev. J. **2**(2), 143–148 (2018)
17. Fontana, H.: Authentication failure reporting using the abuse reporting format. RFC 6591, RFC Editor, April 2012
18. Gojmerac, I., Zwickl, P., Kovacs, G., Steindl, C.: Large-scale active measurements of DNS entries related to e-mail system security. In: IEEE International Conference on Communications (ICC), pp. 7426–7432, June 2015. ISSN: 1938–1883
19. Herzberg, A.: DNS-based email sender authentication mechanisms: a critical review. Comput. Secur. **28**(8), 731–742 (2009)
20. Hu, H., Peng, P., Wang, G.: Towards understanding the adoption of anti-spoofing protocols in email systems. In: IEEE Cybersecurity Development (SecDev), pp. 94–101 (2018)
21. Hu, H., Wang, G.: Revisiting email spoofing attacks. arXiv preprint arXiv:1801.00853 (2018)
22. Izhikevich, L., et al.: ZDNS: a fast DNS toolkit for internet measurement. In: ACM Internet Measurement Conference (IMC), pp. 33–43. ACM (2022)
23. Kitterman, S.: Sender policy framework (SPF) authentication failure reporting using the abuse reporting format. RFC 6652, RFC Editor, June 2012
24. Kitterman, S.: Sender policy framework (SPF) for authorizing use of domains in email, version 1. RFC 7208, RFC Editor, April 2014
25. Klensin, J.: Simple mail transfer protocol. RFC 5321, RFC Editor, October 2008
26. Konno, K., Dan, K., Kitagawa, N.: A spoofed e-mail countermeasure method by scoring the reliability of DKIM signature using communication data. In: IEEE Computer Software and Applications Conference (COMPSAC), vol. 2, pp. 43–48 (2017)
27. Kucherawy, M.: Extensions to domainkeys identified mail (DKIM) for failure reporting. RFC 6651, RFC Editor, June 2012
28. Kucherawy, M., Zwicky, E.: Domain-based message authentication, reporting, and conformance (DMARC). RFC 7489, RFC Editor, March 2015
29. Lever, C., Walls, R., Nadji, Y., Dagon, D., McDaniel, P., Antonakakis, M.: Domain-Z: 28 registrations later measuring the exploitation of residual trust in domains. In: IEEE Symposium on Security and Privacy (SP), pp. 691–706 (2016)
30. Liu, D., Hao, S., Wang, H.: All your DNS records point to us: understanding the security threats of dangling DNS records. In: ACM SIGSAC Conference on Computer and Communications Security (CCS), pp. 1414–1425. ACM (2016)
31. Liu, G., et al.: Dial "N" for NXDomain: the scale, origin, and security implications of DNS queries to non-existent domains. In: ACM Internet Measurement Conference (IMC). ACM (2023)
32. Malatras, A., Coisel, I., Sanchez, I.: Technical recommendations for improving security of email communications. In: International Convention on Information and Communication Technology, Electronics and Microelectronics (MIPRO), pp. 1381–1386 (2016)
33. Maroofi, S., Korczyński, M., Duda, A.: From defensive registration to subdomain protection: evaluation of email anti-spoofing schemes for high-profile domains. In: Traffic Measurement and Analysis Conference (TMA) (2020)

34. Maroofi, S., Korczyński, M., Hölzel, A., Duda, A.: Adoption of email anti-spoofing schemes: a large scale analysis. IEEE Trans. Netw. Serv. Manage. **18**(3), 3184–3196 (2021)
35. Mori, T., Sato, K., Takahashi, Y., Ishibashi, K.: How is e-mail sender authentication used and misused? In: Annual Collaboration, Electronic messaging, Anti-Abuse and Spam Conference (CEAS), pp. 31–37. ACM (2011)
36. Nosyk, Y., Hureau, O., Fernandez, S., Duda, A., Korczyński, M.: Unveiling the weak links: exploring DNS infrastructure vulnerabilities and fortifying defenses. In: IEEE European Symposium on Security and Privacy Workshops (EuroS&PW), pp. 546–557. IEEE Computer Society (2023)
37. Partridge, C., Allman, M.: Ethical considerations in network measurement papers. Commun. ACM **59**(10), 58–64 (2016)
38. Pochat, V.L., Van Goethem, T., Tajalizadehkhoob, S., Korczyński, M., Joosen, W.: Tranco: a research-oriented top sites ranking hardened against manipulation. In: NDSS Symposium (2019)
39. Portier, A., Carter, H., Lever, C.: Security in plain TXT. In: Perdisci, R., Maurice, C., Giacinto, G., Almgren, M. (eds.) DIMVA 2019. LNCS, vol. 11543, pp. 374–395. Springer, Cham (2019). https://doi.org/10.1007/978-3-030-22038-9_18
40. Postel, J.B.: Simple mail transfer protocol. STD 10, RFC Editor, August 1982
41. Scheffler, S., Smith, S., Gilad, Y., Goldberg, S.: The unintended consequences of email spam prevention. In: Beverly, R., Smaragdakis, G., Feldmann, A. (eds.) PAM 2018. LNCS, vol. 10771, pp. 158–169. Springer, Cham (2018). https://doi.org/10.1007/978-3-319-76481-8_12
42. Schlamp, J., Gustafsson, J., Wählisch, M., Schmidt, T.C., Carle, G.: The abandoned side of the internet: hijacking internet resources when domain names expire. In: Traffic Measurement and Analysis Conference (TMA) (2015)
43. Shukla, S., Misra, M., Varshney, G.: Forensic analysis and detection of spoofing based email attack using memory forensics and machine learning. In: Li, F., Liang, K., Lin, Z., Katsikas, S.K. (eds.) Security and Privacy in Communication Networks, vol. 462, pp. 491–509. Springer, Cham (2023). https://doi.org/10.1007/978-3-031-25538-0_26
44. Szalachowski, P., Perrig, A.: Short paper: on deployment of DNS-based security enhancements. In: Kiayias, A. (ed.) FC 2017. LNCS, vol. 10322, pp. 424–433. Springer, Cham (2017). https://doi.org/10.1007/978-3-319-70972-7_24
45. Tatang, D., Flume, R., Holz, T.: Extended abstract: a first large-scale analysis on usage of MTA-STS. In: Bilge, L., Cavallaro, L., Pellegrino, G., Neves, N. (eds.) DIMVA 2021. LNCS, vol. 12756, pp. 361–370. Springer, Cham (2021). https://doi.org/10.1007/978-3-030-80825-9_18
46. Tatang, D., Zettl, F., Holz, T.: The evolution of DNS-based email authentication: measuring adoption and finding flaws. In: International Symposium on Research in Attacks, Intrusions and Defenses (RAID), pp. 354–369. Association for Computing Machinery (2021)
47. Vissers, T., Barron, T., Van Goethem, T., Joosen, W., Nikiforakis, N.: The wolf of name street: hijacking domains through their nameservers. In: ACM SIGSAC Conference on Computer and Communications Security (CCS), pp. 957–970. ACM (2017)
48. Wang, C., Wang, G.: Revisiting email forwarding security under the authenticated received chain protocol. In: ACM Web Conference (WWW), pp. 681–689. ACM (2022)
49. Wang, C., et al.: A large-scale and longitudinal measurement study of DKIM deployment. In: USENIX Security Symposium, pp. 1185–1201 (2022)

50. Wong, M., Schlitt, W.: Sender policy framework (SPF) for authorizing use of domains in e-mail, version 1. RFC 4408, RFC Editor, April 2006
51. Yajima, M., Chiba, D., Yoneya, Y., Mori, T.: A first look at brand indicators for message identification (BIMI). In: Brunstrom, A., Flores, M., Fiore, M. (eds.) International Conference on Passive and Active Network Measurement, vol. 13882. pp. 479–495. Springer, Cham (2023). https://doi.org/10.1007/978-3-031-28486-1_20

Designing a Lightweight Network Observability Agent for Cloud Applications

Pravein Govindan Kannan[1(✉)], Shachee Mishra Gupta[2], Dushyant Behl[3], Eran Raichstein[4], and Joel Takvorian[5]

[1] IBM Research, San Jose, USA
pravein.govindan.kannan@ibm.com
[2] IBM Research, Gurgaon, India
[3] IBM Research, Bangalore, India
[4] IBM Research, Haifa, Israel
[5] Red Hat, Puteaux, France

Abstract. Applications are increasingly being deployed on the cloud as microservices using orchestrators like Kubernetes. With microservices-type deployment, performance and observability are critical requirements, especially given the SLAs and strict business guarantee requirements (latency, throughput, etc.) of requests. Network observability is an imperative feature that every orchestrator needs to incorporate to provide the operators visibility into the network communication between the services deployed and the ability to provide necessary metrics to diagnose problems.

In this paper, we propose a lightweight network observability agent *netobserv-ebpf-agent* built using eBPF, that can be deployed in various environments (K8s, Bare-metal, etc.) and runs independent of the underlying network datapath/ Container Network Interfaces (CNIs) deployed by the orchestrator. *netobserv-ebpf-agent* monitors the network traffic in each host-nodes' interfaces running in the cluster and summarizes the necessary information of the traffic workloads with very minimal overhead. We articulate the design decisions of *netobserv-ebpf-agent* using measurements which maximize the performance of the datapath. Our evaluations show that *netobserv-ebpf-agent* offers significant performance benefits against the existing systems, while keeping the CPU and memory overheads lower by a magnitude. *netobserv-ebpf-agent* is available in open source and is officially released as part of *Red Hat OpenShift* Container Platform. (https://github.com/netobserv/netobserv-ebpf-agent)

1 Introduction

With the growing cloud deployment of applications using microservices [30] running on container orchestration platforms like Kubernetes, more focus has been recently on observability. Observability is the ability to know and interpret the current state of the deployment, and technology to realize if something is amiss. With several applications demanding strict communication guarantees [31] i.e.,

© The Author(s), under exclusive license to Springer Nature Switzerland AG 2024
P. Richter et al. (Eds.): PAM 2024, LNCS 14537, pp. 262–276, 2024.
https://doi.org/10.1007/978-3-031-56249-5_11

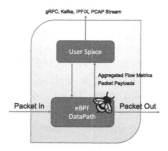

Fig. 1. The architecture of *netobserv-ebpf-agent*

SLAs in terms of down times, latency, throughput, etc, network-level observability is a highly imperative feature that needs to be provided by the orchestration platforms either natively or using third-party plugins/operators. Network observability additionally helps operators to tune network provisioning based on the application workloads, detecting heavy workloads and additionally provide application-level insights (such as percentage of web traffic [1,28], video streaming [27], etc.).

The core part of every network observability tool is the ability to monitor and collect network metrics in a transparent manner. The network metrics typically provide insights like the number of packets/bytes exchanged between two IP endpoints [14]. Traditionally, host-based tools like libpcap-based pmacct citepmacct, and Tcpdump [22] are used. OpenVSwitch (OVS) [29] also has been used to expose information as sFlow or NetFlow records [17] in deployments where the Container Network Interfaces (CNI) are OVS-based [18].

Recently eBPF [8] (extended Berkeley Packet Filter) has emerged as a popular technology to implement various networking features like monitoring, filtering, etc at the end-hosts kernel. eBPF enables custom programs to be run along with the kernel in a safe and sandboxed manner. The major advantages of using eBPF are its performance, programmability, and flexibility. It allows programs to be hooked at certain points along the network data path like socket system calls, Traffic Control (TC) and Express Data Path (XDP [26]) to capture network traffic and insights at different vantage points irrespective of the underlying datapath/CNI. eBPF uses data structures called maps which allow the kernel programs to share data with user-space applications.

Recently, several open source tools [2,4,5,13,16] use eBPF for network observability, by storing network metrics in different eBPF maps, which is a fundamental data structure to store state information in eBPF datapath. However, so far there has been no systematic study on how the type of eBPF maps used affect the performance of the observability tool and end-application traffic.

In this paper, we propose *netobserv-ebpf-agent*, an eBPF-based traffic monitoring tool that we developed to enable Network observability in orchestrators such as Kubernetes. *Netobserv-ebpf-agent* hooks onto the Traffic Control (TC) of the interfaces at the end-hosts (worker nodes) to monitor the network traffic at the flow-level and exports aggregate statistics using gRPC/Kafka/IPFIX (refer Fig. 1). The main primitive of network observability is the monitoring of the necessary packet/flow-level information of the ongoing network packets in the data-path. The type of eBPF maps which maintains the records in the data-path is quite important, since it is accessed on a per-packet basis. Using benchmarks, we study how the eBPF maps used in the eBPF monitoring datapath impacts the performance of the observed traffic as well as affect the overheads. We apply the learnings from the benchmarks to design *netobserv-ebpf-agent* based on a novel architecture using Per-CPU hash maps where the data-structure is maintained per-core. The monitoring data is scattered across different hash buckets in the data-path and is aggregated in the user space.

We implement the *netobserv-ebpf-agent* using Cilium Go [4] eBPF library and evaluate our system with realistic traffic at line-rate and observe that *netobserv-ebpf-agent* can perform better by a magnitude compared against state-of-the-art monitoring systems used in production, while consuming very little overhead in terms of CPU and memory. Finally, we present the deployment model of *netobserv-ebpf-agent* in Kubernetes with enrichment of network metrics with contextual information like namespace, pod names and topology. *netobserv-ebpf-agent* is available open-source and also released along with *Red Hat OpenShift* and its compatible with Kubernetes regardless of the underlying networking datapaths.

2   Background and Related Work

In this section, we give a brief background on network observability with eBPF and enumerate the existing open-source tools available for observability.

eBPF [8] provides a way to run sandboxed programs in the OS kernel and safely extend the capabilities of the kernel. eBPF programs can be attached to several hook points like system calls, socket APIs, Traffic Control (TC), XDP, etc to implement features in security, networking, profiling and observability. eBPF uses datastructure called maps to store & exchange information with the userspace. Several types of eBPF maps exists while the popular types used for network traffic analysis being hash map and ring buffer (as explained in Sect. 3). In the context of network observability, maps are popularly used to store network metrics (flow-id, packet counts, etc.) which the userspace program would pick up and export it to a collector in the necessary format. Over the recent years, driven by adoption of cloud (predominantly running linux [23]), several open source tools have emerged to achieve network observability.

Libebpfflow [16] is an eBPF-based network visibility library. It hooks on to various points in the host stack like kernel probes (e.g. inet_csk_accept) and tracepoints (e.g. net:net_dev_queue) to analyze TCP/UDP traffic states. Its eBPF implementation uses perf event buffer (or ringbuffer) to notify TCP state change events to the user-space.

Cloudflare's ebpf exporter [7] provides APIs for plugging in custom ebpf code to record custom metrics of interest. Pixie [20] uses bpftrace to trace syscalls for application profiling and protocol tracing (TLS). It listens to TCP/UDP state messages to collect necessary information and stores them for querying. Inspektor [12] provides a collection of tools for Kubernetes cluster debugging, added as a daemonset on each node of the cluster to collect traces. These events are written to a ring buffer, which is consumed retrospectively when a fault occurs (for e.g. upon a pod crash).

L3AF [15] provides a set of eBPF packages which can be packaged and chained together using tail-calls. It provides network observability by storing flow records on a hash map in the eBPF datapath to be exported as IPFIX.

Host-INT [13] extends the in-band Network Telemetry [11] to support telemetry for host network stack. Fundamentally, INT embeds the switching delay incurred for each packet into an INT header in the packet. Host-INT does the same for the host network stack and uses a ring buffer to send statistics to the userspace. Skydive [21]. Skydive is a network topology and flow analyzer. It attaches probes to the nodes to collect flow-level information. The probes are attached using PCAP, AF_Packet, OpenVSwitch, etc. Recently, Skydive uses eBPF-based hash maps to capture the flow metrics.

Cilium Tetragon [5] is a recently released extensible framework for security and observability in Cilium. Tetragon stores the recorded metrics in user space using ring buffers. Additionally, eBPF is leveraged to enforce policy spanning various kernel components such as virtual file system (VFS), namespace, system call.

While different tools adopted different data structures to collect and export per-packet metrics, there are no existing performance measurements to study the impact of these data-structure used in the eBPF data-path. We start by first bridging that gap to study how the choice of eBPF maps in the monitoring data-path affects the performance. *netobserv-ebpf-agent* uses the insights from the measurements to use the optimal data-structure to maximize performance of the eBPF data-path.

3   Design and Implementation

3.1   Revisiting the Monitoring Data-Path

In this section, we benchmark the basic primitive of a monitoring data-path which extracts flow-level information per packet (standard 5-tuple {source IP address, destination IP address, source port, destination port, protocol}) and maintains per-flow counters for number of bytes and packets. We implement template eBPF programs (attachable to TC hook-point) using different eBPF maps [24] to collect the same metrics from host traffic. The artefacts of our measurements are open source[1]. We use the following eBPF maps, which are popularly used by existing open source tools to collect and store packet-level and flow-level metrics:

- **Ring Buffer** : Ring buffer is a shared queue between the eBPF datapath and the userspace, where eBPF datapath is the producer and the userspace program is the consumers.

---

[1] https://github.com/netobserv/ebpf-research/tree/main/ebpf-measurements.

- **Array & Per-CPU Array** : (Per-CPU) Array-based map could be used to store per-packet metrics temporarily in the eBPF data-path before sending to user space.
- **Hash & Per-CPU Hash** : (Per-CPU) Hash map could be used in the eBPF datapath by first performing a hash of the 5-tuple flow-id which would point to a specific bucket in the array. Thus, it is possible to aggregate per-flow metrics since a flow-id maps to the same bucket.

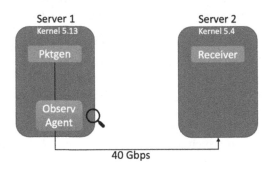

Fig. 2. Testbed Setup used for measurements and evaluation of *netobserv-ebpf-agent*

Measurement Studies. Given the above eBPF map options for implementing the observability data-path, its very imperative to study the empirical performance of a data-path using each of the above choices. To do that, we implemented representative eBPF data-paths which collect flow metrics using each of the above mentioned data structures and study the performance by sending traffic using a custom-built UDP-based packet generator built on top of PcapPlusPlus [19]. The testbed setup for benchmarking is shown in Fig. 2. The observe agent is the eBPF datapath performing flow metric collection, attached to the TC (traffic control) hook-point of the sender. We use two bare-metal servers connected over a 40G link. Packet generation is done using custom-built UDP-based packet generator over PcapPlusPlus [19] using 40 separate cores. To bring these measurements in perspective, libpcap-based Tcpdump (collecting similar flow information) is also used for comparison.

We run the tests by generating bursts of UDP packets belonging to a *single-flow* and *multi-flow*. While *single-flow* generated packets belonging to a single UDP flow using the 40 cores, *multi-flow* generates 40 different UDP flows (1 flow per core). Traffic was generated in bursts to generate maximum packets per seconds, while saturating the cores. As shown in the Fig. 3, native performance without any observe agent is about 4.7 Mpps (Million Packets Per Second), and with tcpdump running, the throughput falls to about 1.8 Mpps. With eBPF-based observe agents, we observed that the performance varies from 1.6 Mpps to 4.7 Mpps based on the eBPF maps used to store the flow metrics. Using a shared data structure such as a single hash map, we observed the most significant drop in performance for a single-flow, because each packet writes to the same hash bucket in the map regardless of the CPU it originated from. However, performance improves when multiple-flows are introduced since the contention reduces for a single bucket. Ring buffer (RB) performs almost equally worse as single Hash Map for burst of packets from a single flow, however fails to improve with multiple flows, since the contention for the memory of the ring buffer remains a bottleneck.

Using a Per-CPU hash map (CpuHash), we observed an increase in throughput for a single flow, because packets arriving from multiple CPUs no longer contend for the same map bucket, and with multiple flows, the performance increases significantly as the contention reduces further. With (Per-CPU) arrays, we see a significant increase in the throughput. We attribute this to the fact there is no contention between packets since each packet takes up a different entry in the array incrementally upon arrival. However, the major drawback is we do not handle the eviction of entries in the array upon full, while it performs writes in a circular fashion. Hence, it stores only the last few packet records observed at any time. Array eviction would require using redundant arrays which are periodically flushed (to userspace) to handle large packet rates and hence complicating the eBPF datapath, which makes it hard to maintain. Nevertheless, it provides us the spectrum of performance gains we can achieve by appropriately using the maps in the eBPF datapath.

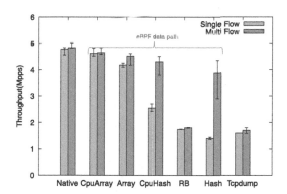

Fig. 3. Throughput observed comparison of different eBPF data-paths built using various data structures

Key Takeways:

- Ringbuffer and hash maps which are popularly used by several tools [2,5,12, 13,16] have a significant effect on the underlying workload's performance.
- Per-CPU hash maps perform much better in handling multiple flows by aggregating flow metrics in multiple per-CPU buckets in the eBPF data-path.
- Arrays perform best due to absence of contention/locking, however it is hard to be implemented to handle millions of packet records at line-rate.

3.2   Design of *netobserv-ebpf-agent*

Flow Capture Agent. Based on the insights gathered in the measurement studies, we design *netobserv-ebpf-agent* using Per-CPU hash maps to aggregate flow metrics in the eBPF datapath, since it offers good performance and is easier to implement and maintain from userspace. *netobserv-ebpf-agent* attaches to the TC hook-point of the individual network interfaces to monitor traffic going through. The architecture of the *netobserv-ebpf-agent* is illustrated in Fig. 1, where *netobserv-ebpf-agent* is composed of an eBPF data-path and the userspace daemon. In the following, we explain the components of *netobserv-ebpf-agent* in detail.

eBPF Datapath. The eBPF Datapath comprises of a Per-CPU hash map which is used to map a flow-id from every incoming packet to a hash bucket in the map, which maintains metrics like bytes/packets counter, and start and last-seen timestamps. Upon a packet arrival, a lookup is performed on the hash map using the flow-id. If the lookup is successful, the corresponding packet/byte counters and last-seen timestamp are updated. The start timestamp is initialized when the bucket gets created or TCP SYN bit is set in the packet. However, the above logic could fail to map to a hash bucket upon certain scenarios : 1) The hash map is full, and 2) The hash map is busy (due to another operation/eviction). To tackle this scenario, we additionally use a ringbuffer map. When we encounter such scenarios, we send the flow-id with counters to user space using the ringbuffer map along with the error-type for the user space to take appropriate action. Hence, under a normal scenario, the flow counters are aggregated in the eBPF datapath using the Per-CPU hash map. Hash collisions are possible in the Per-CPU hash map, and they are handled by libbpf by maintaining an array of key/value pairs per hash bucket and verifying the key upon insertion/retrieval. We represent this logic in Fig. 4.

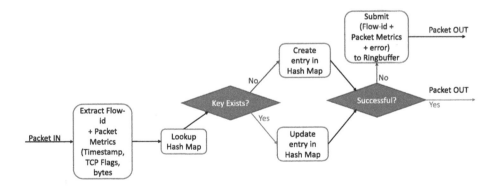

Fig. 4. Logic of the eBPF datapath

User Space. The user space daemon configures the eBPF datapath with settings such as the interfaces to be monitored, hash map size, eviction timeout,

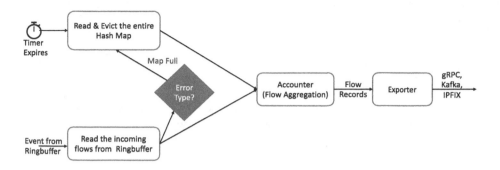

Fig. 5. Logic of the userspace daemon

etc. As show in Fig. 5, the user space daemon is responsible to periodically evict the flow records in Per-CPU hash maps based on the configured eviction time-out. Upon eviction, the user space daemon also needs to aggregate the entries per-flow which could be scattered across different CPU buckets of the Per-CPU hash map, which uses different contiguous buckets for each CPU. The aggregated entries from the hash map are sent to the *accounter*. During eviction, the map bucket might be temporarily unavailable to write in the datapath. In such scenarios, the flow information is written to the ring buffer.

The user space daemon also listens to the ring buffer to receive individual flow entries from the eBPF datapath directly. Upon receiving a flow entry, the user space checks the error which the flow encountered in the eBPF datapath. If the error is due to *map being full*, then the user space daemon, immediately triggers a bulk eviction of the map to minimize the usage of ringbuffer (due to performance). However, if the error is due to the map being busy, then the flow entries are sent to the accounter. The user space daemon maintains mutex to ensure only a single eviction of the hash map is happening at a given time. The accounter performs another aggregation of flow entries from the hash map and ring buffer and temporarily stores the flow entries in a buffer before sending to the exporter. The exporter is pre-configured using configuration to export the flow records as gRPC, Kafka, IPFIX records.

The challenge with using Per-CPU hashmap in the eBPF datapath is that memory is not zeroed when an entry is evicted/removed by the user space daemon. Hence, if an entry is removed and a new flow maps to the same hash bucket from other CPUs, the older entries pertaining to the deleted flow would still be present in the hash bucket. This would produce inaccurate results when aggregating the individual flow entries across per-CPU hash buckets. To solve this in a lightweight manner, we additionally, maintain a timestamp of last eviction in the user space. During aggregation, we discard old flow entries whose last-seen timestamp is before the last eviction time. These old entries would eventually be written over by new flows.

In the following, we show the code snippets of the flow and map declarations. *flow_id* encodes both v4 and v6 addresses in *src_ip* and *dst_ip* to avoid maintaining a separate declaration for v6.

```
1   struct flow_metrics {
2       u32 packets;
3       u64 bytes;
4       u64 start_mono_time_ts; // Flow start monotomic timestamp in ns
5       u64 end_mono_time_ts; // Flow end monotomic timestamp in ns
6       u8 errno; // Positive errno of a failed map insertion
7       u16 flags; // TCP Flags encountered by the flow
8   };
9
10  // Attributes that uniquely identify a flow(flow-id)
11  struct flow_id {
12      u16 eth_protocol;
13      u8 direction;
14      u8 src_mac[ETH_ALEN];
15      u8 dst_mac[ETH_ALEN];
16      struct in6_addr src_ip; // IPv4 addresses are encoded as IPv6
17      struct in6_addr dst_ip; // with prefix ::ffff/96
18      u16 src_port, dst_port;
19      u8 transport_protocol;
20      u32 if_index;
21  };
22
23  // Flow record
24  struct flow_record_t {
25      flow_id id;
26      flow_metrics metrics;
27  };
```

```
1   // eBPF Map declarations for aggregating the flow
2   // Common Ringbuffer as a conduit for flows to userspace
3   struct {
4       __uint(type, BPF_MAP_TYPE_RINGBUF);
5       __uint(max_entries, 1 << 24);
6   } direct_flows SEC(".maps");
7
8   // Key: the flow identifier.
9   // Value: the flow metrics for that identifier.
10  struct {
11      __uint(type, BPF_MAP_TYPE_PERCPU_HASH);
12      __type(key, flow_id);
13      __type(value, flow_metrics);
14  } aggregated_flows SEC(".maps");
15
```

Packet Capture Agent. We additionally design a Packet Capture Agent (PCA) to selectively capture the entire packet payload for further analysis (for e.g. DNS inspection). The user space daemon also configures the eBPF datapath with PCA settings such enabling packet capture, specifying the filters for capture and the target where a collector will listen and receive a PCAP stream.

A Per-CPU Perf buffer is allotted to capture packets and write them to the userspace. The userspace daemon listens on the perf buffers and the packets are streamed as soon as a collector (for e.g. a wireshark client, zeek [25], etc.) connect to the agent on the specified PCA port.

```
1  //PerfEvent Array for Capturing full Packet Payloads
2  // Key: the packet idenitfier
3  // Value: the packet payload metadata
4  struct {
5      __uint(type, BPF_MAP_TYPE_PERF_EVENT_ARRAY);
6      __type(key, u32);
7      __type(value, u32);
8      __uint(max_entries, 256);
9  } packet_record SEC(".maps");
```

Here, we show the code snippet of the packet metadata structure.

```
1  struct payload_metadata {
2      u32 if_index;    // Interface Index
3      u32 pkt_len;     // Length of the packet (headers+payload)
4      u64 timestamp;   // Timestamp when packet is received by eBPF
5  };
6
```

Packet capture being resource intensive is turned off by default and could be turned on by setting $ENABLE\_PCA = true$. This is followed by setting up the filters and the port that packet capture server would listen to. The capture starts

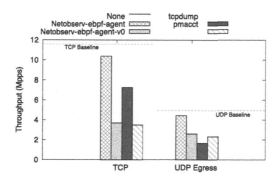

Fig. 6. Throughput observed by *netobserv-ebpf-agent* variants in comparison to existing tools

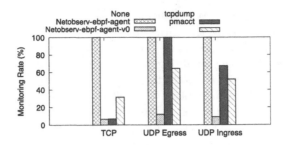

Fig. 7. Monitoring rate observed by *netobserv-ebpf-agent* variants in comparison to existing tools

only when a client (receiver) connects to it. The filter is set using environment variable *PCA_FILTER* and port using *PCA_SERVER_PORT*. A filter is specified as a combination of protocol and port number e.g. `tcp,80`.

4   Evaluation

We perform the evaluation of *netobserv-ebpf-agent* using the setup shown in Fig. 2 with two 80-core Intel(R) Xeon(R) Gold 5218R CPU @ 2.10GHz bare-metals connected using 40 G Mellanox Connect-X5 NICs. We evaluate *netobserv-ebpf-agent* against other Observ agents : 1) pmacct (a popularly deployed libcap based filtering tool), 2) tcpdump, and 3) *netobserv-ebpf-agent*-v0 : An initial version of *netobserv-ebpf-agent* using only ringbuffer in the eBPF datapath, and entire flow aggregation being done in the user space. This version doesn't have a per-CPU hash map which performs flow-aggregation in the eBPF datapath. Hence, each packet's flow-id and packet size is submitted to a ring buffer. Many monitoring tools [2,5,12,13,16] use ring-buffer to submit critical events in the datapath

We evaluate the above *Observ agent*(s) under the three traffic scenarios :

– *TCP* : The *pktgen* in Fig. 2 is located in Server 2 (ingress direction), and it generates multiple short TCP flows with 100-byte packets for a duration of 100 s.
– *UDP-Egress* : The *pktgen* is located in Server 1 along with the *Observ Agent* and generates multiple UDP flows of 75-byte packets. Hence, the packets pass through the *Observ Agent* upon egress.
– *UDP-Ingress* : The *pktgen* is located in Server 2 and generates multiple UDP flows of 75-byte packets. Hence, the packets pass through the *Observ Agent* upon ingress.

We use ingress setup to evaluate the monitoring rate which is calculated by Num(Packets Observed in Observ agent) $/Num$(Actual Packets) and the egress setup to evaluate the overhead of the *Observ agent* on the throughput generated. For TCP we do not have an egress setup, since ingress setup is sufficient to capture both throughput and monitoring rate. While we use iperf3 to generate 128 different TCP flows (-P option), we use PcapPlusPlus to generate 40 UDP flows (1 flow per core). The intention behind the packet generation is to evaluate the performance of *Observ agent* under stress conditions. Performing this evaluation in bare-metal environment provides more control to perform traffic generation, and fine-grained measurements. We initially plot the throughput observed by *pktgen*, when the *Observ agent* is running in the same node (scenarios *TCP*, and *UDP-Egress*) in Fig. 6. *Baseline* refers to the native throughput observed by the *pktgen* without any *Observ agent* running. We observe that native throughput to be about 11.75 Mpps with TCP flows, and about 4.7 Mpps with UDP flows. With *Observ agents* such as pmacct and tcpdump, the throughput degradation is about 50–70%. With *netobserv-ebpf-agent*-v0, we observe a similar degradation in throughput due to usage of only ringbuffer. However with *netobserv-ebpf-agent*, we observe close to only 10% degradation in throughput due to flow aggregation using Per-CPU hash maps in the eBPF datapath.

Next, we measure the monitoring rate of the *Observ agent(s)* , which is calculated by Num(Packets Observed in Observ agent) / Num(Packets sent at line-rate) in Fig. 7. While, *netobserv-ebpf-agent* is able to monitor and provide the flow records for all 100% of the traffic sent over the interfaces (with TCP, UDP Egress and UDP Ingress), we observed pmacct, tcpdump and *netobserv-ebpf-agent*-v0 drop significant portion of the traffic as the user space fails to catch-up. While tcpdump monitors 100% of the traffic in *UDP Egress* scenario, it hampers the throughput of the outgoing traffic (Fig. 6).

Finally, we measure the overheads of the *Observ agent(s)* in terms of additional CPU overhead and memory consumed by the process[2] during line-rate traffic. We observe that *netobserv-ebpf-agent* consumes a magnitude lesser in additional CPU consumption % (over 80 Cores) compared to other *Observ agents*. This is mainly attributable to the usage of Per-CPU hash maps, which perform aggregation in the kernel eBPF datapath, thus keeping the userspace daemon idle periodically. We observe the memory footprint of the *netobserv-ebpf-agent* process is only 12 MB, while it being higher for other *Observ agents*. *netobserv-ebpf-agent*-v0 uses a slightly lesser memory due to absence of hash map in the data path.

Table 1. Overheads of the Observ agents

Observ Agent	Extra CPU Overhead (%)			Memory (MB)
	TCP	UDP Egress	UDP Ingress	
netobserv-ebpf-agent	11.19	0.08	20.17	12
netobserv-ebpf-agent-v0	220.4	13.8	233.24	11
tcpdump	51.48	6.18	670.46	27.4
pmacct	234.23	4.68	416.85	89.2

---

[2] mpstat for CPU consumption and pmap for memory.

Realistic Deployment Scenario. We deployed *netobserv-ebpf-agent* on a multi-node *Red Hat OpenShift* deployment deployed on AWS m6i.4xlarge EC2 instances (16 vCPU x 64 GB memory x 12.5 Gbps network) to capture network metrics from two realistic benchmarking workloads: 1) Node-density-heavy (25 nodes), and 2) cluster-density (120 nodes) [6]. Table 2 captures the average flows processed per minute and the oevrhead incurred in terms of total CPU cores and memory consumed.

Table 2. Performance and Overhead of *netobserv-ebpf-agent* in a 120-node (m6i.4xlarge EC2 instances) *Red Hat OpenShift* deployment

Workload Type	Total Nodes	Flows/Min (Millions)	CPU (Cores)	Mem (GB)
Node-density-heavy	25	0.52	3.32	2.71
Cluster-density	120	1.92	10.14	11.13

netobserv-ebpf-agent incurs a mere 0.83% CPU and 0.16% memory overhead in node-density-heavy scenarios and 0.52% CPU and 0.14% memory overhead in cluster-density workloads, impacting the deployment cost.

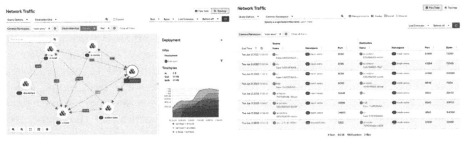

(a) Network Topology with metrics   (b) Network Metrics in dashboard

Fig. 8. Deployment & Visualization of *netobserv-ebpf-agent* in *Red Hat OpenShift*

5   Deployment Model

To deploy *netobserv-ebpf-agent* in *Red Hat OpenShift*, we have released an observability operator in OperatorHub[3]. Upon installing and deploying the tool, *netobserv-ebpf-agent* is deployed in all the nodes in the cluster. The flows records exported by *netobserv-ebpf-agent* (gRPC/Kafka/IPFIX) from *netobserv-ebpf-agent* can be consumed by flowlogs-pipeline [9], which are first enriched with

---

[3] https://operatorhub.io/operator/netobserv-operator.

kubernetes-specific contexts such as pod names, namespace, topology etc, and, in parallel, metrics are derived from the flow records for Prometheus consumption. Alternatively, the enriched metrics could also be exported as IPFIX records. Finally, the metrics are stored in a persistent storage (Loki [10]), and observed using Grafana or our dashboard in the *Red Hat OpenShift* as shown in Fig. 8a. Figure 8b shows how the workload network metrics are displayed along with the contextual information (Namespace, app names, etc.) in the observability dashboard. *netobserv-ebpf-agent* can also be deployed independently in bare-metal and other environments (OpenStack, VMs, etc.) and be configured to export flow records from the host interfaces using IPFIX records.

Use-Cases. *netobserv-ebpf-agent* can be used to auditing network traffic in a cluster, troubleshooting connectivity of applications, cost-planning and provisioning network based on demand and so on.

6   Conclusion

Network observability is gaining more traction with web applications increasingly being refactored as microservices in the cloud. In this paper, we present the design and implementation of *netobserv-ebpf-agent*, an eBPF-based network observability agent that can be readily deployed in existing Kubernetes-based orchestration platforms to gain network insights of the application workloads in a transparent manner with very minimal overhead. In future, we plan to enhance *netobserv-ebpf-agent* with more connection-level performance insights such RTT which would particularly help diagnosing performance issues. We also plan to go beyond the standard headers to derive application-specific insights from the payload like dns analytics, video conferencing, etc. *netobserv-ebpf-agent* is available in opensource and has also been released with *Red Hat OpenShift* [3].

Acknowledgements. We would like to thank the anonymous reviews and our shepherd Ramakrishnan Durairajan for their valuable feedback. We would like to thank the Red Hat development team which lead and foresaw the active development, testing and release of *netobserv-ebpf-agent*. A special shoutout to Nathan Weinberg for benchmarking *netobserv-ebpf-agent* in realistic scenarios, Mario Macias who lead the work during the initial release and Mohammad Mahmoud for his continuous improvements.

References

1. A guide to providing insight with network observability. https://cloud.redhat.com/blog/a-guide-to-providing-insight-with-network-observability
2. Aquasecurity tracee. https://github.com/aquasecurity/tracee
3. Check out the new network observability support in OpenShift 4.12. https://www.redhat.com/en/blog/check-out-the-new-network-observability-support-in-openshift-4.12
4. Cilium eBPF. https://github.com/cilium/ebpf
5. Cilium tetragon. https://github.com/cilium/tetragon

6. CloudBullDozer   workloads.   https://github.com/cloud-bulldozer/e2e-benchmarking/tree/master/workloads/kube-burner
7. Cloudflare ebpf_exporter. https://github.com/cloudflare/ebpf_exporter
8. eBPF. https://ebpf.io
9. Flowlogs-pipeline. https://github.com/netobserv/flowlogs-pipeline
10. Grafana Loki. https://grafana.com/oss/loki/
11. In-band network telemetry. https://github.com/p4lang/p4-applications/blob/master/docs/INT_v2_1.pdf
12. Inspektor-gadget. https://github.com/kinvolk/inspektor-gadget
13. Intel Host-INT. https://github.com/intel/host-int
14. IP flow information export (IPFIX) implementation guidelines. https://datatracker.ietf.org/doc/html/rfc5153
15. l3af-project eBPF IPFIX flow exporter. https://github.com/l3af-project/eBPF-Package-Repository/blob/main/ipfix-flow-exporter/bpf_ipfix_egress_kern.c
16. Libebpfflow. https://github.com/ntop/libebpfflow
17. Monitoring VM traffic using sFlow. https://docs.openvswitch.org/en/stable/howto/sflow/
18. OVN Kubernetes. https://github.com/ovn-org/ovn-kubernetes
19. PcapPlusPlus. https://pcapplusplus.github.io/
20. Pixie-IO Pixie. https://github.com/pixie-io/pixie
21. Skydive. https://github.com/skydive-project/skydive
22. TCPDump and Libpcap. https://www.tcpdump.org
23. The state of linux in the public cloud for enterprises. https://www.redhat.com/en/resources/state-of-linux-in-public-cloud-for-enterprises
24. Types of eBPF maps. https://prototype-kernel.readthedocs.io/en/latest/bpf/ebpf_maps_types.html
25. Zeek. https://zeek.org
26. Høiland-Jørgensen, T., et al.: The express data path: Fast programmable packet processing in the operating system kernel. CoNEXT 2018, New York, NY, USA, Association for Computing Machinery (2018)
27. Michel, O., Sengupta, S., Kim, H., Netravali, R., Rexford, J.: Enabling passive measurement of zoom performance in production networks. In: Proceedings of the 22nd ACM Internet Measurement Conference, IMC 2022, New York, NY, USA, Association for Computing Machinery (2022)
28. Moore, A.W., Papagiannaki, K.: Toward the accurate identification of network applications. In: Proceedings of the 6th International Conference on Passive and Active Network Measurement, PAM 2005 (2005)
29. Pfaff, B., et al.: The design and implementation of open vswitch. In: Proceedings of the 12th USENIX Conference on Networked Systems Design and Implementation, NSDI 2015, USA, USENIX Association (2015)
30. Yu, G., et al.: Microrank: end-to-end latency issue localization with extended spectrum analysis in microservice environments. In: Proceedings of the Web Conference 2021, WWW 2021 (2021)
31. Zhang, Y., et al.: Aequitas: admission control for performance-critical RPCS in datacenters. In: Proceedings of the ACM SIGCOMM 2022 Conference, SIGCOMM 2022, Association for Computing Machinery (2022)

Crawling to the Top: An Empirical Evaluation of Top List Use

Qinge Xie[✉] and Frank Li

Georgia Institute of Technology, Atlanta, GA, USA
{qxie47,frankli}@gatech.edu

Abstract. Domain top lists, such as Alexa, Umbrella, and Majestic, are key datasets widely used by the networking and security research communities. Industry and attackers have also been documented as using top lists for various purposes. However, beyond these scattered documented cases, who actually uses these top lists and how are they used? Currently, the Internet measurement community lacks a deep understanding of real-world top list use and the dependencies on these datasets (especially in light of Alexa's retirement).

In this study, we seek to fill in this gap by conducting controlled experiments with test domains in different ranking ranges of popular top lists, monitoring how network traffic differs for test domains in the top lists compared to baseline control domains. By analyzing the DNS resolutions made to domain authoritative name servers, HTTP requests to websites hosted on the domains, and messages sent to email addresses associated with the websites, we evaluate how domain traffic changes once placed in top lists, the characteristics of those visiting the domain, and the behavioral patterns of these visitors. Ultimately, our analysis sheds light on how these top lists are used in practice and their value to the networking and security community.

1 Introduction

For well over a decade, domain top lists, such as those by Alexa [40], Cisco Umbrella [42], and Majestic [55], have provided a set of purportedly popular or commonly used domains. Anecdotally, these top lists have been critical resources, widely used across both academia and industry. Dozens of prior academic studies [61,67] have used top lists as sources of interesting domains to crawl and evaluate. On the industry side, some security analysis tools and services (e.g., DNSthingy [15] and Quad9 [29]) have incorporated existing top lists into their security offerings. In addition, attackers have manipulated top lists for attracting traffic to their sites [30,68] and offer top list manipulation as a paid service [2,3], suggesting that top list placement provides non-trivial value. However, beyond these scattered documented cases, the research community currently lacks a deeper understanding of how top lists are used in practice and dependencies on these datasets. This understanding is crucial for offering insights to key stakeholders, such as illuminating top list design considerations

P. Richter et al. (Eds.): PAM 2024, LNCS 14537, pp. 277–306, 2024.
https://doi.org/10.1007/978-3-031-56249-5_12

for list providers, improving top list usage by researchers and security tools, and informing domain owners on the impact of being ranked. This limitation has become a more pressing issue of late, as Alexa, one of the most popular top lists in academic research [61,67], has been retired, and it is unclear yet what the consequences of this change will be and what potential alternatives are suitable.

In this paper, we take a step in closing this gap by providing empirical grounding on who actually crawls the domains in top lists, and their behavior when visiting these domains. We measure the usage of top lists, which includes both automated (given the large number of domain names included in a top list, practical usage often involves automated, large-scale crawling) and manual/human-driven uses. We seek to answer three primary research questions.

1. How does top list ranking affect the volume of domain visitors?
2. Who visits a domain once placed in a top list?
3. What are the behaviors of visitors to top list domains?

To answer these questions, we conduct controlled top list experiments comparing test domains that are manipulated into different ranking ranges of top lists commonly used by prior work (Alexa before its retirement, Umbrella, and Majestic) with control baseline domains that remain unlisted. We monitor DNS resolutions for these domains as well as requests to websites hosted on these domains, and messages sent to email addresses associated with those sites (on the webpage, in WHOIS, and in `security.txt`). This data affords analysis of the impact of top list placement, and characterization of the domain visitors and their visit behavior. To evaluate whether different types of domain names may result in different behavior, we experiment with two categories of domains: those with realistic names and those that are long and randomly generated.

From our experiment, we find that placement in a top list does drive consistent DNS and web traffic to domains (including suspicious traffic), although primarily once a domain is in the top 100K. We also find that Alexa domains attract more traffic compared to the other top lists, highlighting the need for alternative top list options given that Alexa is now retired. Furthermore, the scale of traffic observed suggests that academic research accounts for a limited portion of top list use in practice. Once a domain falls out of the top list, traffic quickly returns to pre-listing levels, indicating that most uses of top lists rely on the most recent rankings. By analyzing the ASNs and IP geolocations of visitors to our test websites once ranked, we observe extensive use of cloud infrastructure by visitors, various organizations in both industry and academia, as well as visitors predominantly from the US, the Netherlands, China, and Russia. The HTTP user agent headers of these visitors identify various crawlers of web and security companies, and the resources requests hint at many of their purposes, including for RSS feed aggregation, advertising, potential censorship, and security evaluation.

Ultimately, our study provides a systematic characterization of how top lists are used in practice, shedding light on their value to the networking, web, and security community. Moving forward, our findings can inform the design and deployment of top lists to better support their uses.

2   Background

Here, we provide background on the domain top lists investigated in this study, and summarize the related work.

2.1   Domain Top Lists

In this work, we investigate the use of three public domain top lists that have been widely used in prior research [61,67,72]: Alexa, Umbrella, and Majestic.

Alexa. The Alexa's Top 1 Million Sites has been one of the most widely used domain top lists [61,67,72], and ranks domains based on web traffic telemetry collected from user installs of Alexa's browser extension, as well as participating websites that subscribe to Alexa's Certify service [72]. Alexa's ranking is constructed on daily telemetry snapshots, and ranks second-level domains (SLDs) only, rather than fully qualified domain names (FQDNs).

On Dec. 8, 2021, Alexa suddenly announced the retirement of its top list as of May 1, 2022 [39]. On May 1, it retired its web portal but the URL endpoint [40] for downloading its full CSV list remains active and updating until 2023. As of February 1, 2024, the URL endpoint has become unaccessible. Despite its retirement, we include Alexa in our study as its results can still shed light on how top lists are being used in practice.

Umbrella. The Cisco Umbrella Top Million [42] is another popular top list, whose ranking is constructed using passive DNS (PDNS) requests observed across Cisco's Umbrella global network (including OpenDNS [41], Phish-Tank [58], etc.). Umbrella ranks FQDNs by computing a score for each domain on two-day windows, considering the number of different IP addresses issuing DNS lookups for the domain compared to others [69,72]. Unlike Alexa, Umbrella's traffic data telemetry also accounts for non-web traffic.

Majestic. The Majestic Million [32] is a third domain top list that has been used in several prior studies. Majestic regularly crawls websites and uses the URLs visited within the last 120 days to produce a daily ranking based on a site's backlinks. Specifically, Majestic ranks a site based on the number of referring IPv4/24 subnets hosting other sites that link to it [54,55]. Thus, unlike the prior two lists, Majestic does not consider web traffic to a domain, but rather the amount of backlinks to it. Majestic's list comprises mostly of SLDs, but ranks FQDNs for certain very popular sites [61].

Other Lists. In this study, we do not focus on other top lists that are paid or otherwise restrict usage. For example, the Quantcast Top Million [67] ranks the most visited domains in the United States, but has not been available since April 2020 [72]. Meanwhile, the Chrome User Experience Report (CrUX) [12] does not provide daily fine-grained rankings, instead providing domains in ranking buckets (e.g., top 10K) in monthly releases. There have also been several more recent top lists released, such as SecRank [72], Cloudflare's Radar Ranking [13] and the Farsight Ranking [22]. We did not include these lists in our study as they were released after our experiments and have not yet been widely used by prior work. We also do not explicitly investigate the Tranco top list [61], as at the time of our experiments, it was constructed by aggregating the rankings of the three top lists we study and thus cannot be disentangled from the input lists (discussed further in Sect. 3.6). As of February 1, 2024, the Tranco list also includes data from Google CrUX, the Cloudflare Radar rankings, and the Farsight rankings, and excludes Alexa (which has been retired).

2.2 Related Work

Empirical Investigation of Top Lists. Although used for years in both academia and industry, top lists received little empirical evaluation until late 2018 when Scheitle et al. [67] analyzed the structure, stability, and significance of Alexa, Umbrella, and Majestic. Around the same time, Le Pochat et al. [61] identified various ways for an adversary to manipulate top lists, and created Tranco to account for existing top list shortcomings by aggregating those lists. Rweyemamu et al. [65,66] also identified ways to manipulate Alexa and Umbrella, and investigated the two lists' alphabetically ordering and weekend effects. In 2022, Xie et al. [72] proposed a new top list, SecRank, which serves as an open and transparent ranking method for the research community. Later, Ruth et al. [64] evaluated the relative accuracy of different top lists using popularity metrics derived from a Cloudflare dataset. However, to date, there has not been a systematic investigation of how top lists are actually used in practice, especially beyond surveys of prior academic works, which is the focus of our study.

Internet Service Measurements. Beyond top lists, prior work has evaluated various types of Internet services [37,50,53,71,73,74]. For example, Vallina et al. [70] compared popular domain classification services. Gharaibeh et al. [44] studied the accuracy and consistency of public and commercial IP geolocation databases. Similar to domain top lists, these services are often black-box operations, inhibiting public understanding of their data quality and limitations.

3   Method

In this study, we aim to measure the usage of popular top lists, focusing on Alexa, Umbrella, and Majestic. To answer our core research questions (from Sect. 1), we conduct controlled experiments with newly created domains under our control, manipulating top lists to include our domains at different ranking ranges. We monitor these domains over time to collect traffic telemetry, affording analysis of top list usage. As our study involves testing real-world artifacts, we discuss ethical considerations in Sect. 3.5.

3.1   Top List Manipulation

We aim to manipulate our experiment domains into different portions of top lists, to observe the impact on visitors to these domains. Specifically, we investigate

Table 1. The highest, lowest, and median rankings obtained when manipulating our test domains into the Alexa, Umbrella and Majestic lists.

Range	Alexa			Umbrella			Majestic
	1M	100K	10K	1M	100K	10K	1M
Highest	642,006	44,418	2,968	119,330	20,066	8,325	148,983
Lowest	983,356	62,485	6,393	490,015	54,925	9,683	623,773
Median	879,894	52,289	5,913	197,957	35,432.5	9,127	152,756

how domain visit activity differs when the domain is placed in a top list's top 1M, top 100K, and top 10K. To manipulate the top lists, we rely on existing techniques, which we describe in detail in Appendix A. In short:

- **Alexa:** We manipulate Alexa using the same method from Xie et al. [72], which forges fake visits to a domain by generating requests for that domain to the Alexa Certify service's data collection endpoint [38].
- **Umbrella:** As Umbrella is a PDNS-based ranking, we manipulate it by generating DNS requests for a domain to Umbrella's DNS resolvers [61,66,72].
- **Majestic:** We manipulate Majestic using the method from Le Pochat et al. [61]. The method leverages certain "reflecting" sites, particularly MediaWiki sites, that accept user-provided URLs (i.e., our target domains) in the site's URL query parameters and reflect these user-provided URLs as anchor elements in their web pages. As a result, Majestic's crawler would observe a backlink to the target domain when visiting such reflecting sites. Using the Fofa search engine [17] and the set of reflecting wiki sites used in [61], we found and used 1,642 valid reflecting links for manipulation. We also subscribe to Majestic's service to better trigger Majestic's crawler to visit those links.

All manipulation experiments were conducted from a single server on one IP address within a large academic network, and we rate limited requests to minimize load at receiving endpoints (discussed further in Sect. 3.5).

Table 1 lists the rankings obtained for our Alexa, Umbrella and Majestic experiment for different ranking ranges. We note that manipulating Majestic is more challenging than Alexa and Umbrella though, as its ranking is not based on user traffic/visit, but rather the amount of backlinks to it. The highest ranking Le Pochat et al. obtained was ∼500K [61] and we obtain rankings as high as 150K. Thus, we only consider measuring Majestic's top 1M in this study.

3.2 Experimental Design

Our experiment is a controlled study of the three top lists (Alexa, Umbrella, and Majestic) across three ranking ranges (top 1M, top 100K, and top 10K), started performing from January, 2022 (just after Alexa announced the retirement). Note, as discussed in Sect. 3.1, we only evaluate Majestic on the top 1M. For each top list and ranking range pair, we created and monitored eight domains, split equally between a test set of four domains and a control set of four domains. For each set of four domains, we evaluated two realistic-looking domains and two randomly-generated (RG) domains, to investigate if domain name characteristics may affect its use in top lists. We chose to replicate our experiments across two domains of matching characteristics to identify whether observations are consistent. Here we discuss how those domains are created, grouped, and tested.

Realistic versus RG Domains. As our study focuses on the usage of top lists, we are interested in understanding whether usage may vary based on the domain name. While there are various methods for constructing domain names, as a first exploration, we experiment with two classes of domain names, those that have a realistic domain name and those that are long and generated randomly (akin to those generated by domain generation algorithms).

To generate a realistic domain, we manually created a 9-letter domain using complete English words, although we avoided using words that may imply the site's function/content (e.g., "shopping") to avoid biasing visitors seeking certain classes of sites. For RG domains, we randomly generated a 50-letter domain name composed of randomly selected words (using the `nltk` corpus [26]), similarly avoiding functionality/content-related words.

Control versus Test Group. We manipulated our four test group domains into top lists and observed the traffic they received. All four domains in our control group were configured identically to the manipulated domains and similarly monitored, but were never manipulated into top lists, serving as baselines.

Experiment Phases. For each top list and ranking range, our experiment evaluated eight domains (2 realistic test domains, 2 RG test domains, 2 realistic control domains, and 2 RG control domains) over three phases spanning at least six weeks total. Phase I and II are two weeks each. Phase III is over two weeks, starting from the end of Phase II until the conclusion of our study.

(1) **Preparation Phase (Phase I):** At least one week before Phase I, we configured valid DNS resolutions for all domains, but performed no further activities to avoid characterizing any initial traffic due to DNS registration. No activities (including top list manipulation) were performed during Phase I.

(2) **Active-Manipulation Phase (Phase II):** We manipulated test domains into the target top list and ranking range, and performed continued manipulation throughout this phase to maintain the domain's ranking. We remained inactive with control domains.

(3) **Idle Phase (Phase III):** We halted top list manipulation of our test domains (and remained inactive with control domains).

3.3 Experiment Domain Setup

Here, we describe the setup for the experiment domains, which had valid DNS configurations and hosted websites.

Domain Names. All domains are newly registered with no past registration history. We registered our domains with NameSilo [23], using the " `.xyz`" top-level domain (TLD)[1]. We provided a unique email under our control in the WHOIS registration for each domain, listed as the registrant, admin, and technical contacts (the abuse contact was automatically set to the domain registrar).

For each domain, we configured our own authoritative name servers using BIND9. For each domain, we set up two name servers with NS and A records, at the *ns1* and *ns2* subdomains. We set up A records for the SLD and the FQDN with a "*www*" prefix. We do not configure other DNS record types. We set the Time-to-live (TTL) of each domain's A record to 0 to limit DNS caching, aiming for our name server to observe as many DNS resolutions as possible.

Site Content. Our domains hosted Nginx-based websites that consisted of a simple HTML page that includes one line of text indicating that the site was a research experiment site, and listing an email contact for further information. We also provide a `security.txt` file [43] listing a different email contact. We do not configure a `robots.txt` file [48], allowing crawlers to visit our site. To monitor top list users visiting domains over HTTPS, our web server supports both HTTPS and HTTP (which redirects to HTTPS), using a valid TLS certificate from Let's Encrypt [20]. We note that while enabling TLS may lead to domain names appearing in certificate transparency logs, the potential impact of resulting traffic on the observed differences between the test and control groups should be negligible, as we use the same TLS configurations for all domains.

Web Hosting. We hosted our experiment websites at Vultr Cloud Hosting [34] on static IP addresses, allocating each site to a unique address, allowing us to reliably associate traffic with sites.

Justification of Domain Setup. We intentionally use fresh domains and content-free websites without existing visitors/traffic, to allow us to confidently associate domain traffic with top list placement and avoid confounding factors during analysis. If we used existing domains already receiving traffic, we would lack clean signals to distinguish the traffic driven by top list placement from other traffic sources. Similarly, providing realistic content on our site could attract traffic driven by the content rather than top list placement (e.g., site appearance on social media or search engines due to its content), rendering it infeasible to isolate the impact of top list ranking. Our method should capture both automated and manual/human-driven uses of top lists, although realistically, we expect that top lists are crawled at scale in an automated fashion. As a consequence, our study's results should largely identify and characterize the automated uses of top lists such as by various researchers and organizations.

3.4 Data Collection

We collected three types of telemetry for all experiment sites.

---

[1] The "`.xyz`" TLD is a generic alternative to "`.com`", and has been used in prior web traffic measurement studies [49,60].

DNS Telemetry. For each DNS requests received at our authoritative name server, we recorded the following telemetry: Timestamp, Source IP address, and Requested DNS record type (e.g., A/AAAA/TXT).

Web Telemetry. We recorded the web traffic logs generated by our web servers. Specifically, for each web request, we recorded the following telemetry: Timestamp, Source IP address, Protocol (HTTP vs. HTTPS), HTTP method (e.g., GET, POST), Resource path URL (e.g., /index.html), Host HTTP header, and User-Agent HTTP header. We further used the Maxmind database [21] to geolocate and identify the ASN mapping for source IP addresses.

Email Telemetry. As described in Sect. 3.3, each test site is associated with three unique contact emails (i.e., from the main web page, in security.txt, and in WHOIS records, we will call them the main email, security.txt email, and WHOIS email, respectively). Every site has a distinct set of emails, which we registered at Microsoft Outlook. We monitored emails received at these inboxes.

3.5 Ethics

As our study involved experimenting with real-world top lists, we must account for ethical considerations throughout the experiment design. Here, we discuss these ethical considerations for each component of this study.

Test Domains. All domains used in our experiment were new domains under our own control, specifically set up for this study. We notified our DNS registrar (Namesilo [23]) and hosting provider (Vultr [34]) about our study and received their consent. Our experiment does not affect any other domains. Beyond placing them in top lists, we do not distribute these domains elsewhere. We also signal the research nature of these domains through both the simple website hosted on the domains as well as the domain's WHOIS records. While our domain is associated with multiple emails (as described in Sect. 3.3), we did not receive any organic emails and did not respond to any messages. We did not interact with any human subjects in this study.

Top List Manipulation. Multiple prior studies [61,65,66,72] have conducted top list manipulation on the same set of top lists that we investigated. Our manipulation techniques are adopted from these prior works and the extent of manipulation (i.e., rankings achieved) are commensurate with these previous efforts. As we staggered our study over multiple months, at any given time during our study, we manipulated up to only four domains for a top list, which should have a negligible impact on the list's overall rankings.

For Alexa and Umbrella, we required generating requests to Alexa's data collection endpoint and Umbrella's DNS resolvers, respectively. While these endpoints by nature should be capable of handling heavy traffic load, as they collect the vast amounts of telemetry that feed into the top lists, we heavily rate limited our requests to these endpoints to avoid potentially burdening them and any transit networks. Even for our largest-scale manipulation, we did not generate more than 5 packets per second (with all traffic generated from a single server).

Our manipulation of Umbrella required spoofing the source IP address of DNS requests sent to the Umbrella DNS resolvers. We only spoofed IP addresses within our own local network, which was permitted. Furthermore, all DNS requests were only for test domains involved in our experiment, rather than any real-world online services. Thus, there should be negligible risk or harm to any hosts/individuals residing on a spoofed IP address. For Majestic's manipulation, the reflecting URLs we used were only crawled by Majestic, and did not have any impact on the sites themselves. We only submitted the reflecting URLs to Majestic once, and the number of submitted URLs was within Majestic's quota for our subscription, and should not have overburdened Majestic.

3.6   Limitations

Experimenting on top lists is challenging, as they are live, complex, and opaque. As a result, our study does bear several limitations:

- We lack direct visibility into all top list use, and instead infer use through visits to our test domains. As our experiments are controlled, we can more confidently attribute observed differences between the test and control groups to top list presence. However, we ultimately may not fully capture all top list use (e.g., use of the top list where our test domains may have been filtered), and some differences may be partially driven by external factors.
- For our experiments, we manipulated four domains into a top list. We did not use a more diverse set of domains (e.g., different TLDs), as we aimed to limit our experiment's impact on top lists during this initial study, avoiding manipulating many domains concurrently into each list.
- To limit our experiment's impact on top lists, we chose a two-week duration for Phase II to capture top list usage behaviors within the two-week observation window. Thus, one-off usage occurring outside this window or periodic top-list usage exceeding two weeks may not be captured in this study. Users also may not visit a domain immediately after finding it; our study only captures usage behaviors where the domain visits occur within our observation window.
- For each experiment, our manipulated domains had similar rankings within each range, but the exact rankings varied. Results may differ slightly for sites at different rankings within a given range.
- Our experiment sites provide no meaningful content, and as fresh sites, have no traffic history or existing user base. This experiment decision is **necessary** to control for confounding variables in measuring the impact of top list placement. However, we will not capture top list uses that are restricted to types/sets of sites which exclude our domains. Rather our study will primarily capture automated crawling of the top lists, such as by various researchers and organizations.
- The Tranco top list [61] is now often used, and its ranking aggregates the three top lists we investigate. Domains appearing on one input list may also appear in Tranco, and we lack visibility into which list domain visitors are

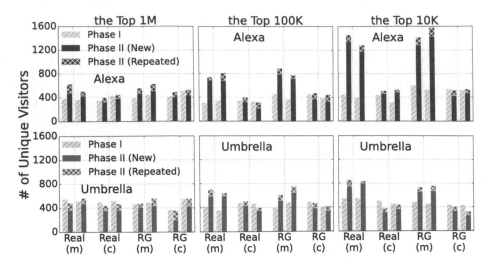

Fig. 1. The number of visitors (unique IP addresses) to each test domain's website observed in HTTP server logs during Phase I and II, across different ranking ranges for Alexa and Umbrella. For Phase II, we distinguish between "New" visitors not previously seen in Phase I, and "Repeated" visitors observed in both phases. ("Real" = realistic domain, "RG" = randomly-generated domain; "c" = control domain, "m" = manipulated domain)

using. Our experiment results include the potential side effect of being listed in Tranco as well (although the Tranco ranking will be much lower).

4   Findings

In this section, we analyze our datasets that comprise of web, DNS, and email telemetry to evaluate how domain traffic changes once placed in top lists (RQ1), the characteristics of those visiting top list domains (RQ2), and the behavioral patterns of these visitors (RQ3). As we expect that top lists are primarily crawled at scale in an automated fashion, our findings will largely characterize the automated use of top lists, such as by various researchers and organizations.

4.1   RQ1: Impact of Top List Placement

We first evaluate the impact of top list placement by comparing the incoming traffic of manipulated domains before and after entering a top list. We compare the DNS and HTTP requests for manipulated domains as well as control group domains between the preparation phase (Phase I) and active-manipulation phase (Phase II). We investigate the long-term effects when a domain falls out of a top list by monitoring traffic during the idle phase (Phase III). We also examine the differences between the three top lists' academic use versus broader use (by observed visitors).

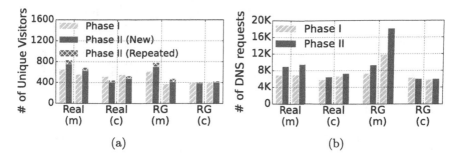

Fig. 2. Majestic top 1M results: (a) the number of unique visitors (unique IP addresses) to each test domain's website; (b) the number of DNS requests for each experiment domain. ("Real" = realistic domain, "RG" = randomly-generated domain; "c" = control domain, "m" = manipulated domain)

Web Traffic. For each experiment domain, we consider the number of visitors observed in HTTP server logs, counting the number of unique IP addresses issuing HTTP requests for the domain and its sub-domains. (We note that individual IP addresses do not necessarily represent unique visitors. Here we utilize unique IP addresses to analyze visiting traffic as we lack the visibility behind IP addresses. We will further analyze IP characteristics in Sects. 4.2 and 4.3.) We analyze how the number of visitors varies in the two phases and across ranking ranges. (We do not consider request volume as visitors can generate varying numbers of requests, although our findings remain consistent for request volume.)

Figure 1 depicts the number of distinct visitors to each experiment domain observed in Phase I and II, across the three ranking ranges of Alexa and Umbrella. The Majestic top 1M result is shown in Fig. 2a. Overall, for all three top lists, we observe more visitors accessed manipulated domains in Phase II compared to I, while control domains observed little to no increases in visitors. Thus, we conclude that top list placement does result in a notable increase in domain visitors, even without meaningful online services provided. (By manually checking the HTTP server logs, we identified that the increased traffic to the control group domains mainly stems from Internet-wide scans. Other cases include traffic resulting from the side effects of enabling HTTPS, as discussed in Sect. 3.3.) We also observe that across lists and ranking ranges, the number of daily visitors is stable throughout Phase II, indicating that the increase in visitors is consistent rather than ephemeral.

Higher rankings resulted in more web traffic, for both realistic and RG domains. In particular, placement in the top 1M resulted in significantly less visitor increases compared to the top 100K and top 10K. For example, placement in the Alexa top 1M produced a 45.1% (179) increase in visitors, averaged across the four manipulated domains. Meanwhile, the number of visitors can double or triple once a domain is in the top 100K or top 10K. Umbrella exhibits a similar pattern, although the increases are less extreme (50.5% increase for the top 100K and 55.6% for the top 10K).

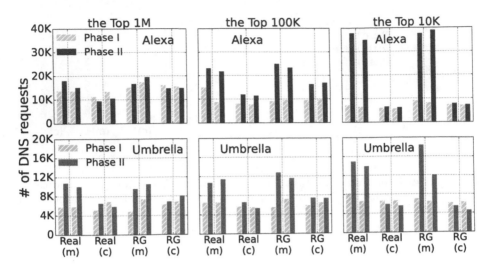

Fig. 3. The number of DNS requests for each experiment domain observed in DNS logs during Phase I and II, across different ranking ranges for Alexa and Umbrella. ("Real" = realistic domain, "RG" = randomly-generated domain; "c" = control domain, "m" = manipulated domain)

We also observe that RG domains typically received more visitors once ranked compared to realistic ones, across lists and ranking ranges, hinting at some focus on odd/suspicious domains (e.g., randomly generated ones).

DNS Traffic. Here, we consider the number of DNS requests to each experiment domain. Unlike with web traffic, we do not consider the number of unique addresses as most observed DNS requests are from recursive resolvers rather than clients. We briefly note that we observed two short massive bursts of DNS traffic for our manipulated domains while listed in the Alexa top 100K (and not for control domains). Based on the distinct request features in these bursts, we identified and filtered them out from our DNS telemetry (discussed more in Sect. 4.3). While we are not certain of this traffic's purpose, its anomalous nature highlights that top list ranking may render a domain as an attack target.

Figure 3 depicts the total number of DNS requests observed in Phase I and II for each experiment domain, across the ranking ranges of Alexa and Umbrella. The Majestic top 1M result is shown in Fig. 2b. The patterns found in our web traffic analysis hold for DNS traffic too, across lists and ranking ranges. Again, DNS telemetry shows that placement in top lists consistently drives more domain traffic, with higher DNS lookup volumes for domains once ranked and minimal increases for control domains. Higher-ranked domains also observe higher DNS lookup volumes, and RG domains on average receive more DNS traffic compared to realistic ones. Thus, both web and DNS telemetry demonstrate that entering top lists positively affects multiple types of incoming traffic.

Long-Term Effects. We investigate the long-term effects when a domain falls out of the top list. Here we focus on characterizing data from our top 100K

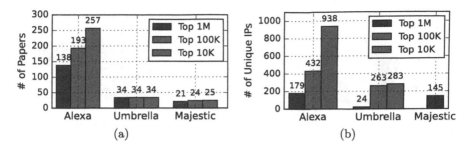

Fig. 4. Academic vs broader top list use in practice: (a) shows the number of papers using each top list and ranking range from 2017 to 2022, across 10 networking and security venues, while (b) depicts the number of distinct new visitors in Phase II across different lists and ranking ranges, averaged across the two types of manipulated domains (note that we did not experiment with the Majestic top 100K and top 10K.)

experiments, which we conducted first and hence had the longest period for Phase III, although we observe similar outcomes for other ranges. We observe that over the four month period after de-listing, web visitors and DNS lookup volumes quickly decreased to pre-listing levels within two weeks, for both lists, indicating that most uses of top lists rely on more recent daily snapshots.

Academic vs Broader Use. Scheitle et al. [67] evaluated top list use by academic studies published in 2017 across 10 networking/security venues, finding that 69 papers relied on top lists: 59 used Alexa, 3 used Umbrella, and none used Majestic. We extended this survey across the same 10 venues from 2017 to 2022 (we list the 10 venues and describe our survey details in Appendix B). Figure 4a shows the number of studies using each list across each ranking range (note, if a study uses a top 1M list, we also include it as using the top 100K and top 10K.) We observe, similar to the previous study, that academic studies have skewed heavily towards using Alexa (particularly higher ranking ranges), although Umbrella and Majestic are both used (primarily the top 1M).

When considering our top list domain visitors, as shown in Fig. 4b, we found significantly more top list use over the two-week observation period compared to use by the academic studies published in the prior 6 years. While our academic literature survey was limited in the venues considered, the scale of the discrepancy suggests that academic research accounts for a minority of broader top list use.

We do see that, similar to academic studies, Alexa was most heavily used, especially the higher ranking ranges. However, we see similar numbers of Majestic top 1M visitors as Alexa top 1M visitors (we were unable to experiment with Majestic top 100K and top 10K). We hypothesize that this similarity arises because broader top list use skews towards investigating websites, as ranked by Alexa and Majestic, even if ranking methods vary significantly. In comparison, we observed minimal use of the Umbrella top 1M (whereas academic studies primarily used the Umbrella top 1M), although we do see elevated usage of the Umbrella top 100K.

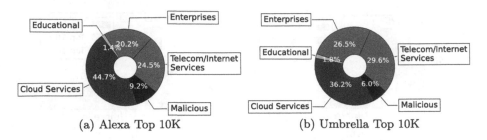

(a) Alexa Top 10K   (b) Umbrella Top 10K

Fig. 5. Distributions of new visitors in Phase II, averaged across the four manipulated domains, for the Alexa top 10K and Umbrella top 10K.

4.2 RQ2: Characteristics of Top Domain Visitors

In Sect. 4.1, we answered our first research question, finding that top list placement can result in significant amounts of traffic to a domain. However, top 1M placement produces relatively limited traffic increases. Thus, moving forward, we focus on analyzing the traffic that results from placement in the higher ranking ranges (also removing Majestic from consideration, as we only experimented with its top 1M).

We now analyze the web traffic logs to evaluate top domain visitors. We do not consider DNS traffic here, as we lack visibility into the DNS lookup clients (as discussed in Sect. 4.1). Specifically, we analyze new IP addresses observed in the HTTP server logs once a domain is ranked (Phase II) but not previously in Phase I, characterizing their ASes, countries, and user agents. We use the Maxmind databases [21] for IP geolocation and ASN mapping.

IP Reputation. Before characterizing visitors, we investigate the reputation of IP addresses newly observed during Phase II. We query the addresses using VirusTotal [33], which aggregates classification results across many third-party security vendors. As some vendors may produce false positive labels, we consider an address as malicious only if classified by at least three vendors (as suggested by prior work [59]).

As shown in Fig. 5, we found that 9.2% of addresses were classified as malicious for the Alexa top 10K and 6.0% for the Umbrella top 10K, averaged across the four manipulated domains. For the top 100K range, we observed that 7.4% and 5.2% of addresses were labeled as malicious for Alexa and Umbrella, respectively. (We omit the top 100K from Fig. 5, as it exhibits similar patterns.) By manually inspecting the malicious addresses, we do find suspicious behavior. We observe addresses with at least 10 vendors classifying as malicious, which issue suspicious requests to our domains (e.g., "\x03\x00\x00/*\xE0\x00\x00\x00\x00\x00Cookie: mstshash=Administr"), potentially searching for web vulnerabilities to exploit. Thus, top list domains do attract malicious visitors, especially for the Alexa list and higher ranking ranges.

ASN. Here we investigate the top ASNs that contribute the most new visitors once a test domain is manipulated into a top list. A new visitor represents an address observed in Phase II that was not observed in Phase I. Through manually inspecting AS names, we categorize visitor ASes into different categories, and depict the distribution of visitors over different AS categories for both the Alexa and Umbrella top 10K in Fig. 5. (We elide a figure for the top 100K, which exhibits a similar distribution.)

Across top lists, rankings, and domain types, we observe that the top ASNs are primarily cloud service and hosting providers, such as Google Cloud (396982, 15169), DigitalOcean (14061), Amazon (16509), and HostRoyale (203020). While these organizations may use top lists themselves (which we do observe during user-agent analysis, discussed shortly), the volume of visitors suggests that many top list users access ranked domains through cloud platforms (even for the malicious users), presumably using automated methods.

Beyond cloud-related ASes, we identify visitors from various enterprise networks (around 20–27% of visitors, as shown in Fig. 5, particularly for security organizations such as Zscaler (22616), Eonscope (208417), and Censys (398324, 398722). Other types of enterprises, such as Hangzhou Alibaba Advertising (37963, advertising), hint at different purposes behind top list uses.

We also find ASes providing telecom and Internet services, potentially serving both residential and enterprise networks (accounting for 24–30% of visitors, as shown in Fig. 5), such as Comcast (7922) in the US, PJSC VimpelCom (3216) in Russia, and TATA Communications (4755) in India.

We do see visitors located in the ASes for educational/research institutions, aligning with known uses of top lists in academic research studies [67]. As examples, we observe MIT (3) and Boston University (111) from the US, Seoul National University (9488) from South Korea, Technische Universitaet Muenchen (209335) from Germany, and China Education and Research Network Center (4538). Such visitors only accounts for 1–2% of all visitors, aligning from our prior analysis showing that academic research likely accounts for only a minority of top list use.

Notably, we find that for Alexa, there is a 40% increase in the number of distinct visitor ASNs (averaged across experiment domains) for the top 10K compared to the top 100K (169 vs 120), indicating more diversity in visitor ASNs for higher-ranked Alexa sites. However, for Umbrella, we do not find a consistent difference in the number of visitor ASNs between the top 100K and the top 10K (107 vs 108). The number of visitor ASNs for the Alexa top 10K is also significantly higher than for Umbrella (169 vs 107), suggesting that Alexa domains not only receive more visitors than Umbrella (as observed in Sect. 4.1), but more diverse visitors.

Country. Table 2 lists the top 5 counties/regions by the number of new visitors in Phase II, using the same definition for a new visitor as with ASNs. We observe that across lists, rankings, and domain types, the top countries overall include the US, the Netherlands, and China (Russia and Germany also frequently appeared).

When inspecting the ASNs of visitors geolocated to the US, the majority are from cloud providers such as Amazon (16%–47% of visitors, across all manipulated domains), Google Cloud (6%–30%), and DigitalOcean (7%–18%).

Table 2. The top 5 countries/regions by their number of new visitors in Phase II, for the four manipulated domains, across Alexa and Umbrella's top 100K and top 10K.

	Alexa Top 100K				Alexa Top 10K			
	Realistic-#1	Realistic-#2	RG-#1	RG-#2	Realistic-#1	Realistic-#2	RG-#1	RG-#2
1	US (224)	US (181)	US (287)	US (248)	US (427)	RU (422)	RU (397)	US (397)
2	NL (211)	NL (196)	NL (209)	NL (206)	RU (391)	US (298)	US (387)	RU (393)
3	CN (76)	CN (63)	BR (83)	BR (80)	CN (316)	CN (228)	CN (227)	CN (383)
4	RU (50)	RU (51)	RU (57)	CN (61)	NL (91)	NL (101)	NL(103)	NL(106)
5	DE (23)	DE (22)	CN (32)	RU (55)	DE (35)	DE (37)	DE (31)	HK (37)
#Countries	33	38	35	40	42	37	42	38
#Cities	114	111	101	110	149	141	158	154
	Umbrella Top 100K				Umbrella Top 10K			
1	NL (190)	NL (193)	US (186)	US (197)	US (289)	CN (329)	US (275)	US (270)
2	CN (164)	CN (172)	NL (166)	NL (191)	CN (182)	US (224)	NL (115)	NL (122)
3	US (159)	US (171)	RU (48)	CN (73)	NL (128)	NL (87)	CN (89)	CN (88)
4	RU (48)	RU (70)	CN (45)	RU (67)	RU (32)	RU (24)	RU (32)	RU (30)
5	DE (20)	DE (27)	DE (17)	FR (31)	DE (28)	DE (16)	DE (21)	DE (24)
#Countries	34	37	35	38	34	28	31	35
#Cities	99	103	81	99	98	108	98	102

Similarly, most visitors from the Netherlands are from Google Cloud (80%–95%) and DigitalOcean (1%–5%) data centers in the Netherlands. Note that as many visitors geolocated to the US and the Netherlands used cloud platforms to host their clients, we could not confidently attribute these visitors to those two countries. Meanwhile, visitors geolocated to other countries are more strongly geographically correlated. Chinese visitors are primarily from two Chinese ASes: ChinaNet (36%–49% of Chinese visitors) and ChinaUnicom (21%–46%).

Table 2 also lists the number of countries and cities that new visitors in Phase II geolocate to. We do not see significant differences in the number of visitor counties across the ranking ranges for both lists. At the city granularity, we observe limited variation between the Umbrella top 100K and 10K. In contrast, visitors to Alexa top 10K domains exhibit significantly higher city diversity compared to Alexa top 100K (151 vs 109, 38.5% higher, averaged across domains), with the variation primarily arising through US and Chinese cities.

User Agent. Finally, we investigate the HTTP user-agent headers in web requests from IP addresses newly observed during Phase II. Note that as user-agent strings can be spoofed, we lack ground truth on the real user-agent used, and our analysis is limited to characterizing the user-agents as is.

Across all manipulated domains for both top lists and ranking ranges, we identify that over 75% of visitor have user-agent strings for various browsers and browser versions. Among browser user agents, the majority were for the Chrome browser (64% of visitors, across all manipulated domains in both top lists and ranking ranges), followed by Firefox (13%), Opera (10%) and IE (6%). (As discussed above, visitors can modify their HTTP header arbitrarily [56], thus the results may show a browser tendency to be set by the visitors, rather than actual browser use.) We see several mobile browsers, where Mobile Safari and

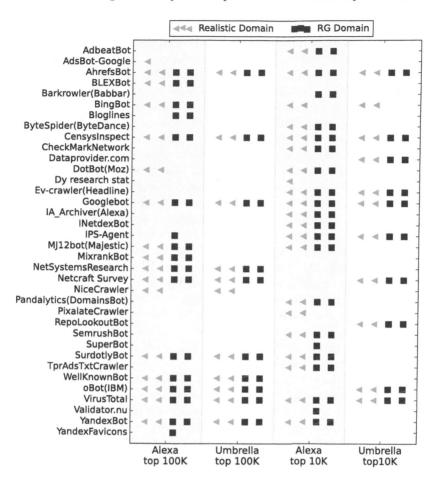

Fig. 6. Crawlers observed as new visitors during Phase II for the four manipulated domains. Each dot represents a crawler observed for a domain.

Chrome Mobile are typically in the top 10 software/browsers used by visitors. (We suspect these are spoofed user agents, as it seems less likely that we would observe organic mobile traffic to our experiment sites.) We also observe the use of different variants of browsers, e.g., Chromium and Waterfox. According to these user agent headers, we found Windows to be the most common OS among visitors, followed by Mac OS X, then Linux variants. For mobile systems, we observe visitors used Android more than iOS (with a long tail of other mobile OSes). By manually inspecting the remaining non-browser user agents, we find common networking tools and programming frameworks used by visitors (e.g., networking libraries for Python and Go, command-line tools such as `curl` and `wget`, scan tools such as `masscan` and `zgrab`).

We also uncover visitors self-identifying as web crawlers (around 9–15% of visitors, across all manipulated domains for both lists and ranking ranges) for various organizations, as shown in Fig. 6. These include for search engines (e.g., Googlebot [18], BingBot [8], YandexBot [36]), web analytics services (e.g., Pandalytics [28], Netcraft Survey [24], Dataprovider.com [14]), advertising/marketing services (e.g., AdbeatBot [5], AdsBot-Google [6], AhrefsBot [7]) and security organizations (e.g., VirusTotal [33], CensysInspect [10], SurdotlyBot [31]), hinting at the purposes behind top list uses. We observe about twice as many crawlers for Alexa as for Umbrella, for both ranking ranges, aligning with our prior observations of Alexa's popularity over Umbrella (see Sect. 4.1). Interestingly, we observe Majestic's crawler on Alexa domains (across both ranking ranges) but not on Umbrella domains, likely due to the web-specific nature of both Alexa and Majestic. Only AhrefsBot, CensysInspect, GoogleBot and Virus-Total crawled all of our test domains across both top lists and ranking ranges. These crawlers are associated with search engine or security services.

Unsurprisingly, some crawlers (e.g., CheckMarkNetwork [11], Ev-crawler [16]) only visited domains within the top 10K. However, we also found crawlers only accessing domains in the top 100K range (e.g., Bloglines [9], NetSystemResearch [4], NiceCrawler [25], and WellKnownBot [35]). We hypothesize that, as our top 100K and top 10K experiments were conducted at different periods of time, this behavior may have arisen due to the crawlers executing infrequently, such that we did not observe them during our top 10K experiments. We believe it is unlikely that many crawlers visit the top 100K domains of a top list but intentionally avoid crawling the top 10K.

We also note minor differences between domain types. For example, Nice-Crawler only accessed realistic domains for both Alexa and Umbrella's top 100K, while Bloglines only accessed RG domains in Alexa's top 100K. Experiment timing and ranking differences cannot account for this behavior, as the domains of both types are concurrently listed with similar rankings. We hypothesize that these top list users focus on only certain types of domain names.

Finally, we observe possible effects from Alexa's retirement, where oBot (from the IBM Security X-Force Threat Intelligence [19]) crawled test domains in all other three groups but was absent in Alexa's top 10K (as our top 10K experiment was close to Alexa's retirement).

4.3   RQ3: Behaviors of Top Domain Visitors

Here, we tackle our final research question on the behavioral patterns of top domain visitors. Again, we specifically investigate new visitors (IP addresses) during Phase II, when a test domain is placed into a top list, who had not previously appeared during Phase I. We again focus on web traffic as observed DNS queries primarily originate from recursive resolvers rather than clients. In this analysis, we focus on visitor access frequency, use of TLS, popular resources requested, and messages sent to domain-associated emails.

Access Frequency. We first study how often visitors access a domain once placed in a top list. Figure 7a depicts the distribution of the number of days a new visitor in Phase II accessed our experiment domains (aggregated across the

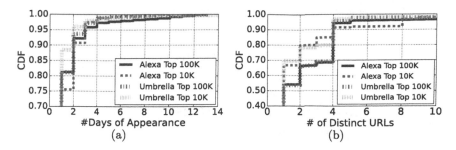

Fig. 7. CDF of (a) # of days that a new visitor accessed a ranked domain in Phase II; (b) # of distinct URLs/resources accessed by new visitors in Phase II.

manipulated domains for each list and ranking range). We observe a dominant pattern across the top lists and ranking ranges, where the majority of visitors (over 75%) only accessed the experiment domains on a single day. This access pattern likely reflects two classes of top list use: 1) one-off/adhoc top list uses, such as single snapshot measurements as often done in prior academic studies (e.g., [46,52]), or 2) repeated periodic top list use, where the crawling periodicity exceeds two weeks (our Phase II period), such as monthly crawls of a top list.

Looking at the outlier visitors that crawled our domains on more than 7 days, we identify that those visitors are either associated with security-related organizations (Forcepoint and VirusTotal), or cloud providers (Google, Azure, and Digital Ocean). Security-related organizations may need to crawl domains more frequently for detecting malicious domains. Meanwhile, cloud provider visitors may include companies hosting their crawling infrastructure on cloud platforms, as well as researchers conducting longitudinal top list measurements. For example, we observe one Digital Ocean visitor repeatedly crawling for the `dnt-policy.txt` of domains, and one visitor from Amazon EC2 crawling `security.txt` files.

HTTP Protocol/Request Method Prevalence. We now investigate the HTTP protocol (HTTP vs HTTPS) and HTTP request methods used by new visitors to top list domains during Phase II. Table 3 lists the percentages of visitors that were seen accessing our domains over HTTP, HTTPS, or both, for each top list and ranking (as the realistic and RG domains exhibit similar patterns, we list averages across manipulated domains). Domains in the Alexa and Umbrella top 100K exhibit similar distributions, with ~40% of visitors only using HTTP and ~25% only using HTTPS. The remaining third accessed the domain using both protocols. For domains in the top 10K, we observe notable differences. Over half of visitors to Alexa top 10K domains used both protocols, almost 20% more than in the other three experiment groups. For Umbrella top 10K domains, the percentage of visitors using both protocols remained similar to the top 100K, but 10% more visitors used only HTTPS. This difference may be driven by the broader TLS adoption observed for higher-ranked domains [67].

Table 3. The averaged percentages of new site visitors during Phase II using only HTTP/only HTTPS/both.

	HTTP	HTTPS	Both
Alexa Top 100K	41.4%	25.6%	33.0%
Umbrella Top 100K	41.2%	26.0%	32.8%
Alexa Top 10K	**19.6%**	**28.8%**	**51.6%**
Umbrella Top 10K	**29.9%**	**36.1%**	**34.0%**

For HTTP request methods, we observe a wide array of methods across domains in the Alexa and Umbrella top 100K and top 10K, including GET, HEAD, POST, CONNECT, OPTIONS, and PRI (HTTP/2.0) methods. The GET method is used by more than 90% of visitors across the two ranking ranges, for both Alexa and Umbrella. The HEAD method is the second most popular, particularly for Alexa, which we observe used by 4.6% and 6.0% of visitors to Alexa top 100K and top 10K domains, respectively (averaged across the manipulated domains). For Umbrella, ∼3% of visitors used the HEAD method across the two ranking ranges. Beyond the top HTTP methods, there is a long tail of other methods used, including PUT and REQMOD (ICAP mode), illustrating diverse purposes behind top domain visits.

Resource Prevalence. We next study what web resources are commonly requested by new visitors in Phase II. We observe similar resources frequently requested from manipulated domains in each top list and ranking range group. In Table 4, we select one of the realistic domain's results as a representative example, and list the top 10 most accessed URL paths by the percentage of new visitors in Phase II requesting it. We observe several interesting cases:

- *Root.* The majority of visitors (58–80% across different lists and ranking ranges) requested the root "/" home page of a domain. This does indicate that a notable fraction of visitors do not crawl the domain root at all, and rather focus on accessing other resources.
- *Favicons.* Across top lists and ranking ranges, another one of the top 3 requested resource is the "/favicon.ico" path, for a domain's favicon. Modern browsers generate favicon requests when visiting a domain, and we hypothesize that many of these requests arise from visitors using real browsers (whether manually or programmatically). Between 10% and 31% of visitors requested the favicon, suggesting only a minority of visitors use real browsers.
- *RSS Feeds.* We observe a large fraction of visitors (up to 16%) requesting "/feed", "/feeds", and "/rss" URL paths, commonly associated with RSS feeds [62]. These visitors cluster within two Google Cloud ASes (396982 and 15169). We note that Google's Feedfetcher [47] similarly crawls these RSS or Atom feeds, but presents a distinct user agent (i.e., "Feedfetcher-Google"). Thus, these visitors are likely other RSS feed aggregators operating on Google Cloud, rather than Google's Feedfetcher.

Table 4. Top URL paths/resources by the percentage of new visitors in Phase II accessing it.

	the Alexa Top 100K		the Alexa Top 10K		the Umbrella Top 100K		the Umbrella Top 10K	
	URL Path	%	URL Path	%	URL Path	%	URL Path	%
1	"/"	80.0	"/"	57.7	"/"	75.8	"/"	75.0
2	"/feed", "/feeds", "/rss"	13.8	"/favicon.ico"	30.8	"/feed", "/feeds", "/rss"	16.0	"/favicon.ico"	9.7
3	"/favicon.ico"	10.3	Russia-Related URLs[c]	8.6	"/favicon.ico"	15.8	"/feed", "/feeds", "/rss"	7.2
4	"/ads.txt"	4.5	"/feed", "/feeds", "/rss"	5.1	"/1jlbdmb"	6.5	"/robots.txt"	6.1
5	"/robots.txt"	4.2	"/gaocc/g445g"	3.7	"/ads.txt "	3.8	"/1jlbdmb"	4.5
6	""	3.9	"/robots.txt"	3.5	""	3.1	"*"	3.0
7	WordPress Scans[a]	3.1	"/1jlbdmb"	2.3	"."	2.5	""	2.3
8	"/1jlbdmb"	2.2	""	1.6	"/robots.txt"	2.3	"/ads.txt"	2.3
9	security.txt[b]	1.1	"/.git/config"	1.4	WordPress Scans[a]	2.0	"MGLNDD_[IP]_443"[d]	1.6
10	"/.env"	0.9	"*"	1.3	security.txt[b]	1.0	WordPress Scans[a]	1.6

[a]We observe a group of IP addresses accessing several WordPress vulnerability URLs, such as "//blog/wpincludes/wlwmanifest.xml", "//wordpress/wp-includes/wlwmanifest.xml", and "//2019/wp-includes/wlwmanifest.xml".
[b]Requests for security.txt were to the "/.well-known/security.txt" path.
[c]Russian-related URL paths as discussed under *Nation-State Related Activity*.
[d]"[IP]" represents the IP address of our sites.

- *.txt Files.* A non-trivial fraction of visitors requested different standard .txt resources, with robots.txt and ads.txt being most frequent overall across top lists and ranking ranges. robots.txt informs crawlers on which site resources are permitted to be crawled, but only a small fraction of visitors (less than 7% for all domains) requested this information, indicating limited adherence to this standard. Meanwhile, ads.txt provides information on advertising relationships, and such visitors crawling this resource (less than 5% for each domains) are likely involved in online advertising. We observe up to ~1% of visitors accessing security.txt files on some domains, suggesting harvesting of security contacts or signals about security postures. Other .txt files were accessed but by less than 10 visitors per domain, including app-ads.txt, humans.txt and dnt-policy.txt.
- *Nation-State Related Activity.* We observe several interesting resources accessed by a notable fraction of visitors that seem related to nation-state activities, specifically for domains in the Alexa top 10K. Approximately 4% of visitors accessing our domains placed in the Alexa top 10K requested the "/gaocc/g445g" URL path, all from Chinese IP addresses. We identify anecdotal evidence that this URL path is related to configuring the V2Ray censorship circumvention tool[2], and that crawls for this resource may indicate Chinese censors attempting to detect servers supporting censorship circumvention[3]. (We also observe "/1jlbdmb" frequently requested. It is unclear what this resource is associated with, although upon Google searches, we do note a large number of query results about odd traffic to this URL path in Chinese, so this resource may also be related to Chinese censorship.) Similarly, we observe that ~9% of visitors requested the "/russianfederation", "/russia-

---

[2] https://github.com/v2fly/v2ray-core/issues/304.
[3] https://twitter.com/germanyorthoped/status/1405413138468536322.

Table 5. The number of distinct contacts that messaged email addresses on our test domains' main pages or `security.txt` files.

#Contacts	Alexa			Umbrella		
	1M	100K	10K	1M	100K	10K
Main (control)	3	2	3	1	1	0
Main (manipulated)	**7**	**6**	**12**	**1**	**4**	**6**
`Security.txt` (control)	0	0	0	0	0	0
`Security.txt` **(manipulated)**	**0**	**3**	**5**	**1**	**4**	**2**

w1", "/lenta", "/aeroflot" URL paths (as well as "/kfc", "/kfccorporationx" and "/blablacar-w", which appear related to US and French corporations), all from Russian IP addresses. We are uncertain of the reason behind requesting these resources, although we suspect that they may be related to either Russian censorship or the ongoing war in Ukraine.

– *WordPress Scans.* Many visitors launching WordPress scans on our ranked domains, specifically requesting for the `wlwmanifest.xml` file under various URL paths. We find anecdotal evidence [1,63] that such scans are often associated with vulnerability scans of WordPress installations, suggesting that security researchers or attackers leverage top lists to find vulnerable sites.

In Fig. 7b, we also depict the distribution of the number of distinct resources requested by new visitors during Phase II (again using a realistic domain for each top list and ranking range as a representative example). Overall, the number of resources requested is low, with at least 55% of visitors only requesting a single resource and over 90% of visitors requesting four resources or less, across both top lists and ranking ranges. Thus, most visitors do not extensively crawl a site (although we note that as our site was simple, it is possible that some visitors would have more extensively crawled had our site contained more links). Looking at the outliers, we observe a small number of visitors crawling hundreds of resources (up to 1.5K). The most extensive crawler scanned for 1,545 Polycom VOIP configuration files (e.g., "/dms/Polycom_VVX_201_000000000000.cfg"). Another visitor accessed over 200 URLs seemingly for vulnerability scanning (e.g., "/error3?msg=30&data=';alert('nuclei');", likely related to the Nuclei vulnerability scanner [27]).

Email Traffic. Finally, we look at how visitors use contact information on top list domains. Table 5 lists the number of unique email addresses that contacted an email associated with our domain once placed in a top list (Phase II). We received few emails throughout our measurement. Interestingly, we did not receive any emails for our Majestic domains nor to our WHOIS contacts.

Overall, we observe that manipulated domains received more emails than control domains, for both emails associated with domain landing pages and `security.txt`. We note that all email addresses that contacted our control domain also contacted our manipulated domain, indicating that these contacts identified our domains through means other than top lists (potentially domain registration information or certificate transparency logs). We also observe that higher ranked domains generally received more messages as well, and that more contacts used the main page emails compared to `security.txt` ones (as discussed earlier, we did observe a small fraction of visitors crawling `security.txt` files, but significantly fewer than the domain root). By manually inspecting all messages received, we classify the emails as either advertising/spam or phishing/scams. Interestingly, all emails to `security.txt` addresses were phishing/scams, suggesting that some visitors crawl `security.txt` to identify valuable security contacts for a site to target. Thus, top list placement does result in additional unwanted/malicious emails to email contacts associated with the page. This is particularly relevant for `security.txt`, as a common concern is that listing security contacts in such files will result in high volumes of spam content [51], although we note that the email volumes we directly observed is small.

Anomalous DNS Traffic. During our Alexa top 100K experiment, we observed two massive floods of DNS requests on two different days. Each manipulated domain received more than 1M requests within a 20-minute window on both days, whereas the domains only received hundreds to thousands of requests per day otherwise. Thus during these bursts, nearly all DNS lookups were due to the flood. By inspecting the DNS requests during the floods, we identified that these queries were for subdomains of our experiment domains, and originated from only three ASes, Google (15169), WoodyNet (42) and Cisco OpenDNS (33692), which all host public DNS services. To prevent these floods from skewing our DNS telemetry, we filtered out all such queries (subdomain queries from the three ASes during the 20-min windows). We briefly note that Google DNS forwards the original DNS client's network through EDNS Client Subnet, and we observed that client IP addresses were all within a DigitalOcean AS (14061). While we are not certain of the purpose behind this traffic, its anomalous and suspicious nature highlights that top list ranking may render a domain a ready target for attacks.

5 Concluding Discussion

In this paper, we empirically investigated real-world top list use by conducting controlled experiments with test domains in different ranking ranges of popular top lists. Here, we synthesize lessons from our study and future directions.

Lessons for Top List Design. Our findings demonstrate ongoing dependencies on top list datasets. While simple, this observation is especially salient in light of Alexa's retirement [39]. While the consequences of Alexa's retirement remain to be seen, there is clearly a need for alternative options. We observed that of the three top lists considered, despite facing impending retirement, domains placed in Alexa received the highest levels of traffic, and prior research studies have depended primarily on Alexa over the other options (see Sect. 4.1).

While the Tranco top list [61] has become more popular of late, at least in academic studies, it is ultimately an aggregator of existing lists rather than its own distinct top list, and the loss of Alexa reduces Tranco's input data. After Alexa's end, Tranco has since replaced it with a new PDNS-based ranking by DomainTools [22]. However, we note that DomainTools' ranking itself combines Umbrella and Majestic, in addition to Netcraft top 100 sites [57] (only containing 100 sites ranked) and Farsight Security's PDNS data [22]. It is unclear currently what the implications are of the new Tranco's heavy dependence on PDNS data, as well as its double dependency on Umbrella and Majestic (both direct dependency as well as indirect dependency via DomainTools).

Given the community's dependence on top lists, there is a need to investigate new top list designs. Recently, Xie et al. [72] proposed a new PDNS-based top list design, SecRank, that achieves desirable top list properties. Such developments may serve as promising alternatives to Alexa in the future, especially as SecRank's design is transparent, although SecRank's current implementation inputs Asia-centric DNS data, and thus exhibits regional skew in its ranking.

Our study's findings can help inform top list design considerations. For example, we observed that traffic to top list domains primarily increases once in the top 100K, suggesting that most uses of top lists are within that ranking range. Thus, top lists should aim for higher-quality rankings at such scales, rather than prioritizing larger ranking quantities (i.e., there may be less value in having millions of domains ranked compared to a 100K). In addition, our findings hint at a preference for website-based top lists (e.g., Alexa, Majestic) regardless of the ranking methods, whereas SecRank and Umbrella (as well as Cloudflare's new Radar ranking [13]) are both DNS-based and contain non-website domains. New top lists may be more broadly used if focusing on collecting web traffic telemetry for ranking websites.

We also identified how geographically diverse top list use is (in Sects. 4.2 and 4.3), with visitors from over 40 countries. However, existing top lists exhibit bias towards certain geographic regions. For example, SecRank is built on PDNS data from a Chinese DNS provider and thus skews towards Asia-centric domains, whereas the other top lists skew towards popular domains in Western countries, particularly due to their US and European-centric data sources. Constructing top lists that focus on different geographic regions could support more geographic diversity in network and security measurements.

Furthermore, our experiments identified various organizations relying on top lists for multiple purposes, including for search engine indexing and security evaluations (as discussed in Sect. 4.2). Given these sensitive use cases, top lists must be designed with robustness against manipulation. The threat of domains manipulated into top lists is not purely hypothetical though, as online websites have been identified offering top list manipulation as a paid service [72] (often with high prices, such as $40/month for entering the Alexa top 100K, and $500/month for its top 10K [3]).

Lessons for Top List Usage. While many security analysis tools/services allowlist domains on existing lists, our results highlight how readily this allowlisting can be abused. We identified in Sect. 4.3 that the majority of list users, including various security organizations, either assessed a site only once after top list placement, or recrawled the site only with a long periodicity (although we did observe a few outliers who recrawled frequently). Thus, an attacker could first manipulate a benign domain into the rankings, resulting in allowlisting by security tools and services, and then subsequently modify that site to a malicious one. Instead, sensitive uses of top lists (such as for security purposes) should regularly revisit sites on top lists, to avoid relying on stale information.

Lessons for Ranked Domains. We observed that ranked domains receive various types of traffic. This traffic, as discussed in Sect. 4.3, includes advertising, spam, scam, and phishing messages to domain-associated emails, potentially by malicious actors looking to exploit sites. Of particular note is that deploying `security.txt` resulted in a small number of malicious emails, aligning with concerns of spam or low-quality reports to `security.txt` contacts [51]. Thus, while `security.txt` remains a promising protocol for providing security contacts for a website, domain owners must be prepared to handle spam reports.

We identified that most visitors to our experiment domains did not crawl `robots.txt` (Sect. 4.3), much less adhere to it, similar to prior findings [45]. Only a small fraction of visitors self-identify as web crawlers, despite the vast majority of visitors arriving from cloud platforms (and thus are likely crawlers). For ranked domains seeking to limit crawling, anti-bot techniques should leverage the AS classifications of visitors, beyond relying on `robots.txt` and signals from the user-agent. We also observed that top list ranking results in a non-trivial number of suspicious visitors and accessing patterns (Sects. 4.2 and 4.3). Thus, ranked domain owners (especially higher-ranked domains) require defense measures, such as DDoS protection and appropriate DNS and web cache configurations.

Lessons for Future Research. Future work can more extensively study top list use in practice, as our work is ultimately a first step. One direction is in better understanding the purposes behind top list use, as our study's experiment did not afford detailed visibility into how top lists domains may be used after crawling. Such investigations may involve user studies, and could investigate interesting use cases such as allow/block-listing and domain classification. Our case studies in Sect. 4.3 also shed light on how top lists could be used as a gateway for measuring censorship (or other scanning behaviors) in a blackbox fashion, as top lists may serve as a source of sites evaluated for potential censorship/scanning. Related, top list usage could be studied over longer periods of time, as our experiments monitored sites only on the order of weeks, rather than months or years. Both ephemeral (e.g., holidays, special events) and long-term effects could be identified through such longitudinal studies, providing deeper insights into top list use in practice. Ultimately, the importance of top lists across various measurement and evaluation use cases motivates deeper future investigation into top list characteristics.

A   Top List Manipulation

Here we detail the top list manipulation methods we employed.

Alexa. We apply the Alexa manipulation method recently developed by Xie et al. [72], which leverages Alexa's Certify service. Xie et al. observed that beyond collecting web traffic telemetry from its browser extension, Alexa also collects data from its paid Certify service [38]. For websites subscribing to the Certify service, they embed a JavaScript snippet[4] provided by Alexa on their own web pages, which uploads visitor information to an Alexa data collection endpoint. Xie et al. identified that the telemetry sent to Alexa differentiated users with a single ID field that could be modified arbitrarily to forge fake visits by distinct users to the site. Furthermore, Alexa did not apply rate limits to the collected telemetry. A single IP address could generate a large volume of visitor telemetry that appeared to represent distinct user visits. As a result, Alexa would more highly rank a domain as it receives more distinct visitors. Thus, to manipulate an experiment domain into the Alexa ranking, we subscribed that site to the Certify service, and then applied this same technique of generating data telemetry to Alexa's data collection endpoint with distinct visitor ID values.

Umbrella. We use IP spoofing for Umbrella manipulation, as its ranking is constructed with PDNS and heavily depends on the number of IP addresses issuing DNS lookups for a domain [61,66,72]. Spoofing only addresses within our institution's local network (ethical considerations are discussed in Sect. 3.5), we generate DNS A record requests to Umbrella's DNS resolvers for our manipulated domains from different source IP addresses, causing Umbrella to more highly rank our domains due to higher request volume and IP diversity.

Majestic. We apply the Majestic manipulation method of Le Pochat et al. [61], which uses reflecting sites (described shortly). Majestic ranks a domain based on the IP subnet diversity of other websites linking back to the domain. It collects data on these website backlink relationships through regular large-scale web crawls. The authors identified that certain *reflecting* sites, particularly MediaWiki sites, will accept user-provided URLs as values in the site's URL query parameters and embed (reflect) these user-provided values as anchor elements in their webpages. When Majestic's crawler analyzes such reflecting links with a target domain provided as the URL query value, it observes a backlink to the target domain.

To trigger Majestic's crawler to visit certain links, we subscribe to Majestic's online service that accepts submitted URLs for crawling. To find reflecting sites, we use the set of reflecting wiki sites used by Le Pochat et al. [61]. We also crawled 12,920 MediaWiki-related domains from the Fofa search engine [17], checking whether a URL provided as a URL query value is reflected in the returned webpage. In total, we found 1,642 wiki pages that reflected URLs.

---

[4] https://web.archive.org/web/20220322000324/https://certify-js.alexametrics.com/atrk.js.

For manipulating our test domains into Majestic, we submitted wiki links that reflected URLs to the Majestic service, with our test domain provided as the links' URL query value.

B Survey of Top List Use in Academic Papers

We evaluate the use of our three investigated top lists in academic research by surveying research papers published at 10 networking and security-related venues from 2017 to 2022, choosing the same set of venues previously surveyed by Scheitle et al. [67]:

– Measurement (3): ACM IMC, PAM, and TMA.
– Security (4): USENIX Security, IEEE S&P, ACM CCS and NDSS.
– Systems (2): ACM CoNEXT and ACM SIGCOMM.
– Web Technology (1): WWW.

To do the survey, we searched all papers published in the 10 venues from 2017 to 2022 for keywords such as "top list", "toplist", "Alexa", "Umbrella", "Cisco", and "Majestic". We manually reviewed the matching papers and counted the studies that relied upon a subset of a top list as input for part of the study, such as for measurements, data analysis, or experiment deployments. If a study used multiple top lists, we count them separately for each list used.

References

1. Weird GET and POST requests node (2021). https://www.digitalocean.com/community/questions/weird-get-and-post-requests-node
2. RankStore (2022). https://web.archive.org/web/20220314142408/http://www.rankstore.com/
3. Alexa Specialist (2023). https://web.archive.org/web/20230607092454/http://improvealexaranking.com/
4. Net Systems Research (2023). https://web.archive.org/web/20230219081618/http://netsystemsresearch.com/
5. AdbeatBot (2024). https://www.adbeat.com/policy
6. AdsBot (2024). https://developers.google.com/search/docs/crawling-indexing/overview-google-crawlers#adsbot
7. AhrefsBot (2024). http://ahrefs.com/robot/
8. BingBot (2024). https://www.bing.com/webmasters/help/which-crawlers-does-bing-use-8c184ec0
9. Bloglines (2024). http://www.bloglines.com
10. CensysInspect (2024). https://about.censys.io/
11. CheckMarkNetwork (2024). http://www.checkmarknetwork.com/spider.html
12. Chrome UX Report (2024). https://developer.chrome.com/docs/crux/
13. Cloudflare Radar Domain Rankings (2024). https://radar.cloudflare.com/domains
14. Dataprovider.com (2024). https://www.dataprovider.com/
15. Dnsthingy (2024). https://www.dnsthingy.com/
16. ev-crawler (2024). https://headline.com/legal/crawler

7. Fofa (2024). https://fofa.info/
8. GoogleBot (2024). http://www.google.com/bot.html
9. IBM X-Force Exchange (2024). https://exchange.xforce.ibmcloud.com/
10. Let's Encrypt (2024). https://letsencrypt.org/
21. MaxMind (2024). https://www.maxmind.com/
22. Mirror, Mirror, on the Wall, Who's the Fairest (website) of Them all? (2024) (2024). https://web.archive.org/web/20240124161803/https://www.domaintools.com/resources/blog/mirror-mirror-on-the-wall-whos-the-fairest-website-of-them-all/
23. NameSilo (2024). https://www.namesilo.com/
24. Netcraft Web Server Survey (2024). https://www.netcraft.com/
25. Nicecrawler (2024). http://www.nicecrawler.com/
26. nltk.corpus Package (2024). https://www.nltk.org/api/nltk.corpus.html
27. Nuclei (2024). https://nuclei.projectdiscovery.io/
28. Pandalytics (2024). https://domainsbot.com/pandalytics/
29. Quad9 (2024). https://www.quad9.net/
30. Rankboostup (2024). https://rankboostup.com/
31. SurdotlyBot (2024). http://sur.ly/bot.html
32. The Majestic Million (2024). https://majestic.com/reports/majestic-million
33. VirusTotal (2024). https://www.virustotal.com/
34. Vultr Cloud Hosting (2024). https://www.vultr.com/
35. WellKnownBot (2024). https://well-known.dev/about/#bot
36. YandexBot (2024). https://yandex.com/support/webmaster/robot-workings/robot.html
37. Ahmad, S.S., Dar, M.D., Zaffar, M.F., Vallina-Rodriguez, N., Nithyanand, R.: Apophanies or Epiphanies? How crawlers impact our understanding of the web. In: The World Wide Web Conference (WWW) (2020)
38. Alexa: How do I get my site's metrics Certified? (2021). https://web.archive.org/web/20211127215835/https://support.alexa.com/hc/en-us/articles/200450354-How-do-I-get-my-site-s-metrics-Certified-
39. Alexa: We will be retiring Alexa.com on May 1, 2022 (2021). https://web.archive.org/web/20221126132843/https://support.alexa.com/hc/en-us/articles/4410503838999
40. Alexa: Alexa Top 1 Million (2022). https://web.archive.org/web/20220701000000*/https://s3.amazonaws.com/alexa-static/top-1m.csv.zip
41. Cisco: OpenDNS (2024). https://www.opendns.com/
42. Cisco: Umbrella Popularity List (2024). http://s3-us-west-1.amazonaws.com/umbrella-static/index.html
43. EdOverflow, Shafranovich, Y.: security.txt (2024). https://securitytxt.org/
44. Gharaibeh, M., Shah, A., Huffaker, B., Zhang, H., Ensafi, R., Papadopoulos, C.: A look at router geolocation in public and commercial databases. In: Internet Measurement Conference (IMC) (2017)
45. Giles, C.L., Sun, Y., Councill, I.G.: Measuring the web crawler ethics. In: The World Wide Web Conference (WWW) (2010)
46. Giotsas, V., Smaragdakis, G., Dietzel, C., Richter, P., Feldmann, A., Berger, A.: Inferring BGP blackholing activity in the internet. In: Internet Measurement Conference (IMC) (2017)
47. Google: Feedfetcher (2024). https://developers.google.com/search/docs/advanced/crawling/feedfetcher
48. Google: Introduction to robots.txt (2024). https://developers.google.com/search/docs/advanced/robots/intro

49. Halvorson, T., Der, M.F., Foster, I., Savage, S., Saul, L.K., Voelker, G.M.: From. academy to. zone: an Analysis of the New TLD Land Rush. In: Internet Measurement Conference (IMC) (2015)
50. Khan, M.T., DeBlasio, J., Voelker, G.M., Snoeren, A.C., Kanich, C., Vallina-Rodriguez, N.: An empirical analysis of the commercial VPN ecosystem. In: Internet Measurement Conference (IMC) (2018)
51. Krebs, B.: Does your organization have a security.txt file? (2021). https://krebsonsecurity.com/2021/09/does-your-organization-have-a-security-txt-file/
52. Kuchhal, D., Li, F.: Knock and talk: investigating local network communications on websites. In: Internet Measurement Conference (IMC) (2021)
53. Li, V.G., Dunn, M., Pearce, P., McCoy, D., Voelker, G.M., Savage, S.: Reading the tea leaves: a comparative analysis of threat intelligence. In: USENIX Security Symposium (2019)
54. Majestic: Majestic Million - Reloaded! (2011). https://blog.majestic.com/company/majestic-million-reloaded/
55. Majestic: Majestic Million now free for all (2012). https://blog.majestic.com/development/majestic-million-csv-daily/
56. Mendoza, A., Chinprutthiwong, P., Gu, G.: Uncovering HTTP header inconsistencies and the impact on desktop/mobile websites. In: The World Wide Web Conference (WWW) (2018)
57. Netcraft: Most Visited Websites (2024). https://trends.netcraft.com/topsites
58. OpenDNS: PhishTank (2024). http://phishtank.org/
59. Oprea, A., Li, Z., Norris, R., Bowers, K.: Made: security analytics for enterprise threat detection. In: Annual Computer Security Applications Conference (ACSAC) (2018)
60. Peng, P., Yang, L., Song, L., Wang, G.: Opening the blackbox of virustotal: analyzing online phishing scan engines. In: Internet Measurement Conference (IMC) (2019)
61. Pochat, V.L., Van Goethem, T., Tajalizadehkhoob, S., Korczyński, M., Joosen, W.: Tranco: a research-oriented top sites ranking hardened against manipulation. In: Network and Distributed System Security Symposium (NDSS) (2019)
62. Pot, J.: How to Find the RSS Feed URL for Almost Any Site (2019). https://zapier.com/blog/how-to-find-rss-feed-url/
63. PumpkinSeed: I Wanted to Play and I Got Hacked (2021). https://medium.com/swlh/i-wanted-to-play-and-i-got-hacked-e5314fd5b27f
64. Ruth, K., Kumar, D., Wang, B., Valenta, L., Durumeric, Z.: Toppling top lists: evaluating the accuracy of popular website lists. In: Internet Measurement Conference (IMC) (2022)
65. Rweyemamu, W., Lauinger, T., Wilson, C., Robertson, W., Kirda, E.: Clustering and the weekend effect: recommendations for the use of top domain lists in security research. In: International Conference on Passive and Active Network Measurement (PAM) (2019)
66. Rweyemamu, W., Lauinger, T., Wilson, C., Robertson, W., Kirda, E.: Getting under Alexa's umbrella: infiltration attacks against internet top domain lists. In: International Conference on Information Security (ISC) (2019)
67. Scheitle, Q., et al.: A long way to the top: significance, structure, and stability of internet top lists. In: Internet Measurement Conference (IMC) (2018)
68. Spaventa, L.: Behind the Scenes Part II: What Makes HARO So Successful in Getting You Media Coverage (2012). https://www.cision.com/blogs/2012/10/behind-the-scenes-part-ii-what-makes-haro-so-successful-in-getting-you-media-coverage/

69. Cisco Umbrella: Cisco Umbrella 1 Million (2016). https://web.archive.org/web/20230218105309/https://umbrella.cisco.com/blog/cisco-umbrella-1-million
70. Vallina, P., et al.: Mis-shapes, mistakes, misfits: an analysis of domain classification services. In: Internet Measurement Conference (IMC) (2020)
71. Wan, G., et al.: On the origin of scanning: the impact of location on internet-wide scans. In: Internet Measurement Conference (IMC) (2020)
72. Xie, Q., et al.: Building an open, robust, and stable voting-based domain top list. In: USENIX Security Symposium (2022)
73. Zeber, D., et al.: The representativeness of automated web crawls as a surrogate for human browsing. In: The World Wide Web Conference (WWW) (2020)
74. Zhao, B., et al.: A large-scale empirical study on the vulnerability of deployed IoT devices. IEEE Trans. Dependable and Secure Comput. (TDSC) **19**, 1826–1840 (2020)

Author Index

A
Arlitt, Martin II-37, II-293

B
Bailey, Brad II-170
Baltra, Guillermo II-132
Bayer, Jan I-232
Behl, Dushyant I-262
Belding, Elizabeth II-153
Bischof, Zachary S. I-189
Bruhner, Carl Magnus II-293

C
Candela, Massimo II-88
Cardenas, Alvaro A. I-3
Carle, Georg II-273
Carlsson, Niklas II-37, II-293
Cerenius, David II-293
Chakravaty, Sambuddho II-19
Chandrasekaran, Balakrishnan II-249
Choffnes, David II-322
Chung, Jae II-153
Dainotti, Alberto I-189

D
den Hartog, Jerry I-3
Dubois, Daniel J. II-322
Duda, Andrzej I-206, I-232
Durairajan, Ramakrishnan II-170

E
Esrefoglu, Rasit II-104

F
Fainchtein, Rahel A. II-228
Fathalli, Seifeddine II-249
Feldmann, Anja II-249
Fernandez, Simon I-206
Finamore, Alessandro I-159

Fontugne, Romain I-32, II-88, II-199
Fukuda, Kensuke I-95, II-199

G
Gallo, Massimo I-159
Gasser, Oliver I-112
Gebauer, Florian II-273
Gosain, Devashish II-19
Gupta, Arpit II-153
Gupta, Shachee Mishra I-262

H
Haddadi, Hamed II-322
Hasselquist, David II-37
Heidemann, John II-104, II-132
Hsu, Amanda I-112
Huang, Tingshan II-104
Hureau, Olivier I-206, I-232

I
Iradukunda, Blaise II-170

J
Jonker, Mattijs II-3

K
Kaller, Martin II-293
Kannan, Pravein Govindan I-262
Kobayashi, Satoru I-95
Korczyński, Maciej I-206, I-232

L
Lerner, David II-153
Li, Frank I-112, I-277
Li, Zhenyu I-133
Liu, Jiamo II-153
Livadariu, Ioana II-88
Lyu, Minzhao I-61

M
Madanapalli, Sharat Chandra   I-61
Mandalari, Anna Maria   II-322
Michiardi, Pietro   I-159

O
Ortiz, Neil   I-3

P
Paul, Udit   II-153
Pearce, Paul   I-112
Phokeer, Amreesh   II-88

R
Raichstein, Eran   I-262
Rizvi, A. S. M.   II-104
Rosenquist, Hampus   II-37
Rossi, Dario   I-159
Rosso, Martin   I-3

S
Safronov, Vadim   II-322
Sattler, Patrick   II-273
Schulmann, Haya   II-69
Sethuraman, Manasvini   I-189
Sharma, Rishi   II-19
Sherr, Micah   II-228
Singh, Kartikey   II-19
Sivaraman, Vijay   I-61
Song, Xiao   II-132
Sosnowski, Markus   II-273

Sperotto, Anna   II-3
Stevens, Aleksandr   II-170
Stucchi, Massimiliano   II-88
Suresh Babu, Jithin   II-19

T
Takvorian, Joel   I-262
Tashiro, Malte   II-199
Tian, Yu   I-133

V
Vishwanath, Arun   I-61
Visser, Christoff   I-32

W
Wang, Chao   I-159
Weyulu, Emilia N.   II-249

X
Xie, Qinge   I-277

Y
Yazdani, Ramin   II-3

Z
Zambon, Emmanuele   I-3
Zeynali, Danesh   II-249
Zhao, Liang   I-95
Zhao, Shujie   II-69
Zirngibl, Johannes   II-273